THE BOOK OF LIBEL

The Book of Libel

Revised Edition

BY CHARLES ANGOFF

with an Introduction by Martin Gansberg

New York: A. S. Barnes and Co., Inc.
London: Thomas Yoseloff Ltd

Library of Congress Catalogue Card Number: 65-14635

A.S. Barnes and Company, Inc.
South Brunswick, New Jersey

Thomas Yoseloff Ltd
18 Charing Cross Road
London W.C.2, England

6260
Printed in the United States of America

Preface

LIBEL is one of the most extensive and complicated subjects in the law. This volume makes no pretense whatever to being exhaustive or to contain any philosophic contribution to the subject. It is purely a practical book, aiming to be of help to all who deal with the printed word, particularly editors in newspaper, magazine and book offices.

Strangely enough, there has not been one handy volume that the practicing journalist and editor could consult for the basic facts about libel. This lack the present volume hopes to fill. It begins with an essay on the underlying principles of libel. Then follow the libel laws—and other pertinent information—of all the states and the District of Columbia. Then come seventeen decisions by high courts on various aspects of libel. Each case is prefaced by a summary of the important points of law in it. Finally, there is a very detailed index.

The more intricate and technical aspects of libel, such as the meaning of "implied malice" and the difference between punitive and compensatory damages, are not discussed in this book because they have no place in it. An editor is more interested in avoiding being sued than in the fine points of the law once he is haled into court. A practicing magazine editor of twenty years' experience, I have tried to answer most of the questions regarding libel that any other practicing editor is likely to ask. It is impossible to give definite "rules" to avoid libel, but there are several "rules of thumb" that help, and I have tried to state these rules of thumb in the Introduction—and then to show them in operation in the court decisions I quote near the end of the volume.

The book has been checked by several members of the New York bar and the Massachusetts bar.

I shall, of course, be grateful to all readers who send in suggestions for the improvement of this book. I can be reached in care of my publisher.

CHARLES ANGOFF

Preface to Second Edition

FIRST PUBLISHED in 1946 *The Book of Libel* has had a strange history. It did not get widely reviewed at the time of its appearance, certainly not in the general newspaper and periodical press. But I did get many letters about it from editors and professors of journalism, and I do know that the book was used as a text in several courses in journalism. The letters from journalists and professors of journalism were almost uniformly favorable; my correspondents told me how helpful they found it. At the beginning lawyers were rather cautious in their comments. They appeared to wish I had been more "positive" in what I said about consulting lawyers in times of libel trouble. I did not say (as can readily be seen by reading my introductory essay on Essentials of the Law of Libel) that journalists should not consult lawyers. I said and I still say that they should consult lawyers. But I added that there are times when an editor must also pay attention to his journalistic conscience. It's easy for a lawyer (it's probably his duty to do so) to tell a client not to print something. But it's nobler for an editor to print it nevertheless, if he feels that he is in possession of enough of the truth about a situation and that he owes it to his public to let them know about it.

Slowly, even lawyers began to see virtues in the book. Compiled by a layman (though checked by lawyers), it nevertheless did contain, as several of them told me, useful information and "guidelines for one in libel-trouble." I was told that my book was listed as an authoritative work in various legal pamphlets and also in the section on libel and slander in no less a work than the Encyclopedia Britannica, written by Mitchell Dawson, former editor of the *Chicago Bar Record.* Then came a time when an editor of one of the largest newspapers in the United States called me long distance one night to ask for advice on a libel matter. I did (perhaps foolishly) give it to him, and for my trouble I didn't get even a note. I say this, not by way of carping, but only to present some of the history of *The Book of Libel.* A few months ago Mr. Martin Gansberg, staff reporter for *The New York Times* and former managing editor of the International edition of that paper, did a story on a libel issue, and quoted me on it. Whereupon it occurred to my publisher, Mr. Thomas Yoseloff, that perhaps it would be a good idea to revise the book and put it out in a fresh edition.

The present edition is a bit larger than the first one. There have been changes in the laws of the various states; I have added the new states of Hawaii and Alaska, and also Puerto Rico and the Virgin Islands; and I have added a long case, decided by the United States Supreme Court, dealing with the criticism of public officials. In this edition, as in the previous one, I make no claim that my book is an exhaustive one. A one-volume edition of all the laws of libel of the fifty states plus all the important cases would be unwieldy and really would be of little use to the working editor. I am not addressing lawyers; I am addressing editors and journalists and other lay readers who want some basic information, and in a hurry, about the matter of libel. An editor or journalist in libel trouble should, of course, see a lawyer, as a man with a physical illness should see a physician. But just as a layman's book on medicine has its uses, so, I believe, does a layman's book on libel.

A few words seem called for with respect to the subject of "republication." Like "publication" it is rather technical, and in this area the advice of a lawyer who really knows the intricacies of libel should be especially sought. The problems are many and complicated and they vary from state to state. Does a new edition of a printed work constitute "republication" and therefore revive a possible libel? Is a new edition merely a continuous "publication"? What about the reprinting of selections from a work under question—does that constitute "republication"? Does the sale of each book constitute a "republication"? Respectable opinions can be found on various sides of these and similar questions.

My listings are a bit unorthodox in that I give the notations of both older Codes and newer Codes. Of course, where only an older one is given, its equivalent in a newer Code can be determined by consulting the conversion tables. Why, then, have I listed, at times, both the Old and the New? Because, I believe, it is useful for the practicing editor to see how the judicial mind is working, how the consciences of the various legislators are working, and so on. Sometimes, as I have said, I list only an old Code, simply because the newer one is pretty much the same, and the changes are minor and of little concern to the rushed editor.

There is one area where there have been some important changes throughout the land. That is in the area of radio-television defamation. In 1946 the legal world was still in state of flux on the issues involved. The thinking has been crystallizing, as I point out in the Introduction. Yet, I have not given all the radio-television laws of all the fifty states, simply because to do so would make the book too bulky, and also (and chiefly) because the radio-television laws, in the main, are so very much alike. The radio-television laws I have given may serve as an indication how the legislatures and courts have been thinking in other states. Of course, when one is pressed for the precise law and its precise application one should consult a lawyer. There are other areas, where I have followed the same procedure. One important such area is the defamation of financial institutions and other corporations. Some of the states are quite clear on this, some are less clear. The laws I present indicate the general direction of the thinking of the various states. Here, too, when an editor needs specific information he should consult his lawyer. And what about dead people? Can they be libeled? The answer is yes, and no, as can readily be seen by glancing at the relevant laws. The memory of one dead is dear to some or all of his survivors, and any reflection upon him can conceivably be injurious to them. So it's wise to be cautious when discussing dead people. When discussing dead people, as when discussing living ones, one must make sure of the truth of the allegations. The truth is the mightiest weapon of all in the armamentarium of a defendant in a libel action.

It is worth noting how little the libel laws, in essentials, have changed through the past nineteen years. Sections have been rewritten and combined, but the basic content remains. A movement started long ago continues, namely, the reduction in the term of the statute of limitations, which in the not too distant future will probably be one or two years throughout the country. And the difference between the United States and England is now as it was in 1946: English courts and juries are readier to find for the defendant than are our courts and juries.

What about the future of the whole subject of libel? This question is not as pointless as it may sound on first encounter. No less a person than Associate Justice Hugo L. Black of the United States Supreme Court had some relatively novel things to say about it on April 14, 1962, at the biennial convention of the American Jewish Congress, in an interview with the late Professor Edmond Cahn of the New York University School of Law. (The Interview is published in the *New York University Law Review,* Vol. 37, June, 1962, pp. 549-563). Professor Cahn asked the Justice whether, in his adherence to the First Amendment he made "an exception in freedom of speech and press for the law of defamation? That is, are you willing to allow people to sue for damages when they are subjected to libel and slander?"

The Justice said: "My view of the First Amendment, as originally ratified, is that it said Congress should pass none of these kinds of laws. As written at that time, the Amendment applied only to Congress. I have no doubt myself that the provision, as written and adopted, intended that there should be no libel or defamation law in the United States under the United States government, just absolutely none as far as I am concerned. That is, no federal law. . . . My belief is that the First Amendment was made applicable to the states by the Fourteenth. I do not hesitate, so far as my own view is concerned, as to what should be and what I hope will sometime be the constitutional doctrine that just as it was not intended to authorize damage suits for mere words as distinguished from conduct as far as the Federal Government is concerned, the same rule should apply to the states. . . . I believe with Jefferson that it is time enough for government to step in to regulate people when they *do* something, not when they *say* something, and I do not believe myself that there is *any* halfway ground if you enforce the protections of the First Amendment. . . . My view is, without deviation, without exception, without any ifs, buts, or whereases, that freedom of speech means that you shall not do something to people either for the views they have or the views they express or the words they speak or write."

Perhaps it should be added here Justice Black did not go this far in his concurring opinion in the celebrated New York Times vs. L.B. Sullivan case, decided on March 9, 1964, and reprinted in the present volume.

Contents

CASES

Introduction

by MARTIN GANSBERG of *The New York Times*

TWO THINGS HAVE HAPPENED in recent years that make it mandatory that an understanding of libel—that mysterious tort which is interpreted fifty different ways in the fifty states—be more widespread. The two items that are responsible for this are the advent of television as a major source of tidings and the bugaboo called inflation.

Briefly, these two factors have broadened the scope of libel by making it possible for more people to note a wrongdoing and for juries to award fantastic sums of money to those who have been wronged. Television's very magnitude has made it possible to present a news event or the background of a news event to a tremendous audience at a single time. Since most experts have placed television in the same field as newspapers, magazines, and books, when the medium errs it is put in the same legal category as those sources of information. Thus, a television program that defames a person is held as having libeled that person, injured him in visual presentation, instead of having slandered him, or injured him in oral presentation, such as radio is said to do when it slips.

Juries have demonstrated in many cases in the last five years that they feel money is the only salve, and they have awarded two or three million dollars in cases where publications affected would have to have gone out of business if they had to pay the sums. This, many experts feel, is because juries have lost track of the value of money in this inflationary age of ours. Men and women dream green; they are unrealistic when they make awards in libel cases. They would give huge sums to the injured and forget that the publisher might have to go out of business as a result.

It is a dangerous thing. It is dangerous because it could stifle freedom of speech and freedom of the press. It is dangerous because it is a voluntary act, not one of compulsion by a Governmental source. In fact, judges and courts have strived to hold the line by reducing jury awards where possible or by alerting Americans to the dangers of eliminating honest, important criticism by putting fear into the hearts—and typewriters—of the men and women who speak out in the press. It takes courage to speak out, but courage is useless when the means of speaking out—the vehicle of expression, the newspaper or magazine or book or television outlet—is destroyed because of a financial noose. In our society, money can be used for good and bad; compensation in libel suits well fits our way of life.

This is not to say that we must not have means of making certain that the irresponsible can be punished when they viciously distort fact to injure the reputation of any individual. And this is not to say that money is not the best deterrent, for if it is the source of publishing, it is also the thing most understood by the publisher—particularly when it is taken from him rather than given to him. But there are those who believe that there must be a relationship between the amount of money taken from the publisher and the extent of damage done to the person libeled. In fact, it has been suggested that damages should equal one dollar for each person who has seen the wrongdoing. Thus, a magazine of two million circulation would pay two million dollars to an injured person.

Opponents feel this is too strong. Should the man earning sixty-five dollars a week get as much as the man earning sixty-five hundred dollars a week if libeled? Should a magazine on the verge of bankruptcy pay as much as a magazine that is prospering? Should the man in the public eye get as much as the man who leads a quiet life?

These are just a scant few of the questions. But they point

up something that is coming to the fore more and more: that is, quite simply, isn't it about time more people understood the subject before we allowed huge awards, before we condemned, before we acted?

Educators, lawyers, publishers, and editors would, no doubt, join forces in answering the last question affirmatively. Vincible ignorance should not be permitted to persist in judgments on the written word or the television picture of an event. The men and women who sit in judgment of mistakes bound to happen should understand the legal pyrotechnics that may ensue.

How best to educate the public to the meaning of libel and to its concomitant problems? It would appear to be a rather simple task to begin in the colleges, in the journalism courses, in the creative writing courses, in the pre-law and law courses. For once the college student grasps the subject, it is quite likely that he will pass the information along to his friends, to his family, and to the future student. To achieve this, we must have educators who understand the subject and are willing to explore it. And, naturally, there should be a text that would go into it thoroughly, clearly, forcefully. It may very well be that the pages herein fit that need, for the author, Charles Angoff, is well schooled in the subject, having been author, editor, and educator.

But a book for college students would, of necessity, have a limited audience and, as a result, fail to achieve the broader goal—be more widespread, more popular.

No, a limited venture would not suffice. It is important that the entire reading public grasp the meaning of libel and the legal machinations that go with it. That is why an effective book would need not only history and definitions but examples, examples that can bring the whole of the subject into perspective. Once you have all three of these elements between the covers of a book you have the answer to a problem that has vexed the courts: How do you get the public to understand the meaning of a libel action?

Charles Angoff has faced up to this in his book. History, definitions, and examples are all employed skillfully to pinpoint for the reader the courses of action of the past and to emphasize the alternates for the future. Mr. Angoff's use of specific cases is a strong feature of his book, and it should help the neophyte, the student, and the veteran gain a fuller understanding of the meaning of libel and its defenses.

There have been historic court decisions in libel actions, and there have been startling victories by famous authors. These have made the newspaper headlines. And these have influenced our way of disseminating information. Many an editor has told a writer that the best defense against libel is: "When in doubt, leave it out." This has applied the world over, for let us not forget that France and England, too, have figured prominently in the development of laws governing publishing. On the following pages, you will find the role of these nations ably plotted.

It takes questions to get answers, especially in libel. For example, when a plaintiff sues a defendant in a libel case, do we understand the implications? Do we know what the differences are in the varied decisions that have been rendered? Do we know why we need libel laws, and why they must be sectional instead of national or international?

The Book of Libel answers these questions in a way that should make it easier for all of us to understand what is happening in the courtroom and why the public news media must be careful—not cautious, mind you, but careful. Mr. Angoff has not attempted a literary masterpiece, for he has been alert to the need for fact rather than fiction in documenting his study of the problem. But what he has done in this book is to make it possible for all of us who would sit in judgment some day—whether as a reader or on a jury—on the question of whether some individual has been defamed, to come up with an objective answer based on history, fact, and reality.

His book is now more necessary than at any time in the past. This is so because there are not enough of us who understand what type of injury in print can lead to a suit in court and how much that injury really is worth in dollars and cents when its intent was malicious. Mr. Angoff is telling us by recalling what has happened and by linking the past with the present.

Libel is making the headlines these days. Huge sums of money accompany courtroom rulings. But not enough of us understand the implications. Perhaps this book will help more of us to be better informed. That is why it is being published at this time.

Introduction

ESSENTIALS OF THE LAW OF LIBEL

BOTH LIBEL AND SLANDER constitute defamation of character, which is a civil offence and sometimes also a criminal offence. Slander is spoken defamation, and in a conviction generally carries little more than a small fine plus a reprimand from the judge. Libel is written defamation, and because of the permanency of the record and its greater possible currency, it is far more serious. As Mr. Justice Cardozo said: "Many things that are defamatory may be said with impunity through the medium of speech. Not so, however, when the speech is caught upon the wing and transmuted into print. What gives the sting to the writing is its permanence of form. The spoken word dissolves, but the written one abides and 'perpetuates the scandal.'" (Ostrover v. Lee, reported in Vol. 256, New York Reports, p. 39)

The problem of libel is obviously related to the principle of free speech. All the states and the Federal government, of course, provide for freedom of expression in their constitutions. The articles on this point read about the same:

"Every citizen may freely speak, write, and publish his sentiments on all subjects, being responsible for the abuse of that right; and no law shall be passed to restrain or abridge the liberty of speech or of the press." (Constitution of the State of California, Art. I, Section 9)

The laws of libel do not contradict this provision. They deal merely with the abuse of the right of free speech.

The definition of libel is pretty much identical in all the states and the Federal government. In New York, for example, libel is defined as follows:

"A malicious publication, by writing, printing, picture, effigy, sign or otherwise than by mere speech, which exposes any living person, or the memory of any person deceased, to hatred, contempt, ridicule or obloquy, or which causes, or tends to cause any person to be shunned or avoided, or which has a tendency to injure any person, corporation or association of persons, in his or their business or occupation, is a libel." (New York Consolidated Laws, 1909. Section 1340)

In Iowa, to pick a state in mid-America, libel is defined thus:

"A libel is the malicious defamation of a person, made public by any printing, writing, sign, picture, representation or effigy, tending to provoke him to wrath or expose him to public hatred, contempt, or ridicule, or to deprive him of the benefits of public confidence and social intercourse; or any malicious defamation, made public as aforesaid, designed to blacken and vilify the memory of one who is dead, and tending to scandalize or provoke his surviving relatives or friends." (Code of Iowa, 1939. 737.1)

A libel, to be actionable, must first of all be "published," that is, written or printed in language or drawing and transmitted to a third person or so transmitted or exposed that a third person might see it. A libel, therefore, can be published in a newspaper, a magazine, a poster, a billboard, a letter or postcard sent through the mail, or even by leaving an unsealed note on one's desk. The New York law defines "publication" very clearly:

"To sustain a charge of publishing a libel, it is not necessary that the matter complained of should have been seen by another. It is enough that the defendant knowingly displayed it, or parted with its immediate custody, under circumstances which exposed it to be seen or understood by another person than himself." (New York Consolidated Laws, 1909. Section 1343)

This definition of "publication" holds pretty much for all the other states and the District of Columbia.

Once "publication" has been proved, the questions of truth and motive have to be decided. The use of such phrases as "it is alleged" do not absolve a publisher or editor of being responsible for a libel. Truth is generally an adequate defence "if the publication is for good motives and for justifiable ends." There are times, as Lord Coke said, when "the greater the truth the greater the libel." This applied particularly in proceedings involving "criminal libel," which, as will be pointed out, are very rare in the United States.

The New York law says:

"The publication is justified when the matter charged as libelous is true, and was published with good motives and for justifiable ends." (New York Consolidated Laws, 1909. Section 1342)

The Iowa law says:

"In all prosecutions or indictments for libel, the truth thereof may be given in evidence to the jury and if it appear to them that the matter charged as libelous was true and was published with good motives and for justifiable ends, the defendant shall be acquitted." (Code of Iowa, 1951. 737.4)

And in the District of Columbia the law is that "Any publication of a libel shall be justified if it appear that the matter charged as libelous was true and was published with good motives and for justifiable ends." (District of Columbia Code, 1940 edition. 22. 2303)

Alabama, however, does not provide for motive. Its Supreme Court has ruled that "The truth is no 'libel' under the laws of Alabama, no matter what motive may have prompted its publication." (Supreme Court of Alabama. Ripps v. Herrington. 1 Div. 90, March 27, 1941)

In asking for "good motives" and "justifiable ends" in the publication of a "truthful libel" the law appears to be on the side of mercy and deters many publishers, editors and authors from using the printed page for blackmail purposes. If Mr. X was convicted of burglary ten years ago and a newspaper publshes the fact for no reason whatever, save perhaps to hurt him in his occupation or to estrange some of his friends who did not know of his previous conviction, the publisher and editor are on dangerous ground. When Mr. X was convicted and sentenced, and had served his sentence, he had paid his debt to society, and to hound him further would be sheer cruelty.

In the realm of sexual and marital irregularity and immorality the truth can be a defence, but it is safest to stay clear of such charges. It is, for example, risky to call a woman a Lesbian, a prostitute, a nymphomaniac, an adultress, a cradle-snatcher, a grave-digger, or a gold-digger. Similarly it is risky to call a man a homosexual, a lecher, an adulterer, a gigolo, or a pervert. Juries are likely to feel that one's sexual practices, manners and preferences, however out of the ordinary, are so tremendously important to one's self-respect that it's well to make sure that they remain as private as possible, unless there is good reason to do otherwise.

Such facts may be published with impunity only if they appear in "privileged" documents or are stated during legislative or judicial proceedings. The New York law on this point is as follows:

"A prosecution for libel can not be maintained against a reporter, editor, publisher, or proprietor of a newspaper, for the publication therein, of a fair and true report of any judicial, legislative or other public and official proceeding, or of any statement, speech, argument or debate in the course of the same, without proving actual malice in making the report.

"This section does not apply to a libel contained in the heading of the report, or in any other matter added by any other person concerned in the publication; or in the report of anything said or done at the time and place of the public and official proceeding, which was not a part thereof." (New York Consolidated Laws, 1909. Sec. 1345) The law is substantially the same now.

The Texas law is somewhat more specific and extensive:

"It is no libel:

"1. To make any publication respecting a body politic or corporate as such.

"2. To make publications respecting the merits or doctrines

of any particular religion, system of morals or politics, or of any particular form of government.

"3. To publish any statement respecting any legislative or judicial proceedings, whether in fact true or not, unless in such statement a charge of corruption is made against some person acting in a legislative or judicial capacity.

"4. To publish any criticism or examination of any work of literature, science or art or any opinion as to the qualifications or merits of the author of such work.

"5. To publish true statements of fact as to the qualifications of any person for any occupation, profession or trade.

"6. To make true statements of fact or express opinions as to the integrity or other qualifications of a candidate for any office or public place of appointment." (Vernon's Annotated Statutes of the State of Texas. PC 1284)

Subsection 4, dealing with literary and art criticism, is of especial interest to newspaper and magazine editors who employ critics of violent prejudices and vigorous pens. A critic can say almost anything about a work of art—a book, a painting, a statue, a musical composition—with impunity, and he is permitted much leeway in airing his opinions about the artist, but it is safest to limit the expression of one's displeasure to the work of art and to let the reader form his own opinion about the artist. A close reading of pertinent cases seems to indicate that the law is eager to protect a man's earning capacity. Thus it is safe to say that Mr. Y's novel, "Purple Patches," is "horrendous garbage," but it is unsafe to say that Mr. Y is "an incompetent novelist." The apparent legal philosophy involved is sound enough: Mr. Y, in the case of "Purple Patches," may have done a bad job, but that does not necessarily mean that he is "incompetent." It may only mean that in this instance he failed; in the future, indeed, he might write a masterpiece.

Subsection 5, dealing with occupational qualifications, is to safeguard those making honest but unfavorable reports on people applying for jobs of any kind. To quote a high authority:

"The law accords a qualified privilege to communications

passing between persons having a mutual interest in the subject matter thereof or a mutual duty in reference thereto, even though they contain matter of a defamatory nature, and no criminal prosecution can ordinarily be based upon them unless malice is definitely made to appear." (33 American Jurisprudence, Libel and Slander, Section 318)

Subsection 6, dealing with remarks about candidates for public office, or office holders, appears in one form or another in the libel laws of all the states. It is of the highest importance, since it protects free and open discussion during elections. The law, in general, is that a candidate for public office or a man or woman in office seeks to be the beneficiary of so much trust and to enjoy so much responsibility, or already has this trust and responsibility, that the public has a right to know more about him than they otherwise would, and that here the libel laws should be relaxed. If Mr. B was convicted of embezzlement fifteen years ago, it would be libelous to print that fact, in most states, for no good motive or justifiable end. But if Mr. B runs for public office it would be safe to print the fact. The people have a right to know this item in Mr. B's past; it is important information regarding his qualifications as a potential public servant. The Utah Supreme Court has held:

". . . the rule appears to be well settled by an unbroken line of authority that every candidate for public office is amenable to public and private criticism, made in good faith, and based upon reasonable or probable cause: and when a person becomes such candidate he is regarded in law as putting his character in issue in respect to his qualifications and fitness for the office for which he is a candidate. This rule is founded in public policy, which demands that the conduct, qualifications, and fitness of persons seeking public positions of trust and confidence shall be subject to criticism, upon proper occasion, from proper motives, because the community has a right, and it is to its interests, to know the character, habits, mental and moral qualifications of its public servants." (People vs. Glassman, 12 Utah 238, 42 Pac. 956)

And in Kansas the court has gone even further:

"If the supposed libelous article was circulated only among the voters of Chase county, and only for the purpose of giving what the defendants believed to be truthful information, and only for the purpose of enabling such voters to cast their ballots more intelligently, and the whole thing was done in good faith, we think the article was privileged, and the defendants should have been acquitted, although the principal matters contained in the article were untrue in fact and derogatory to the character of the prosecuting witness. . . . Generally we think a person may in good faith publish whatever he may honestly believe to be true, and essential to the protection of his own interests or the interests of the person or persons to whom he makes the publication, without committing any public offense, although what he publishes may in fact not be true, and may be injurious to the character of others. And we further think that every voter is interested in electing to office none but persons of good moral character, and such only as are reasonably qualified to perform the duties of the office. This applies with great force to the election of county attorneys." (Coleman vs. MacLennan, 78 Kansas 711, 98 Pac. 281, 20 L.R.A. (N.S.) 361)

In all states one may say practically anything about a candidate for public office or an incumbent official provided such statements are made "in good faith and on reasonable grounds." So jealous is the law of the freedom of democratic discussion that it puts the factual truth of an allegation beneath the accuser's "justifiable ends."

A most significant victory for freedom of press with respect to candidates for public office and the freedom of discussion of public affairs was won on March 9, 1964, when the United States Supreme Court handed down its unanimous decision in the case of New York Times vs. Sullivan. Mr. Justice Brennan, writing the opinion of the Court, held that "debate on public issues should be uninhibited, robust and wide open, and that it may well include vehement, caustic, and sometimes unpleasantly sharp attacks on government and public officials." Mr.

Justice Hugo Black said that while he agreed with the opinion of the Court as a whole he was for "granting the press an absolute immunity for criticism of the way public officials do their public duty."

Libeling a bank, trust company, insurance company or any similar financial institution is a serious offence in all states, on the obvious ground that to defame such an institution is to endanger the safety of the savings of the people. A typical law is that of Indiana, which follows:

"Any person who shall wilfully and maliciously make, circulate or transmit to another or others, any false statement, rumor or suggestion, written, printed or by word of mouth, which is directly or by inference derogatory to the financial condition or affects the solvency or financial standing of any bank, savings bank, banking institution, trust company, credit union, or building and loan association doing business in this state, or who shall counsel, aid, procure or induce another to start, transmit or circulate any such statement or rumor, shall be deemed guilty of a misdemeanor and upon conviction thereof shall be punished by a fine of not more than one thousand dollars ($1,000) or by imprisonment for a term of not more than one (1) year, or both." (Burns Indiana Statutes, Annotated, 1933. 10-3203)

With regard to libeling religious systems, fraternal organizations, or "races" of mankind, the legislatures of most states have been reluctant to pass any laws, for fear that in trying to achieve a good end they would end by achieving a greater harm, to wit, the limitation of the rights of a free press. But some states seem to have definite ideas on this subject. The law in New Mexico is:

"It is no libel to make publication respecting the merits or doctrines of any particular religion, system of morals or politics, or of any particular form of government." (New Mexico Statutes, 1941, Annotated. 41-2719)

"Any person who, with intent to injure, publishes or circulates any malicious statement in writing, with reference to or concerning any fraternal or religious order or society, shall be guilty of criminal libel.

"The written or printed or published statement to come within the definition of libel must convey the idea either:

a. That said fraternal or religious order or society has been guilty as an order or society of some penal offense or has conspired to commit some penal offense.

b. That said fraternal or religious order or society has, as an order or society, been guilty of some act or omission which, though not a penal offense, is disgraceful and the natural consequences of which act or omission are to bring such order or society into contempt among honorable persons.

"Any person found guilty of libel under the provisions of this act (Secs. 41-2725–41-2727) shall be punished by a fine of not more than two thousand dollars ($2,000), nor less than two hundred dollars ($200), or by imprisonment in the county jail for a term of three (3) months, or by both such fine and imprisonment." (New Mexico Statutes, 1941, Annotated. 41-2725–41-2727)

In Massachusetts the law is:

"Whoever publishes any false written or printed material with intent to maliciously promote hatred of any group of persons in the Commonwealth because of race, color or religion shall be guilty of libel and shall be punished by a fine of not more than one thousand dollars or by imprisonment for not more than one year, or both. The defendant may prove in defense that the publication was privileged or was not malicious. Prosecutions under this section shall be instituted only by the attorney general or by the district attorney for the district in which the alleged libel was published." (1943, 223, appvd. April 31, 1943) (Annotated Laws of Massachusetts. C. 273, Sec. 98C.)

Newspapers and magazines sometimes put wrong pictures or wrong names in their reports or advertising, but the admission of the error, however honest, does not prevent prosecution for libel by the people who consider themselves defamed. The classic decision on this subject was written by the late Mr. Justice Oliver Wendell Holmes in 1909. It is so important in the libel literature that it is worth quoting at considerable length:

Peck vs. Tribune Co., 214 U.S. 185(1909). Holmes, J., for the Court:

This is an action on the case for a libel. The libel alleged is found in an advertisement printed in the defendant's newspaper The Chicago Sunday Tribune, and so far as is material is as follows: "Nurse and Patients Praise Duffy's—Mrs. A. Schuman, One of Chicago's Most Capable and Experienced Nurses, Pays an Eloquent Tribute to the Great Invigorating Life-Giving and Curative Properties of Duffy's Pure Malt Whiskey. . . ." Then followed a portrait of the plaintiff, with the words "Mrs. A. Schuman" under it. Then, in quotation marks, "After ten years of constant use of your Pure Malt Whiskey, both by myself and as given to patients in my capacity as nurse, I have no hesitation in recommending it as the very best tonic and stimulant for all weak and run-down conditions," &c., &c., with the words "Mrs. A. Schuman, 1576 Mozart St., Chicago, Ill.," at the end, not in quotation marks, but conveying the notion of a signature, or at least that the words were hers. The declaration alleged that the plaintiff was not Mrs. Schuman, was not a nurse and was a total abstainer from whiskey and all spirituous liquors. There was also a count for publishing the plaintiff's likeness without leave. The defendant pleaded not guilty. At the trial, subject to exceptions, the judge excluded the plaintiff's testimony in support of her allegations just stated, and directed a verdict for the defendant. His action was sustained by the Circuit Court of Appeals. . . .

Of course the insertion of the plaintiff's picture in the place and with the concomitants that we have described imported that she was the nurse and made the statements set forth, as rightly was decided in *Wandt vs. Hearst's Chicago American,* 129 Wisconsin, 419, 421. *Morrison vs. Smith,* 177 N. Y. 366. Therefore the publication was of and concerning the plaintiff, notwithstanding the presence of another fact, the name of the real signer of the certificate, if that was Mrs. Schuman, that was inconsistent, when all the facts were known, with the plaintiff's having signed or adopted it. Many might recognize the plaintiff's face without knowing her name, and those who did know it might be led to infer that she had sanctioned the publication under an alias. There was some suggestion that the defendant published the portrait by mistake, and without knowledge that it was the plaintiff's portrait or was not what it purported to be. But the fact, if it was one, was no excuse. If the publication was libellous the defendant took the risk. As was said of such matters by Lord Mansfield, "Whatever a man publishes, he publishes at his peril." The *King vs. Woodfall*, Lofft, 776, 781. See further *Hearne vs. Stowell*, 12 A. & E. 719, 726; *Shepheard vs. Whitaker*, L. R. 10 C. P. 502; *Clark vs. North American Co.*, 203 Pa. St. 346, 351, 352. The reason is plain. A libel is harmful on its face. If a man sees fit to publish manifestly hurtful statements concerning an individual, without other justification than exists for an advertisement or a piece of news, the usual principles of tort will make him liable, if the statements are false or are true only of some one else. See *Morasse vs. Brochu*, 151 Massachusetts, 567, 575.

The question, then, is whether the publication was a libel. It was held by the Circuit Court of Appeals not to be, or at most to entitle the plaintiff only to nominal damages, no special damage being alleged. It was pointed out that there was no general consensus of opinion that to drink whiskey is wrong or that to be a nurse is discreditable. It might have been added that very possibly giving a certificate and the use of one's portrait in aid of an advertisement would be regarded with irony, or a stronger feeling, only by a few. But it appears to us that such inquiries are beside the point. It may be that the action for libel is of little use, but while it is maintained it should be governed by the general principles of tort. If the advertisement obviously would hurt the plaintiff in the estimation of an important and respectable part of the community, liability is not a question of a majority vote.

We know of no decision in which this matter is discussed upon principle. But obviously an unprivileged falsehood need not entail universal hatred to constitute a cause of action. No falsehood is thought about or even known by all the world. No conduct is hated by all. That it will be known by a larger number and will lead an appreciable fraction of that number to regard the plaintiff with contempt is enough to do her practical harm. Thus if a doctor were represented as advertising, the fact that it would affect his standing with others of his profession might make the representation actionable, although advertising is not reputed dishonest and even seems to be regarded by many with pride. See *Martin vs. The Picayune*, 115 Louisiana, 979. It seems to us impossible to say that the obvious tendency of what is imputed to the plaintiff by this advertisement is not seriously to hurt her standing with a considerable and respectable class in the community. Therefore it was the plaintiff's right to prove her case and go to the jury, and the defendant would have got all that it could ask if it had been permitted to persuade them, if it could, to take a contrary view. . . .

It is unnecessary to consider the question whether the publication of the plaintiff's likeness was a tort *per se*. It is enough for the present case that the law should at least be prompt to recognize the injuries that may arise from an unauthorized use in connection with other facts, even if more subtlety is needed to state the wrong than is needed here. In this instance we feel no doubt.

Judgment reversed.

An apparently slight mistake in printing the name of a man can lead to serious litigation. The Boston *Globe* reported that an H. P. Hanson, a real estate and insurance broker of South Boston, was arrested for drunkenness. The actual person arrested was A.P.H. Hanson. But there was an H.P. Hanson, who also lived in South Boston and who also was a real estate and insurance broker. This H.P. Hanson sued the *Globe* for libel. The majority of the Massachusetts Supreme Court held there was no libel since the news item obviously referred to A.P.H. Hanson. Justice Oliver Wendell Holmes, who was then a member of that court, thought otherwise, and in a very short time his dissent became the accepted doctrine on this phase of libel. His opinion is so basic, and takes up so many fundamental questions in the realm of libel in general, that it is worth close study on the part of the practicing journalist, and hence is here quoted:

Hadley P. Hanson vs. Globe Newspaper Company. 159 Mass. 293, 299 (1893).

I am unable to agree with the decision of the majority of the court, and as the question is of some importance in its bearing on legal principles, and as I am not alone in my views, I think it proper to state the considerations which have occurred to me.

The first thing to determine is what question is presented. If we were to stop with the words in which the conclusion of the report is couched there would be no question at all. "The court found as a fact that the alleged libel declared on by the plaintiff was not published by the defendant of or concerning the plaintiff." But it is not to be supposed that a justice of the Superior Court would send a report to this court in which he did not intend to present a question of law. The so-called finding either is a ruling on the effect of the facts previously found, or at least, putting it in the most favorable way for the defendant, is a conclusion drawn from those facts alone. Whether the conclusion be one of fact or of law, the question is whether it is justified by the facts set forth, without other facts or evidence.

The facts are that libellous matter was published in an article by the defendant about "H. P. Hanson, a real estate and insurance broker of South Boston," that the plaintiff bore that name and description, and, so far as appears, that no one else did, but that the defendant did not know of his existence, and intended to state some facts about one Andrew P. H. Hanson, also a real estate and insurance broker of South Boston, concerning whom the article was substantially true.

The article described the subject of it as a prisoner in the criminal dock, and states that he was fined, and this makes it possible to speak of the article as one describing the conduct of a prisoner. But this mode of characterization seems to me misleading. In form it describes the plight and conduct of "H. P. Hanson, a real estate and insurance broker of South Boston." The statement is, "H. P. Hanson, a real estate and insurance broker of South Boston, emerged from the seething mass of humanity that filled the dock," etc. In order to give it any different subject, or to give the subject any further qualifications or description, you have to resort to the predicate, to the very libellous matter itself. It is not necessary to say that this never can be done, but it must be done with great caution. The very substance of the libel complained of is the statement that the plaintiff was a prisoner in the criminal dock, and was fined. The object of the article, which is a newspaper criminal court report, is to make that statement. The rest of it amounts to nothing, and is merely an attempt to make the statement amusing. If an article should allege falsely that A. murdered B. with a knife, it would not be a satisfactory answer to an action by A. that it was a description of the conduct of the murderer of B., and was true concerning him. The public, or all except the few who may have been in court on the day in question, or who consult the criminal records, have no way of telling who was the prisoner except by what is stated in the article, and the article states that it was "H. P. Hanson, a real estate and insurance broker of South Boston."

If I am right so far, the words last quoted, and those words alone, describe the subject of the allegation, in substance as well as in form. Those words also describe the plaintiff, and no one else. The only ground, then, on which the matters alleged of and concerning the subject, can be found not to be alleged of and concerning the plaintiff, is that the defendant did not intend them to apply to him, and the question is narrowed to whether such a want of intention is enough to warrant the finding, or to constitute a defence, when the inevitable consequence of the defendant's acts is that the public, or that part of it which knows the plaintiff, will suppose that the defendant did use its language about him.

On general principles of tort, the private intent of the defendant would not exonerate it. It knew that it was publishing statements purporting to be serious, which would be hurtful to a man if applied to him. It knew that it was using as the subject of those statements words which purported to designate a particular man, and would be understood by its readers to designate one. In fact, the words purported to designate, and would be understood by its readers to designate, the plaintiff. If the defendant had supposed that there was no such person, and had intended simply to write an amusing fiction, that would not be a defence, at least unless its belief was justifiable. Without special reason, it would have no right to assume that there was no one within the sphere of its influence to whom the description answered. The case would be very like firing a gun into a street, and, when a man falls, setting up that no one was known to be there. *Commonwealth vs. Pierce,* 138 Mass. 165, 178. *Hull's case,* Kelyng, 40. *Rex vs. Burton,* 1 Strange, 481. *Rigmaidon's case,* 1 Lewin, 180. *Regina vs. Desmond,* Steph. Cr. Law, 146. So, when the description which points out the plaintiff is supposed by the defendant to point out another man whom in fact it does not describe, the defendant is equally liable as when the description is supposed to point out nobody. On the general principles of tort, the publication is so manifestly detrimental that the defendant publishes it at the peril of being able to justify it in the sense in which the public will understand it.

But in view of the unfortunate use of the word "malice" in connection with libel and slander, a doubt may be felt whether actions for these causes are governed by general principles. The earliest forms of the common law known to me treat slander like any other tort, and say nothing about malice. 4 Seld. Soc. Pub. 40, 48, 61. Probably the word was borrowed at a later, but still early date, from the *malitia* of the canon law. By the canon law, one who maliciously charged another with a grave sin incurred excommunication, *ipso facto*. Lyndw., Provinciale, lib. 5, tit. 17 (*De Sent Excomm. c.* 1, *Auctoritate Dei*). Oughton, *Ordo Judiciorum,* tit. 261. Naturally *malitia* was defined as *cogitatio malae mentis,* coming near to conscious malevolence. Lyndw., *ubi supra,* note f. Naturally also for a time the common law followed its leader. Three centuries ago it seems to have regarded the malice alleged in slander and libel as meaning the malice of ethics and the spiritual law.

In the famous case where a parson in a sermon repeated, out of Foxe's *Book of Martyrs,* the story "that one Greenwood, being a perjured person, and a great persecutor, had great plagues inflicted upon him, and was killed by the hand of God, whereas in truth he never was so plagued, and was himself present at that sermon," and afterwards sued the parson for the slander, Chief Justice Wray instructed the jury "that, it being delivered but as a story, and not with any malice or intention to slander any, he was not guilty of the words maliciously; and so was found not guilty. . . ."

But that case is no longer law. . . . The law constantly is tending towards consistency of theory. For a long time it has been held that the malice alleged in an action of libel means no more than it does in other actions of tort. . . . Indeed, one of the earliest cases to state modern views was a case of libel. . . . Accordingly, it was recently laid down by this court that the liability was the usual liability in tort for the natural consequences of a manifestly injurious act. A man may be liable civilly, and formerly, at least by the common law of England, even criminally, for publishing a libel without knowing it. . . . And it seems he might be liable civilly for publishing it by mistake, intending to publish another paper. . . . So, when by mistake the name of the plaintiff's firm was inserted under the head "First Meetings under the Bankruptcy Act," instead of under "Dissolution of Partnerships." . . . So a man will be liable for a slander spoken in jest, if the bystanders reasonably understand it to be a serious charge. . . . Of course it does not matter that the defendant did not intend to injure the plaintiff, it lies upon him "only to show that this construction, which they've put in the paper, is such as the generality of readers must take it in, according to the obvious and natural sense of it." . . . In *Smith vs. Ashley,* 11 Met. 367, the jury were instructed that the publisher of a newspaper article written by another, and supposed and still asserted by the defendant to be fiction, was not liable if he believed it to be so. Under the circumstances of the case, "believed" meant "reasonably believed." Even so qualified, it is questioned by Mr. Odgers if the ruling would be followed in England. . . . But it has no application to this case, as here the defendant's agent wrote the article, and there is no evidence that he or the defendant had any reason to believe that H. P. Hanson meant any one but the plaintiff.

The foregoing decisions show that slander and libel now, as in the beginning, are governed by the general principles of the law of tort, and, if that be so, the defendant's ignorance that the words which it published identified the plaintiff is no more an excuse, than ignorance of any other fact about which the defendant has been put on inquiry. To hold that a man publishes such words at his peril, when they are supposed to describe a different man, is hardly a severer application of the law, than when they are uttered about a man believed on the strongest grounds to be dead, and thus not capable of being the subject of a tort. It has been seen that by the common law of England such a belief would not be an excuse. . . .

I feel some difficulty in putting my finger on the precise point of difference between the minority and majority of the court. I understand, however, that a somewhat unwilling assent is yielded to the general views which I have endeavored to justify, and I should gather that the exact issue was to be found in the statement that the article was one describing the conduct of a prisoner brought before the Municipal Court of Boston, coupled with the later statement that the language, taken in connection with the publicly known circumstances under which it was written, showed at once that the article referred to A. P. H. Hanson, and that the name H. P. Hanson was used by mistake. I have shown why it seems to me that these statements are misleading. I only will add, on this point, that I do not know what the publically known circumstances are. I think it is a mistake of fact to suppose that the public generally know who was before the Municipal Criminal Court on a given day. I think it is a mistake of law to say that, because a small part of the public have that knowledge, the plaintiff cannot recover for the harm done him in the eyes of the greater part of the public, probably including all his acquaintances who are ignorant of the matter, and I also think it no sufficient answer to say that they might consult the criminal records, and find out that probably there was some error. . . . If the case should proceed further on the facts, it might appear that, in view of the plaintiff's character and circumstances, all who knew him would assume that there was a mistake, that the harm to him was merely nominal, and that he had been too hasty in resorting to an action to vindicate himself. But that question is not before us.

With reference to the suggestion that, if the article, in addition to what was true concerning A. P. Hanson, had contained matter which was false and libellous as to him, he might have maintained an action, it is unnecessary to express an opinion. I think the proposition less obvious than that the plaintiff can maintain one. If an article should describe the subject of its statements by two sets of marks, one of which identified one man and one of which identified another, and a part of the public naturally and reasonably were led by the one set to apply the statements to one plaintiff, and another part were led in the same way by the other set to apply them to another, I see no absurdity in allowing two actions to be maintained. But that is not this case.

Even if the plaintiff and A. P. H. Hanson had borne the same name, and the article identified its subject only by a proper name, very possibly that would not be enough to raise the question. For, as every one knows, a proper name always purports to designate one person and no other, and although, through the imperfection of our system of naming, the same combination of letters and sounds may be applied to two or more, the name of each, in theory of law, is distinct, although there is no way of finding out which person was named but by inquiring which was meant. *Licet idem sit nomen, tamen diversum est propter diversitatem personae. . . .*

Mr. Justice Morton and Mr. Justice Barker agree with this opinion.

In libel the jury is of particular importance. In state after state it is made very clear that "the jury shall have the right to determine the law and the fact." (Minnesota Statutes, 1941.

634.05)

In libel an apology or a retraction cannot prevent a suit, but it can mitigate damages considerably. The Indiana law is pretty inclusive on this point:

"Before any suit shall be brought for the publication of a libel in any newspaper in this state, the aggrieved party shall, at least three (3) days before filing the complaint in such suit, serve notice in writing on the publisher or publishers of such newspaper, at their principal office of publication, specifying the statements in said article which he or they allege to be false and defamatory. If it shall appear upon trial of said action that said article was published in good faith, that its falsity was due to mistake or misapprehension of the facts, and that a full and fair retraction of any statement therein alleged to be erroneous was published in a regular issue of such newspaper, within three (3) days, if such newspaper be a daily publication, or within ten (10) days, if such newspaper be a weekly publication, after such mistake or misapprehension was brought to the knowledge of such publisher or publishers, in as conspicuous place and type in the same place where said original item appeared in such newspaper as was the article complained of, then the plaintiff in such case shall recover only actual damages: Provided, however, That the foregoing provisions of sec. one of this act shall not apply to the case of any libel against any candidate for a public office in this state, unless the retraction of the charge is made in a conspicuous manner at least three (3) days before the election. (Burns Indiana Statutes, Annotated, 1933. 2-1043)

"The words 'actual damages' in the foregoing section shall be construed to include all damages that the plaintiff may have suffered in respect to his character, property, business, trade, profession or occupation, and no other damages whatever." (Burns Indiana Statutes, Annotated, 1933. 2-1044)

The State of Florida puts much more value upon an apology or retraction:

"If it appears upon the trial that said article was published in good faith, that its falsity was due to an honest mistake of the facts, and that there were reasonable grounds for believing that the statements in said article were true, and that within ten days after the service of said notice a full and fair correction, apology and retraction was published in the same editions or corresponding issues of the newspaper or periodical in which said article appeared, and in as conspicuous place and type as was said original article, and if, in a criminal proceeding, a verdict of 'guilty' is rendered on such a state of facts, the defendant shall be fined one dollar and costs, and no more." (Florida Statutes, 1941. 836. 08)

Radio broadcasting and television have been coming more and more within the province of the libel law, though the various states are still feeling their way in this respect. It is wise, however, for the practical radio official to assume that the law of libel for radio is about the same as the law of libel applied to the printed page. Perhaps even more so, for defamation by radio reaches a wider audience generally than defamation by the printed word.

The Oregon law is:

"If any person shall wilfully, by any means other than words orally spoken, except as herein provided, publish or cause to be published of or concerning another any false and scandalous matter, with intent to injure or defame such other person, or if any person shall wilfully use or utter over, through or by means of the radio commonly called broadcasting, of or concerning another any false and scandalous matter, with intent to injure or defame such other person, upon conviction thereof, he shall be punished by imprisonment in the county jail not less than three months nor more than one year, or by fine of not less than $100 nor more than $500. Any allusion to any person or family, with intent to injure, defame or maliciously annoy such person or family, shall be deemed to come within the provisions of this section; and it hereby is made the duty of the prosecuting attorney of each judicial district to see that the provisions of this section are enforced, whether the party injured desire to prosecute such offense or not." (Oregon Compiled Laws, 1940, Annotated. Sec. 23-437)

The Indiana law is:

"Before any suit shall be brought for the publishing, speaking, uttering or conveying by words, acts, or in any other manner of a libel or slander by any radio or television station or company in this state, the aggrieved party shall, at least three (3) days before filing the complaint in such suit, serve notice in writing on the manager or managers of such radio or television station, at their principal office, specifying the words or acts which he or they allege to be false and defamatory. If it shall appear, upon trial of such action, that such words or acts were conveyed and broadcast in good faith, that its falsity was due to mistake or misapprehension of the facts, and that a full and fair retraction of any words or acts therein alleged to be erroneous was conveyed or broadcast on a regular program of such radio or television company, within ten (10) days after such mistake or misapprehension was brought to the knowledge of such manager or managers, at approximately the same time and by the same sending power so as to be as visible and audible as the original acts or words complained of, then the plaintiff in such case shall recover only actual damages. The foregoing provisions of this act shall not apply to the case of any libel or slander against any candidate for a public office in this state, unless the retraction of the charge is made in an audible or visible manner at least three (3) days before the election." (Burns Indiana Statutes, Annotated, 1933. 2-518)

The laws of the various states are now generally pretty much of one intent with respect to defamation on the radio and on television. They consider it a libel rather than a slander, and they offer safeguards to the radio-television stations, especially with alleged defamation of candidates for public office. The following statute from the State of Massachusetts (Supplement to Vol. 8, Mass., 1958, 231 §91A) is typical:

"The owner, operator, or licensee of a radio or television station or network of such stations or the agent or servant of any such person shall not, in action for slander, or for publishing a libel, be held liable in damages for or on account of any defamatory matter uttered, broadcast, telecast, or published over the radio or television facilities of any such station or network by any person whose utterance, broadcast, telecast, or publication is not, under the provisions of any law of the United States or any regulation, ruling or order of the Federal Communications Commission, subject to censorship or control by such station or network. (Added by 1957, 378, approved May 15, 1957; effective 90 days thereafter)."

So is the following law from the State of Missouri:

"The owner, licensee, or operator of a visual or sound radio broadcasting station or network of stations, or the agents or employees of such owner, licensee, or operator of such a station or network of stations, shall not be liable for any damages for any defamatory statement uttered over the facilities of such station or network by or on behalf of any candidate for public office when such statement is not subject to censorship or control by reason of any federal statute or any ruling or order of the Federal Communications Commission made pursuant thereto. (Laws, 1951, 537.105)"

Most libel actions are civil actions. Criminal libel is a rare phenomenon in this country. It involves a "breach of peace," and is extremely difficult to prove, since defamation is hardly ever of so horrifying a nature that it arouses a community to a state of violence. Some states, in their statutes, ignore "criminal libel"; others do mention it, but they do not always draw a sharp distinction between "criminal libel" and "civil libel." The law in Indiana, for instance, says:

"Whoever makes, composes, dictates, prints or writes a libel to be published, or procures the same to be done, and whoever publishes or knowingly aids in publishing or communicating a libel, or whoever maliciously publishes any false charge of and concerning another, accusing such other person of any crime, or of any degrading or infamous act, or whoever, by such means, maliciously and falsely charges any woman with want of chastity, shall be deemed guilty of criminal libel, and, on conviction, shall be fined not less than five dollars ($5.00) nor more than one thousand dollars ($1,000), to which may be added imprisonment in the county jail for not more than six (6) months." (Burns Indiana Statutes, Annotated, 1933. 10-3201)

There are probably fewer libel cases in this country than in England, certainly fewer successful ones in proportion to publications. In England the libel laws are much more severe than here, and hence libel suits are so much more serious. American juries are inclined, on the whole, to find against the plaintiff, or to place damages at a ridiculously small amount, unless there is obviously gross, malicious defamation.

Libel suits, however, are plentiful enough and can be dreadful nuisances, involving the expenditure of considerable time and money. The libel laws themselves are not always as clear as they might be; they vary from state to state, courts reverse themselves, and lawyers are inclined to be too cautious. Most of them, when consulted, generally advise against the publication of any questionable item on the ground that they can't guarantee that a jury won't find against the publication. The courageous editor has to consult his own conscience, instincts, and experience. He may not always be one hundred per cent sure of the truth of an article, but if he is, say, seventy-five per cent sure, and his instinct tells him that the other twenty-five per cent of the truth can somehow be dug up, and if the content of the article is of vital interest to the community, then he is duty-bound to publish the "libel." An editor who has not had such possible "libel" suits on his hands is unworthy of his calling.

There is always risk involved, but the experienced editor knows when it's minor and he can always do much to minimize it. He knows that libel generally means defamation of character, but if a man has very little character he can hardly be defamed. There is a whole class of proven corrupt politicians and convicted felons who can barely be libeled no matter what is said about them. Then there is a class of people who hesitate to sue for fear of exposing aspects of their careers and character that they prefer to keep hidden. A plaintiff in a libel suit has to submit to embarrassing probing into his record, for the defendant has a right to know what sort of character he is charged with having defamed.

There are a few rules of thumb to remember in the realm of libel. It is wise never to question a man's or woman's sexual regularity or integrity, or to impugn his or her earning capacity. When criticizing a work of art, criticize the *work,* not the artist. If you must say something about the artist, do so in relation to the specific work of art that you are discussing. As has been said, there is greater leeway in the discussion of public servants or candidates for public office.

Lord Mansfield's celebrated dictum, "Whatever a man publishes, he publishes at his peril," has been a nightmare to editors and publishers for almost 175 years. In the general run of publishing, a reasonable amount of care and regard for the ordinary decencies is all that is needed to avoid nearly all danger of libel. In the few remaining cases the worthy editor will gladly assume the risk in the public interest, thereby turning Lord Mansfield's dictum from a nightmare into a challenge.

Alabama

CODE OF ALABAMA, 1940, 1958

Basic Statutes. §908. *Truth of charges against public men may be proved.*—In civil actions for the publication of papers, investigating the official conduct of officers or men in public capacity, or when the matter published is proper for public information, the truth thereof may be given in evidence.

§909. *Truth of the words, etc., evidence under the general issue.*—In all actions of slander or libel, the truth of the words spoken or written, or the circumstances under which they were spoken or written, may be given in evidence under the general issue in mitigation of the damages.

§910. *Libel or slander; defamatory matter.*—In an action for libel or slander, it shall be sufficient to state, generally, that the defamatory matter was published or spoken of the plaintiff; and if the allegation be denied, the plaintiff must prove, on the trial, the facts showing that the defamatory matter was published or spoken of him.

§911. *Import of words*—Every accusation of false swearing presumptively imports a charge of perjury, and every accusation importing the commission of a crime punishable by indictment must be held presumptively to mean what the language used ordinarily imports.

§912. *Charges of unchastity actionable.*—Any words, written, spoken or printed, of any woman, falsely imputing to her a want of chastity, are actionable without proof of special damages.

§913. *Retraction mitigates damages.*—The defendant in an action of slander or libel may prove under the general issue in mitigation of damages that the charge was made by mistake or through inadvertence, and that he has retracted the charge and offered amends before suit by publishing an apology in a newspaper when the charge had been thus promulgated, in a prominent position; or verbally, in the presence of witnesses, when the accusation was verbal or written, and had offered to certify the same in writing.

§914. *Aggrieved person must give notice to publishers of alleged libel before vindictive damages can be recovered.*—Vindictive or punitive damages shall not be recovered in any action for libel on account of any publication concerning the official conduct or actions of any public officer, or for the publication of any matter which is proper for public information, unless five days before the bringing of the suit the plaintiff shall have made written demand upon the defendant for a public retraction of the charge or matter published; and the defendant shall have failed or refused to publish within five days in as prominent and public a place or manner as the charge or matter published occupied, a full and fair retraction of such charge or matter.

§915. *When actual damages only recoverable.*—If it shall appear on the trial of an action for libel that an article complained of was published in good faith, that its falsity was due to mistake and misapprehension, and that a full correction or retraction of any false statement therein was published in the next regular issue of said newspaper, or in case of daily newspapers, within five days after service of said notice aforesaid, in as conspicuous a place and type in said newspaper as was the article complained of, then the plaintiff in such case shall recover only actual damages.

§916. *Recantation and tender; effect of.*—If the defendant, after or before suit brought, make the recantation and amends recited in the preceding sections, and also tender to the plaintiff a compensation in money, and bring the same into court, the plaintiff can recover no costs, if the jury believe and find the tender was sufficient.

§917. *Effect of tender received.*—The receipt of the money

tendered, if before suit brought, is a bar to the action; if after suit, releases the defendant from all damages and costs, except the costs which accrued before the tender and receipt of the money.

TITLE 7

Limitations. §26. *Limitation of one year.*—The following must commence within one year:

"Actions for malicious prosecution.

"Actions for seduction.

"Actions qui tam, or for a penalty given by statute to the party aggrieved, unless the statute imposing it prescribes a different limitation.

"Actions of libel or slander.

"Actions for any injury to the person or rights of another, not arising from contract, and not herein specifically enumerated."

Alaska

FROM THE ALASKA CONSTITUTION

Article I, Section 5. Freedom of Speech. Every person may freely speak, write, and publish on all subjects, being responsible for the abuse of that right.

Section 6. *Immunities.*—Legislators may not be held to answer before any other tribunal for any statement made in the exercise of their legislative duties while the legislature is in session. Members attending, going to, or returning from legislative sessions are not subject to civil process and are privileged from arrest except for felony or breach of the peace.

Section 11.15.310. *Libel and Slander.*—A person who wilfully speaks, writes, or in any other manner publishes defamatory or scandalous matter concerning another with intent to injure or defame him is guilty of a misdemeanor, and upon conviction is punishable by imprisonment in a jail for not less than six months nor more than one year, or by a fine of not less than $50 nor more than $500, or by both. This section applies to an allusion to person or family, with intent to injure, defame, or maliciously annoy the family. (§65-4-28 ACLA 1949; am §4 ch 2 SLA 1964)

Section 09.50.250. *Actionable claims against the state.*—A person or corporation having a claim against the state may bring an action against the state in the superior court. However, no action may be brought under this section if the claim . . .

(3) arises out of assault, battery, false imprisonment, false arrest, malicious prosecution, abuse of process, libel, slander, misrepresentation, deceit, or interference with contract rights.

Section 06.05.515. *Slander and libel of bank.*—Any person who wilfully or maliciously makes, circulates, or transmits to another any statement, rumor or suggestion, written, printed or by word of mouth, which is directly or by implication derogatory to the financial condition or affects the solvency or financial standing of any bank or trust company doing business in the state, or who counsels, aids, procures, or induces another to start, transmit, or circulate such a statement or rumor is guilty of a felony, and upon conviction is punishable by a fine of not more than $5,000, or by imprisonment for not less than one year nor more than five years, or by both. (§3.508 ch 129 SLA 1951; am §2 ch 43 SLA 1964)

Section 11.15.320. *Truth as a defense.*—In prosecutions under §310 of this chapter, the truth of the defamatory or scandalous matter is a defense only when uttered or published with a good motive and for a justifiable end. (§65-4-29 ACLA 1949)

Section 11.15.330. *Presumption of malice in prosecution for libel and slander.*—An injurious publication is presumed malicious if no justifiable end or good motive is shown for making it.

Section 09.10.070. *Actions to be brought in two years.*—No person may bring an action for libel, slander, assault, battery, seduction, . . . unless commenced within two years. (§1.07 ch. 101 SLA 1962)

Arizona

ARIZONA CODE, 1939, 1956

Basic Statutes. Sec. 18-107. *Actions for publications made in compliance with law prohibited.*—An action for damages shall not lie against the editor, publisher, or proprietor of any newspaper or periodical for the publication of any report, proceedings, or other matter, published at the instance of a public officer acting in compliance with a requirement of law.

Sec. 21-101. *Venue of actions.*—No person shall be sued out of the county in which he resides, except: . . .

10. Where the foundation of the action is a crime, offense or trespass for which an action in damages may lie, the action may be brought in the county in which the crime, offense or trespass was committed or in the county in which the defendant or any of the several defendants reside or may be found; provided, however, that any action for damages against the editor, proprietor or publisher of any newspaper or periodical published in the state for the publication therein of any alleged libelous statement shall be brought in the county in which the principal publication office of such newspaper or periodical is located or in the county where the plaintiff resided at the time of the publication of such statement.

Sec. 21-420. *Complaint in action for libel.*—In an action for libel or slander, the complaint need not state the extrinsic facts applying to the plaintiff the defamatory matter out of which the cause of action arose; but may allege generally that the same was published or spoken concerning the plaintiff, and if such allegation be controverted the plaintiff shall establish on the trial that it was so published or spoken.

Sec. 43-3501. *Libel defined—punishment.*—A libel is any malicious falsehood expressed by writing, printing, or by signs or pictures, which tends to bring any person into disrepute, contempt or ridicule, or to blacken the memory of one who is dead; or any malicious defamation expressed by writing, printing, or by signs or pictures, which tends to impeach the honesty, integrity, virtue or reputation, or publish the natural or alleged defects of one who is alive, and thereby to expose him to public hatred, contempt or ridicule. Libel is punishable by a fine not exceeding five thousand dollars ($5,000) or imprisonment in the state prison not exceeding one (1) year.

Sec. 43-3502. *When malice presumed—Justification—Jury tries law and facts.*—An injurious publication is presumed to have been malicious if no justifiable motive for making it is shown. In a criminal prosecution for libel, the truth may be given in evidence to the jury, and if it appears to the jury that the matter charged as libelous is true, and was published with good motives and for justifiable ends, the party shall be acquitted. The jury have the right to determine the law and the fact.

Sec. 43-3503. *Publication—Publisher liable.*—To sustain the charge of publishing it is not necessary that the words or things complained of should have been read or seen by another; it is enough that the accused knowingly parted with the immediate custody of the libel, under circumstances which exposed it to be read or seen by any other person than himself. The author, editor and proprietor of any book, newspaper or serial publication, is chargeable with the publication of any words contained in any part of such book, newspaper or serial.

Sec. 43-3504. *Reporting public proceedings.*—No reporter, editor, or proprietor of any newspaper is liable to any prosecution for a fair and true report of any judicial, legislative or other public official proceedings, or of any statement, speech, argument or debate in the course of the same, except upon proof of malice in making such report, which shall not be implied from the mere fact of publication. Libelous remarks or comments connected with such privileged matter receive no privilege by reason of their being so connected.

Sec. 43-3505. *Communication to interested person, privileged.*—A communication made to a person interested in the communication, by one who was also interested, or who stood in such relation to the former as to afford a reasonable ground for supposing his motive innocent, is not presumed to be malicious and is a privileged communication.

Sec. 43-3506. *Threatening to publish libel.*—Every person who threatens another to publish libel concerning him, or any parent, husband, wife or child of such person, or member of his family, and every person who offers to prevent the publication of any libel upon another person, with intent to extort any money or other valuable consideration from any person is guilty of a misdemeanor.

Sec. 43-704. *Circulating false rumor of insolvency of bank.*—Any person who wilfully and knowingly makes, circulates or transmits to another any statement or rumor, written, printed or by word of mouth, which is untrue in fact and is directly or by inference derogatory to the financial condition, or affects the solvency or financial standing of any bank, doing business in this state; or who knowingly counsels, aids, procures or induces another to start, transmit or circulate any such statement or rumor, is guilty of a crime and punishable by a fine of not more than one thousand dollars ($1,000) or by imprisonment for not more than one (1) year, or both.

Sec. 43-5407. *Sending threatening or anonymous letter.*—Every person who knowingly and wilfully sends or delivers to another any letter or writing, whether subscribed or not, threatening to accuse him or another of a crime, or to expose or publish any of his failings or infirmities, and every writer or sender of any anonymous letter or writing calculated to create distrust of another or tending to impute dishonesty, want of chastity, drunkenness or any crime or infirmity to the receiver of the letter, or to any other person, is guilty of a misdemeanor.

Sec. 44-741. *Libel.*—No indictment or information for libel shall be invalid or insufficient for the reason that it does not set forth extrinsic facts for the purpose of showing the application to the party alleged to be libelled of the defamatory matter on which the indictment is founded.

Sec. 44-753. *Forms of specific offenses.*—The following forms may be used in the cases in which they are applicable:

Libel.—A. B. published a libel concerning C. D. in the form of a letter (book, picture, or as the case may be) (the particulars should specify the pages and lines constituting the libel, when necessary, as where it is contained in a book or pamphlet).

Sec. 51-623. *Untrue or derogatory statements, circulating a misdemeanor.*—Any person who wilfully makes, circulates or transmits to any other person, except to any public officer, any statement written, printed or by word of mouth, which is untrue in fact and known by such person to be untrue or which is directly derogatory to the financial condition or affects the solvency or financial standing of any building and loan association is guilty of a misdemeanor.

Constitution of Arizona, Art. II, Sec. 6. *Freedom of speech and press.*—Every person may freely speak, write, and publish on all subjects, being responsible for the abuse of that right.

Limitations. Sec. 12-541. *One-year limitation.*—There shall be commenced and prosecuted within one (1) year after the cause of action shall have accrued, and not afterward, the following actions:

1. For malicious prosecution, or for false imprisonment, or for injuries done to the character or reputation of another by libel or slander;

2. For damages for seduction or breach of promise of marriage;

3. Upon a liability created by statute, other than a penalty of forfeiture.

Arkansas

THE STATUTES OF ARKANSAS, 1937, 1947, 1962

Basic Statutes. Constitution of Arkansas. Art. II, Sec. 6. *The liberty of the press shall forever remain inviolate.*—The free communication of thoughts and opinions is one of the invaluable rights of man; and all persons may freely write and publish their sentiments on all subjects, being responsible for the abuse of such right. In all criminal prosecutions for libel the truth may be given in evidence to the jury; and, if it shall appear to the jury that the matter charged as libelous is true, and was published with good motives and for justifiable ends, the party charged shall be acquitted.

Sec. 3015. *Definition.*—A libel is a malicious defamation, expressed either by writing, printing or by signs or pictures or the like, tending to blacken the memory of one who is dead, or to impeach the honesty, integrity, veracity, virtue or reputation, or to publish the natural defects of one who is living, and thereby expose him to public hatred, contempt and ridicule. Rev. Stat., chap. 44, div. 8, art. 2, sec. 1.

Sec. 3016. *Punishment.*—Every person, whether writer, printer, or publisher, convicted of the crime of libel shall be fined in any sum not exceeding five thousand dollars and may also be imprisoned not exceeding one year. Id. sec. 2.

Sec. 3107. *Justification.*—In all prosecutions for libel, under the provisions of the preceding sections, the truth thereof may be given in evidence in justification.

Sec. 3018. *Proclaiming one as a coward for not accepting challenge.*—If any person shall in any newspaper, or handbill or other advertisement printed or written, publish or proclaim any other person as a coward, or use any other opprobrious or abusive language, for not accepting a challenge to fight a duel, or for not fighting a duel, such person on conviction shall be fined in any sum not less than three hundred dollars, not more than one thousand dollars, or be imprisoned in the penitentiary at hard labor for a term of not less than two months or more than one year, or both fine and imprisonment. The publisher or printer of any newspaper, handbill, or other publication may be summoned as a witness, and shall be required to testify against the writer of such handbill or publication; and if any such publisher or printer shall refuse to testify in relation to the premises, either before the grand or petit jury, or any other judicial officer, he shall be deemed guilty of a flagrant contempt of court, and may be punished by fine and imprisonment or either. Provided, however, that the testimony given by such witness shall in no case be used in any prosecution or civil suit against such witness.

Sec. 3844. *Indictment for libel.*—An indictment for libel need not set forth any extrinsic facts for the purpose of showing the application, to the party libeled, of the defamatory matter; but it is sufficient to state generally that the same was published concerning him.

Sec. 1452. *Complaint in libel and slander.*—In an action for libel or slander, it shall not be necessary to state in the complaint any extrinsic facts for the purpose of showing the application to the plaintiff of the defamatory matter out of which the cause of action arose; but it shall be sufficient to state generally that the same was published or spoken concerning the plaintiff; and if such allegation is not controverted as stated in Sec. 1450 in regard to judgments, it shall not be necessary to prove it on trial.

Sec. 1453. *Answer in Libel and Slander.*—In the action mentioned in the last section, the defendant may, in his answer, allege both the truth of the matter charged as defamatory and any mitigating circumstances, legally admissible in evidence, to reduce the amount of damages, and whether he proves the justification or not, he may give in evidence the mitigating circumstances.

Limitations. Sec. 8928. The following actions shall be commenced within three years after the cause of action shall accrue, and not after:

Second. All actions for trespass on lands (b) or for libels.

California

CALIFORNIA CODES, GENERAL LAWS AND CONSTITUTION, 1941, 1962
CIVIL CODE OF CALIFORNIA, 1941, 1962
CIVIL PROCEDURE AND PROBATE CODES, 1941, 1962
PENAL CODE OF CALIFORNIA, 1941, 1962

Basic Statutes. Constitution of the State of California. Art. I, Sec. 9. *Liberty of Speech and of the Press.*—Every citizen may freely speak, write, and publish his sentiments on all subjects, being responsible for the abuse of that right; and no law shall be passed to restrain or abridge the liberty of speech or of the press. In all criminal prosecutions for libels, the truth may be given in evidence to the jury; and if it shall appear to the jury that the matter charged as libelous is true, and was published with good motives and for justifiable ends, the party shall be acquitted; and the jury shall have the right to determine the law and the fact. Indictments found, or information laid, for publications in newspapers shall be tried in the county where such newspapers have their publication office, or in the county where the party alleged to be libeled resided at the time of the alleged publication, unless the place of trial shall be changed for good cause.

CCP Sec. 460. *Libel and slander, how stated in complaint: Not necessary to allege or prove special damages.*—In an action for libel or slander it is not necessary to state in the complaint any extrinsic facts for the purpose of showing the application to the plaintiff of the defamatory matter out of which the cause of action arose; but it is sufficient to state, generally, that the same was published or spoken concerning the plaintiff; and if such allegation be controverted, the plaintiff must establish on the trial that it was so published or spoken. (Enacted 1872.)

CCP Sec. 461. *Answer in such cases.*—In the actions mentioned in the last section the defendant may, in his answer, allege both the truth of the matter charged as defamatory, and any mitigating circumstances, to reduce the amount of damages; and whether he prove the justification or not, he may give in evidence the mitigating circumstances. (Enacted 1872.)

CCP Sec. 370. *Married women as parties to actions.*—A married woman may be sued without her husband being joined as a party, and may sue without her husband being joined as a party in all actions, including those for injury to her person, libel, slander, false imprisonment, or malicious prosecution, or for the recovery of her earnings, or concerning her right or claim to the homestead property. (Enacted 1872; Am. Code Amdts. 1873–74, p. 293; Stats. 1901, p. 126 (unconstitutional); Stats. 1913, p. 217; Stats. 1921, p. 102.)

CC Sec. 44. *Defamation, what is.*—Defamation is affected (effected) by:

1. Libel;
2. Slander. (Enacted 1872.)

CC Sec. 45. *Libel, what is.*—Libel is a false and unprivileged publication by writing, printing, picture, effigy, or other fixed representation to the eye, which exposes any person to hatred, contempt, ridicule, or obloquy, or which causes him to be shunned or avoided, or which has a tendency to injure him in his occupation.

CC Sec. 46. *Slander, what is.*—Slander is a false and unprivileged publication other than libel, which:

1. Charges any person with crime, or with having been indicted, convicted, or punished for crime;
2. Imputes in him the present existence of an infectious, contagious, or loathsome disease;
3. Tends directly to injure him in respect to his office, profession, trade, or business, either by imputing to him general disqualification in those respects which the office or other occupation peculiarly requires, or by imputing something with

reference to his office, profession, trade, or business that has a natural tendency to lessen its profits;

4. Imputes to him impotence or a want of chastity; or,

5. Which, by natural consequence, causes actual damage. (Enacted 1872.)

CC Sec. 47. *Privileged publications.*—A privileged publication is one made—

1. In the proper discharge of an official duty.

2. In any (1) legislative or (2) judicial proceeding, or (3) in any other official proceeding authorized by law; provided, that an allegation or averment contained in any pleading or affidavit filed in an action for divorce or an action prosecuted under section 137 of this code made of or concerning a person by or against whom no affirmative relief is prayed in such action shall not be a privileged publication as to the person making said allegation or averment within the meaning of this section unless such pleading be verified or affidavit sworn to, and be made without malice, by one having reasonable and probable cause for believing the truth of such allegation or averment and unless such allegation or averment be material and relevant to the issues in such action.

3. In a communication, without malice, to a person interested therein, (1) by one who is also interested; or (2) by one who stands in such relation to the person interested as to afford a reasonable ground for supposing the motive for the communication innocent, or (3) who is requested by the person interested to give the information.

4. By a fair and true report, without malice, in a public journal, of (1) a judicial, (2) legislative, or (3) other public official proceeding, or (4) of anything said in the course thereof, or (5) of a verified charge or complaint made by any person to a public official, upon which complaint a warrant shall have been issued.

5. By a fair and true report, without malice, of (1) the proceedings of a public meeting, if such meeting was lawfully convened for a lawful purpose and open to the public, or (2) the publication of the matter complained of was for the public

benefit. (Enacted 1872; Amended by Code Amdts. 1873–74, p. 184; Stats. 1895, p. 167; Stats. 1927, p. 1881.)

CC Sec. 48. *Malice not inferred.*—In the cases provided for in subdivisions three, four, and five, of the preceding section, malice is not inferred from the communication or publication. (Enacted 1872; Amended by Stats. 1895, p. 168.)

48a. *Libel in newspaper; slander by broadcast.*—

1. *Special damages; notice and demand for correction.* In any action for damages for the publication of a libel in a newspaper, or of a slander by radio broadcast, plaintiff shall recover no more than special damages unless a correction be demanded and be not published or broadcast, as hereinafter provided. Plaintiff shall serve upon the publisher, at the place of publication or broadcaster at the place of broadcast, a written notice specifying the statements claimed to be libelous and demanding that the same be corrected. Said notice and demand must be served within 20 days after knowledge of the publication or broadcast of the statements claimed to be libelous.

2. *General, special and exemplary damages.* If a correction be demanded within said period and be not published or broadcast in substantially as conspicuous a manner in said newspaper or on said broadcasting station as were the statements claimed to be libelous, in a regular issue thereof published or broadcast within three weeks after such service, plaintiff, if he pleads and proves such notice, demand and failure to correct, and if his cause of action be maintained, may recover general, special and exemplary damages; provided that no exemplary damages may be recovered unless the plaintiff shall prove that defendant made the publication or broadcast with actual malice and then only in the discretion of the court or jury, and actual malice shall not be inferred or presumed from the publication or broadcast.

3. *Correction prior to demand.* A correction published or broadcast in substantially as conspicuous a manner in said newspaper or on said broadcasting station as the statements claimed in the complaint to be libelous, prior to receipt of a demand therefor, shall be of the same force and effect as

though such correction had been published or broadcast within three weeks after a demand therefor.

4. *Definitions.* As used herein, the terms "general damages," "special damages," "exemplary damages" and "actual malice," are defined as follows:

(a) "General damages" are damages for loss of reputation, shame, mortification and hurt feelings;

(b) "Special damages" are all damages which plaintiff alleges and proves that he has suffered in respect to his property, business, trade, profession or occupation, including such amounts of money as the plaintiff alleges and proves he has expended as a result of the alleged libel, and no other;

CC Sec. 43. *General personal rights.*—Besides the personal rights mentioned or recognized in the Penal Code, every person has, subject to the qualifications and restrictions provided by law, the right of protection from bodily restraint or harm, from personal insult, from defamation, and from injury to his personal relations. (Enacted 1872.)

Pen. Sec. 248. *Libel defined.*—A libel is a malicious defamation, expressed either by writing, printing, or by signs or pictures, or the like, tending to blacken the memory of one who is dead, or to impeach the honesty, integrity, virtue, or reputation, or publish the natural or alleged defects of one who is alive, and thereby to expose him to public hatred, contempt, or ridicule. (Enacted 1872; Am. Code Amdts. 1873–74, p. 428.)

Pen. Sec. 249. *Punishment of libel.*—Every person who willfully, and with a malicious intent to injure another, publishes or procures to be published any libel, is punishable by fine not exceeding five thousand dollars, or imprisonment in the county jail not exceeding one year. (Enacted 1872.)

Pen. Sec. 250. *When malice presumed.*—An injurious publication is presumed to have been malicious if no justifiable motive for making it is shown. (Enacted 1872.)

Pen. Sec. 251. *Truth may be given in evidence: (Effect): Jury to determine law and fact.*—In all criminal prosecutions for libel, the truth may be given in evidence to the jury, and if it appears to the jury that the matter charged as libelous is true, and was published with good motives and for justifiable ends, the party shall be acquitted. The jury have the right to determine the law and the fact. (Enacted 1872.)

Pen. Sec. 252. *Publication defined.*—To sustain a charge of publishing a libel, it is not needful that the words or things complained of should have been read or seen by another. It is enough that the accused knowingly parted with the immediate custody of the libel under circumstances which exposed it to be read or seen by any other person than himself.

Pen. Sec. 253. *Liability of authors, editors and publishers.*—Each author, editor, and proprietor of any book, newspaper, or serial publication, is chargeable with the publication of any words contained in any part of such book, or number of such newspaper or serial. (Enacted 1872.)

Pen. Sec. 254. *When publishing a true report of public official proceedings privileged.*—No reporter, editor, or proprietor of any newspaper is liable to any prosecution for a fair and true report of any judicial, legislative, or other public official proceedings, or of any statement, speech, argument, or debate in the course of the same, except upon proof of malice in making such report, which shall not be implied from the mere fact of publication. (Enacted 1872.)

Pen. Sec. 255. *Extent of privilege: Connected matters.*—Libelous remarks or comments connected with matter privileged by the last section receive no privilege by reason of their being so connected. (Enacted 1872.)

Pen. Sec. 256. *Other privileged communications.*—A communication made to a person interested in the communication, by one who was also interested or who stood in such relation to the former as to afford a reasonable ground for supposing his motive innocent is not presumed to be malicious, and is a privileged communication. (Enacted 1872.)

Pen. Sec. 257. *Threatening to publish libel: Offer to prevent publication, with intent to extort money.*—Every person who threatens another to publish a libel concerning him, or any parent, husband, wife, or child of such person, or member of his family, and every person who offers to prevent the publication of any libel upon another person, with intent to extort any money or other valuable consideration from any person, is guilty of a misdemeanor. (Enacted 1872.)

Pen. Sec. 1150. *General or special verdict may be rendered: Exception.*—The jury may render a general verdict, or, when they are in doubt as to the legal effect of the facts proved, they may, except upon a trial for libel, find a special verdict. (Enacted 1872; Am. Code Amdts. 1880, p. 24.)

DA Act. 4317. *Concerning Actions for Libel and Slander.*—(Stats. 1871–72, p. 533; Amended by Stats. 1880, p. 81.)

Sec. 1. *Undertaking.*—In an action for libel or slander the clerk shall, before issuing the summons therein, require a written undertaking on the part of the plaintiff in the sum of five hundred (500) dollars, with at least two competent and sufficient sureties, specifying their occupations and residences, to the effect that if the action be dismissed or the defendant recover judgment, that they will pay such costs and charges as may be awarded against the plaintiff by judgment or in the progress of the action, or on an appeal, not exceeding the sum specified in the undertaking. An action brought without filing the undertaking required shall be dismissed.

Sec. 2. *Sureties.*—Each of the sureties on the undertaking mentioned in the first section shall annex to the same an affidavit that he is a resident and householder or freeholder within the county, and is worth double the amount specified in the undertaking, over and above all his just debts and liabilities, exclusive of property exempt from execution.

Sec. 3. *Exception to sureties.*—Within ten days after the service of the summons, the defendants, or either of them, may give to the plaintiff, or his attorney, notice that they or he except to the sureties and require their justification before a judge of the court at a specified time and place, the time to be not less than five or more than ten days thereafter, except by consent of parties. The qualifications of the sureties shall be as required in their affidavits. (Amended by Stats. 1880, p. 81.)

Sec. 4. *Justification.*—For the purpose of justification each of the sureties shall attend before the judge at the time and place mentioned in the notice, and may be examined on oath touching his sufficiency in such manner as the judge in his discretion shall think proper. The examination shall be reduced to writing if either party desires it.

Sec. 5. *Approval: New undertaking.*—If the judge find the undertaking sufficient, he shall annex the examination of the undertaking and indorse his approval thereon. If the sureties fail to appear, or the judge finds the sureties or either of them insufficient, he shall order a new undertaking to be given. The judge may also at any time order a new or additional undertaking upon proof that the sureties have become insufficient. In case a new or additional undertaking is ordered, all proceedings in the case shall be stayed until such undertaking is executed and filed, with the approval of the judge.

Sec. 6. *Failure to file bond.*—If the undertaking as required be not filed in five days after the order therefor, the judge or court shall order the action to be dismissed.

Sec. 7. *Costs.*—In case plaintiff recovers judgment, he shall be allowed as costs one hundred (100) dollars, to cover counsel fees, in addition to the other costs. In case the action is dismissed, or the defendant recover judgment, he shall be allowed one hundred (100) dollars, to cover counsel fees, in addition to the other costs, and judgment therefor shall be entered accordingly.

Section 48.5. *Defamation by radio; non-liability of owner, licensee or operator of broadcasting station or network.*—

1) The owner, licensee or operator of a visual or sound radio broadcasting station or network of stations, and the agents or employees of any such owner, licensee or operator, shall not be liable for any damages for any defamatory statement or matter published or uttered in or as part of visual or sound radio broadcast by one other than such owner, licensee or operator, or agent or employee thereof, if it shall be alleged and proved by such owner, licensee or operator, or agent or employee thereof, that such owner, licensee or operator, or such agent or employee has exercised due care to prevent the publication or utterance of such statement or matter in such

broadcast.

2) If any defamatory statement or matter is published or uttered in or as part of a broadcast over the facilities of a network of visual or sound radio broadcasting stations the owner, licensee or operator of any such stations, or network of stations, and the agents or employees thereof, other than the owner, licensee or operator of the station, or network of stations originating such broadcast, and the agents or employees thereof, shall in no event be liable for any damages for any such defamatory statement or matter.

3) In no event, however, shall any owner, licensee or operator of any such station or network of stations or agents or employees thereof, be liable for any damages for any defamatory statement or matter published or uttered, by one other than such owner, licensee or operator, or agent or employee thereof, in or as part of a visual or sound radio broadcast by or on behalf of any candidate for public office, which broadcast cannot be censored by reason of the provisions of federal statue or regulation of the Federal Communications Commission.

4) As used in this Part 2, the terms "radio," "radio broadcast," and "broadcast" are defined to include both visual and sound radio broadcasting.

5) Nothing in this section contained shall deprive any such owner, licensee or operator or agent or employee thereof, of any rights under any other section of the Part 2. (Added stats. 1949, C. 1258, P. 2213, section 1.)

Limitation of Action. CCP Sec. 340. *Within one year:—*

1. An action upon a statute for a penalty or forfeiture, when the action is given to an individual, or to an individual and the State, except when the statute imposing it prescribes a different limitation;

2. An action upon a statute, or upon an undertaking in a criminal action, for a forfeiture or penalty to the people of this State;

3. An action for libel, slander, assault, battery, false imprisonment, seduction of a person below the age of legal consent,

or for injury to or for the death of one caused by the wrongful act or neglect of another, or by a depositor against a bank for the payment of a forged or raised check, or a check that bears a forged or unauthorized indorsement;

4. An action against a sheriff or other officer for the escape of a prisoner arrested or imprisoned on civil process;

5. An action against a municipal corporation for damages or injuries to property caused by a mob or riot.

Colorado

COLORADO STATUTES, 1935, 1953

Basic Statutes. Chapter 48, Sec. 199. *Libel—What Constitutes —Truth When May be Proved—Penalty.*—A libel is a malicious defamation expressed either by printing, or by signs, or pictures or the like, tending to blacken the memory of one who is dead, or to impeach the honesty, integrity, virtue or reputation, or publish the natural defects of one who is alive, and thereby to expose him or her to public hatred, contempt or ridicule. Every person, whether writer or publisher, convicted of this offense, shall be fined in a sum not exceeding five hundred dollars or imprisoned in the penitentiary not exceeding one year. In all prosecutions for a libel the truth thereof may be given in evidence in justification, except libels tending to blacken the memory of the dead or expose the natural defects of the living.

Chapter 176, Sec. 247. *What Actions Survive.*—All actions in law whatsoever, save and except actions on the case for slander or libel, or trespass for injuries done to the person, and actions brought for the recovery of real estate, shall survive to and against executors, administrators and conservators.

Chapter 87, Sec. 96. *Defamation of Rival Companies.*—It shall be unlawful for any insurance company now, or hereafter doing business in this state, or any officer, director, clerk, employee or agent thereof, to make, verbally or otherwise, publish, print, distribute, or circulate, or cause the same to be done, or in any way to aid, abet or encourage the making, printing, publishing, distributing or circulating of any pamphlet, circular, article, literature, or statement of any kind which is defamatory of any other insurance company now or hereafter doing business in this state, or now or hereafter licensed to sell its capital stock within this state, which contains any false and malicious criticism or false and malicious statement calculated to injure such company in its reputation or business, and any officer, director, clerk, employee or agent of any insurance company violating the provision of this section shall be deemed guilty of a misdemeanor, and upon conviction thereof shall be punished by a fine of not more than five hundred dollars, or by imprisonment in the county jail for a term of not more than twelve months, or by both fine and imprisonment.

Limitations. Chapter 102, Section 2. *Actions Barred in One Year.*—Assaults, Slander, False Imprisonment. All actions for assault and battery, and for false imprisonment, and all actions for slanderous words and for libels, shall be commenced within one year next after the cause of action shall accrue and not afterwards.

CONNECTICUT LAW OF LIBEL, 1939, 1958

Basic Statutes. *Criminal Libel; penalty.* Sec. 1440e (S. 6194, 1930) 1939.

Breach of Peace. Intimidation. Libel.

Any person who shall disturb or break the peace by tumultuous and offensive carriage, noise or behavior, or by threatening, traducing, quarreling with, challenging, assaulting or striking another or shall disturb or break the peace, or provoke contention, by following or mocking any person, with abusive or indecent language, gestures or noise, or shall,*** with intent to *frighten* any person, threaten to commit any crime against him or his property or shall write or print and publicly exhibit or distribute, or shall publicly exhibit, post up or advertise, any offensive, indecent or abusive matter concerning any person, shall be fined not more than five hundred dollars or imprisoned in jail not more than one year or both.

Damages in actions for libel.

In any action for a libel the defendant may give proof of intention; and unless the plaintiff shall prove either malice in fact or that the defendant, after having been requested by him in writing to retract the libelous charge, in as public a manner as that in which it was made, failed to do so within a reasonable time, he shall recover nothing but such actual damage as he may have specially alleged and proved.

In all prosecutions or indictments for libels, the truth may be given in evidence, and the jury shall have the right to determine the law and the facts, under the direction of the court.

§52-239. *Nonliability for damages of broadcasting in slander actions.*—The owner, licensee or operator of a visual or sound radio broadcasting station or network of stations, or the agents or employees of any such owner, licensee or operator of such station or network of stations shall not be liable for any damages for any defamatory statement uttered over the facilities of such stations or network by or on behalf of a candidate for public office or by any other such person; but this section shall not apply to any such owner, licensee, operator, agent or employee who wilfully, knowingly and with intent to defame participates in such broadcast.

Limitations. §52-597. *Actions for libel or slander.*—No action for libel or slander shall be brought but within two years from the date of the act complained of. (1951 Supp. §3233d)

Delaware

LAWS OF DELAWARE, 1943, 1953

Basic Statutes. Constitution of the State of Delaware. Art. I, Sec. 5. The press shall be free to every citizen who undertakes to examine the official conduct of men acting in a public capacity; and any citizen may print on any subject, being responsible for the abuse of that liberty. In prosecutions for publications, investigating the proceedings of officers, or where the matter published is proper for public information, the truth thereof may be given in evidence; and in all indictments for libels the jury may determine the facts and the law, as in other cases.

120-4692 (Sec. 7). *Proof of Truth of Libel, When, Effect of*—On the trial of indictments for writing or publishing a libel, the truth of the matter charged as libelous may be given in evidence; and if the jury, in any such case, shall find that the act was induced by good motives, and with no malicious intent, and that the matter so charged is true, it shall operate to the acquittal of defendant or defendants.

129-4693 (Sec. 8). *Actions for Damages for Libel; Plea of Truth of; Effect if Proved*—In actions for damages for the writing or publishing of a libel, where the truth is pleaded and given in evidence, if it be found that the same was written or published properly for public information, and with no malicious or mischievous motives, the jury may find for the defendant or defendants.

Laws of Delaware, 1943: Chapter 177, Libel.

An Act to Limit the Liability of Newspapers for Libel.

Section 1. *Libel Against Newspaper: Notice Before Action.*—

Before any action, either civil or criminal, is brought for the publication, in a newspaper of a libel, the plaintiff or prosecutor shall at least five days before instituting such action serve notice in writing on the defendant specifying the article and the statements therein which he alleges to be false and defamatory.

(a) Effect of Publication in Good Faith and Retraction.

If it appears upon the trial that said article was published in good faith, that its falsity was due to an honest mistake of the facts, and that there were reasonable grounds for believing that the statements in said article were true, and that within ten days after the service of said notice a full and fair correction, apology and retraction was published in the same editions or corresponding issues of the newspaper in which said article appeared, and in as conspicuous a place and type as was said in the original article, then the plaintiff in such case, if a civil action, shall recover only actual damages, and if, in a criminal proceeding, a verdict of "guilty" is rendered on such a state of facts, the defendant shall be fined a penny and the costs, and no more.

Approved April 15, 1943.

Limitations. 146-5133 (Sec. 10). *Action for Personal Injuries.* —No action for the recovery of damages upon a claim for alleged personal injuries shall be brought after the expiration of one year from the date upon which it is claimed that such alleged injuries were sustained. (Libel not specifically mentioned.)

District of Columbia

DISTRICT OF COLUMBIA CODE, 1961

Basic Statutes. 22.2301. *Libel.*—Whoever publishes a libel shall be punished by a fine not exceeding one thousand dollars or imprisonment for a term not exceeding five years, or both.

22.2302. *Libel—Publication—Sufficiency.*—To knowingly send or deliver any libelous communication to the party libeled is a sufficient publication to subject the person sending or delivering the same to punishment as provided in section 22.2301.

22.2303. *Libel—Justification.*—Any publication of a libel shall be justified if it appear that the matter charged as libelous was true and was published with good motives and for justifiable ends.

22.2305. *Blackmail.*—Whoever verbally or in writing accuses or threatens to accuse any person of a crime or of any conduct which, if true, would tend to disgrace such other person, or in any way subject him to the ridicule or contempt of society, or threatens to expose or publish any of his infirmities or failings, with intent to extort from such other person anything of value or any pecuniary advantage whatever, or to compel the person accused or threatened to do or to refrain from doing any act, and whoever with such intent publishes any such accusation against any other person shall be imprisoned for not more than five years or be fined not more than one thousand dollars or both.

Limitations. 12-201. *Recovery of real property—Executor's or administrator's bond—Instruments under seal—Simple contract—Property damage—Statutory penalty or forfeiture—Cer-*

tain torts—Actions not specified—Persons under disabilities.—No action shall be brought for the recovery of lands, tenements, or hereditaments after fifteen years from the time the right to maintain such action shall have accrued; nor on any executor's or administrator's bond after five years from the time of the right of action accrued thereon; nor on any other bond or single bill, covenant, or other instrument under seal after twelve years after the accruing of the cause of action thereon; nor upon any simple contract, express or implied, or for the recovery of damages for any injury to real or personal property, or for the recovery of personal property or damages for its unlawful detention after three years from the time when the right to maintain any such action shall have accrued; nor for any statutory penalty or forfeiture, or for libel, slander, assault, battery, mayhem, wounding, malicious prosecution, false arrest, or false imprisonment after one year from the time when the right to maintain any such action shall have accrued; and no action the limitation of which is not specially prescribed in this section shall be brought after three years from the time when the right to maintain such action shall have accrued: *Provided,* That if any person entitled to maintain any of the actions aforesaid shall be at the time of the accruing of such right of action under twenty-one years of age, non compos mentis, or imprisoned, such person or his proper representative shall be at liberty to bring such action within the respective times in this section limited after the removal of such disability, except that where any person entitled to maintain an action for the recovery of lands, tenements, or hereditaments, or upon any instrument under seal, shall be at the time such right of action shall accrue under any of the disabilities aforesaid, such person or his proper representative, except where otherwise provided herein, may bring such action within five years after the removal of such disability, and not thereafter.

§12-301. *Limitations of time for bringing actions.*—Except as otherwise specifically provided by law, actions for the following purposes may not be brought after the expiration of the period specified below from the right to maintain the action accrues: . . .

(4) for libel, slander, assault, battery, mayhem, wounding, malicious prosecution, false arrest, or false imprisonment—1 year.

Florida

FLORIDA STATUTES, 1941, 1964

Basic Statutes. Const. Decl. of Rights, Sec. 13. Every person may fully speak and write his sentiments on all subjects, being responsible for the abuse of that right, and no laws shall be passed to restrain or abridge the liberty of speech, or of the press. In all criminal prosecutions and civil actions for libel, the truth may be given in evidence to the jury, and if it shall appear that the matter charged as libellous is true, and was published for good motives, the party shall be acquitted or exonerated.

836.01. *Punishment for libel.*—Any person convicted of the publication of a libel shall be punished by imprisonment not exceeding one year, or by fine not exceeding one thousand dollars.

836.02. *Must give name of the party written about.*—No person shall print, write, publish, circulate or distribute within this state any newspaper, magazine, periodical, pamphlet or other publication of any character, either written or printed, wherein the alleged immoral acts of any person are stated or pretended to be stated, or wherein it is intimated that any person has been guilty of any immorality, unless such written or printed publication shall in such article publish in full the true name of the person intended to be charged with the commission of such acts of immorality.

Any person convicted of any violation of this section shall be punished by a fine not to exceed five hundred dollars, or by imprisonment not to exceed one year. Any person who shall aid in any way in the writing or printing of any literature in violation of this section shall be punished in the same manner as the principal might be punished upon conviction; provided, nothing in this section shall apply to mechanical employees in printing offices, or to newsboys.

836.07. *Notice condition precedent to prosecution for libel.* —Before any criminal action is brought for publication, in a newspaper periodical, of a libel, the prosecutor shall at least five days before instituting such action serve notice in writing on defendant, specifying the article and the statements therein which he alleges to be false and defamatory.

836.08. *Correction, apology, or retraction by newspaper.*— If it appears upon the trial that said article was published in good faith, that its falsity was due to an honest mistake of the facts, and that there were reasonable grounds for believing that the statements in said article were true, and that within ten days after the service of said notice a full and fair correction, apology and retraction was published in the same editions or corresponding issues of the newspaper or periodical in which said article appeared, and in as conspicuous place and type as was said original article, and if, in a criminal proceeding, a verdict of "guilty" is rendered on such a state of facts, the defendant shall be fined one dollar and costs, and no more.

836.09. *Communicating libelous matter to newspapers; penalty.*—If any person shall state, deliver, or transmit by any means whatsoever, to the manager, editor, publisher or reporter of any newspaper or periodical for publication therein any false and libelous statement concerning any person, then and there known by such person to be false or libelous, and thereby secure the publication of the same he shall be guilty of a misdemeanor.

770.01. *Notice condition precedent to action or prosecution for libel.*—Before any civil action is brought for publication, in a newspaper or periodical, of a libel, the plaintiff shall, at least five days before instituting such action, serve notice in writing on defendant, specifying the article, and the statements therein, which he alleges to be false and defamatory.

770.02. *Correction, apology, or retraction by newspaper.*—If it appears upon the trial that the said article was published in good faith, that its falsity was due to an honest mistake of the facts, and that there were reasonable grounds for believing that the statements in said article were true, and that within ten days after the service of said notice a full and fair correction, apology and retraction was published in the same editions or corresponding issues of the newspaper or periodical in which said article appeared, and in as conspicuous place and type as was said original article, then the plaintiff in such case shall recover only actual damages.

770.03. *Civil liability of radio broadcasting stations, etc.*—The owner, lessee, licensee or operator of a radio broadcasting station shall have the right, but shall not be compelled, to require the submission of a written copy of any statement intended to be broadcast over such station twenty-four hours before the time of the intended broadcast thereof; and when such owner, lessee, licensee or operator has so required the submission of such copy, such owner, lessee, licensee or operator shall not be liable in damages for any libelous or slanderous utterance made by or for the person or party submitting a copy of such proposed broadcast which is not contained in such copy; but this section shall not be construed to relieve the person or party, or the agents or servants of such person or party, making any such libelous or slanderous utterance from liability therefor.

51.05. *Declaration; statement of causes in libel and slander cases.*—In actions of libel and slander the plaintiff may aver that the words or matter complained of were used in a defamatory sense, specifying such defamatory sense without any prefatory averment to show how such words or matter were used in that sense, and such averment shall be put in issue by the denial of the alleged libel or slander; and when the words or matter set forth, with or without the alleged meaning, show a cause of action, the declaration shall be sufficient.

45.11. *Abatement by death or change of parties; personal injuries.*—All actions for personal injuries shall die with the person, to-wit: Assault and battery, slander, false imprisonment, and malicious prosecution; all other actions shall and may be maintained in the name of the representatives of the deceased.

37.02. *Justice of the peace, no jurisdiction.*—No justice of the peace shall have jurisdiction of civil actions:

(3) For false imprisonment, libel, slander, malicious prosetion, criminal conversation or seduction.

Limitations. 95.11. *Limitation upon actions other than real actions.*—Actions other than those for the recovery of real property can only be commenced as follows:

(6) Within two years.—An action by another than the state upon a statute for a penalty or forfeiture; an action for libel, slander, assault, battery or false imprisonment: An action arising upon account of an act causing a wrongful death.

Georgia

CODE OF GEORGIA, 1939, 1963

Basic Statutes. Constitution of Georgia, 2-201. *Libel; jury in criminal cases; new trials.*—In all prosecutions or indictments for libel the truth may be given in evidence; and the jury in all criminal cases, shall be the judges of the law and the facts. The power of the Judges to grant new trials in case of conviction, is preserved.

26-2101. *Libel defined; punishment.*—A libel is a malicious defamation, expressed either by printing or writing, or signs, pictures or the like, tending to blacken the memory of one who is dead, or the honesty, virtue, integrity, or reputation of one who is alive and thereby expose him to public hatred, contempt, or ridicule. Every person convicted of this offense shall be punished as for a misdemeanor.

26-2102. *Printer or publisher a competent witness.*—In all prosecutions under the preceding section, the printer or publisher of a newspaper, handbill, or other publication containing offensive or criminal matter shall be a competent witness; and if such printer or publisher shall refuse to testify in the cause, or to give up the real name of the author or person authorizing and causing the publication, so that he may be indicted, such printer or publisher shall be deemed and considered the author himself, and may be indicted and punished as such, and may be punished for contempt of the court, as any other witness refusing to testify.

26-2103. *The truth in evidence.*—In all cases of indictment for a libel, the person prosecuted shall be allowed to give the truth in evidence.

105-701. *Libel defined; necessity of publication.*—A libel is a false and malicious defamation of another, expressed in print, or writing, or pictures, or signs, tending to injure the reputation of an individual, and exposing him to public hatred, contempt, or ridicule. The publication of the libelous matter is essential to recovery.

105-703. *Newspaper libel defined; necessity of publication.*—Any false and malicious defamation of another in any newspaper, magazine, or periodical, tending to injure the reputation of any individual and expose him to public hatred, contempt, or ridicule, shall constitute a newspaper libel, the publication of such libelous matter being essential to recovery.

105-704. *Same; what privileged.*—A fair and honest report of the proceedings of legislative or judicial bodies, or of court proceedings, or a truthful report of information received from any arresting officer or police authorities, shall be deemed a privileged communication; and in any action brought for newspaper libel the rule of law as to privileged communication shall apply.

105-705. *Publication, what constitutes.*—A libel is published as soon as it is communicated to any person other than the party libeled.

105-706. *Malice; inference; rebuttal.*—In all actions for printed or spoken defamation, malice is inferred from the character of the charge. The existence of malice may be rebutted by proof, which in all cases shall go in mitigation of damages, and in cases of privileged communication it shall be in bar of the recovery.

105-708. *Truth as justification.*—The truth of the charge made may always be proved in justification of the libel or slander.

105-709. *The following are deemed privileged communications:*—

1. Statements made bona fide in the performance of a public duty.

2. Similar statements in the performance of a private duty, either legal or moral.

3. Statements made with the bona fide intent, on the part of the speaker, to protect his own interest in a matter where it is concerned.

4. Fair and honest reports of the proceedings of legislative or judicial bodies.

5. Comments of counsel, fairly made, on the circumstances of his case, and the conduct of parties in connection therewith.

6. Comments upon the acts of public men in their public capacity and with reference thereto.

105-710. *Malicious use of privilege.*—In every case of privileged communications, if the privilege is used merely as a cloak for venting private malice, and not bona fide in promotion of the object for which the privilege is granted, the party defamed shall have a right of action.

105-711. *Allegations in pleadings privileged.*—All charges, allegations, and averments contained in regular pleadings filed in a court of competent jurisdiction, which are pertinent and material to the relief sought, whether legally sufficient to obtain it or not, are privileged. However false and malicious, they are not libelous.

105-713. *True or privileged articles; effect of retraction as to damages recoverable.*

If it appears upon the trial of any case in which such notice has been given that the article published was true or that the same was privileged, the same shall be governed by all the laws of Georgia now in force in reference to such actions, and the truth shall be a complete defense and the privileged communication, if there be no malice, as is now provided, shall be a complete defense, but in all other cases if it appears upon the trial that said article was published in good faith, that its publication was due to an honest mistake of the facts; that there were reasonable grounds for believing that the statements in said article were true, and that within 10 days after the service of said notice a full and fair correction or retraction was published in the same editions or corresponding issues of the newspaper, magazine or periodical in which said article appeared and in as conspicuous a place and type as was said original article, then the plaintiff in such case shall recover only such special or actual damages as the plaintiff shows he has sustained.

24-3405. *No more costs than damages, when.*—In all actions for slanderous words, in any court having jurisdiction of the same, if the jury shall render a verdict under $10, the plaintiff shall have and recover no more costs than damages. In actions of assault and battery, and in all other personal actions, wherein the jury upon the trial thereof shall find the damages to be less than $10, the plaintiff shall recover no more costs than damages, unless the judge, at the trial thereof, shall find and certify on the record that an aggravated assault and battery was proved.

13-9931. *Libel of bank.*—Any person who shall publish or cause to be published any false statement, expressed either by printing or writing, or signs, pictures, or the like, of or concerning any bank, as to the assets or liabilities of said bank, or as to its solvency or ability to meet its obligations, or as to its soundness, or who shall publish or cause to be published any other false statement so expressed, calculated to affect the credit or standing of said bank, or to cast suspicion upon its solvency, soundness, or ability to meet its deposits or other obligations, in due course, shall be guilty of a misdemeanor.

16-9904. *Libel of savings and/or building and loan association.*—Any person who shall publish or cause to be published any false statement, expressed either by printing or writing, or sign, or pictures, or the like of, or concerning any State chartered association, or Federal savings and loan association, or as to its solvency or ability to meet its obligations, or as to its soundness, or who shall publish or cause to be published any other false statement so expressed, calculated to affect the credit or standing of any such State chartered association or Federal savings and loan association, or to cast suspicion upon its solvency, soundness, or ability to meet its obligations in due course, shall be guilty of a misdemeanor, and shall be punished as provided in section 27-2506 of the Code.

105-712. *Radio broadcasting stations; liability for defamatory statements.*—The owner, licensee or operator of a visual or sound radio broadcasting station or network of stations, and agent or employee of any such owner, licensee or operator shall not be liable for any defamatory statement published or uttered in or as part of a visual or sound radio broadcasting, by one other than such owner, licensee, or operator, or agent or employee thereof, unless it shall be alleged and proved by the complaining party, that such owner, licensee, operator or such agent or employee, has failed to exercise due care to prevent the publication or utterance of such statement in such broadcast. (Acts 1949, p. 1137)

(Editorial note—This section formerly related to notice to newspapers publishing libelous articles. The subject matter of the section was repealed by Acts 1949 pp. 915, 916)

Limitations. Injuries to the person. 3-1004. Actions for injuries to the person shall be brought within two years after the right of action accrues, except for injuries to the reputation, which shall be brought within one year.

105-712. *Notice to defendant specifying libelous article, etc., as condition precedent to civil action.*

Before any civil action shall be brought because of any publication of a libel in any newspaper, magazine or periodical, the plaintiff shall, within the period of the statute of limitations for such actions and at least five days before instituting such action, give notice in writing to the defendant specifying the article and the statements therein which he claims to be false and defamatory and further stating in said notice what the complaining party claims to be the true state of facts.

Hawaii

FROM THE HAWAII CONSTITUTION

Section 3. Freedom of religion, speech, press, assembly and petition. No law shall be enacted respecting an establishment of religion or prohibiting the free exercise thereof, or abridging the freedom of speech or of the press, or the right of the people peaceably to assemble and to petition the government for a redress of grievances.

Ch. 294-1. Libel defined. A libel is a publication by writing, print or by a picture, statue, sign or representation, other than words merely spoken, which directly tends to injure the fame, reputation or good name of another person, and bring him into disgrace, abhorrence, odium, hatred, contempt or ridicule, or to cause him to be excluded from society.

§294-4. Publishing defined. The publishing of a libel is the maliciously putting of it into circulation, or the promulgating, exhibiting or distributing of it for the purpose of making it known to others; and thereby in fact making it known to others; or aiding or assisting therein, or the causing or promoting thereof.

§294-5. Malice. Malice is shown, in respect of libel, by making a publication or communicating it to others, wilfully and purposely, to the prejudice and injury of another. Hatred or ill will towards the party injured is not essential to libel.

§294-6. Truth as defense. In every prosecution for writing or publishing a libel, the defendant may give in evidence in his defense upon the trial the truth of the matter contained in the publication charged to be libelous: provided, that such evidence shall not be deemed a justification, unless it is further made to appear on the trial that the matter was published with good motives and for justifiable ends.

§294-7. Penalty. Whoever is guilty of the offense of making or publishing a libel shall be fined not more than $1,000 or imprisoned not more than one year.

§294-8. Libeling the dead. A libel on the dead is subject to a like punishment as one on the living, where the same is malicious in respect to persons living, and defamatory of, or an outrage against, or an injury to, persons living, and is intended so to be by the maker or publisher.

§294-9. Libeling a body of persons. A libel may be of a body, board, class, society or association of individuals, public or private, no less than of one or more persons individually.

§294-11. No defamation by radio, etc., when. The owner, licensee or operator of a visual or sound radio broadcasting station or network of stations, and the agents or employees of any such owner, licensee or operator of such a station or network of stations, shall not be liable for any damages for any defamatory statement published or uttered over the facilities of such station or network by any candidate for public office.

§241-1. Personal actions. Six years. The following actions shall be commenced within six years next after the cause of such action accrued, and not after: . . .

b. Special actions on the case for criminal conversation, for libels or for any other injury to the person or rights of any . . .

§241-4. Two years; Slander, etc.: against high sheriff, etc. The following actions shall be commenced within two years after the cause of action accrued, and not after:

(a) Actions for words spoken slandering the character or title of any person: . . .

Idaho

LAWS OF IDAHO, 1931, 1947

Basic Statutes. 17-1501. *Libel defined.*—A libel is a malicious defamation, expressed either by writing, printing, or by signs or pictures, or the like, tending to blacken the memory of one who is dead, or to impeach the honesty, integrity, virtue or reputation, or publish the natural or alleged defects, of one who is alive, and thereby to expose him to public hatred, contempt or ridicule.

17-1502. *Punishment for libel.*—Every person who wilfully, and with a malicious intent to injure another, publishes, or procures to be published, any libel, is punishable by fine not exceeding $5000, or imprisonment in the county jail not exceeding six months.

17-1503. *Malice presumed.*—An injurious publication is presumed to have been malicious if no justifiable motive for making it is shown.

17-1504. *Truth may be proved.*—In all criminal prosecutions for libel, the truth may be given in evidence to the jury, and if it appears to the jury that the matter charged as libelous is true, and was published with good motives and for justifiable ends, the party shall be acquitted. The jury has the right to determine the law and the fact.

17-1505.—*Sufficiency of publication.*—To sustain a charge of publishing a libel, it is not needful that the words or things complained of should have been read or seen by another. It is enough that the accused knowingly parted with the immediate custody of the libel under circumstances which exposed it to be read or seen by any other person than himself.

17-1506.—*Liability of authors, editors and proprietors.*—Each, author, editor and proprietor of any book, newspaper or serial publication, is chargeable with the publication of any words contained in any part of such book, or number of such newspaper or serial.

17-1507. *Report of public proceeding.*—No reporter, editor or proprietor of any newspaper is liable to any prosecution for a fair and true report of any judicial, legislative, or other public official proceedings, or of any statement, speech, argument, or debate in the course of the same, except upon proof of malice in making such report, which shall not be implied from the mere fact of publication.

17-1508. *Limitation on privilege.*—Libelous remarks or comments connected with matter privileged by the last section receive no privilege by reason of their being so connected.

17-1509. *Threats to publish libel.*—Every person who threatens another to publish a libel concerning him, or any parent, husband, wife, or child of such person, or member of his family, and every person who offers to prevent the publication of any libel upon another person, with intent to extort any money or other valuable consideration from any person, is guilty of a misdemeanor.

Limitations. Compiled Statutes, Vol. 2, 1919. 6612 (4055). *Miscellaneous limitations.*—Actions against officers, for penalties, on bonds and for personal injuries, within two years:

5. An action for libel, slander, assault, etc.

Illinois

ILLINOIS STATUTES, 1931, 1957, 1964
REVISED 1959, 1961

Basic Statutes. Constitution of Illinois, 1870. Art. II, Sec. 4. *Freedom of speech and publication.*—Every person may freely speak, write and publish on all subjects, being responsible for the abuse of that liberty; and in all trials for libel, both civil and criminal, the truth, when published with good motives and for justifiable ends, shall be a sufficient defense.

126 §3. *Proof of malice—Unproved allegation of truth is not.*—In actions for slander or libel, an unproved allegation of the truth of the matter charged shall not be deemed proof of malice, unless the jury, on the whole case, find that such defense was made with malicious intent.

——. *Truth provable by preponderance.*—And it shall be competent for the defendant to establish the truth of the matter charged by a preponderance of testimony.

402 §177. *Libel defined.*—A libel is a malicious defamation, expressed either by printing, or by signs or pictures, or the like, tending to blacken the memory of one who is dead, or to impeach the honesty, integrity, virtue or reputation or publish the natural defects of one who is alive, and thereby to expose him to public hatred, contempt, ridicule, or financial injury.

403 §178. *Punishment.*—Every person, whether writer or publisher, convicted of libel, shall be fined not exceeding $500, or confined in the county jail not exceeding one year.

404 §179. *Justification.*—In all prosecutions for libel, the truth, when published with good motives, and for justifiable ends, shall be a sufficient defense.

3.339. *Actions which survive.*—In addition to the actions

which survive by the common law, the following also survive; actions of replevin, actions to recover damages for an injury to the person (except slander and libel), actions to recover damages for an injury to real or personal property or for the detention or conversion of personal property, actions against officers for misfeasance, malfeasance, or nonfeasance of themselves or their deputies, and actions for fraud or deceit.

38 §707a. *Libel in newspaper or magazine circulated in county other than that of publication.*—Where a libel expressed in a newspaper or magazine of general circulation is printed in one county of this State and thereafter is circulated or published in another county of this State, the jurisdiction in any prosecution for such libel of the owner, publisher, editor, author or printer of the newspaper or magazine shall be in the county in which the libel was composed or printed, except when the defendant resides or the article was printed without this State, and thereafter was circulated or published in this State, in which cases the jurisdiction shall be in any county in which the libel was circulated or printed.

30.58. *Misdemeanor to spread false reports about the finances or management thereof.*—Any person who maliciously and knowingly spreads false reports about the finances or management or activity of an association organized hereunder or organized under a similar statute of another state with similar restrictions, and operating in this State under due authority shall be guilty of a misdemeanor and be subject to a fine of not less than one hundred ($100) dollars and not more than one thousand ($1000) dollars for each such offense; and shall be liable to the association aggrieved in a civil suit in the penal sum of five hundred ($500) dollars for each such offense.

38 §405. *Statements derogatory to banking institutions.*—§1. Any person who shall willfully and maliciously make, circulate, or transmit to another or others, any statements, rumor or suggestion, written, printed or by word of mouth, which is directly or by inference derogatory to the financial condition, with intent to affect the solvency or financial standing of any corporation doing a banking or trust business in this State, or any

building and loan association or federal savings and loan association doing business in this State, or who shall counsel, aid, procure or induce another to start, transmit or circulate any such statement, rumor or suggestion, shall be punished by a fine of not more than $500.00, or by imprisonment in the county jail not exceeding one year, or both: Provided, that the truth of said statement, established by the maker thereof, shall be a complete defense in any prosecution under the provisions of this Act.[1] As amended by act approved July 21, 1947. L.1947, p. 801.

404.1. *Definition.* §179.1. A libel by radio or television is a malicious defamatory broadcast by means of what is commonly known as the radio or television, tending to blacken the memory of one who is dead, or to impeach the honesty, integrity, virtue or reputation, or to publish the natural defects of one who is alive, and thereby to expose him to public hatred, contempt, ridicule or financial injury. As amended by act approved July 11, 1955.

404.2. §179.2. *Liability by radio or television.*—Every person, firm, corporation, or unincorporated or voluntary association owning or operating a radio or television station within the State of Illinois, which shall broadcast a libel by radio or television, as defined above, directly or indirectly, or by means electrical or other form of transcription, and every person who shall maliciously and knowingly participate in the publication or the broadcast of such libel, shall be guilty of libel, provided, however, that

a) no such person, firm, corporation, or unincorporated or voluntary association owning or operating a radio or television station in the State of Illinois, or employee thereof, shall be guilty of libel for the broadcast of any defamatory matter of which such person, firm, corporation, or unincorporated or voluntary association or employee thereof had no advance knowledge of opportunity or right to prevent; and

b) no such person, firm or unincorporated or voluntary

[1] This section.

association, or employee thereof shall be found guilty of libel for any statement uttered over the facilities of such station by any candidate for public office.

404.3. *Punishment.* 179.3. Every person convicted of libel by radio or television shall be fined not exceeding $500.00 or confined in the county jail for one year.

404.4. *Truth as defense.* 179.4. In all prosecutions for libel by radio or television, the truth, when published with good motives and for justifiable ends, shall be sufficient defense.

126. §11. *Remedy—Damages.*—No person shall have more than one cause of action for damages for libel or slander or invasion of privacy or any other tort founded upon any single publication or exhibition or instance or utterance, such as any one edition of a newspaper or book or magazine or any other presentation to an audience or any one broadcast over radio or television or any one exhibition of a motion picture. Recovery in any action shall include all damages for any such tort suffered by the plaintiff in all jurisdictions.

Limitations. 83 §14. *Slander and libel.*—Actions for slander or libel shall be commenced within one year next after the cause of action accrued.

Indiana

INDIANA STATUTES, 1933, 1954

Basic Statutes. Constitution of Indiana. Art. I, Sec. 9. No law shall be passed, restraining the free interchange of thought and opinion, or restricting the right to speak, write, or print, freely, on any subject whatever: but for the abuse of that right, every person shall be responsible.

Art. I, Sec. 10. In all prosecutions for libel, the truth of the matters alleged to be libellous may be given in justification.

2-301. *What causes of action joined.*—The plaintiff may unite several causes of action in the same complaint, when they are included in either of the following classes:

First. Money demands on contract.

Second. Injuries to property.

Third. Injuries to person or character.

2-1041. *Libel or slander—Defamatory matter.*—In an action for libel and slander, it shall be sufficient to state generally that defamatory matter was published or spoken of the plaintiff; and if the allegation be denied, the plaintiff must prove on the trial the facts showing that the defamatory matter was published or spoken of him.

2-1042. *Libel and slander—Justification and mitigation—Evidence.*—In all actions mentioned in the last section, the defendant may allege the truth of the matter charged as defamatory and mitigating circumstances to reduce the damages, and give either or both in evidence.

2-1043. *Libel in newspaper—Action and notice by aggrieved party—Good faith and retraction—Actual damages—Candidate for public office.*—Before any suit shall be brought for the publication of a libel in any newspaper in this state, the aggrieved party shall, at least three (3) days before filing the complaint in such suit, serve notice in writing on the publisher or publishers of such newspaper, at their principal office of publication, specifying the statements in said article which he or they allege to be false and defamatory. If it shall appear upon trial of said action that said article was published in good faith, that its falsity was due to mistake or misapprehension of the facts, and that a full and fair retraction of any statement therein alleged to be erroneous was published in a regular issue of such newspaper, within three (3) days, if such newspaper be a daily publication, or within ten (10) days, if such newspaper be a weekly publication, after such mistake or misapprehension was brought to the knowledge of such publisher or publishers, in as conspicuous place and type in the same place where said original item appeared in such newspaper as was the article complained of, then the plaintiff in such case shall recover only actual damages: Provided, however, That the foregoing provisions of section one of this act shall not apply to the case of any libel against any candidate for a public office in this state, unless the retraction of the charge is made in a conspicuous manner at least three (3) days before the election.

2-1044. *Libel in newspaper—"Actual damages" defined.*—The words "actual damages" in the foregoing section shall be construed to include all damages that the plaintiff may have suffered in respect to his character, property, business, trade, profession or occupation, and no other damages whatever.

2-1045. *Libel or slander—Proof of justification.*—The rule requiring that an answer of justification in cases of libel and slander shall be proved beyond a reasonable doubt, is hereby abrogated; and after the taking effect of this act, the proof of such answer shall be controlled by the rule now applying to the proof of issues in other civil cases.

2-3004. *Recovery under five dollars—Actions for damages solely—Exceptions.*—In all actions for damages solely, not arising out of contract, if the plaintiff do not recover five dollars ($5.00) damages, he shall recover no more costs than damages, except in actions for injuries to character and false imprisonment, and where the title to real estate comes in question.

2-518. *Libel or slander by radio or television—Bringing of suits—Procedure—Proviso.*—Before any suit shall be brought for the publishing, speaking, uttering or conveying by words, acts, or in any other manner of a libel or slander by any radio or television station or company in this state, the aggrieved party shall, at least three (3) days before filing the complaint in such suit, serve notice in writing on the manager or managers of such radio or television station, at their principal office, specifying the words or acts which he or they allege to be false and defamatory. If it shall appear, upon trial of such action, that such words or acts were conveyed and broadcast in good faith, that its falsity was due to mistake or misapprehension of the facts, and that a full and fair retraction of any words or acts therein alleged to be erroneous was conveyed or broadcast on a regular program of such radio or television company, within ten (10) days after such mistake or misapprehension was brought to the knowledge of such manager or managers, at approximately the same time and by the same sending power so as to be as visible and audible as the original acts or words complained of, then the plaintiff in such case shall recover only actual damages. The foregoing provisions of this act shall not apply to the case of any libel or slander against any candidate for a public office in this state, unless the retraction of the charge is made in an audible or visible manner at least three (3) days before the election.

2-519. *Libel or slander by radio or television—"Actual damages," defined.*—The words "actual damages" in the foregoing section shall be construed to include all damages that the plaintiff may have suffered in respect to his character, property, business, trade, profession, or occupation, and no other damages whatever.

9-214. *Libel by publication.*—When the offense of libel is committed by publication in this state, against any person, the jurisdiction is in any county where the libel is published or circulated by the accused. In no case, however, can the accused be prosecuted for the publication of the same libel in more than one county of this state.

10-3201. *Criminal libel.*—Whoever makes, composes, dictates, prints or writes a libel to be published, or procures the same to be done, and whoever publishes or knowingly aids in publishing or communicating a libel, or whoever maliciously publishes any false charge of and concerning another, accusing such other person of any crime, or of any degrading or infamous act, or whoever, by such means, maliciously and falsely charges any woman with want of chastity, shall be deemed guilty of criminal libel, and, on conviction, shall be fined not less than five dollars ($5.00) nor more than one thousand dollars ($1,000), to which may be added imprisonment in the county jail for not more than six (6) months.

10-3203. *Making false statements concerning financial institutions—Penalty.*—Any person who shall wilfully and maliciously make, circulate or transmit to another or others, any false statement, rumor or suggestion, written, printed or by word of mouth, which is directly or by inference derogatory to the financial condition or affects the solvency or financial standing of any bank, savings bank, banking institution, trust company, credit union, or building and loan association doing business in this state, or who shall counsel, aid, procure or induce another to start, transmit or circulate any such statement or rumor, shall be deemed guilty of a misdemeanor and upon conviction thereof shall be punished by a fine of not more than one thousand dollars ($1,000) or by imprisonment for a term of not more than one (1) year, or both.

38-115. *Suits for injury to wife's person or character.*—A married woman may bring and maintain an action in her own name against any person or body corporate for damages for any injury to her person or character the same as if she were sole; and the money recovered shall be her separate property, and her husband, in such case, shall not be liable for costs.

39-5017. *Defamation of companies.*—It shall be unlawful for any person to make, verbally or otherwise use, publish, print, distribute or circulate, or cause the same to be done, or in any way to aid, abet or encourage the making, using, printing, publishing, distributing or circulating, of, any pamphlet, circular, article, literature, comparison or rating of companies or statement of any kind concerning any company which contains any false statement or criticism or false or misleading or incomplete statement or comparison tending to injure such company in its reputation or business or which is otherwise defamatory thereof.

39-5024. *General penalty.*—Any person who shall violate any of the provisions of this act, for the violation of which a specific penalty is not herein otherwise provided, shall be deemed guilty of a misdemeanor and upon conviction thereof shall be fined in any sum not less than one hundred dollars ($100) and not more than five hundred dollars ($500), to which may be added imprisonment for any determinate period of time not exceeding six (6) months.

Limitations. 2-602. *Limitation of actions.*—Two, five, six, ten and twenty years.

The following actions shall be commenced within the periods herein prescribed after the cause of action has accrued, and not afterward:

First: For injuries to person or character, and for a forfeiture or penalty given by statute, within two (2) years.

Iowa

CODE OF IOWA, 1939, 1951

Basic Statutes. Constitution of Iowa, Art. I, Sec. 7. Every person may speak, write, and publish his sentiments on all subjects, being responsible for the abuse of that right. No law shall be passed to restrain or abridge the liberty of speech, or of the press. In all prosecutions or indictments for libel, the truth may be given in evidence to the jury, and if it appear to the jury that the matter charged as libellous was true, and was published with good motives and for justifiable ends, the party shall be acquitted.

737.1 *Libel defined.*—A libel is the malicious defamation of a person, made public by any printing, writing, sign, picture, representation, or effigy, tending to provoke him to wrath or expose him to public hatred, contempt, or ridicule, or to deprive him of the benefits of public confidence and social intercourse; or any malicious defamation, made public as aforesaid, designed to blacken and vilify the memory of one who is dead, and tending to scandalize or provoke his surviving relatives or friends.

737.2 *Punishment.*—Every person who makes, composes, dictates, or procures the same to be done, or who wilfully publishes or circulates such libel, or in any way knowingly or wilfully aids or assists in making, publishing, or circulating the same, shall be imprisoned in the county jail not more than one year, or be fined not exceeding one thousand dollars.

737.3 *Indictment for libel.*—An indictment for a libel need not set forth any extrinsic facts for the purpose of showing the application to the party libeled of the defamatory matter upon which the indictment is founded, but it is sufficient to state generally that the same was published concerning him, and the fact that it was so published must be established on the trial.

737.4 *Truth given in evidence.*—In all prosecutions or indictments for libel, the truth thereof may be given in evidence to the jury, and if it appear to them that the matter charged as libelous was true, and was published with good motives and for justifiable ends, the defendant shall be acquitted.

737.5 *Publication.*—No printing, writing, or other thing is a libel unless there has been a publication thereof.

737.6 *What constitutes publication.*—The delivering, selling, reading, or otherwise communicating a libel, or causing the same to be delivered, sold, read, or otherwise communicated, to one or more persons or to the party libeled, is a publication thereof.

737.7 *Jury determines law and fact.*—In all prosecutions for libel, the jury, after having received the direction of the court, shall have the right to determine at its discretion the law and the fact.

659.1 *Pleading.*—In an action for slander or libel, it shall not be necessary to state any extrinsic facts for the purpose of showing the application to the plaintiff of any defamatory matter out of which the cause of action arose, or that the matter was used in a defamatory sense; but it shall be sufficient to state the defamatory sense in which such matter was used, and that the same was spoken or published concerning the plaintiff.

659.2 *Libel—retraction—actual damages.*—In any action for damages for the publication of a libel in a newspaper, if the defendant can show that such libelous matter was published through misinformation or mistake, the plaintiff shall recover no more than actual damages, unless a retraction be demanded and refused as hereinafter provided. Plaintiff shall serve upon the publisher at the principal place of publication a notice specifying the statements claimed to be libelous, and requesting that the same be withdrawn.

659.3 *Retraction—actual, special, and exemplary damages.*—

If a retraction or correction thereof be not published in as conspicuous a place and type in said newspaper as were the statements complained of, in a regular issue thereof published within two weeks after such service, plaintiff may allege such notice, demand, and failure to retract, in his complaint and may recover both actual, special, and exemplary damages if his cause of action be maintained. If such retraction be so published, he may still recover such actual, special, and exemplary damages, unless the defendant shall show that the libelous publication was made in good faith, without malice and under a mistake as to the facts.

659.4 *Candidate for office—retraction—time.*—If the plaintiff was a candidate for office at the time of the libelous publication, no retraction shall be available unless published in a conspicuous place on the editorial page, nor if the libel was published within two weeks next before the election; provided that this and sections 12413 and 12414 shall not apply to any libel imputing unchastity to a woman.

659.5 *Defamatory statement by radio.*—The owner, lessee, or operator of a radio broadcasting station, and the agents or employees of any such owner, lessee, licensee or operator, shall not be liable for any damages for any defamatory statement published or uttered in or as a part of a radio broadcast, by one other than such owner, lessee, licensee or operator, or agent or employee thereof, if such owner, lessee, licensee, operator, agent or employee shall prove the exercise of due care to prevent the publication or utterance of such statement in such broadcast.

659.6 *Proof of malice.*—In actions for slander or libel, an unproved allegation of the truth of the matter charged shall not be deemed proof of malice, unless the jury on the whole case finds that such defense was made with malicious intent.

11166. *Verification not required.*—Verifications shall not be required to any pleading of a guardian, executor, or prisoner in the penitentiary, nor to any pleading controverting the answer of a garnishee, nor to one grounded on an injury to the person or the character.

619.7 *Mitigating facts.*—In any action brought to recover

damages for an injury to person, character, or property, the defendant may set forth, in a distinct division of his answer, any facts, of which evidence is legally admissible, to mitigate or otherwise reduce the damages, whether a complete defense or justification be pleaded or not, and he may give in evidence the mitigating circumstances, whether he proves the defense or justification or not.

619.8 *Necessity to plead.*—No mitigating circumstances shall be proved unless pleaded, except such as are shown by or grow out of the testimony introduced by the adverse party.

Limitations. 11007 (3). *Limitation of actions.*—Actions may be brought within the times herein limited, respectively, after their causes accrue, and not afterwards, except when otherwise specially declared:

3. Injuries to person or reputation—relative rights—statute penalty—setting aside will. Those founded on injuries to the person or reputation, including injuries to relative rights, whether based on contract or tort, or for a statute penalty, within two years; and those brought to set aside a will, within two years from the time the same is filed in the clerk's office for probate and notice thereof is given; provided that after a will is probated the executor may cause personal service of an original notice to be made on any person interested, which shall contain the name of decedent, the date of his death, the court in which and the date on which the will was probated, together with a copy of said will; said notice shall be served in the same manner as original notices and no action shall be instituted by any person so served after one year from date of service.

Kansas

GENERAL STATUTES OF KANSAS, 1935
1943 SUPPLEMENT TO GENERAL STATUTES OF KANSAS, 1935 LAWS OF KANSAS, 1963

Basic Statutes. Constitution of Kansas. Bill of Rights, Sec. 11. *Liberty of press and speech; libel.*—The liberty of the press shall be inviolate: and all persons may freely speak, write or publish their sentiments on all subjects, being responsible for the abuse of such right; and in all civil and criminal actions for libel, the truth may be given in evidence to the jury, and if it shall appear that the alleged libelous matter was published for justifiable ends, the accused party shall be acquitted.

60-3202. *What causes of action survive; exceptions; actions abated by death.*—No action pending in any court shall abate by the death of either or both the parties thereto, except an action for libel, slander, malicious prosecution, for a nuisance, or against a justice of the peace for misconduct in office, which shall abate by the death of the defendant.

60-745. *Libel or slander; pleading and proof.*—In an action for libel or slander, it shall be sufficient to state, generally, that the defamatory matter was published or spoken of the plaintiff; and if the allegation be denied, the plaintiff must prove, on the trial, the facts, showing that the defamatory matter was published or spoken of him.

60-746. *Same; truth or mitigating circumstances.*—In the actions mentioned in the last section, the defendant may allege the truth of the matter charged as defamatory, and may prove the same and any mitigating circumstances to reduce the amount of damages, or he may prove either.

60-307. *Same (limitation of actions); persons under legal disability; exception.*—If a person entitled to bring an action other than for the recovery of real property, except for a penalty or a forfeiture, be at the time the case of action accrued under any legal disability, every such person shall be entitled to bring such action within one year after such disability shall be removed.

21-2401. *Libel defined.*—A libel is the malicious defamation of a person, made public by any printing, writing, sign, picture, representation or effigy, tending to provoke him to wrath or expose him to public hatred, contempt or ridicule, or to deprive him of the benefits of public confidence and social intercourse, or any malicious defamation made public as aforesaid, designed to blacken and vilify the memory of one who is dead, and tending to scandalize or provoke his surviving relatives and friends.

21-2402. *Penalty for libel.*—Every person who makes or composes, dictates or procures the same to be done, or who wilfully publishes or circulates such libels, or in any way knowingly and wilfully aids or assists in making, publishing or circulating the same, shall be punished by imprisonment in the county jail not more than one year, or by a fine not exceeding one thousand dollars.

21-2403. *Truth as defense in libel prosecution.*—In all prosecutions or indictments for libels the truth thereof may be given in evidence to the jury, and if it appears to them that the matter as charged as libelous was true, and was published with good motives and for justifiable ends, the defendant shall be acquitted.

21-2404. *Necessity of publication.*—No printing, writing or other thing is libel, unless there has been a publication thereof.

21-2405. *What constitutes publication.*—The delivery, selling, reading, or otherwise communicating a libel, or causing the same to be delivered, sold, read or otherwise communicated to one or more persons, or to the party libeled, is a publication thereof.

21-2406. *Jury may determine law and the fact.*—In all indictments or prosecutions for libel, the jury after having received the direction of the court, shall have the right to determine, at their discretion, the law and the fact.

60-746a. *Defamation by means of radio, liability, when.*—The owner, licensee or operator of a visual or sound radio broadcasting station or network of stations, and agents or employees of any such owner, licensee or operator, shall not be liable for any damages for any defamatory statement published or uttered in or as part of a visual or sound radio broadcast, by one other than such owner, licensee or operator, or agent or employee thereof, unless it shall be alleged and proved by the complaining party that such owner, licensee, operator or such agent or employee, has failed to exercise due care to prevent the publication or utterance of such statement in such broadcast. (L. 1949, ch. 320, §1. June 30).

Limitations. 60306. *Civil actions other than for recovery of real property.*—Civil action, other than for the recovery of real property, can only be brought within the following periods, after the cause of action shall have accrued, and not afterwards:

Fourth. Within one year: An action for libel, slander, assault, battery; malicious prosecution, or false imprisonment; an action upon a statute for penalty or forfeiture, except where the statute imposing it prescribes a different limitation.

Kentucky

KENTUCKY REVISED STATUTES, 1944, 1963

Basic Statutes. Constitution of Kentucky, Sec. 8. *Freedom of speech and of the press.*—Printing presses shall be free to every person who undertakes to examine the proceedings of the General Assembly or any branch of government, and no law shall ever be made to restrain the right thereof. Every person may freely and fully speak, write and print on any subject, being responsible for the abuse of that liberty.

411.050. *Action for libel; retraction of statement; effect.*—In any civil action for libel, charging the publication of an erroneous statement alleged to be libelous, it shall be relevant and competent evidence for either party to prove that the plaintiff requested retraction or omitted to request retraction. The defendant may allege and give proof that the matter alleged to have been published and to be libelous was published without malice, and that the defendant in the next regular issue of the newspaper or publication, after receiving demand in writing or within seven days if no such demand was made, did correct and retract the statement, or in the next regular issue of the newspaper or publication did publish a sufficient correction, retraction or explanation as conspicuously and publicly as that in which the alleged libelous statement was published, in the same type and in the same place in at least two successive issues of the same periodical publication, accompanied by editorials in which the allegedly libelous statement was specifically repudiated. Upon proof of such facts the plaintiff shall not be entitled to punitive damages, and the defendant shall be liable only to pay actual damages. The defendant may plead the publication of the correction, retraction or explanation in mitigation of damages.

411.060. *Action for libel; privileged communications.*—The publication of a fair and impartial report of any proceeding before any state or city legislative or executive body, board or officer, or the whole or a fair synopsis of any bill, report, resolution, bulletin, notice, petition, or other document presented, filed or used in any proceeding before any state or city legislative or executive body, board or officer, shall be privileged, unless it is proved that the publication was maliciously made. The publication of a fair and impartial report or the whole or a synopsis of any indictment, warrant, affidavit, pleading or other document in any criminal or civil action in any court of competent jurisdiction shall be privileged, unless it is proved that it was published maliciously, or that the defendant after request by the plaintiff has failed to publish a reasonable explanation or contradiction thereof, giving the explanation or contradiction the same prominence and space as the original publication, or that the publisher refused after request by the plaintiff to publish the subsequent determination of the proceeding. This section shall not authorize the publication of any indecent matter.

411.140. *What actions shall survive.*—No right of action for personal injury or for injury to real or personal property shall cease or die with the person injuring or injured, except actions for assault, slander, libel, criminal conversation, and so much of the action for malicious prosecution as is intended to recover for the personal injury. For any other injury an action may be brought or revived by the personal representative, or against the personal representative, heir or devisee, in the same manner as causes of action founded on contract.

432.280. *Court may bring criminal action for libel or slander; punish resistance to judicial order.*—Nothing in KRS 432.-230 to 432.270 shall prevent any court or judge from proceeding against any person writing or publishing a libel or slanderous words concerning such court or judge in relation to his judicial conduct in court by indictment, nor prevent any court from punishing any person guilty of a contempt in resisting or disobeying any judicial order or process issued by or under the authority of such court.

411.060. *Action for libel; privileged communications.*—The publication of a fair and impartial report of any proceeding before any state or city legislative or executive body, board or officer, or the whole or a fair synopsis of any bill, report, resolution, bulletin, notice, petition, or other document presented,

411.062. *Defense to actions for damages for publication of a defamatory statement against a radio or television broadcasting station.*—If in any action for damages for the publication of a defamatory statement on a visual or sound radio broadcast, the defendant prove that such defamatory statement has been uttered by one other than the owner, licensee or operator of the broadcasting station or one acting as the agent or employee of said owner, licensee or operator, the action shall be dismissed unless the plaintiff shall allege and prove that such owner, licensee, operator, agency or employee has failed to exercise due care to prevent the publication of said statement in said broadcast; provided, however, that bona fide compliance with any federal law or regulation of any federal regulatory agency shall be construed as the exercise of due care; and provided, further, that in no event shall the owner, operator or licensee of a radio or television broadcasting station, or one acting as the agent or employee of such owner, operator or licensee, be held liable for the utterance of a defamatory statement in a visual or sound radio broadcast over the facilities of such station by any person speaking as a legally qualified candidate for public office, or on behalf of any such candidate.

Limitations. 413.140. *Actions to be brought within one year.*—

(1) The following actions shall be commenced within one year after the cause of action accrued:

(d) An action for libel or slander.

Louisiana

LOUISIANA CIVIL CODE, SECOND EDITION
LOUISIANA CODE OF CRIMINAL LAW AND PROCEDURE, 1943
LOUISIANA GENERAL STATUTES, 1939, 1952
LOUISIANA CONSTITUTION, 1921

Basic Statutes. Constitution. Art. I, Sec. 3. *Free speech and press.*—No law shall ever be passed to curtail or restrain the liberty of speech or of the press; any person may speak, write and publish his sentiments on all subjects, being responsible for the abuse of that liberty.

Art. XIX, Sec. 9. *Criminal libel, truth may be given in evidence—Criminal cases, jury judges of law and facts.*—In all proceedings or indictments for libel, the truth thereof may be given in evidence. The jury in all criminal cases shall be the judges of the law and of the facts on the question of guilt or innocence, having been charged as to the law applicable to the case by the presiding judge.

Cr. 740-47. *Defamation.*—Defamation is the malicious publication or expression in any manner, to anyone other than the party defamed, of anything which tends:

(1) To expose any person to hatred, contempt, or ridicule, or to deprive him of the benefit of public confidence or social intercourse; or

(2) to expose the memory of one deceased to hatred, contempt, or ridicule; or

(3) To injure any person, corporation, or association of persons in his or their business or occupation.

Whoever commits the crime of defamation shall be fined not

more than three thousand dollars, or imprisoned for not more than one year, or both.

Cr. 740-48. *Presumption of malice.*—Where a nonprivileged defamatory publication or expression is false it is presumed to be malicious unless a justifiable motive for making it is shown.

Where such a publication or expression is true, actual malice must be proved in order to convict the offender.

Cr. 740-49. *Qualified privilege.*—A qualified privilege exists and actual malice must be proved, regardless of whether the publication is true or false, in the following situations:

(1) Where the publication or expression is a fair and true report of any judicial, legislative, or other public or official proceeding, or of any statement, speech, argument or debate in the course of the same.

(2) Where the publication or expression is a comment, made in the reasonable belief of its truth, upon

(a) The conduct of a person in respect to public affairs; or

(b) A thing which the proprietor thereof offers or explains to the public.

(3) Where the publication or expression is made to a person interested in the communication, by one who is also interested or who stands in such a relation to the former as to afford a reasonable ground for supposing his motive innocent.

(4) Where the publication or expression is made by an attorney or party in a judicial proceeding.

Cr. 740-50. *Absolute privilege.*—There shall be no prosecution for defamation in the following situations:

(1) When a statement is made by a legislator or judge in the course of his official duties.

(2) When a statement is made by a witness in a judicial proceeding, or in any other legal proceeding where testimony may be required by law, and such statement is reasonably believed by the witness to be relevant to the matter in controversy.

Cr. 247. *Defamation—Charging offense.*—An indictment for

defamation need not set forth any extrinsic facts for the purpose of showing the application to the party defamed of the defamatory matter on which the indictment is founded, but it is sufficient to state generally that the same was published or expressed concerning him.

Cr. 443. *Prosecutions for defamation.*—In all prosecutions for defamation, the truth thereof may be given in evidence.

G.S. 2026. *Slander or libel—Truth as a defense—Pleading and proof.*—Whenever any civil suit for slander, defamation, or for a libel, shall be instituted in any court of this state, it shall be lawful for the defendant to plead in justification the truth of the slanderous, defamatory or libelous words or matter, for the uttering or publishing of which he may be sued; and in the trial of the issue in such suit, to maintain and prove his said plea by all legal evidence.

Limitations. C.C. 2315 (2294) (N 1382). *Torts—Liability—Survival of action.*—Every act whatever of man that causes damage to another, obliges him by whose fault it happened to repair it; the right of this action shall survive in case of death in favor of the children, including adopted children, or spouse of the deceased, or either of them, and in default of these in favor of the surviving brothers and sisters, or either of them, for the space of one year from the death; provided that should the deceased leave a surviving spouse, together with minor children, the right of action shall accrue to both the surviving spouse and minor children; provided further, that the right of action shall accrue to the major children only in those cases where there is no surviving spouse or minor child or children.

If the above right of action exists in favor of an adopted person, such right of action shall survive in case of death in favor of the children or spouse of the deceased, or either of them, and in default of these in favor of the surviving adoptive parents, or either of them, and in default of any of these, then in favor of the surviving brothers and sisters of the adopted person, or either of them, for the space of one year from the death.

The survivors above mentioned may also recover the damages sustained by them by the death of the parent or child or husband or wife or brothers or sisters or adoptive parent, or parents, or adopted person, as the case may be.

1351. *Civil liability of station owner, licensee, or operator for defamation.*—Any owner, licensee or operator of a visual or sound radio broadcasting station or network of stations, and the agents or employees of such owner, licensee or operator shall not be liable for damages for defamatory statement published or uttered in or as a part of a visual or sound radio broadcast, by one other than such owner, licensee or operator, or agent or employee thereof, unless it shall be alleged and proved by the complaining party, that such owner, licensee or operator, or such agent or employee, has failed to exercise due care to prevent the publication or utterance in such broadcast. Acts. 1950, No. 468, §1.

1352. *Defamatory statement by or on behalf of, or opposition to candidate for public office.*—In no event shall any owner, licensee or operator, or the agents or employees of any such owner, licensee or operator of such a station or network of stations be held liable for damages for any defamatory statement uttered over the facilities of such station or network by or on behalf of or in opposition to any candidate for public office.

§1353. *Damages recoverable for defamatory statements.*—In any action against any owner, licensee or operator, or the agents or employees of any owner, licensee or operator, of a visual or sound radio broadcasting station or network of stations for damages for any defamatory statement published or uttered in or as a part of a visual or sound radio broadcast, the complaining party shall be allowed only such actual damages as he may prove. Acts 1950, No. 468, §3.

§1354. *Responsibility of persons making defamatory statements.*—This Chapter is not intended to change the responsibility under the laws of this state, of any person or persons for any defamatory utterance made by such person or persons over a visual or sound radio broadcasting station or network of stations. Acts 1950, No. 468, §4.

C.C. 3536 (3501). *Tort, possessory and damage actions.*– The following actions are also prescribed by one year:

That for injurious words, whether verbal or written, and that for damages caused by animals, or resulting from offenses or quasi offenses.

Maine

THE REVISED STATUTES OF THE STATE OF MAINE, 1930, 1954, 1964

Basic Statutes. Chap. 141, Sec. 1. *Definition of a libel and of a publication.*—R.S.c. 131, Sec. 1. A libel is the malicious defamation of a living person, made public by any printing, writing, sign, picture, representation, or effigy, tending to provoke him to wrath, expose him to public confidence and social intercourse; or of a deceased person, thus made public, designed to blacken and vilify his memory, and tending to scandalize or provoke his relatives or friends; but nothing shall be deemed a libel unless there is publication thereof; and the delivery, selling, reading, or otherwise communicating a libel directly or indirectly to any person, including the person libeled is a publication.

Chap. 141, Sec. 2. *Penalty for libel.* R.S.c. 131, Sec. 2.—Whoever makes, composes, dictates, writes, or prints a libel; directs or procures it to be done; wilfully publishes or circulates it, or knowingly and wilfully aids in doing either, shall be punished by a fine of not more than one thousand dollars, and by imprisonment for less than one year.

Chap. 141, Sec. 3. *Responsibility for libels printed or published.* R.S.c. 131, Sec. 3.—Whoever manages or controls the business of a printing-office, bookstore, or shop, as principal or agent, or is, in whole or in part, proprietor, editor, printer, or publisher of a newspaper, pamphlet, book, or other publication, is responsible for any libel printed or published therein, unless he proves on trial that it was printed and published without his knowledge, consent, or suspicion, and that by reasonable care and diligence, he could not have prevented it.

Chap. 141, Sec. 4. *Punishment for securing the publication of any false or libelous statement.* R.S.c. 131, Sec. 4.—Whoever wilfully and maliciously states, delivers, or transmits by any means whatever to the manager, editor, publisher, or reporter of any newspaper, magazine; publication, periodical, or serial, for publication therein, any false or libelous statement concerning any person or corporation, and thereby secures the actual publication of the same, shall be punished by a fine of not more than five hundred dollars, or by imprisonment for not more than eleven months, or by both fine and imprisonment.

Chap. 141, Sec. 5. *How far the truth of a publication is a justification.* R.S.c. 131, Sec. 5.—In prosecutions for any publication relative to the official conduct of men in their public capacities, or to the qualifications of candidates for popular suffrages, or where the matter published is proper for public information, the truth thereof may be given in evidence, and if proved, shall be a complete justification; and in prosecutions for all other libels, the truth thereof, thus proved, shall be a complete justification, unless it appears that such publication originated in corrupt and malicious motives; and if any alleged libel is not justified in either of said modes, it shall be deemed malicious, unless the contrary is clearly proved.

Chap. 141, Sec. 6. *Jury to judge law and fact.* R.S.c. 131, Sec. 6.—In all indictments for libel, the jury after receiving the direction of the court, may determine at their discretion, the law and the fact. Const. Me., Art. 1, Sec. 4.

Chap. 141, Sec. 7. *Publishing lists of debtors prohibited.* R.S.c. 131, Sec. 7.—No person, firm or corporation shall publicly advertise for sale in any manner whatever, or for any purpose whatever, any list or lists of debts, dues, accounts, demands, notes, or judgments, containing the names of any of the persons who owe the same. Any such public advertisement containing the name of but one person who owes as aforesaid, shall be construed as a list within the meaning of this section. Any person, firm, or corporation violating any of the provisions of this section shall be liable in an action of debt to a penalty of not less than twenty-five dollars, nor more than one hundred dollars, to each and every person, severally and not jointly, whose name appears in any such list.

Chap. 141, Sec. 8. *Section seven does not apply to executors, etc., or officials.* R.S.c. 131, Sec. 8.—The provisions of the preceding section shall not apply to executors, administrators, guardians, trustees in bankruptcy, assignees in insolvency, sheriffs, deputy sheriffs, constables, collectors of taxes, town treasurers, or any other officials whose official duties require them to publish any such list or lists.

Chap. 26, Sec. 48. *Mitigation of damages in action for libel.* R.S.c. 87, Sec. 46.—The defendant in an action for libel may prove under the general issue, in mitigation of damages, that the charge was made by mistake or through error or by inadvertence, and that he has in writing, within a reasonable time after the publication of the charge, retracted the charge and denied its truth, as publicly and as fully as he made the charge; and he may also prove in mitigation of damages that the plaintiff has already recovered or has brought action for damages for, or has received or has agreed to receive compensation for, substantially the same libel as that for which said action was brought.

Chap. 96, Sec. 49. *Unproved allegations; effect.* R.S.c. 87, Sec. 47.—In actions for libel or slander, an unproved allegation in the pleadings that the matter charged is true, shall not be deemed proof of malice unless the jury on the whole case find that such allegation or the defense thereunder, is made with malicious intent.

Chap. 100, Sec. 1. *Actions in which trustee process may be used.* R.S.c. 91, Sec. 1.—All personal actions, except those of detinue, replevin, actions on the case for malicious prosecution, for slander by writing or speaking, and for assault and battery, may be commenced by trustee process in the superior court; or when the amount demanded in damages is not less than five dollars, nor more than twenty dollars, before a municipal or police court, or a trial justice unless otherwise limited in the act establishing such court.

Constitution of the State of Maine.—Article I, Section 4.—Every citizen may freely speak, write and publish his sentiments on any subject, being responsible for the abuse of this liberty; no laws shall be passed regulating or restraining the freedom of the press; and in prosecutions for any publication respecting the official conduct of men in public capacity, or the qualifications of those who are candidates for the suffrages of the people, or where the matter published is proper for public information, the truth thereof may be given in evidence, and in all indictments for libels, the Jury, after having received the direction of the Court, shall have a right to determine, at their discretion, the law and the fact.

Chap. 130 Sec. 32. *Responsibility for libel by radio.*—A person shall be responsible for any libel published or uttered in or as part of a visual or sound radio broadcast unless he prove on trial that it was broadcast and published without his knowledge, consent, or suspicion, and that by reasonable care and diligence he could not have prevented it.

In no event, however, shall any person be held liable for any damages for any defamatory statement uttered by another over the facilities of a visual or sound radio station or network by or on behalf of any candidate for public office, or in discussion of any matter referred to referendum, if such person shall have no power of censorship over the material broadcast. (1949 c. 134)

Limitations. Chap. 112, Sec. 93' ***Assault, libel, etc., in two years.*** R.S.c. 86, Sec. 87.—Action for assault and battery, and for false imprisonment, slander and libel, shall be commenced within two years after the cause of action accrues.

Maryland

CODE OF MARYLAND, 1939, 1957

Basic Statutes. Constitution of Maryland. Art. 40.—That the liberty of the press ought to be inviolably preserved; that every citizen of the State ought to be allowed to speak, write, and publish his sentiments on all subjects, being responsible for the abuse of that privilege.

Art. 75, Sec. 19. *Truth as justification for libel.*—In case any person shall be prosecuted by indictment or any other criminal prosecution for a libel the party so prosecuted shall be entitled to give the truth of the matter charged in the said indictment or other prosecution, in evidence under the general issue by way of justification.

Art. 75, §6. *Liability of broadcasting stations for libelous statements of candidates for public office.*—

a) Statements as to opponents.—The owner, licensee or operator of a visual or sound radio broadcasting station or network of stations, and the agents or employees of any such owner, licensee or operator shall not be liable for any damages for any defamatory or libelous statement published or uttered over the facilities of such station or network of stations by any candidate for public office, as to his opponent or opponents for the particular office he seeks, which publication or utterance cannot be censored by such owner, licensee or operator under any regulations of the Federal Communications Commission or any statute of the United States.

b) Statements as to persons other than opponents. As to a possibly defamatory or libelous statement made by any such candidate about any person or persons other than an opponent or opponents for the particular office he seeks, any such other person shall be limited and restricted in any suit or suits for defamation or libel brought against such owner, licensee or operator or against such agents or employees to such damages as may be compensatory for actual injury suffered; except that upon proof of actual malice on the part of any such owner, licensee or operator or on the part of any such agents or employees in allowing or permitting such statement to be made, punitive damages therefor may be allowed to the person aggrieved against the said owner or licensee, operator, agent, or employee. (An. Code, 1951 19a; 1952 ch. 51)

Limitations. Act. 57, Sec. 1.—All actions of account, actions of assumpsit, or on the case, except as hereinafter provided, actions of debt on simple contract, detinue or replevin, all actions for trespass for injuries to real or personal property, all actions for illegal arrest, false imprisonment, or violation of the twenty-third, twenty-sixth, thirty-first and thirty-second articles of the declaration of rights, or any of them, or of the existing, or any future provisions of the code touching the writ of habeas corpus, or proceedings thereunder, and all actions, whether of debt, ejectment or of any other description whatsoever, brought to recover rent in arrear, reserved under any form of lease, whether for ninety-nine years renewable forever, or for a greater or lesser period, and all distraints issued to recover such rent shall be commenced, sued, or issued within three years from the time the cause of action accrued; and all actions on the case for libel and slander and all actions of assault, battery and wounding, or any of them, within one year from the time the cause of action accrued.

Massachusetts

LAWS OF MASSACHUSETTS, 1958

Basic Statutes. Constitution of Massachusetts. Art. XVI. *Liberty of the Press.*—The liberty of the press is essential to the security of free speech in a state: it ought not, therefore, to be restrained in this commonwealth. The right of speech shall not be abridged.

Art. XXI. *Freedom of deliberation, speech and debate in the legislature.*—The freedom of deliberation, speech and debate, in either house of the legislature, is so essential to the rights of the people, that it cannot be the foundation of any accusation or prosecution, action or complaint, in any other court or place whatsoever.

C. 231, Sec. 84. *Consolidation of Action for Libel.*—If two or more actions for substantially the same libel, brought by the same plaintiff, are pending in the same court, either in the same or in different counties, any justice thereof may in his discretion make an order that some or all of them be tried together. A separate verdict, or, if the action tried without a jury, a separate finding, shall be rendered in each action, and judgment shall be rendered in each as if it had been tried separately. If the plaintiff recovers judgment in two or more actions, the court shall make an order for the apportionment of cost between the defendants.

C. 231, Sec. 91. *Justification in Slander Not Proof of Malice; Evidence of Statements of Defendant Not Declared on.*—If the defendant in an action for slander or for publishing a libel justifies that the words spoken or published were true, such allegation, although not maintained by the evidence, shall not of itself be proof of the malice alleged in the declaration, nor shall statements of the defendant differing in import from those declared on be admissible to establish his malice unless such statements were published in pursuance of a general scheme to defame or otherwise injure the plaintiff. If the plaintiff proposes to introduce evidence of statements of the defendant other than those declared on, he shall give the defendant written notice of such intention, specifying the date and content of each such statement, at least fourteen days before trial begins, or earlier if the court so orders; and, if any such statement is introduced in evidence, the defendant shall be permitted to prove that it was true, or was privileged, or any other facts relating thereto which tend to negative malice.

C. 231, Sec. 92. *Truth of Libel Admissible.*—The defendant in an action for writing or for publishing a libel may introduce in evidence the truth of the matter contained in the publication charged as libellous; and the truth shall be a justification unless actual malice is proved.

C. 231, Sec. 93. *Retraction of Libel.*—Where the defendant in an action for libel, at any time after the publication of the libel hereinafter referred to, either before or after such action is brought, but before the answer is required to be filed therein, gives written notice to the plaintiff or to his attorney of his intention to publish a retraction of the libel, accompanied by a copy of the retraction which he intends to publish, and the retraction is published, he may prove such publication, and, if the plaintiff does not accept the offer of retraction, the defendant may prove such non-acceptance in mitigation of damages. If within a reasonable time after receiving notice in writing from the plaintiff that he claims to be libelled the defendant makes such offer and publishes a reasonable retraction, and such offer is not accepted, he may prove that alleged libel was published in good faith and without actual malice, and, unless the proof is successfully rebutted, the plaintiff shall recover only for any actual damage sustained. In no action of slander or libel shall exemplary or punitive damages be allowed, whether because of actual malice or want of good faith or for any other reason. Proof of actual malice shall not enhance the damages recoverable for injury to the plaintiff's reputation.

C. 231, Sec. 94. *Evidence in Mitigation of Damages.*—In an action for libel, the defendant may allege and prove in mitigation of damages that the plaintiff already has brought action for or recovered damages for, or has received or has agreed to receive compensation in respect of, substantially the same libel as that for which such action was brought. In an action for libel or slander, he may introduce in evidence, in mitigation of damages and in rebuttal of evidence of actual malice, acts of the plaintiff which create a reasonable suspicion that the matters charged against him by the defendant are true.

C. 231, Sec. 147. *Forms.*—The following forms of pleadings may be used for the purposes therein indicated, and similar forms with the necessary changes may be used for other like purposes, subject to such changes as the supreme judicial court may from time to time by general rules prescribe; but any other suitable forms may also be used:

20. Libel

And the plaintiff says that the defendant falsely and maliciously printed and published (or wrote and published) of the plaintiff in a newspaper called   the words following: "He is a regular prover in bankruptcies," the defendant meaning thereby that the plaintiff had proved and was in the habit of proving fictitious debts against the estates of bankrupts, with the knowledge that such debts were fictitious; (or, if it is a picture, describe it, e.g.) falsely and maliciously composed and published of the plaintiff and a court-martial of which he was a member a lithograph picture and caricature of the said court-martial in which the plaintiff is represented in an awkward, ludicrous and contemptible light and posture and as saying of A B the respondent then on trial upon certain charges before the said court-martial the words following: (here set out the words) the defendant thereby meaning to impute to the plaintiff low, vulgar and contemptible language, views and motives.);

(or, if it is a letter) falsely and maliciously wrote and published of the plaintiff in a letter addressed to W D, by whom the plaintiff was employed as bookkeeper, the words following: "There is a duplicity about your bookkeeper in serving your interest in this affair of ours which is sadly too transparent. I conceive there is nothing too base for him to be guilty of."

43. Slander or Libel

The defendant denies that he accused the plaintiff of the crime of perjury as alleged in the first count.

And answering the second count, the defendant says that (the plaintiff feloniously stole ten dollars the property of S. T. and so) the words alleged to have been written (or spoken) and published of the plaintiff by the defendant were true.

C. 224, Sec. 4. *No Arrest on Mesne Process for Slander or Libel.*—No person shall be arrested on mesne process in a civil action for slander or libel.

C. 278, Sec. 8 *Justification in Cases of Libel.*—The defendant in a prosecution for writing or publishing a libel may introduce in evidence the truth of the matter contained in the publication charged as libellous, and the truth shall be a justification, unless actual malice is proved.

C. 112, Sec. 12. *Disclosure of Certain Information by Registered Physician Not Slander or Libel.*—Any registered physician or surgeon who knows or has reason to believe that any person is infected with gonorrhoea or syphilis may disclose such information to any person from whom the infected person has received a promise of marriage or to the parent or guardian of such person if a minor. Such information given in good faith by a registered physician or surgeon shall not constitute a slander or libel. (1918, 111.) (1948 amendment broadened this section by making it apply to all venereal diseases.)

C. 272§98c *Libel of Groups of Persons Because of Race, Color, or Religion.*—Whoever publishes any false written or printed material with intent to maliciously promote hatred of any group of persons in the commonwealth because of race, color or religion shall be guilty of libel and shall be punished by a fine of not more than one thousand dollars or by imprisonment for not more than one year, or both. The defendant may prove in defense that the publication was privileged or was not malicious. Prosecutions under this section shall be instituted only by the attorney general or by the district attorney for the district in which the alleged libel was published. (1943, 223, appvd. April 30, 1943.)

231 §91A. (Supplement to Vol. 8.) *Radio, etc., Stations, etc., Exempt from Liability for Damages for Defamatory Matter Uttered by Certain Persons.*—The owner, operator, or licensee of a radio or television station or network of such stations or the agent or servant of any such person shall not, in action for slander, or for publishing a libel, be held liable in damages for or on account of any defamatory matter uttered, broadcast, telecast, or published over the radio or television facilities of any such station or network by any person whose utterance, broadcast, telecast or publication is not, under the provisions of any law of the United States or any regulation, ruling or order of the Federal Communications Commission, subject to censorship or control by such station or network. (Added by 1957, 378, approved May 15, 1957; effective 90 days thereafter.)

Limitations. C. 260, Sec. 4. *Limitation of Two Years; Limita-*

tion of One Year for Certain Actions.—Actions for assault and battery, false imprisonment, slander, actions against sheriffs, deputy sheriffs, constables or assignees in insolvency for the taking or conversion of personal property, actions of tort for injuries to the person against counties, cities and towns, and actions of contract or tort for malpractice, error or mistake against physicians, surgeons, dentists, optometrists, hospitals, and sanitaria, shall be commenced only within two years next after the cause of action accrues; and actions for libel and actions of tort for bodily injuries or for death the payment of judgments in which is required to be secured by chapter ninety and also such actions against officers and employees of the commonwealth, of the metropolitan district commission, and of any county, city or town, arising out of the operation of motor vehicles owned by the commonwealth, including those under the control of said commission, or by any such county, city or town, suits by judgment creditors in such actions of tort under section one hundred and thirteen of chapter one hundred and seventy-five and clause (10) of section three of chapter two hundred and fourteen and suits on motor vehicle liability bonds under section thirty-four G of said chapter ninety shall be commenced only within one year next after the cause of action accrues.

Michigan

COMPILED LAWS OF MICHIGAN, 1962

Basic Statutes. Constitution of Michigan, Art. II, Sec. 18. *Libels; truth as defense.*—In all prosecutions for libels the truth may be given in evidence to the jury; and, if it shall appear to the jury that the matter charged as libelous is true and was published with good motives and for justifiable ends, the accused shall be acquitted.

3322. *False statement, penalty for publication or circulation.*—Sec. 17. If any letter, circular, poster, bill, publication or placard shall contain any false statement or charges reflecting on any candidate's character, morality or integrity, the author thereof and every person knowingly assisting in the circulation thereof, shall, upon conviction thereof, be subject to the penalties provided for the violation of this act: *Provided,* That this shall in nowise deprive the injured party of any other action for libel given by law.

14469. *Civil action for slander or libel; notice of justification.*—Sec. 19. If the defendant in any action for slander or for publishing a libel, shall give notice in his justification, that the words spoken or published were true, such notice, though not maintained by the evidence, shall not, in any case, be of itself proof of the malice charged in the declaration.

14471. *Same; damages.*—Sec. 21. In suits brought for the recovery of damages for libel or slander in this state, the plaintiff shall be entitled to recover only such actual damages as he may have suffered in respect to his property, business, trade, profession, occupation or feelings.

27A.2911. *Actions for slander and libel; damages; justifi-*

cation; privilege; contribution; defenses prior to action for related cause.—

(1) Words imputing a lack of chastity to any female are actionable in themselves and subject the person who uttered or published them to a civil action for the slander in the same manner as the uttering or publishing of words imputing the commission of a criminal offense.

(2) (a) Except as provided in (b), in actions based on libel or slander the plaintiff is entitled to recover only for the actual damages which he has suffered in respect to his property, business, trade, profession, occupation, or feelings.

(b) Exemplary and punitive damages shall not be recovered in actions for libel unless the plantiff, before instituting his action, gives notice to the defendant to publish a retraction and allows a reasonable time to do so, and proof of the publication or correction shall be admissible in evidence under a denial on the question of the good faith of the defendant, and in mitigation and reduction of exemplary or punitive damages. The retraction shall be published in the same size type, in the same editions and as far as practicable, in substantially the same position as the original libel.

(3) If the defendant in any action for slander or libel gives notice in his justification that the words spoken or published were true, this notice shall not be of itself proof of the malice charged in the complaint though not sustained by the evidence. In any action for slander or for publishing a libel even though the defendant has pleaded or attempted to prove a justification he may prove mitigating circumstances including the sources of his information and the ground for his belief. No damages shall be awarded in any libel action brought against a reporter, editor, publisher, or proprietor of a newspaper for the publication in it of a fair and true report of any public and official proceeding, or for any heading of the report which is a fair and true headnote of the article published. This privilege shall not apply to a libel which is contained in any matter added by any person concerned in the publication or contained in the report of anything said or done at the time and place of the public

and official proceeding which was not a part of the public and official proceeding.

(4) Any person or persons against whom a judgment is recovered for damages arising out of the authorship or publication of a libel is entitled to recover contribution in a civil action from all persons who were originally jointly liable for the libel with the defendant or defendants, whether joined as defendants or not, to the same extent as and with the same effect that joint sureties are liable to contribute to each other in cases where they are sureties in the same contract. Where the libel has been published in any newspaper, magazine, or other periodical publication the servants and agents of the publisher of the periodical, and the news agents and other persons who have been connected with the libel only by selling or distributing the publication containing the libel and who have not acted maliciously in selling or publishing the libel, shall not be required to contribute and shall not be taken into account in determining the amount that any joint tort feasor is required to contribute under the provisions of this section. And if the author of the libel acted maliciously in composing or securing the printing or the publication of the libel and the printer, publisher, or distributor of the libel acted in good faith and without malice in printing and publishing the libel the author of the libel is liable in a civil action to that printer, publisher, or distributor for the entire amount of the damages which are recovered against and paid by that printer, publisher, or distributor.

(5) In actions brought for the recovery of damages for libel in this state, it is competent for the defendant or defendants in such action to show in evidence upon the trial of such action that the plaintiff in such action has heretofore recovered a judgment or judgments for damages in an action or actions for libel or libels to the same, or substantially the same purport or effect as the libel for the recovery of damages for which such action has been brought, or that the plaintiff in such action has heretofore brought an action or actions for such libel or has received or agreed to receive compensation for such a libel.

§27.1405 *Liability of visual or sound radio broadcaster for defamatory statements made in or as part of broadcast.*—Section 1. The owner, licensee or operator of a visual or sound radio broadcasting station or network of stations, and the agents or employees of any such owner, licensee or operator, shall not be liable for any damages for any defamatory statement published or uttered in or as a part of a visual or sound radio broadcast, by other than such owner, licensee or operator, or agent or employee thereof, unless it shall be alleged and proved by the complaining party that such owner, licensee, operator or such agent or employee has failed to exercise due care to prevent the publication or utterance of such statement in such broadcast. (CL '48, §484.331.)

§27.1406. *Liability for defamatory statements made by or on behalf of candidate for public office.* Sec. 2. The owner licensee or operator, or the agents or employees of any such owner, licensee or operator of such a station or network of stations, shall not be liable for any damages for any defamatory statement uttered over the facilities of such station or network by or on behalf of any candidate for public office where such statement is not subject to censorship or control by reason of any federal statute or any ruling or order of the federal communications commission made pursuant thereto. (CL '48, §484.332.)

Limitations. Revised Judicature Act. §27. A. 5805. Limits in actions to recover damages for injuries to persons or property. No person may bring or maintain any action to recover damages for injuries to persons or property unless, after the claim first accrued to himself or to someone through whom he claims, he commences the action within the periods of time prescribed by this action.

(6) The period of limitations is 1 year for actions charging libel or slander.

Minnesota

MINNESOTA STATUTES, 1941, 1962

Basic Statutes. Minnesota Constitution, Art. I, Sec. 3. *Liberty of the press.*—The liberty of the press shall forever remain inviolate, and all persons may freely speak, write and publish their sentiments on all subjects, being responsible for the abuse of such right.

619.51. *Libel; Gross Misdemeanor; Punishment; Prosecutions by County Attorneys or Attorney General.*—Every malicious publication, by writing, printing, picture, effigy, sign, or otherwise than by mere speech, which shall expose any living person, or the memory of one deceased, to hatred, contempt, ridicule, or obloquy, or which shall cause or tend to cause any person to be shunned or avoided, or which shall have a tendency to injure any person, corporation, or association of persons in his or their business or occupation, shall be a libel. Every person who publishes a libel shall be guilty of a gross misdemeanor; and, upon conviction, punished by a fine of not less than $100.00, and not more than $1,000, or by imprisonment in the county jail for not more than six months.

It shall be the duty of the county attorney of any county where any such offense was committed to prosecute the offender or offenders.

In any case wherein the county attorney shall fail or refuse to commence a prosecution upon the complaint of the person claiming to have been libeled, the attorney general may commence such prosecution and carry it to final conclusion, or on application the court may appoint an attorney to prosecute.

619.52. *How Justified or Excused; Malice, When Presumed.*

—Every publication having the tendency or effect mentioned in section 619.51 shall be deemed malicious if no justification or excuse therefor is shown. Such publication is justified when the matter charged as libelous is true and was published with good motives and for justifiable ends. It is excused when honestly made, in belief of its truth, and upon reasonable ground for such belief, and consists of fair comments upon the conduct of a person in respect of public affairs.

619.53. *Publication.*—To sustain the charge of publishing a libel it is not necessary that the matter complained of should have been seen by another. It is enough that the defendant knowingly displayed it, or parted with its immediate custody, under circumstances which exposed it to be seen or understood by a person other than himself.

619.54. *Liability of Editors and Others.*—Every editor or proprietor of a book, newspaper, or serial, and every manager of a copartnership or corporation by which any book, newspaper, or serial is issued, is chargeable with the publication of any matter contained in such book, newspaper, or serial. In every prosecution for libel the defendant may show in his defense that the matter complained of was published without his knowledge or fault, and against his wishes, by another who had no authority from him to make such publication, and whose act was disavowed by him as soon as known.

619.55. *Reports of Proceedings Privileged.*—No prosecution for libel shall be maintained against a reporter, editor, publisher, or proprietor of a newspaper for the publication therein of a fair and true report of any judicial, legislative, or other public and official proceeding, or of any statement, speech, argument, or debate in the course of the same, without proving actual malice in making the report. The foregoing shall not apply to a libel contained in the heading of the report, or in any matter added by another person concerned in the publication, or in the report of anything said or done at the time and place of the public and official proceeding, which was not a part thereof.

619.56. *Where indicted; Punishment restricted.*—Every indictment for a libel contained in a newspaper published in the state may be found in any county where the paper was published or circulated, but a person shall not be indicted or tried for the publication of the same libel against the same person in more than one county.

619.57. *Privileged communications.*—Every communication made to a person entitled to or interested in such communication, by one also interested in or entitled to make it, or who stood in such relation to the former as to afford a reasonable ground for supposing his motive innocent, shall be presumed not to be malicious, and shall be termed a privileged communication.

619.63. *Certain Statements Unlawful.*—Subdivision 1. Regarding banks and savings institutions. It shall be unlawful for any person, firm, or corporation to falsely and maliciously state, utter, publish, or cause to be falsely and maliciously stated, uttered, or published, any report, rumor, or statement directly or indirectly tending to disclose that any bank, public or savings institution is in an existing or probable insolvent financial condition.

Subdivision 2. Penalty. Any person, firm, or corporation violating any of the provisions of subdivision 1 shall be guilty of a gross misdemeanor, and shall be punished by imprisonment in the county jail of any county wherein such false, slanderous declarations are made or published, for a term of not less than 30 days, nor more than six months, or by a fine of not less than $100.00, or by both.

548.06. *Damages for libel.*—In an action for damages for the publication of a libel in a newspaper, the plaintiff shall recover no more than special damages, unless a retraction be demanded and refused as hereinafter provided. He shall serve upon the publisher at the principal place of publication, a notice, specifying the statements claimed to be libelous, and requesting that the same be withdrawn. If a retraction thereof be not published on the same page and in the same type and the statement headed in 18 point type or larger "Retraction," as were the statements complained of, in a regular issue thereof published within one week after such service, he may allege such notice, demand, and failure to retract in his complaint and recover both special and general damages, if his cause of action be maintained. If such retraction be so published, he may still recover general damages, unless the defendant shall show that the libelous publication was made in good faith and under a mistake as to the facts. If the plaintiff was a candidate for office at the time of the libelous publication, no retraction shall be available unless published on the same page and in the same type and the statement headed in 18 point type or larger "RETRACTION," as were the statements complained of, in a regular issue thereof published within one week after such service and in a conspicuous place on the editorial page, nor if the libel was published within one week next before the election. This section shall not apply to any libel imputing unchastity to a woman.

210.11. *Defamatory Circulars.*—Every person who writes, prints, posts, or distributes, or causes to be written, printed, posted, or distributed, any circular, poster, or other written or printed matter, which is designed or tends to injure or defeat any candidate for nomination or election to a public office by reflecting on his personal or political character or acts, shall be guilty of a gross misdemeanor.

634.05. *In prosecutions for libel; Right of jury.*—In all criminal prosecutions for libel, the truth may be given in evidence, and if it appears to the jury that the matter charged as libelous is true, and was published with good motives and justifiable ends, the party shall be acquitted; and the jury shall have the right to determine the law and the fact.

544.25. *Pleadings in slander and libel.*—In actions for libel or slander, it shall be sufficient instead of stating extrinsic facts showing the application to plaintiff of the defamatory matter complained of, to allege, generally, that the same was published or spoken concerning the plaintiff; and if such allegation is controverted, the plaintiff is bound to establish on the trial that it was so published or spoken. The defendant may allege, in his answer, both the truth of the matter charged as defamatory and any circumstances in mitigation of damages, and, whether he proves the justification or not, he may give in evidence the mitigating circumstances.

530.06. *Actions not within jurisdiction.*—The jurisdiction conferred by section 530.05 (justice of the peace) does not extend to a civil action:

(1) In a cause involving the title to real estate;

(2) Nor for false imprisonment, libel, slander, malicious prosecution, criminal conversation, or seduction, or upon a promise to marry;

(3) Nor for an action against an executor, administrator, or guardian, as such.

628.22. *Indictment for libel.*—An indictment for libel need not set forth any extrinsic facts for the purpose of showing the application to the party libeled of the defamatory matter on which the indictment is founded, but it shall be sufficient to state generally that the same was published concerning him, and the fact that it was so published shall be established on the trial.

631.06. *Questions of law and fact, how decided.*—On the trial of an indictment for any offense, questions of law shall be decided by the court, except in cases of libel, saving the right of the defendant to except, and questions of fact by the jury; and, although the jury may find a general verdict which shall include questions of law as well as of fact, it shall receive as law what shall be laid down by the court as such.

Minnesota 1964 (Cumulative Annual Packet) 544.043. *Defamation by television and radio; defense.*—The owner, licensee or operator of a visual or sound radio broadcasting station, or network of stations, or any agent or employee of any such owner, licensee, or operator, is not liable for damages for any defamatory statement published or uttered in or as part of a visual or sound radio broadcast, by any one other than such owner, licensee or operator, or agent or employee thereof, if such owner, licensee, operator, or such agent or employee, shows that he has exercised due care to prevent the publication or utterance of the statement in that broadcast. Provided, however, the exercise of due care shall be construed to include a bona fide compliance with any federal law or the regulation of any federal regulatory agency.

Limitations. 541.07. *Two year limitations. The following actions shall be commenced within two years:*—(1) For libel, slander, assault, battery, false imprisonment, or other tort, resulting in personal injury, and all actions against physicians, surgeons, dentists, hospitals, sanitariums, for malpractice, error, mistake, or failure to cure, whether based on contract or tort; provided, a counterclaim may be pleaded as a defense to any action for services brought by a physician, surgeon, dentist, hospital or sanitarium, after the limitations herein described notwithstanding it is barred by the provisions of this chapter, if it was the property of the party pleading it at the time it became barred and was not barred at the time the claim sued on originated, but no judgment thereof except for costs can be rendered in favor of the party so pleading it.

Mississippi

MISSISSIPPI CODE, 1943

Basic Statutes. Constitution. Art. III, Sec. 13.—The freedom of speech and of the press shall be held sacred; and in all prosecutions for libel the truth may be given in evidence, and the jury shall determine the law and the facts under the direction of the court; and if it shall appear to the jury that the matter charged as libelous is true, and was published with good motives and for justifiable ends, the party shall be acquitted.

Sec. 1059. *Certain words actionable.*—All words which, from their usual construction and common acceptation, are considered as insults, and calculated to lead to a breach of the peace, shall be actionable; and a plea, exception or demurrer shall not be sustained to preclude a jury from passing thereon, who are the sole judges of the damages sustained; but this shall not deprive the courts of the power to grant new trials, as in other cases.

Sec. 1473. *Declaration for libel or slander.*—In actions for libel or slander the plaintiff may aver that the words or matter complained of were used in a defamatory sense, specifying such sense, without any prefatory averment to show how such words or matter were used in that sense; and such averment shall be put in issue by the denial of the alleged libel or slander; and where the words or matter set forth, with or without the alleged meaning, show a cause of action, the declaration shall be sufficient.

Sec. 1479. *Mitigating circumstances.*—In actions for libel or slander, assault and battery, and false imprisonment, the defendant, under the plea of not guilty, may give in evidence any mitigating circumstances to reduce the damages, notwithstanding he may also have pleaded a justification.

Sec. 1582. *Costs not recovered in some cases–limited in others.*–In actions of assault, assault and battery, libel and slander, if the plaintiff recover less than ten dollars, costs shall not be awarded to him. In all other actions sounding damages, where the plaintiff sues for more than ten dollars and recovers less than that sum, no more costs than the amount of damages recovered shall be awarded to him, unless the court be of the opinion that the plaintiff had reasonable cause to expect to recover more, and that the action was brought for no other purpose than to be compensated for the wrong done, and enter the same on its minutes. If more costs be awarded, the judgment may be amended on motion at any time.

Sec. 2094. *Dueling–posting or publishing or vilifying another.*–If any person shall post or publish another for not fighting a duel or for not sending or accepting a challenge to fight a duel or shall use any reproachful or contemptuous language, whether oral, written, or printed, to or concerning another for not accepting or sending a challenge to fight a duel, or with intent to provoke a duel, he shall be guilty of a misdemeanor, and be punished accordingly.

Sec. 2268. *Libel–Punishment therefor.*–Any person who shall be convicted of writing or publishing any libel, shall be fined in such sum or imprisoned in the county jail for such term as the court, in its discretion, may adjudge, having regard to the nature and enormity of the offense, or be punished by both such fine and imprisonment.

Sec. 2269. *Libel–truth, good motive, justiable ends.*–In every criminal prosecution for libel it shall be lawful for the defendant, upon the trial, to give in evidence the truth of the matter written or published, and if it shall appear to the jury that the matter charged as libelous is true, and was published with good motives and for justifiable ends, the defendant shall be acquitted.

Sec. 2455. *Indictment–requisites in cases of libel.*–An indictment for libel need not set forth any extrinsic facts to show the application of the defamatory matter charged in the indictment to the party libeled, but it shall be sufficient to charge generally that the same was published of or concerning him, and the fact that it was so published must be proved on the trial.

Limitations. Sec. 732. *Other actions commenced in one year.* —All actions for assault, assault and battery, maiming, false imprisonment, malicious arrest, or menace, and all actions for slanderous words concerning the person or title, and for libels, shall be commenced within one year next after the cause of such action accrued, and not after.

Missouri

MISSOURI REVISED STATUTES, 1931, 1949, 1952

Constitution adopted February 27, 1945. Art. I. Section 8. *Freedom of speech—evidence of truth in defamation actions—province of jury.*—That no law shall be passed impairing the freedom of speech, no matter by what means communicated; that every person shall be free to say, write or publish, or otherwise communicate whatever he will on any subject, being responsible for all abuses of that liberty; and that in all suits and prosecutions for libel or slander the truth thereof may be given in evidence; and in suits and prosecutions for libel the jury, under the direction of the court, shall determine the law and the facts.

Sec. 918. *Punitive Damages, amount sought separately stated.* —In all actions where exemplary or punitive damages are recoverable, the petition shall state separately the amount of such damages sought to be recovered.

Sec. 960. *Libel and slander, actions on.*—In an action for libel or slander, it shall not be necessary to state in the petition any extrinsic facts for the purpose of showing the application to the plaintiff of the defamatory matter out of which the cause of action arose, but it shall be sufficient to state, generally, that the same [was] published or spoken concerning the plaintiff; and if such allegation be not controverted in the answer, it shall not be necessary to prove it on the trial; in other cases it shall be necessary.

Sec. 961. *Defense, mitigating circumstances, separate statement.*—In the actions mentioned in the last preceding section, the defendant may, in his answer, allege both the truth of the matter charged as defamatory and any mitigating circumstances admissible in evidence to reduce the amount of damages; and whether he prove the justification or not, he may give in evidence the mitigating circumstances; but such matters of justification and mitigation shall be separately stated.

Sec. 2554. *Shall not have jurisdiction in certain cases.*—No justice of the peace shall have jurisdiction to hear or try any action against any executor or administrator, nor of any action of slander, libel, malicious prosecution or false imprisonment, nor of any action where the title to any lands or tenements shall come in question and be in issue, nor of any strictly equitable proceedings.

Sec. 3651. *What words are actionable.*—It is actionable to publish falsely and maliciously, in any manner whatsoever, that any person has been guilty of fornication or adultery.

Sec. 4758. *Libel defined.*—A libel is the malicious defamation of a person made public by any printing, writing, sign, picture, representation or effigy tending to provoke him to wrath or expose him to public hatred, contempt or ridicule, or to deprive him of the benefits of public confidence and social intercourse, or any malicious defamation made public as aforesaid, designed to blacken and vilify the memory of one who is dead, and tending to scandalize or provoke his surviving relatives and friends.

Sec. 4759. *Libel a misdemeanor.*—Every person who shall make or compose, dictate or procure the same to be done, or shall wilfully publish or circulate any such libel or libels specified in the preceding section, or shall in any way knowingly and wilfully aid or assist in making, publishing, or circulating the same shall be deemed guilty of a misdemeanor.

Sec. 4760. *Libel, continued.*—No printing, writing, or other thing is a libel unless there has been a publication thereof, by delivering, selling, reading or otherwise communicating the same or causing the same to be delivered, sold, read, or otherwise communicated to one or more persons or to the party libeled, or by exposing or exhibiting such libelous thing or matter in some public place, or where it may be seen or observed by the public.

Sec. 4761. *Evidence in prosecutions.*—In all prosecutions for libel or verbal slander, the truth thereof may be given in evidence to the jury, and shall constitute a complete defense; and the jury, under the direction of the court, shall determine the law and the fact.

Sec. 4455. *Blackmail construed as an attempt to rob.*—Every person who shall knowingly send or deliver, or shall make, and for the purpose of being delivered or sent, shall part with the possession of any paper, letter or writing with or without a name subscribed thereto, or signed with a fictitious name, or with any letter, mark or other designation, threatening therein to accuse any person of any crime or felony whatever, or to do injury to the person or property of anyone with a view or intent to extort or gain any money or property of any description, belonging to another; and every person who shall publish or threaten to publish any libel upon any other person, or shall, directly or indirectly, propose to abstain from printing or publishing, or shall directly or indirectly offer to prevent the printing or publishing of any matter or thing or security for money, or any valuable thing from such or any other person, or with intent to induce any person to confer upon or procure for any person any appointment or office of profit or trust, shall, on conviction, be adjudged guilty of an attempt to rob, and shall be punished by imprisonment in the penitentiary not exceeding five years, or not less than six months in the county jail.

537.105. *Radio stations not liable for defamation, when.*—The owner, licensee or operator of a visual or sound radio broadcasting station or network of stations, or the agents or employees of such owner, licensee, or operator of such a station or network of stations, shall not be liable for any damages for any defamatory statement uttered over the facilities of such station or network by or on behalf of any candidate for public office when such statement is not subject to censorship or control by reason of any federal statute or any ruling or order of the Federal Communications Commission made pursuant thereto. (Laws, 1951)

Limitations. 516.140. What actions within two years. Within two years: An action for libel, slander, assault, battery, false imprisonment or criminal conversation. (R. S. 1939, §1016, A. L. 1945, p. 644)

Montana

THE REVISED CODES OF MONTANA OF 1935, 1947

Basic Statutes. Constitution of Montana, Art. III, Sec. 10. *No law shall be passed impairing the freedom of speech;*—every person shall be free to speak, write, or publish whatever he will on any subject, being responsible for all abuse of that liberty; and that in all suits and prosecutions for libel, the truth thereof may be given in evidence; and the jury, under the direction of the court, shall determine the law and the facts.

5689. *Defamation—how effected.*—
Defamation is effected by:

1. Libel;
2. Slander.

5690. *Libel defined.*—Libel is a false and unprivileged publication by writing, printing, picture, effigy, or other fixed representation to the eye, which exposes any person to hatred, contempt, ridicule, or obloquy, or which causes him to be shunned or avoided, or which has a tendency to injure him in his occupation.

5692. *What communications are privileged.*—A privileged publication is one made:

1. In the proper discharge of an official duty;

2. In any legislative or judicial proceeding, or in any other official proceeding authorized by law;

3. In a communication, without malice, to a person interested therein, by one who is also interested, or by one who stands in such relation to the person interested as to afford a reasonable ground for supposing the motive for the communication innocent, or who is requested by the person interested to give the information;

4. By a fair and true report, without malice, of a judicial, legislative or other public official proceeding, or of anything said in the course thereof.

5692.1. *Liability of owner or operator of radio station for libel and defamation, extent of.*—No person, firm, or corporation owning or operating a radio broadcasting station shall be liable under the law of libel and defamation on account of having made its broadcasting facilities available to any person, whether a candidate for public office or any other person, for discussion of controversial or any other subjects, in the absence of proof of actual malice on the part of such owner or operator.

5692.2 *Copy of proposed radio address may be required prior to broadcast.*—Any person, firm or corporation owning or operating a radio broadcasting station shall have the right, but shall not be compelled, to require the submission and permanent filing, in such station, of a copy of the complete address, or other form of expression, if in words, intended to be broadcast over such station, not more than 48 hours before the time of the intended broadcast thereof.

5692.3. *Construction of act—liability.*—Nothing in this act contained shall be construed to relieve any person broadcasting over a radio station from liability under the law of libel and defamation. Nor shall anything in this act be construed to relieve any person, firm or corporation owning or operating a radio broadcasting station from liability under the law of libel and defamation an account of any broadcast prepared or made by any such firm, person, or corporation or by any officer or employee thereof in the course of his employment; and in any case where liability shall exist on account of any broadcast as declared in the first clause of this sentence, in that event where two or more broadcasting stations were connected together simultaneously or by transcription, film, metal tape or other approved or adapted use for joint operation, in the making of such broadcast, such liability shall be confined and limited solely to the person, firm or corporation owning or operating the radio station which originated such broadcast.

10800. *Political criminal libel.*—It shall be unlawful to write, print, or circulate through the mails or otherwise any letter, circular, bill, placard, or poster relating to any election or to any candidate in any election, unless the same shall bear on its face the name and address of the author, and of the printer and publisher thereof; and any person writing, printing, publishing, circulating, posting, or causing to be written, printed, circulated, posted, or published any such letter bill, placard, circular, or poster as aforesaid, which fails to bear on its face the name and address of the author and of the printer or publisher, shall be guilty of an illegal practice, and shall on conviction thereof be punished by a fine of not less than ten dollars nor more than one thousand dollars. If any letter, circular, poster, bill, publication, or placard shall contain any false statement or charges reflecting on any candidate's character, morality, or integrity, the author thereof, and every person printing or knowingly assisting in the circulation, shall be guilty of political criminal libel, and upon conviction thereof shall be punished by imprisonment in the penitentiary for not less than one nor more than three years. If the person charged with such crime, shall prove on his trial that he had reasonable ground to believe such charge was true, and did believe it was true, and that he was not actuated by malice in making such publication, it shall be a sufficient defense to such charge. But in that event, and as a part of such defense, the author and the printer or publisher or other person charged with such crime shall also prove that, at least fifteen days before such letter, circular, poster, bill, or placard containing such false statement or statements was printed or circulated, he or they caused to be served personally and in person upon the candidate to whom it relates a copy thereof in writing, and calling his attention particularly to the charges contained therein, and that, before printing, publishing, or circulating such charges, he received and read any denial, defense, or explanation, if any, made or offered to him in writing by the accused candidate within ten days after the service of such charge upon the accused person.

10989. *Libel defined.*—A libel is a malicious defamation, expressed either by writing, printing, or by signs or pictures, or the like, tending to blacken the memory of one who is dead, or to impeach the honest, integrity, virtue, or reputation, or to publish the natural or alleged defects of one who is alive, and thereby to expose him to public hatred, contempt, or ridicule.

10990. *Punishment of libel.*—Every person who wilfully, and with a malicious intent to injure another, publishes, or procures to be published, any libel, is punishable by fine not exceeding five thousand dollars, or imprisonment in the county jail not exceeding one year.

10991. *Malice presumed.*—An injurious publication is presumed to have been malicious if no justifiable motive for making it is shown.

10992. *Truth may be given in evidence—jury to determine law and fact.*—In all criminal prosecutions for libel, the truth may be given in evidence to the jury, and if it appears to the jury that the matter charged as libelous is true, and was published with good motives and for justifiable ends, the party shall be acquitted. The jury have the right to determine the law and the fact.

10993. *Publication defined.*—To sustain a charge of publishing a libel, it is not needful that the words or things complained of should have been seen or read by another. It is enough that the accused knowingly parted with the immediate custody of the libel, under circumstances which exposed it to be read or seen by any other person than himself.

10994. *Liability of editors and publishers.*—Each author, editor, or proprietor of any book, newspaper, or serial publication, is chargeable with the publication of any words contained in any part of such book, or number of such newspaper or serial.

10995. *Publishing a true report of public proceedings privileged.*—No reporter, editor or proprietor of any newspaper is liable to any prosecution for a fair and true report of any judicial, legislative, or other public official proceedings, or of any statement, speech, argument, or debate in the course of the same, except upon proof of malice in making such report, which is not implied from the mere fact of publication.

10996. *Extent of privilege.*—Libelous remarks or comments connected with matter privileged by the last section receive no privilege by reason of their being so connected.

10997. *Other privileged communications.*—A communication made to a person interested in the communication, by any one who was also interested, or who stood in such relation to the former, as to afford a reasonable ground for supposing his motive innocent, is not presumed to be malicious, and is a privileged communication.

10998. *Threatening to publish libel—offer to prevent publication, with intent to extort money.*—Every person who threatens another to publish a libel concerning him, or any parent, husband, wife, or child of such person, or member of his family, and every person who offers to prevent the publication of any libel upon another person, with intent to extort money or other valuable consideration from any person is guilty of a misdemeanor.

10999. *Giving false information for publication.*—Any person who wilfully states, delivers, or transmits, by any means whatsoever, to the manager, editor, publisher, or reporter of any newspaper, magazine, publication, periodical, or serial, for publication therein, any false or libelous statement concerning any person or corporation, and thereby secures the actual publication of the same, is hereby declared guilty of a misdemeanor, and, upon conviction, shall be sentenced to pay a fine not exceeding five hundred dollars, or confined in the county jail not exceeding six months, or both.

11857. *Pleading for libel.*—An indictment or information for libel need not set forth any extrinsic facts for the purpose of showing the application to the party libeled, of the defamatory matter on which the indictment or information is founded; but it is sufficient to state generally, that the same was published concerning him, and the fact that it was so published must be established on the trial.

12003. *On indictment for libel, jury to determine law and*

fact.—On a trial for libel, the jury has the right to determine the law and the fact.

Limitations. 9032. *Within Two Years.*—

3. An action for libel, slander, assault, battery, false imprisonment, or seduction.

Nebraska

COMPILED STATUTES OF NEBRASKA, 1950

Basic Statutes. Constitution of Nebraska, Art. I, sec. 5.—Every person may freely speak, write and publish on all subjects, being responsible for the abuse of that liberty; and in all trials for libel, both civil and criminal, the truth when published with good motives, and for justifiable ends, shall be a sufficient defense.

Art. III, sec. 26.—No member of the Legislature shall be liable to any civil or criminal action whatever for words spoken in debate.

28.440. *"Libel" defined, penalty.*—Whoever writes, prints or publishes any false and malicious libel of or concerning another, or causes or procures any such libel to be written or published, shall upon conviction thereof be fined in any sum not exceeding five hundred dollars, or be imprisoned in the county jail not exceeding six months, or both, and moreover shall be liable to the party injured: Provided, if such libel is published in a newspaper having a general circulation, the person so offending shall be punished by imprisonment in the penitentiary not less than one year nor more than three years.

20-701. *Causes of Action, When Joined.*—The plaintiff may unite several causes of action in the same petition, whether they be such as have heretofore been denominated legal or equitable, or both, when they are included in either of the following classes: First. The same transaction or transactions connected with the same subject of action; Second. Contracts, express or implied; Third. Injuries with or without force to person and property or either; Fourth. Injuries to character; Fifth. Claims to recover possession of personal property, with or without damages for the withholding thereof; Sixth. Claims to recover real property with or without damages for the withholding thereof and the rents and profits of the same; Seventh. Claims against a trustee by virtue of a contract, or by operation of a law.

20-839. *Libel or slander, how sufficiently started by plaintiff.*—In an action for a libel or slander it shall be sufficient to state, generally, that the defamatory matter was published or spoken of the plaintiff, and if the allegation be denied, the plaintiff must prove on the trial the facts, showing that the defamatory matter was published or spoken of him.

25-840. *Same, allegation of truth, mitigating circumstances, proper Pleading by Defendant.*—In the actions mentioned in the next preceding section, the defendant may allege the truth of the matter charged as defamatory, and may prove the same and any mitigating circumstances to reduce the amount of damages, or he may prove either.

25-1402. *What causes of Action Survive—Exceptions, Actions Abated by Death.*—No action pending in any court shall abate by the death of either or both the parties thereto, except an action for libel, slander, malicious prosecution, assault, or assault and battery, for a nuisance, or against a justice of the peace for misconduct in office; which shall abate by the death of the defendant.

25-1709. *Plaintiff's costs, when allowed—when no recovery.*—If it shall appear that a justice of the peace has jurisdiction of an action and the same has been brought in district court the plaintiff shall not recover costs; and in all actions for libel, slander, malicious prosecution, assault, assault and battery, false imprisonment, criminal conversation, seduction, actions for nuisance, or against a justice of the peace for misconduct in office, if the damages assessed be under Five Dollars ($5.00), the plaintiff shall not recover any costs.

27-105. *Actions not Cognizable Before Justice of Peace.*—Justices shall not have cognizance of any action; First. To recover damages for an assault, or assault and battery; Second. In any action for malicious prosecution; Third. In actions against justices of the peace, or other officers, for misconduct in office, except in the cases provided for in this chapter; Fourth. In actions for slander, verbal or written; Fifth. In actions on contracts for real estate; Sixth. In actions in which the title to real estate is sought to be recovered or may be drawn in question, except actions for trespass on real estate, which are provided for in this chapter.

28-440. *Libel, Penalty.*—Whoever writes, prints, or publishes any false and malicious libel of or concerning another, or causes, or procures, any such libel to be written or published, shall, upon conviction thereof, be fined in any sum not exceeding five hundred dollars, or be imprisoned in the county jail not exceeding six months, or both, and moreover, be liable to the party injured: *Provided,* if said libel is published in a newspaper having a general circulation, the person so offending shall be punished by imprisonment in the penitentiary not less than one year nor more than three years.

Limitations. 25-208. *Libel, Slander, Assault and Battery, Malicious Prosecution, Malpractice, Penalty, Forfeiture.*—Within one year an action for libel, slander, assault and battery, false imprisonment, malicious prosecution; and for malpractice two years; an action upon a statute for penalty or forfeiture but where the statute giving such action prescribes a different limitation, the action may be brought within the period so limited. In the absence of any other shorter applicable statute of limitations, any action for the recovery of any excise or other tax, which has been collected under any statute of the state of Nebraska, which has been finally adjudged to be unconstitutional, shall be brought within one year after the final decision of the court declaring it to be unconstitutional.

Nevada

NEVADA COMPILED LAWS, 1929
NEVADA COMPILED LAWS, SUPPLEMENT, 1931–1941
NEVADA STATUTES REVISED, 1957

Basic Statutes. Constitution of Nevada. Sec. 30. *Freedom of Speech and Press.*—Every citizen may freely speak, write and publish his sentiments on all subjects, being responsible for the abuse of that right; and no law shall be passed to restrain or abridge the liberty of speech or of the press. In all criminal prosecutions and civil actions for libels the truth may be given in evidence to the jury, and if it shall appear to the jury that the matter charged as libelous is true, and was published with good motives, and for justifiable ends, the party shall be acquitted or exonerated.

Sec. 8630. *Idem.—Truth and Mitigating Circumstances.—Evidence.*—Sec. 132. In the actions mentioned in the last section, the defendant may, in his answer, allege both the truth of the matter charged as defamatory, and any mitigating circumstances to reduce the amount of the damages; and, whether he prove the justification or not, he may give in evidence the mitigating circumstances.

Sec. 10110. *Libel Defined.—Penalty.*—Sec. 163. A libel is a malicious defamation, expressed by printing, writing, signs, pictures, or the like, tending to blacken the memory of the dead, or to impeach the honesty, integrity, virtue, or reputation, or to publish the natural defects, of a living person or persons, or community of persons, or association of persons, and thereby to expose them to public hatred, contempt, or ridicule. Every person, whether the writer or the publisher, convicted of the offense, shall be fined in a sum not exceeding five thousand dollars, or imprisonment in the county jail not exceeding one year, or in the state prison not exceeding five years. In all prosecutions for libel the truth may be given in evidence to the jury, and if it shall appear to the jury that the matter charged as libelous is true, and was published for good motive and for justifiable ends, the party shall be acquitted, and the jury shall have the right to determine the law and the fact. (Revised statutes, 1957, Sec. 510)

Sec. 10111. *Publication Defined.*—Sec. 164. Any method by which matter charged as libelous may be communicated to another shall be deemed a publication thereof.

Sec. 10112. *Liability of Editors and Others.*—Sec. 165. Every editor or proprietor of a book, newspaper or serial, and every manager of a copartnership or corporation by which any book, newspaper or serial is issued, is chargeable with the publication of any matter contained in any such book, newspaper or serial, but in every prosecution for libel the defendant may show in his defense that the matter complained of was published without his knowledge or fault and against his wishes by another who had no authority from him to make such publication, and was retracted by him as soon as known with an equal degree of publicity.

Sec. 10113. *Venue, Punishment Restricted.*—Sec. 166. Every other person publishing a libel in this state may be proceeded against in any county where such libelous matter was published or circulated, but a person shall not be proceeded against for the publication of the same libel against the same person in more than one county.

Sec. 10114. *Furnishing Libelous Information.*—Sec. 167. Every person who shall wilfully state, deliver, or transmit by any means whatever, to any manager, editor, publisher, reporter or other employee or a publisher of any newspaper, magazine, publication, periodical or serial, any statement concerning any person or corporation, which, if published therein, would be a libel, shall be guilty of a misdemeanor.

Sec. 10115. *Threatening to Publish Libel.*—Sec. 168. Every

person who shall threaten another with the publication of a libel concerning the latter, or his spouse, parent, child, or other member of his family, and every person who offers to prevent the publication of a libel upon another person upon condition of the payment of, or with intent to exhort money or other valuable consideration from any person, shall be guilty of a gross misdemeanor.

Sec. 10506. *Denial of Libelous Article Must Be Published.*—Sec. 561. If in any newspaper or other periodical published or circulated within this state any matter is published regarding a person named or otherwise designated in such a manner as to be identified therein, it shall be the duty of the editor, publisher, or proprietor to publish gratuitously any denial or correction of the matter so published that may be received from the person so named or designated when the denial or correction is signed by the person so making the same; *provided, however,* that the denial or correction shall be made and presented by mail or otherwise to such editor, publisher, or proprietor within one week after the original publication in the case of daily newspapers published in this state, or thirty days in case of other periodicals. Such denial or correction shall be published in the next issue after the receipt thereof, or if presented less than two days prior to the next issue shall be published in either the next or the succeeding one, and shall be given a like position and space and as much display as had the statement which provoked it; but if the denial or correction exceed the length of the original article, the charge for publishing the excess shall be computed and paid for in advance at the regular advertising rates for the periodical in question. Failure to comply with the provisions of this section by any editor, publisher or proprietor of any newspaper or periodical shall be punished by a fine of not less than one hundred dollars nor more than one thousand dollars, or by imprisonment in the county jail not exceeding six months.

Sec. 10862. *Requisites of Indictment or Information for Libel.*—Sec. 214. An indictment or information for libel need not set forth any intrinsic facts for the purpose of showing the application to the party libeled of the defamatory matter on which the indictment or information is founded; but it is sufficient to state generally that the same was published concerning him and the fact that it was so published must be established on the trial.

Sec. 10994. *Jury Determines Law and Facts in Libel.*—Sec. 346. On a trial for libel the jury shall have the right to determine the law and the facts.

Limitations. Sec. 8524. *Limitations of various actions.*—Actions other than those for the recovery of real property, can only be commenced as follows:

Within two years: 3. An action for libel, slander, assault, battery, false imprisonment or seduction.

New Hampshire

REVISED STATUTES OF NEW HAMPSHIRE, 1942, 1955

Basic Statutes. Constitution of New Hampshire, Art. 22d. The *liberty of the press* is essential to the security of freedom in a state: It ought, therefore, to be inviolably preserved.

Chap. 515, Sec. 6. *General Issue in Libel.*—In actions for libel or slander, under the general issue, the defendant may prove, in mitigation of damages and to rebut evidence of actual malice, that the writing or words complained of were the repetition of common report, and that the conduct of the plaintiff was such as to create suspicion of the truth of the matters therein charged against him.

Limitations. Chap. 385, sec. 3 Actions of trespass to the person, actions for malpractice, and actions for defamatory words may be brought within two years, and all other personal actions within six years, after the cause of action accrued, and not afterward.

New Jersey

NEW JERSEY STATUTES, 1940, 1952, 1957, 1960, 1964

Basic Statutes. Constitution of New Jersey, Art. I, Sec. 6.— Every person may freely speak, write and publish his sentiments on all subjects, being responsible for the abuse of that right. No law shall be passed to restrain or abridge the liberty of speech or of the press. In all prosecutions or indictments for libel, the truth may be given in evidence to the jury; and if it shall appear to the jury that the matter charged as libelous is true, and was published with good motives and for justifiable ends, the party shall be acquitted; and the jury shall have the right to determine the law and the fact.

2A:43-1 *Privileged communications.*—The privileged character attaching to the publication of judicial or other proceedings shall extend to the publication in any newspaper of official statements issued by police department heads, county prosecutors and coroners in investigations in progress or completed by them, and which are accepted in good faith by the publisher of any newspaper, and the privileged character thereof shall be a good defense to any action for libel, unless malice in fact be shown by the plaintiff therein.

2A:43-2 *Damages recoverable.*—The defendant, in an action for libel against the owner, manager, editor, publisher or reporter of any newspaper, magazine, periodical, serial or other publication in this state, may give proof of intention, and plaintiff, unless he shall prove either malice in fact or that defendant, after having been requested by plaintiff in writing to retract the libelous charge in as public a manner as that in which it was made, failed to do so within a reasonable time, shall recover only his actual damage proved and specially alleged in the complaint.

2:59-3. *Pleading.*—In an action for libel or slander, plaintiff may aver that the words or matter complained of were used in a defamatory sense, specifying such sense, without a prefatory averment to show how the words or matter were used in that sense. Such an averment shall be put in issue by a denial of the alleged libel or slander. If the words or matter set forth, with or without the alleged meaning, show a cause of action, the complaint shall be sufficient.

2A: 15-63 *Actions for assault, battery or imprisonment, libel or slander.*—If, in an action for assault, battery or imprisonment, or for slander, or libel, plaintiff does not recover damages to the amount of fifty dollars, his costs shall not exceed the damages recovered.

2A: 120.1. (New Jersey Statutes 1952) *Securing publication, broadcasting or televising defamatory statements on representations.*—Any person who knowingly and wilfully states, delivers, or transmits to any owner, manager, editor, publisher, reporter or employee of, or connected with, any newspaper, magazine, periodical, or other publication, or of any radio or television station, any false, defamatory, libelous, or untrue statement or representation as though it were fact, concerning any person, and thereby secures the publication, broadcasting or televising of the statement or representation, is guilty of a misdemeanor.

2A: 43-3. (New Jersey Statutes 1964) *Broadcasters: liability for statements of candidates for public office.*—The owner, licensee or operator of a visual or sound radio broadcasting station or network of stations, hereinafter referred to as a broadcaster, and any agent or employee of any such broadcaster, shall not be liable for any damages for any statement published or uttered in or as part of a visual or sound radio broadcast, by any legally qualified candidate for public office, when such broadcast is made under the provisions of Federal law and regulations governing broadcasts by candidates for public office, which deny to a broadcaster the power of censorship over the material broadcast. (L. 1956., c.50, p. 101,§1)

Limitations. 2A: 14-3. *One year; libel or slander.*—Every action at law for libel or slander shall be commenced within one year next after the publication of the alleged libel or slander.

New Mexico

NEW MEXICO STATUTES, 1941, 1953

Basic Statutes. Constitution of New Mexico, Art. II, Sec. 17. *Freedom of speech and press—Libel.*—Every person may freely speak, write and publish his sentiments on all subjects, being responsible for the abuse of that right; and no law shall be passed to restrain or abridge the liberty of speech or of the press. In all criminal prosecutions for libels, the truth may be given in evidence to the jury; and if it shall appear to the jury that the matter charged as libelous is true and was published with good motives and for justifiable ends, the party shall be acquitted.

40A-11-1. *Libel.*—Libel consists of making, writing, publishing, selling or circulating without good motives and justifiable ends, any false and malicious statement affecting the reputation, business or occupation of another, or which exposes another to hatred, contempt, ridicule, degradation or disgrace.

Whoever commits libel is guilty of a misdemeanor.

The word "malicious," as used in this article, signifies an act done with evil or mischievous design and it is not necessary to prove any special facts showing ill-feeling on the part of the person who is concerned in making, printing, publishing or circulating a libelous statement against the person injured thereby.

A. A person is the maker of a libel who originally contrived and either executed it himself by writing, printing, engraving or painting, or dictated, caused or procured it to be done by others.

B. A person is the publisher of a libel who either of his own will or by the persuasion or dictation, or at the solicitation or employment for hire of another, executes the same in any of the modes pointed out as constituting a libel; but if anyone by force or threats is compelled to execute such libel he is guilty of no crime.

C. A person is guilty of circulating a libel who, knowing its contents, either sells, distributes or gives, or, who, with malicious design, reads or exhibits it to others.

D. The written, printed or published statement to come within the definition of libel must falsely convey the idea either:

(1) that the person to whom it refers has been guilty of some penal offense;

(2) that he has been guilty of some act or omission which, though not a penal offense, is disgraceful to him as a member of society, and the natural consequence of which is to bring him into contempt among honorable persons;

(3) that he has some moral vice or physical defect or disease which renders him unfit for intercourse with respectable society, and as such should cause him to be generally avoided;

(4) that he is notoriously of bad or infamous character; or

(5) that any person in office or a candidate therefor is dishonest and therefore unworthy of such office, or that while in office he has been guilty of some malfeasance rendering him unworthy of the place.

E. It shall be sufficient to constitute the crime of libel if the natural consequence of the publication of the same is to injure the person defamed although no actual injury to his reputation need be proven.

F. No statement made in the course of a legislative or judicial proceeding, whether true or false, although made with intent to injure and for malicious purposes, comes within the definition of libel.

41-2718. *Criticisms of works of literature, science or art, and opinions as to qualifications of authors are not libel.*—It is no offense to publish any criticism or examination of any work of literature, science or art, or any opinion as to the qualifications or merits of the author of such work.

41-2719. *Publication respecting religion, morals, politics, or forms of government not libel.*—It is no libel to make publication respecting the merits or doctrines of any particular religion, system of morals or politics, or of any particular form of government.

41-2720. *Publications respecting legislative or judicial proceedings not libel—Exception.*—It is not libel to publish any statement respecting any legislative or judicial proceeding, whether the statement be in fact true or not, unless in such statement a charge of corruption is made against some person acting in legislative or judicial capacity.

41-2721. *Statements made in legislative or judicial proceedings not libel.*—No statement made in the course of a legislative or judicial proceeding, whether true or false, although made with intent to injure and for malicious purposes, comes within the definition of libel.

41-2722. *Truth as a defense.*—In the following cases, the truth of any statement charged as a libel may be shown in justification of the defendant:

1. Where the publication purports to be an investigation of the official conduct of officers or men in a public capacity.
2. Where it is stated in the libel that a person has been guilty of some penal offense, and the time, place and nature of the offense is specified in the publication.
3. Where it is stated in the libel that a person is of a notoriously bad or infamous character.
4. Where the publication charges any person in office, or a candidate therefor, with a want of honesty, or having been guilty of some malfeasance in office, rendering him unworthy of the place. In other cases the truth of the facts stated in the libel can not be inquired into.

41-2723. *Jury to decide facts—Rules governing determination of verdict.*—In all cases of libel the jury shall be the judges of the facts under the direction of the court, and of the intent with which a libel may have been published or circulated, subject to the rules prescribed in this article (secs. 41-2701—41-2724), and in rendering their verdict, they are to be governed by a a consideration of the nature of the charge contained in the libel, the general reputation of the person said to be defamed and the degree of malice exhibited by the defendant in the commission of the offense.

41-2724. *Civil remedy for libel unaffected.*—This article (41-2701—41-2724) shall regulate the law with regard to libel when prosecuted as a penal offense, and shall have no operation upon the subject so far as relates to civil remedies for the recovery of damages.

41-2725. *Malicious writings concerning fraternal or religious orders or societies as libel.*—Any person who, with intent to injure, publishes or circulates any malicious statement in writing, with reference to or concerning any fraternal or religious order or society, shall be guilty of criminal libel.

41-2726. *Statements which constitute libel against religious or fraternal societies.*—The written or printed or published statement to come within the definition of libel must convey the idea either:

a. That said fraternal or religious order or society has been guilty as an order or society of some penal offense or has conspired to commit some penal offense.

b. That said fraternal or religious order or society has, as an order or society, been guilty of some act or omission which, though not a penal offense, is disgraceful and the natural consequences of which act or omission are to bring such order or society into contempt among honorable persons.

41-2727. *Penalty for libel of religious or fraternal society.*—Any person found guilty of libel under the provisions of this act (Secs. 41-2725—41-2727) shall be punished by a fine of not more than two thousand dollars ($2,000), nor less than two hundred dollars ($200), or by imprisonment in the county jail for a term of three (3) months, or by both such fine and imprisonment.

41.6.31. *Libel.*—No indictment or information for libel shall be invalid or insufficient for the reason that it does not set forth extrinsic facts for the purpose of showing the application to the party alleged to be libeled of the defamatory matter on which the indictment is founded.

42-641. *Forms for specific offenses.*—The following forms may be used in the cases in which they are applicable:

LIBEL.—A. B. published libel concerning C. D. in the form of a letter (book, picture, or as the case may be) (the particulars should specify the pages and lines constituting the libel, when necessary, as where it is contained in a book or pamphlet).

60-709. *Penalty for libeling insurance company.*—Any person who shall make, utter, circulate, or transmit to another or others any statement untrue in fact, derogatory to the financial condition of any insurance company licensed to transact business in this state with intent to injure such insurance company, or who shall counsel, aid, procure, or induce another to originate, make, transmit or circulate any such statement with like intent, shall be guilty of a misdemeanor, and upon conviction shall be punished by a fine not to exceed $500.00.

50-802. *False statements as to financial condition—Penalty.*—Any person who shall wilfully and maliciously make, circulate or transmit to another or others any statement, rumor, or suggestion written, printed or by word of mouth, which is derogatory to the financial condition or affects the solvency or financial standing of any bank, banking institution or trust company doing business in this state, with intent to injure such bank, or who shall wilfully, and maliciously and with the intent aforesaid, counsel, aid, procure, or induce another to start, transmit, or circulate any such statement or rumor, shall be guilty of a felony, and punishable by a fine not less than five hundred ($500.00) dollars, or by imprisonment in the state penitentiary for a period not less than one (1) year, or both such fine and imprisonment.

19-408. *Libel and slander—Extrinsic facts showing application of defamatory matter to plaintiff.*—In an action for libel or slander, it shall not be necessary to state in the complaint any extrinsic facts for the purpose of showing the application to the plaintiff of the defamatory matter out of which the cause of action arose, but it shall be sufficient to state generally that the same was published or spoken concerning the plaintiff, and if such allegations be not controverted in the answer, it shall not be necessary to prove it on the trial; in other cases it shall be necessary.

19-409. *Truth and mitigating circumstances in action for libel or slander.*—In the actions mentioned in the last preceding section, the defendant may, in his answer, allege both the truth of the matter charged as defamatory and any mitigating circumstances admissible in evidence, to reduce the amount of damages, and whether he prove the justification or not, he may give mitigating circumstances in evidence.

21.7.4. *Death of party to pending action—No abatement—Exceptions.*—No action pending in any court shall abate by the death of either, or both, the parties thereto, except an action for libel, slander, malicious prosecution, assault, or assault and battery, for a nuisance, or against a justice of the peace for misconduct in office, which shall abate by the death of the defendant.

Limitations. 23.1.8. *Action against sureties on official or fiduciary bonds—Two year limitation—Actions against county or state officers—Injuries to person or reputation—Three year limitation.*—Those against sureties on official bonds and on bonds of guardians, executors, administrators and persons acting in a fiduciary capacity, within two (2) years after the liability of the principal or the person for whom they are sureties, shall have been finally established or determined by a judgment or decree of the court and those brought against any county or state officer for or on account of any liability incurred in the doing of any act in an official capacity or by the omission of any official duty and for an injury to the person or reputation of any person, within three years.

New York

NEW YORK CONSOLIDATED LAWS, 1909
CIVIL PRACTICES, 1944, 1964

Basic Statutes. Sec. 1340. *Libel defined.*—A malicious publication, by writing, printing, picture, effigy, sign or otherwise than by mere speech, which exposes any living person, or the memory of any person deceased, to hatred, contempt, ridicule or obloquy, or which causes, or tends to cause any person to be shunned or avoided, or which has a tendency to injure any person, corporation or association of persons, in his or their business or occupation, is a libel.

Constitution. Art 1 §8. *Freedom of speech and press; criminal prosecution for libel.*—Every citizen may freely speak, write and publish his sentiments on all subjects, being responsible for the abuse of that right; and no law shall be passed to restrain or abridge the liberty of speech or of the press. In all criminal prosecutions or indictments for libels, the truth may be given in evidence to the jury; and if it shall appear to the jury that the matter charged as libelous is true, and was published with good motives and for justifiable ends, the party shall be acquitted; and the jury shall have the right to determine the law and the fact.

NEW YORK CIVIL RIGHTS LAW 1964

§74. *Privilege in actions for libel.*—A civil action cannot be maintained against any person, firm or corporation for the publication of a fair and true report of any judicial proceeding, legislative proceeding or other official proceeding, or for any heading of the report which is a fair and true headnote of the statement published.

This section does not apply to a libel contained in any other matter added by any person concerned in the publication, or in the report of anything said or done at the time or place of such a proceeding which was not a part thereof.

§78. *Mitigating circumstances in action for libel or slander*—In an action for libel or slander the defendant may prove mitigating circumstances, including the sources of his information and the ground for his belief, whether or not he has pleaded or attempted to prove any defense. A defendant in default for want of an answer may prove such mitigating circumstances upon a reference or inquiry to ascertain the amount of the plaintiff's damages. Matter tending only to mitigate or reduce damages is a partial defense and may be set forth in the answer.

§78a. At the trial of any civil action for libel the defendant may prove for consideration by the jury in fixing the amount of the verdict, that the plaintiff has already recovered damages or has received or agreed to receive compensation in respect of a libel or libels of a similar purport or effect as the libel for which such action has been brought.

§138. *Jurisdiction in prosecution for libel.*—

1. When a crime of libel is committed by publication in any paper in this state, against a person residing in the state, the jurisdiction is in either the county where the paper is published, or in the county where the party libeled resides. But the defendant is entitled to an order of the supreme court, directing the indictment against him to be tried in the county in which the paper is published, upon compliance with the following conditions:

(a) He must apply for the order within thirty days, after being committed upon, or giving bail to answer, the indictment;

(b) He must execute a bond to the complainant, with two sufficient sureties, approved by the judge hearing his application, in a penal sum fixed by the judge, not less than two hundred and fifty nor more than one thousand dollars, conditioned for the payment, in case the defendant is convicted, of all the complainant's reasonable expenses in going to and from his place of residence and the place of trial, and in attendance upon the trial;

(c) He must, within ten days after the granting of the order, file the order and deposit the bond with the clerk of the county in which the indictment is pending.

2. Whenever the crime of libel is committed against a person not a resident of this state, the defendant must be indicted and the trial had in the county where the paper purports upon its face to be published. But if the paper does not, upon its face, purport to be published in a particular county of this state, the defendant may be indicted and the trial had, in any county where the paper was circulated.

3. In no case can the defendant be indicted for the publication of the same libel against the same person in more than one county of this state.

4. Nothing contained herein shall be construed to abridge, or in any manner affect, the power of a competent court to change the place of trial of an indictment for libel, in the same manner as may lawfully be done in respect to any other indictment. As amended L.1940, c.561, §7, eff. April 17, 1940.

Sec. 1341. *Libel a misdemeanor.*—A person who publishes a libel, is guilty of a misdemeanor.

Sec. 1342. *Malice presumed; defense to prosecution.*—A publication having the tendency or effect, mentioned in section thirteen hundred and forty, is to be deemed malicious, if no justification or excuse therefor is shown.

The publication is justified when the matter charged as libelous is true, and was published with good motives and for justifiable ends.

The publication is excused when it is honestly made, in the belief of its truth and upon reasonable grounds for this belief, and consists of fair comments upon the conduct of a person in respect of public affairs, or upon a thing which the proprietor thereof offers or explains to the public.

Sec. 1343. *Publication defined.*—To sustain a charge of publishing a libel, it is not necessary that the matter complained of should have been seen by another. It is enough that the defendant knowingly displayed it, or parted with its immediate custody, under circumstances which exposed it to be seen or understood by another person than himself.

Sec. 1344. *Liability of editors and others.*—Every editor, or proprietor of a book, newspaper or serial, and every manager of a partnership or incorporated association, by which a book, newspaper or serial is issued, is chargeable with the publication of any matter contained in such book, newspaper or serial. But in every prosecution for libel the defendant may show in his defense that the matter complained of was published without his knowledge or fault and against his wishes, by another who had no authority from him to make the publication and whose act was disavowed by him as soon as known.

Sec. 1345. *Publishing a true report of public official proceedings.*—A prosecution for libel cannot be maintained against any person, firm or corporation for the publication of a fair and true report of any judicial, legislative or other public and official proceedings, or for any heading of the report which is a fair and true headnote of the statement published.

This section does not apply to a libel contained in the heading of the report, or in any other matter added by any other person concerned in the publication; or in the report of any thing said or done at the time and place of the public and official proceeding, which was not a part thereof.

Sec. 138. *Jurisdiction in prosecution for libel.*—An indictment for a libel, contained in a newspaper published within this state, against a resident thereof, may be found either in the county where the paper was published, or in the county where the person libeled resided when the offense was committed. In the latter case the defendant is entitled to an order of the supreme court, directing the indictment against him to be tried in the county in which the paper was printed and published, upon compliance with the following conditions:

1. He must apply for the order within thirty days after being

committed upon, or giving bail to answer the indictment;

2. He must execute a bond to the complainant, with two sufficient sureties, approved by the judge hearing his application, in a penal sum fixed by the judge, not less than two hundred and fifty nor more than one thousand dollars, conditioned for the payment in case the defendant is convicted, of all the complainant's reasonable expenses in going to and from his place of residence and the place of trial, and in attendance upon the trial;

3. He must, within ten days after the granting of the order, file the order and deposit the bond with the clerk of the county in which the indictment is pending.

Sec. 1347. *Indictment for libel published against nonresident.*—An indictment for a libel published against a person not a resident of this state, must be found and tried in the county, where the paper containing the libel purports upon its face to be published; or, if no county is indicated upon the face of the paper, in any county where the paper was circulated.

Sec. 1348. *Restriction on indictment for libel.*—A person can not be indicted or tried for the publication of the same libel, against the same person, in more than one county.

Sec. 1349. *Power of court; place of trial.*—Nothing contained in this article shall be construed to abridge, or in any manner affect, the power of a competent court, to change the place of trial of an indictment for libel, in the same manner as may lawfully be done, in respect to any other indictment.

Sec. 1346. *Privileged communications.*—A communication made to a person entitled to, or interested in, the communication, by one who was also interested in or entitled to make it, or who stood in such relation to the former as to afford a reasonable ground for supposing his motive innocent, is presumed not to be malicious, and is called a privileged communication.

Sec. 1347. *Threatening to publish libel.*—A person who threatens another with the publication of a libel, concerning the latter or concerning any parent, husband, wife, child or other member of the family of the latter, and a person who offers to prevent the publication of a libel upon another person upon condition of the payment of, or with intent to extort, money or other valuable consideration from any person, is guilty of a misdemeanor.

Sec. 1349. *Furnishing false (libelous) information.*—Any person who wilfully states, delivers or transmits by any means whatever to any manager, editor, publisher, reporter or other employee of a publisher of any newspaper, magazine, publication, periodical or serial, any statement, concerning any person or corporation which, if published therein, would be a libel, is guilty of a misdemeanor.

NEW YORK CIVIL RIGHTS LAW 1964

§75. *Defamation by radio or television.*—

1. The owner, licensee or operator of a visual or sound radio broadcasting station or network of stations, and the agents or employees of any such owner, licensee or operator, shall not be liable for any damages for any defamatory statement published or uttered in or as a part of a visual or sound radio broadcast, by any legally qualified candidate for public office whose utterances, under rules and regulations of the federal communications commission may not be subject to censorship by such owner, licensee or operator of such visual or sound radio broadcasting station or network of stations, or their agents or employees.

2. A "legally qualified candidate" means any person who has publicly announced that he is a candidate for nomination by a convention of a political party or for nomination or election in a primary, special, or general election, municipal, county, state or national, and who meets the qualifications prescribed by the applicable laws to hold the office for which he is a candidate, so that he may be voted for by the electorate directly or by means of delegates or electors and who (a) has qualified for a place on the ballot or (b) is eligible under the applicable law to be voted by writing in his name on the ballot, or other method, and who has been nominated by a political party which is commonly known and regarded as such or makes a

substantial showing that he is a bona fide candidate for nomination or office, as the case may be.

3. In order to be absolved from liability for damages for any utterance by a legally qualified candidate as herein defined in or as part of a visual or sound radio broadcast, the owner, licensee or operator of such visual or sound radio broadcasting station or network of stations, or the agents or employees thereof, shall announce, in substance, at the beginning and end of each such political broadcast of more than five minutes duration, and at the beginning of each such political broadcast of five minutes duration or less, that the remarks about to be made, or made, as the case may be, by the speaker are not to be construed as reflecting the opinions or beliefs of the station, its ownership or management. Added L.1962, c. 310, §62, eff. Sept. 1, 1963.

Section derived from CPA §337 a, added by L.1955, c. 50, amended by L. 1956, c. 452; repealed by CPLR §10001. Another section 337 a, which contained related matter, was added by L.1939, c. 415 and repealed by L.1939, c. 415.

Criminal prosecutions for libel, see Penal Law, §1340 et seq.

§76. *Action for libel: evidence, separate verdicts.*—

At the trial of any civil action for libel, the defendant may prove, for consideration by the jury in fixing the amount of the verdict, that the plaintiff has already recovered damages; or has received, or agreed to receive, compensation in respect of a libel or libels of a similar purport or effect as the libel for which such action has been brought. In consolidated actions based on libels of similar purport or effect the jury shall assess the whole amount of the plaintiff's damages in one sum, but a separate verdict shall be taken for or against each defendant and the jury shall apportion the amount of damages among the defendants against whom it found a verdict. Added L.1962, c. 310, §63, eff. Sept. 1, 1963.

Section derived from CPA §97 a, added by L.1924, c. 637, amended by L.1939, c. 359 and CPA §338 a, added by L.1924, c. 635; repealed by CPLR §10001.

Criminal prosecutions for libel, see Penal Law, §1340 et seq.

Limitations. Act. 2. Sec. 215. Actions to be commenced within one year after the cause of action has accrued:

3. An action to recover damages for libel or slander.

Testamentary Libel.—A testator may properly give the reasons for disinheriting the natural objects of his bounty, but such statements are not privileged. The estate may be called upon to respond for any libel, although the estate has the defense of justification. The executor, however, is privileged and may not be held liable for publication of the libel through probating of the will (*Brown v. Mack,* Sup. Ct., Special Term, N.Y. County, Walsh, J., July 10, 1945)

North Carolina

NORTH CAROLINA–GENERAL STATUTES, 1960

Basic Statutes. §99-1. *Libel against newspaper; defamation by or through radio or television station; notice before action.*

(a) Before any action, either civil or criminal, is brought for the publication in a newspaper or periodical, of a libel, the plaintiff or prosecutor shall at least 5 days before instituting such action serve notice in writing on the defendant, specifying the article and statements therein which he alleges to be false and defamatory.

(b) Before any action, either civil or criminal, is brought for the publishing, speaking, uttering, or conveying by words, acts or in any other manner of a libel or slander by or through any radio or television station, the plaintiff or prosecutor shall at least 5 days before instituting such action serve notice in writing on the defendant, specifying the time of and the words or acts which he or they allege to be false or defamatory.

§99-2. *Effect of publication or broadcast in good faith and retraction.*

(a) If it appears upon the trial that said article was published in good faith, that its falsity was due to an honest mistake of the fact, and that there were reasonable grounds for believing that the statements in said article were true, and that within ten days after the service of said notice a full and fair correction, apology and retraction was published in the same editions or corresponding issues of the newspaper or periodical in which said article appeared, and in as conspicuous place and type as was said original article, then the plaintiff in such case, if a civil action, shall recover only actual damages, and if, in a criminal proceeding, a verdict of "guilty" is rendered on such a statement of facts, the defendant shall be fined a penny and the costs and no more.

(b) If it appears upon the trial that such words or acts were conveyed and broadcast in good faith, that their falsity was due to an honest mistake of the facts, or without prior knowledge or approval of such station, and if with prior knowledge or approval that there were reasonable grounds for believing that the words or acts were true, and that within 10 days after the service of said notice a full and fair correction, apology, and retraction was conveyed or broadcast by or over such radio or television station at approximately the same time of day and by the same sending power so as to be as visible and audible as the original acts or words complained of, then the plaintiff in such case, if a civil action, shall recover only actual damages, and if, in a criminal proceeding, a verdict of "guilty" is rendered on such state of fact, the defendant shall be fined a penny and costs, and no more.

§99-3. *Anonymous Communications.* The preceding sections shall not apply to anonymous communications and publications.

§99-4. *Charging innocent woman with incontinency.* Whereas doubts have arisen whether actions of slander can be maintained against persons who may attempt, in a wanton and malicious manner, to destroy the reputation of innocent and unprotected women, whose very existence in society depends upon the unsullied purity of their character, therefore any words written or spoken of a woman, which may amount to a charge of incontinency, shall be actionable.

§28-175. *Actions which do not survive.* The following rights of action do not survive:

1. Causes of action for libel and for slander, except slander of title.

2. Causes of action for false imprisonment and assault and battery.

3. Causes where the relief sought could not be enjoyed, or granting it would be nugatory, after death.

§1-410 *In what cases arrest allowed.* The defendant may be arrested, as hereinafter prescribed, in the following cases:

1. In an action for the recovery of damages on a cause of action not arising out of contract where the action is for wilful, wanton, or malicious injury to person or character, or for wilfully, wantonly or maliciously injuring, taking, detaining, or converting real or personal property.

2. In an action for a fine or penalty, for seduction, for money received, or property embezzled or fraudulently misapplied by a public officer, attorney, solicitor, or officer or agent of a corporation or banking association in the course of his employment, or by any factor, agent, or broker or other person in a fiduciary capacity, or for any misconduct or neglect in office, or in a professional employment.

3. In an action to recover the possession of personal property, unjustly detailed, where all or any part of the property has been concealed, or disposed of, so that it cannot be found or taken by the sheriff and with the intent that it should not be so found or taken, or with the intent to deprive the plaintiff of the benefit thereof.

4. When the defendant has been guilty of a fraud in contracting the debt or incurring the obligation for which the action is brought, in concealing or disposing of property for the taking, detention or conversion of which the action is brought, or when the action is brought to recover damages for fraud or deceit.

§53-128. *Derogatory reports, wilfully and maliciously making.* Any person who shall wilfully and maliciously make, circulate, or transmit to another or others any statement, rumor or suggestion, written, printed, or by word of mouth, which is directly or by inference derogatory to the financial condition, or affects the solvency or financial standing of any bank, or who shall counsel, aid, procure, or induce another to state, transmit, or circulate any such statement or rumor shall be guilty of a misdemeanor, and upon conviction thereof shall be fined or imprisoned, or both, in the discretion of the court.

§53-129. *Misapplication, embezzlement of funds, etc.* Whoever being an officer, employee, agent or director of a bank with intent to defraud or injure the bank, or any person or corporation, or to deceive an officer of the bank or an agent appointed to examine the affairs of such bank, embezzles, abstracts, or misapplies any of the money, funds, credit or property of such bank, whether owned by it or held in trust, or who, with such intent, wilfully and fraudulently issues or puts forth a certificate of deposit, draws an order for bill of exchange, makes an acceptance, assigns a note, bond, draft, bill of exchange, mortgage, judgment, decree or fictitiously borrows or solicits, obtains or receives money for a bank, not in good faith, intended to become the property of such bank; or whoever being an officer, employee, agent or director of a bank, makes or permits the making of a false statement or certificates, as to a deposit, trust fund or contract, or makes or permits to be made a false entry in a book, report, statement or record of such bank, or conceals or permits to be concealed by any means or manner, the true and correct entries of said bank, or its true and correct transactions, who knowingly loans, or permits to be loaned, the funds or credit of any bank to any insolvent company or corporation, or corporation which has ceased to exist, or which never had any existence, or upon collateral consisting of stocks or bonds of such company or corporation, or who makes or publishes or knowingly permits to be made or published a false report, statement, or certificate as to the true financial condition of such bank, shall be guilty of a felony and upon conviction thereof shall be fined not more than ten thousand dollars or imprisoned in the State's prison not more than 30 years, or both.

§14-47. *Communicating libelous matter to newspapers.* If any person shall state, deliver or transmit by any means whatever, to the manager, editor, publisher or reporter of any newspaper or periodical for publication therein any false and libelous statement concerning any person or corporation and thereby secure the publication of the same, he shall be guilty of a misdemeanor.

§14-48. *Slandering innocent women.* If any person shall attempt in a wanton and malicious manner, to destroy the reputation of an innocent woman by words, written or spoken, which amount to a charge of incontinency, every person so offending shall be guilty of a misdemeanor.

§1-158. *Pleadings in libel and slander.* In an action for libel or slander it is not necessary to state in the complaint any extrinsic facts for the purpose of showing the application to the plaintiff of the defamatory matter out of which the cause of the action arose, but it is sufficient to state generally that the same was published or spoken concerning the plaintiff; and if such allegation is controverted, the plaintiff is bound to establish on trial that it was so published or spoken.

The defendant may in his answer allege both the truth of the matter charged as defamatory, and any mitigating circumstances to reduce the amount of damages; and whether he proves the justification or not, he may give in evidence the mitigating circumstances. (Revised SS. 501, 502; C.S., 5.542)

§15-168. *Justification as defense to libel.* Every defendant who is charged by indictment with the publication of a libel may prove on the trial for the same the truth of the facts alleged in the indictment; and if it shall appear to the satisfaction of the jury that the facts are true, the defendant shall be acquitted of the charge.

Limitations. Civil Procedure Limitations. Chap. 1, §54. *One Year.*—Within one year an action:

3. For libel, assault, etc.

North Dakota

1943 REVISED CODE OF THE STATE OF NORTH DAKOTA

NORTH DAKOTA CENTURY CODE, 1960

Basic Statutes. Section 14-02-01. *General Personal Rights.*—Every person, subject to the qualifications and restrictions provided by law, has the right of protection from bodily restraint or harm, from personal insult, from defamation, and from injury to his personal relations.

Section 14-02-03. *Civil Libel Defined.*—Libel is a false and unprivileged publication by writing, printing, picture, effigy, or other fixed representation to the eye which exposes any person to hatred, contempt, ridicule, or obloquy, or which causes him to be shunned or avoided, or which has a tendency to injure him in his occupation.

Section 14-02-05. *Privileged Communications.*—A privileged communication is one made:

1. In the proper discharge of an official duty;
2. In any legislative or judicial proceeding, or in any other proceeding authorized by law;
3. In a communication, without malice, to a person interested therein by one who also is interested, or by one who stands in such relation to the person interested as to afford a reasonable ground for supposing the motive for the communication innocent, or who is requested by the person interested to give the information; and
4. By a fair and true report, without malice, of a judicial, legislative, or other public official proceeding, or of anything said in the course thereof.

In the cases provided for in subsections 3 and 4 of this section, malice is not inferred from the communication or publication.

Section 14-02-08. *Libel Suits Against Newspapers: Retraction.*—Before any suit for libel can be brought against a newspaper, other than for the libel of or concerning a female, the party aggrieved, at least three days before filing his complaint, must serve notice on the publisher of such newspaper at the principal office of its publication, specifying the statement alleged to be false and defamatory. If on the trial it appears that the article was published in good faith, and its falsity was due to a misapprehension in regard to the facts, and a full and fair retraction of the erroneous statement was published in the next issue of the paper, or in the case of a daily paper, within three days after the mistake was brought to the attention of the publisher, in as conspicuous a place and type as the original article, the plaintiff will be entitled to recover only such damage as he can show he has sustained to his property, business, trade, profession, or occupation. If the libel is against a candidate for office, the retraction also must be made editorially, and in the case of a daily paper, at least three days before the election, and in the case of a weekly paper, at least ten days before the election.

Section 12-28-01. *Criminal Libel Defined.*—A libel is a malicious defamation of a person made public by any printing, writing, sign, picture, representation, or effigy tending to expose such person to public hatred, contempt, or ridicule, or to deprive him of the benefits of public confidence and social intercourse, or any malicious defamation made public as aforesaid designed to blacken and vilify the memory of one who is dead and tending to scandalize or provoke his surviving relatives and friends.

Section 12-28-02. *When Publication is Presumed to be Malicious.*—A publication having the tendency or effect mentioned in s.12-2801 is deemed malicious if no justification or excuse therefor is shown.

Section 12-28-03. *Publication of Criminal Libel Misdemeanor.*—Every person who makes, composes, or dictates a libel, or who procures the same to be done, or who wilfully publishes or circulates a libel, or who in any way knowingly or wilfully aids or assists in making, publishing, or circulating a libel, is guilty of a misdemeanor.

Section 12-28-04. *Truth as a Defense of Libel.*—In all prosecutions for libel, the truth thereof may be given in evidence to the jury, and if it appears to the jury that the matter charged as libelous is true and was published with good motives and for justifiable ends, the defendant shall be acquitted.

Section 12-28-05. *Jury May Determine Law and Fact on Trial for Libel: No Special Verdict Permitted.*—On the trial of an information or indictment for libel, the jury shall have the right to determine the law and facts under the direction of the courts as in other cases, and shall return a general verdict.

Section 12-28-06. *Conspiracy to Publish Libel; Felony.*—If two or more persons conspire together to publish maliciously by writing, printing, picture, effigy, sign, or otherwise than by mere speech, anything which exposes any living person or the memory of any deceased person to hatred, contempt, ridicule, or obloquy, or which causes or tends to cause any person to be shunned or avoided, or which has a tendency to injure any person or association of persons in his or their business, each of them is guilty of a felony.

Section 12-28-07. *Publication Defined.*—To sustain a charge of publishing a libel, it is not necessary that the matter complained of should have been read or seen by another. It is enough that the accused knowingly displayed it, or parted with its immediate custody under circumstances which exposed it to be read or seen or understood by a person other than himself.

Section 12-28-08. *Liability of Editors and Others: Defense.*—Every editor or proprietor of a book, newspaper, or serial publication, and every manager of a partnership or incorporated association by which a book, newspaper, or serial publication is issued, is chargeable with the publication of any libelous matter contained in such book, newspaper or serial. But in every such prosecution for libel, the accused may show in his defense that the matter complained of was published without his knowledge or fault and against his wishes by another who had no authority from him to make the publication and whose act was disavowed by him as soon as known.

Section 12-28-09. *Publishing True Report of Public Official Proceedings: Proof of Malice Required.*—A prosecution for libel cannot be maintained against a reporter, editor, publisher, or proprietor of a newspaper, for the publication therein of a fair and true report of any judicial, legislative, or other public and official proceeding, or of any statement, speech, argument, or debate in the course of the same, without proving actual malice in making the report.

Section 12-28-10. *Publication of Additional Matter. Malice Presumed.*—The requirement for the proof of actual malice does not apply to libel contained in the heading of the report of a public and official proceeding, or in any other matter added by any other person concerned in the publication or in the report of anything said or done at the time and place of the public and official proceeding which was not a part thereof.

Section 12-28-11. *Other Privileged Communications.*—A communication made to a person entitled to or interested in the communication by one who also was entitled or interested or who stood in such relation to the former as to afford a reasonable ground for supposing his motive innocent, is not presumed to be malicious, and is a privileged communication.

Section 12-28-12. *Threatening to Publish Libel; Offer to Prevent Publication for Consideration; Misdemeanor.*—Every person who threatens another with the publication of a libel concerning the latter, or concerning any parent, husband, wife, child, or other member of his family, and every person who offers to prevent the publication of a libel upon another person upon the condition of the payment of, or with intent to extort money or other valuable consideration from any person, is guilty of a misdemeanor.

Section 12-28-13. *Furnishing Libelous Information: Misdemeanor.*—Every person who wilfully states, or transmits by any means whatever to any manager, editor, publisher, reporter, or other employee of a publisher of any newspaper, magazine, publication, periodical, or serial any statement concerning any person or corporation which if published therein would be a libel, is guilty of a misdemeanor.

Section 12-28-15. *Slander by Means of the Radio; Punishment.*–Every person who falsely uses, utters, or publishes words over, through, or by means of the radio, which in their common acceptance tend to blacken the memory of one who is dead or to impeach the honesty, integrity, virtue, or reputation, or to publish the natural defects of one who is alive and thereby to expose him or her to public hatred, contempt, ridicule, or financial injury, is guilty of slander and shall be punished by a fine of not more than one hundred dollars.

Limitations. 28-01-08. Actions having two-years limitations.

1. An Action for libel, slander, assault, battery, or false imprisonment.

Ohio

OHIO CODE, 1940 AND 1945
OHIO REVISED CODE, 1953

Basic Statutes. Constitution of the State of Ohio. Art. I, Sec. 11. *Freedom of Speech; of the Press; Libels.* —Every citizen may freely speak, write, and publish his sentiments on all subjects, being responsible for the abuse of the right; and no law shall be passed to restrain or abridge the liberty of speech, or of the press. In all criminal prosecutions for libel, the truth may be given in evidence to the jury, and if it shall appear to the jury, that the matter charged as libellous is true, and was published with good motives, and for justifiable ends, the party shall be acquitted.

Sec. 2739.01. *Libel and slander.*—In an action for a libel or slander, it is sufficient to state, generally, that the defamatory matter was published or spoken of the plaintiff. If the allegation be denied the plaintiff must prove the facts, showing that the defamatory matter was published or spoken of him. In such action it shall not be necessary to set out any obscene word, but it shall be sufficient to state its import. (R.S. Sec. 5093.)

Sec. 2739.02. *Defenses in actions for libel or slander.*—In an action for a libel or a slander, the defendant may allege and prove the truth of the matter charged as defamatory. Proof of the truth thereof shall be a complete defense. In all such actions any mitigating circumstances may be proved to reduce damages.

Sec. 11343. *Malice must be proved.*—If it appears at the trial, that the publication complained of was made in good faith, through mistake of fact, but with reasonable ground for believing the statements therein contained were true, and that the publisher, upon demand, within a reasonable time thereafter published a full and complete retraction in as public a manner as that in which the original publication was made, the presumption of malice attaching to or growing out of such publication shall thereby be rebutted. Nothing contained in this section shall prevent the person libelled from alleging and proving actual malice on the part of the publisher and any special damages resulting to him therefrom.

§2739.14. *Publishing corrected statements.* (GC §6319-4) Whenever demand has been made for the publication of statements or articles under section 2739.13 of the Revised Code, the newspaper company shall print and circulate the same in the next regular issue or within forty-eight hours following the receipt of such statement or article. Such statement or article shall be phrased in proper language and be printed without any additions to, or omissions therefrom, in the same color of ink, from like type, with headlines of equal prominence, occupying a like space in the same portion of the newspaper as was used in printing the original article complained of, and shall be given the same publicity in all respects and, as nearly as possible, the same circulation as such original article. Such company shall print and publish such statements or articles without cost to such persons or their representatives; and such publication may be proved at the trial of a suit for damages as a mitigating circumstance to reduce damages, provided that any voluntary publication made without demand may be used to rebut any presumption of malice or injury on the part of such company growing out of the original publication to which the same related. This section does not prevent the injured party from alleging and proving actual malice on the part of the publisher and any special damages resulting to him therefrom.

History: GC §6319-4; 103 v 854 (855), §3. Eff. 10-1-53.

§2739.15. *Published statements shall be sworn to.* (GC §6319-5)

(A) Every statement or article which newspaper companies are required to publish under sections 2739.13 to 2739.18, inclusive, of the Revised Code, shall be sworn to by the person offering the same for publication, but the certificate of the notary or other official showing that the statement was so made under oath, shall not be published.

(B) No person shall willfully swear falsely to any such statement or article and whoever does so, is guilty of perjury.

No newspaper company shall be held liable in any civil or criminal proceedings for anything in any such statement or article.

§2739.16. *Refusal or failure to publish.* (GC §6319-6)

(A) No newspaper company shall refuse or fail to print, publish, and circulate any statement or article if true as required by sections 2739.13 to 2739.18, inclusive, of the Revised Code.

(B) Any person responsible for refusing to print, publish, and circulate any statement or article mentioned in division (A) of this section shall be fined as provided in division (C) of section 2739.99.

The prosecuting attorney of the county in which such newspaper is published, when complaint is made to him in writing of the refusal or failure of any newspaper company or persons to comply with sections 2739.13 to 2739.18, inclusive, of the Revised Code relative to the publication of such statements or articles, shall investigate said complaint and upon reasonable cause begin proceedings against such newspaper company or person and prosecute the same.

§2739.17. *Prohibition against furnishing false news item.* (GC §6319-7) No person shall contribute or furnish any statement, allegation, or news item to a newspaper, knowing that such statement, allegation, or news item is untrue. Prosecution under this section shall be upon complaint of such newspaper company or of any person injured in property, person, or reputation by the publication of such statement, allegation, or news item.

History: GC §6319-7; 103 v 854 (856), §6. Eff. 10-1-53.

Penalty, RC §2739.99 (D).

§2739.18. *Prohibition against threats of publication to influence official action* (GC §6319-8) No newspaper company, or owner, officer, editor, writer, or representative thereof, shall attempt improperly to influence any public official for or against any public measure or official action by threats of publication of articles derogatory to such public official, or seek improperly to influence such public official on the floor or in the cloakrooms or committee rooms of any general assembly or other legislative body, to which he has access because of his connection with the newspaper, for or against any proposed law, ordinance, or other legislative act.

History: GC §6319-8; 102 v 854 (856), §7. Eff. 10-1-53.

Penalty, RC §2739.99 (E).

§2739.99. *Penalties.*

(A) Whoever violates division (B) of section 2739.15 of the Revised Code shall be fined not more than five hundred dollars or imprisoned not more than one year, or both.

(B) Whoever violates division (A) of section 2739.16 of the Revised Code shall be fined not more than one thousand dollars.

(C) Whoever violates division (B) of section 2739.16 of the Revised Code shall be fined not more than five hundred dollars.

(D) Whoever violates section 2739.17 of the Revised Code shall be fined not more than five hundred dollars or imprisoned not more than six months, or both.

(E) Whoever violates section 2739.18 of the Revised Code shall be fined not more than one thousand dollars or imprisoned not more than one year, or both.

(F) Whoever violates division (E) of section 2739.03 of the Revised Code shall be fined not more than five hundred dollars or imprisoned not more than one year, or both.

(G) Whoever violates division (F) of section 2739.03 of the Revised Code shall be fined not more than one thousand dollars.

(H) Whoever violates division (G) of section 2739.03 of the Revised Code shall be fined not more than five hundred dollars.

Sec. 2317.04 *Impartial report of proceedings privileged.*—The publication of a fair and impartial report of the proceedings before state or municipal legislative bodies, or before state or municipal executive bodies, boards or officers, or the whole or a fair synopsis of any bill, ordinance, report, resolution, bulletin, notice, petition or other document presented, filed or issued in any proceeding before such legislative or executive body, board or officer, shall be privileged, unless it shall be proved that such publication was made maliciously.

Sec. 2317.05 Ohio Revised Code 1953. *Impartial report of proceedings or arrest, privileged.*—The publication of a fair and impartial report of the return of any indictment, the issuing of any warrant, the arrest of any person accused of crime, or the filing of any affidavit, pleading other document in any criminal or civil cause in any court of competent jurisdiction, or of a fair and impartial report of the contents thereof, shall be privileged unless it be proved that the same was published maliciously, or that the defendant has refused or neglected to publish in the same manner in which the publication complained of appeared, a reasonable written explanation or contradiction thereof by the plaintiff, or that the publisher has refused, upon request of the plaintiff, to publish the subsequent determination of such suit or action; provided, that nothing in this act shall authorize the publication of blasphemous or indecent matter.

Sec. 2311.21*Abatement by death of party.*—Unless otherwise provided, no action or proceeding pending in any court shall abate by the death of either or both of the parties thereto, except actions for libel, slander, malicious prosecution, for a nuisance, or against a justice of the peace for misconduct in office, which shall abate by the death of either party.

Sec. 2323.41. *Cases in which plaintiff may not recover costs.*—If it appears that a justice of the peace has jurisdiction of an action brought in any other court and the judgment is less than one hundred dollars, unless the recovery be reduced below that sum by counter-claim, each party shall pay his own costs.

Sec. 2323.42 *Costs when damages less than five dollars.*—In all actions for libel, slander, malicious prosecution, assault, assault and battery, false imprisonment, criminal conversation or seduction, actions for nuisance, or against a justice of the peace for misconduct in office, when the damage assessed is under five dollars, the plaintiff shall not recover costs.

Sec. 2901.37 *Definition.* Whoever writes, prints, or publishes a false or malicious libel of, or concerning, another, or utters or publishes a false or malicious slander of, or concerning, a female of good repute, with intent to cause it to be believed that such a female is unchaste, shall be fined not more than five hundred dollars or imprisoned not less than one or more than five years, or both. Nothing written or printed is a libel unless there is publication thereof.

§2739.03. *Slander by radio or television station.*

(A) The owner, licensee, or operator of a visual or sound radio broadcasting station or network of stations, shall not be liable for any damages for any defamatory statement uttered over the facilities of such station or network by or on behalf of any candidate for public office where such statement is not subject to censorship or control by reason of any federal statute or any ruling or order of the Federal Communications Commission made pursuant thereto, provided, however, that this section shall not apply to any owner, licensee or operator of such visual or sound radio broadcasting station, or network of stations, when such owner, licensee, or operator is a candidate for public office or speaking on behalf of a candidate for public office.

(B) The owner, licensee, or operator, shall not be liable for any damages for any defamatory statement published or uttered in or as a part of a visual or sound radio broadcast, by one other than such owner, licensee, or operator, or agent or employee thereof, if it shall be proved by such owner, licensee, or operator, that he exercised reasonable care to prevent the publication or utterance of such statement in such broadcast time.

(C) If any broadcasting station, at any time, broadcasts, publishes, or circulates any false statement, allegation, or rumor pertaining or relating to any individual or association of individuals, or to any trade, labor, business, social, economic or religious organization or to any firm, corporation, or business, or to any public official or candidate for a public office, the said broadcasting station upon demand of any person or persons affected or of their representatives, shall broadcast any statement setting forth in proper language the truth pertaining to such statement, allegation, or rumor, which said person or persons or their representatives shall offer to said broadcasting station for broadcast.

(D) Whenever demand has been made for the broadcast of a statement under division (C) of this section, the broadcasting station shall broadcast the same within forty-eight hours following the receipt of such statement. Such statement shall be phrased in proper language and be broadcast without any additions to, or omissions therefrom, in as prominent a manner and at as prominent a time as the original broadcast to which the statement relates. Said broadcasting station shall broadcast such statements without cost to such persons or their representatives; and such broadcast may be proved at the trial of a suit for damages as a mitigating circumstance to reduce damages, provided that any voluntary broadcast made without demand may be used to rebut any presumption of malice or injury on the part of such station growing out of the original broadcast to which the same related. This section does not prevent the injured party from alleging and proving actual malice on the part of the owner, licensee, or operator, and any special damages resulting to him therefrom.

(E) Every statement which broadcasting stations are required to broadcast under division (C) of this section shall be sworn to by the person offering the same for broadcast, but the certificate of the notary or other official showing that the statement was so made under oath, shall not be broadcast.

No person shall willfully swear falsely to any such statement and whoever does so, is guilty of perjury and shall be punished as provided in division (F) of section 2739.99 of the Revised Code.

No broadcasting station shall be held liable in any civil or criminal proceedings for anything in any such statement.

(F) No broadcasting station shall refuse or fail to broadcast and circulate any statement or article if true as required by division (C) of this section.

(G) Any person responsible for refusing to broadcast and circulate any statement mentioned in division (C) of this section shall be fined as provided in division (H) of section 2739.99 of the Revised Code.

The prosecuting attorney of the county in which such broadcasting station is located when complaint is made to him in writing of the refusal or failure of any such broadcasting station or persons to comply with divisions (C), (D), (E), (F), and (G) of this section, relative to the broadcasting of such statements, shall investigate said complaint and upon reasonable cause begin proceedings against such broadcasting station or person and prosecute the same.

Limitations. Sec. 2305.11 Ohio Revised Code 1953. An action for libel, slander, assault, battery, malicious prosecution, false imprisonment or malpractice, or upon a statute for a penalty or forfeiture, shall be brought within one year after the cause thereof accrued, provided that an action by an employee for the payment of unpaid minimum wages, unpaid overtime compensation or liquidated damages by reason of the nonpayment of minimum wages or overtime compensation, shall be brought within three years after the cause thereof accrued.

Oklahoma

OKLAHOMA STATUTES, 1941, 1952, 1961

Basic Statutes. Title 12, also in 21: §771, §1441. *Libel defined.* —Libel is a false or malicious unprivileged publication by writing, printing, picture or effigy or other fixed representation to the eye, which exposes any person to public hatred, contempt, ridicule or obloquy, or which tends to deprive him of public confidence, or to injure him in his occupation, or any malicious publication as aforesaid, designed to blacken or vilify the memory of one who is dead, and tending to scandalize his surviving relatives and friends.

Art 2§22. *Liberty of speech and press—Truth as evidence in prosecution for libel.*—Every person may freely speak, write or publish his sentiments on all subjects, being responsible for the abuse of that right; and no law shall be passed to restrain or abridge the liberty of speech or of the press. In all criminal prosecutions for libel, the truth of the matter alleged to be libelous may be given in evidence to the jury, and if it shall appear to the jury that the matter charged as libelous be true, and was written or published with good motives and for justifiable ends, the party shall be acquitted.

§1443. *Privileged communication defined—Presumption of malice in absence of privilege.*—A privileged publication or communication is one made: First. In any legislative or judicial proceeding or any other proceeding authorized by law;

Second. In the proper discharge of an official duty;

Third. By a fair and true report of any legislative or judicial or other proceeding authorized by law, or anything said in the course thereof, and any and all expressions of opinion in regard thereto, and criticisms thereon, and any and all criticisms upon the official acts of any and all public officers, except where the matter stated of and concerning the official act done, or the officer, falsely imputes crime to the officer so criticised.

In all cases of publication of matter not privileged under this section, malice shall be presumed from the publication, unless the fact and the testimony rebut the same. No publication which, under this section, would be privileged, shall be punished as a libel.

§1444. *Pleading–Proof and defenses.*–In all civil actions to recover damages for libel or slander, it shall be sufficient to state generally what the defamatory matter was, and that it was published or spoken of the plaintiff, and to allege any general or special damage caused thereby, and the plaintiff to recover shall only be held to prove that the matter was published or spoken by the defendant concerning the plaintiff. As a defense thereto, the defendant may deny and offer evidence to disprove the charges made, or he may prove that the matter charged as defamatory was true, and in addition thereto, that it was published or spoken under such circumstances as to render it a privileged communication.

§1445. *Malice presumed.*–An injurious publication is presumed to have been malicious if no justifiable motive for making it is shown.

§1446. *Minimum judgment.–Judgment for defendant.*–If there be a verdict by a jury or finding by the court in favor of the plaintiff, the verdict and judgment shall in no case be less than one hundred dollars and costs, and may be for a greater sum if the proof justifies the same. And if there be a verdict in favor of the defendant, and the jury find that the action was malicious or without reasonable provocation, judgment shall be rendered against the plaintiff and in favor of the defendant for his costs, including an attorney's fee of one hundred dollars.

§1446a. *Good faith in publishing libel–Retraction–Actual damages only–Jury question–Exemptions.*–In an action for damages for the publication of a libel in a newspaper or periodical, if the evidence shows that the article was published in good faith and that its falsity was due to an honest mistake of the facts, and the question of "honest mistake" shall be a question of fact to be determined by a jury, unless a jury be waived by the parties, the plaintiff shall be entitled to recover actual damages only unless a retraction be requested and refused as hereinafter provided. The person claiming to have been libeled shall notify the publisher, either orally or in writing, stating or setting forth the particular matter claimed to be libelous and requesting that the same be retracted. If a retraction, headed "RETRACTION" in eighteen point type or larger, be published on the same page and in the same type as were the statements complained of, in two regular issues of said newspaper or periodical, published within a reasonable time, but not to exceed two weeks after such notice in a weekly newspaper, or not to exceed one week in a daily newspaper, the publication of said retraction shall be full and complete satisfaction as to all other than damages, and the plaintiff shall not be entitled to recover other than actual damages on account of such erroneous published matter. If such a retraction be not so published, plaintiff may recover such damages as are provided by the statutes of this State, if his cause of action is maintained. This section shall not apply to any libel imputing unchastity to a woman, nor in any case in which the evidence shows the publication was made maliciously or with a premeditated intention and purpose to injure, defame or destroy the reputation of another or to injuriously alter a person's reputation; nor to anonymous communications or publications, and provided further that this Section shall not apply to any article pertaining to any candidate for any public office when said article is published within 3 weeks of the date of the primary, run-off primary, special or general election, as the case may be.

21:§772 *Privileged publications.*—A privileged publication is one made:

First: In any legislative or judicial proceeding or any other proceeding authorized by law;

Second: In the proper discharge of an official duty;

Third: By a fair and true report of any legislative or judicial or other proceeding authorized by law, or anything said in the course thereof, and any and all expressions of opinion in regard thereto, and criticisms thereon, and any and all criticisms upon the official acts of any and all public officers, except where the matter stated of and concerning the official act done, or of the officer, falsely imputes crime to the officer so criticised.

In all cases of publication of matter not privileged under this section, malice shall be presumed from the publication; unless the fact and the testimony rebut the same. No publication which, under this section, would be privileged, shall be punishable as libel.

21: §773.*Penalty–Civil liability.*–Every person who makes, composes or dictates such libel or procures the same to be done; or who wilfully publishes or circulates such libel; or in any way knowingly or wilfully aids or assists in making, publishing or circulating the same, shall be punishable by imprisonment in the county jail not more than one year or by fine not exceeding one thousand dollars, or both, and shall also be civilly liable to the party injured.

21: §774.*Defenses in Criminal Libel Action.*–In all criminal prosecutions or indictments for libel, the truth thereof may be given in evidence to the jury, and if it be made to appear by the defendant that the matter charged as libelous was true, and in addition thereto was published with good motives, and for justifiable ends, or was a privileged communication, the defendant shall be acquitted.

21: §775.*Indictment or information–Requirements.*–In criminal prosecutions for libel, the indictment or information need not set forth any extrinsic facts for the purpose of showing the application to the party libeled of the defamatory matter upon which the indictment is founded, but it is sufficient to state generally that the same was published concerning the party named and the fact that it was published must be established on the trial.

21: §776 *Publication, what constitutes.*–To sustain the charge of publishing libel it is not needful that the words complained of should have been read by any person; it is enough and sufficient evidence that the accused knowingly parted with the immediate custody of the libel under circumstances which exposed it to be read by any person other than himself.

21: §777 *Newspapers reporting official proceedings.*—No editor or proprietor of any newspaper shall be liable to prosecution for a fair and true report of any judicial, legislative or other public official proceedings except upon proof of malice in making such report, and in making such report of public official proceedings, malice shall not be implied from publication; but libelous remarks connected with matter privileged under the last section, shall not be privileged by reason of their being connected therewith.

21: §778*Threatened Libel.*—Any person who threatens to publish a libel concerning any other person, or concerning any relative, wife or child or dead relative of such person, or member of his family, shall be liable civilly and criminally to have the same intent as though the publication had been made. But if the [threat?] be not in writing, the threat and character of the libelous matter must be proven by at least two witnesses, or by one witness and corroborating circumstances.

21: §779*Imputing unchastity to females.*—If any person shall orally or otherwise, falsely and maliciously, or falsely and wantonly impute to any female, married or unmarried, a want of chastity, he shall be deemed guilty of slander, and upon conviction shall be fined not less than twenty-five dollars nor more than five hundred dollars, or by imprisonment in the county jail not less than thirty days nor more than ninety days, or by both such fine and imprisonment.

1447.1 *Defamation by radio and television—Limitation of liability.*—The owner, licensee or operator of a television and/or radio broadcasting station or network of stations, and the agents or employees of any such owner, licensee or operator, shall not be liable for any damages for any defamatory statement published or uttered in or as part of a television and/or radio broadcast, by one other than such owner, licensee or operator, or agent or employee thereof, unless it shall be alleged and proved by the complaining party, that such owner, licensee, operator or such agent or employee, has failed to exercise due care to prevent the publication or utterance of such statement in such broadcast.

Limitation. Civil procedure. 12. §95. Limitation of action. (4) for libel, slander, etc., one year.

Oregon

OREGON REVISED STATUTES, 1940, 1963

Basic Statutes. Sec. 7-301. *When defendant may be arrested.*—No person shall be arrested in an action at law, except as provided in this section. The defendant may be arrested in the following cases:

(1) In an action for the recovery of money or damages on a cause of action arising out of contract, when the defendant is not a resident of the state, or is about to remove therefrom, or when the action is for an injury to person or character, or for injuring or wrongfully taking, detaining, or converting property.

Sec. 1-908. *Libel and slander, how alleged in complaint.*—In an action for libel or slander it shall not be necessary to state in the complaint any extrinsic facts for the purpose of showing the application to the plaintiff of the defamatory matter out of which the cause of action arose; but it shall be sufficient to state generally that the same was published or spoken concerning the plaintiff, and if such allegation be controverted, the plaintiff shall be bound to establish on trial that it was so published or spoken.

Sec. 1-909. *Pleading justification and mitigation in same answer.*—In the actions mentioned in the last section, the defendant may, in his answer, allege both the truth of the matter charged as defamatory, and any mitigating circumstances, to reduce the amount of damages; and whether he prove the justification or not, he may give in evidence the mitigating circumstances.

Sec. 1-909a. Allegation and proof in action for defamatory statement over radio broadcasting station.

Sec. 23-437. *Publishing words with intent to defame.*—Radio broadcasting: Enforcement of law by prosecuting attorney.

If any person shall wilfully, by any means other than words orally spoken, except as herein provided, publish or cause to be published of or concerning another any false and scandalous matter, with intent to injure or defame such other person, or if any person shall wilfully use or utter over, through or by means of the radio commonly called broadcasting, of or concerning another any false and scandalous matter, with intent to injure or defame such other person, upon conviction thereof, he shall be punished by imprisonment in the county jail not less than three months nor more than one year, or by fine of not less than $100 nor more than $500. Any allusion to any person or family, with intent to injure, defame or maliciously annoy such person or family, shall be deemed to come within the provisions of this section; and it hereby is made the duty of the prosecuting attorney of each judicial district to see that the provisions of this section are enforced, whether the party injured desire to prosecute such offense or not.

Sec. 163.420. *Truth as defense: Admissibility of evidence: Motive of defendant.*—In all criminal prosecutions for libel, the truth may be given in evidence, and if it appears to the jury that the matter charged as libelous is true and was published with good motives and justifiable ends, the defendant must be found not guilty.

Sec. 163.420 (2). An injurious publication is presumed to have been malicious if no justifiable end or good motive is shown for making it.

Sec. 132.670. ***Libel: Application of defamatory publication.***—An indictment for libel need not set forth any extrinsic facts, for the purpose of showing the application to the party libeled of the defamatory matter on which the indictment is founded; but it is sufficient to state that the same was published concerning him; and the fact that it was so published must be established on the trial.

Sec. 81-2533. *Unlawful publications: Punishment: Anonymous publications: Criminal libel: False statement, charge or comment as to candidate.*—It shall be unlawful to write, print or circulate or cause to be circulated through the mails or otherwise any letter, circular, bill, placard, poster or other publication relating to any election or to any candidate at any election, unless the same shall bear on its face the name and address of the author and of the printer and publisher thereof; and any person writing, printing, publishing, circulating, posting or causing to be written, printed, circulated, posted or published any such letter, bill, placard, circular, poster or other publication, as aforesaid, which fails to bear on its face the name and address of the author and of the printer or publisher, shall be guilty of an illegal practice, and shall, on conviction thereof, be punished by a fine of not less than twenty-five dollars ($25) nor more than one thousand dollars ($1,000), or by imprisonment in the county jail for more than six months, or by both such fine and imprisonment in the discretion of the court. If any letter, circular, poster, bill, publication or placard shall contain any false statement or charges reflecting on the candidate's character, morality or integrity, the author thereof and every person printing or knowingly assisting in the circulation thereof shall be guilty of political criminal libel, and upon conviction thereof, shall be punished by imprisonment in the penitentiary for not less than one nor more than three years. Any person or persons who shall write, print or circulate, or who shall cause to be written, printed or circulated, any letter, circular, bill, placard or poster, or who shall cause any paid advertisement to be placed in a newspaper or any other publication, or who shall singly or with others pay for any such advertisement, knowing said letter, circular, bill, placard, poster, publication or paid advertisement to contain any false statement, charge or comment relating to any candidate, shall be guilty of corrupt political practice and, upon conviction thereof, shall be punished by a fine of not less than one hundred dollars ($100) nor more than one thousand dollars ($1,000), or by imprisonment in the county jail not less than three months nor more than one year, or by both such fine and imprisonment.

Sec. 102-806. *Blacklisting prohibited.*—No corporation, company, or individual shall blacklist or publish, or cause to be blacklisted or published, any employee, mechanic, or laborer, discharged by such corporation, company, or individual, with intent and for the purpose of preventing such employee, mechanic, or laborer from engaging in or securing similar or other employment from any other corporation, company or individual.

Sec. 102-807. *Penalty.*—If any officer or agent of any corporation, company, or individual, or other person, shall blacklist or publish, or cause to be blacklisted or published, any employee, mechanic, or laborer, with intent and for the purpose of preventing such employee, mechanic, or laborer from engaging in or securing similar or other employment from any corporation, company, or individual, or shall, in any manner, conspire or contrive by correspondence or otherwise, to prevent such discharged employee from securing employment, he shall be deemed guilty of a misdemeanor, and upon conviction thereof shall be fined in a sum not less than $50 nor more than $250, or imprisoned in the county jail not less than thirty nor more than ninety days, or both, at the discretion of the court.

Sec. 103-293. *Attachment of privilege to reports and communications.*—The reports and communications of all officers and members of the national guard in the line of their military duty shall be privileged communications and shall not be competent evidence against the writer in any civil or criminal action in the courts of this state, and in case any suit or action shall be brought against any officer or member of the national guard because of such reports or communications it shall be the duty of the judge advocate or the attorney general of this state, or both of them, at the direction of the governor, to appear in behalf of such officer or member of the national guard and defend such suit or action without cost to him.

Limitations. Sec. 12:120 *Within one year:*—Action for escape or for libel or slander.

Within one year:

(2) An action for libel or slander.

Pennsylvania

PENNSYLVANIA STATUTES, 1940, 1953, 1961

Basic Statutes. 19-Sec. 801. *Defenses to prosecutions for libel; truth as evidence.*—In all criminal prosecutions or indictments for libel, no conviction shall be allowed if the subject matter of the publication, whether contained in newspapers or otherwise, relates to candidates for public office or the official conduct of public officers, and is found to the satisfaction of the jury to be proper for public information or investigation and not to have been maliciously or negligently made. In all such cases the truth may be given in evidence to the jury.

18-Sec. 4840. *False statements concerning financial institutions.*—Whoever makes, utters, publishes, writes, circulates, or transmits to another, any statement or rumor, untrue in fact, in reference to the solvency or derogatory to the financial condition of any national or state bank, bank and trust company, trust company, surety company, guarantee company, insurance company, building and loan association, or other financial institution, in this Commonwealth, or counsels, aids, procures, or induces another to originate, make, utter, publish, write, transmit, or circulate to another, any such statement or rumor, is guilty of a misdemeanor, and upon conviction thereof, shall be sentenced to pay a fine not more than two thousand dollars ($2,000), or to undergo imprisonment at hard labor for a term not exceeding three (3) years, or both.

The falsity of the statement or rumor shall be prima facie evidence of intent to violate the provisions of this section.

18 Sec. 4412. *Libel.*—Whoever writes, prints, publishes or exhibits any malicious or defamatory libel, tending either to

blacken the memory of one who is dead, or the reputation of one who is alive, thereby exposing him to public hatred, contempt or ridicule, is guilty of libel, a misdemeanor, and on conviction, shall be sentenced to pay a fine not exceeding five hundred dollars ($500), or undergo imprisonment not exceeding one (1) year, or both.

No person shall be indicted for the same libel in more than one county.

18 §4413. *Furnishing false or libelous statements.*—Whoever maliciously states, delivers or transmits by any means whatever to the manager, editor, publisher, reporter, or agent of any newspaper, magazine, publication, periodical, or to the writer or author of any editorial or article for publication therein, any false or libelous statement shall be imprisoned not exceeding one (1) year or fined not exceeding one thousand ($1000) dollars, or both.

18 §4413.1. *Furnishing false or libelous matter for broadcasting.* Whoever maliciously states, delivers or transmits by any means whatever to the owner, agent or employee of a radio, television or fascimile broadcasting station or studio, or to any person intending the same for broadcasting, any false or libelous statement, view, scene or matter, shall be imprisoned not exceeding one (1) year or fined not exceeding one thousand ($1000) dollars, or both.

18 Sec. 4414. *Anonymous communications.*—Whoever, without appending his proper signature thereto, sends or causes to be sent to another, any written or printed communication or matter, which is either libelous, defamatory, scurrilous, or opprobrious, is guilty of a misdemeanor, and on conviction thereof, shall be sentenced to pay a fine not exceeding five hundred dollars ($500), or undergo imprisonment for not more than one (1) year, or both.

18 Sec. 4415. *Libel on candidates.*—Whoever writes, prints, posts or distributes, or causes to be written, printed, posted or distributed, a circular or poster, cartoon or other written or printed paper, designed or tending to injure or defeat any

candidate for nomination or election to public office, by reflecting upon his personal character or political actions, unless the same is published in a newspaper avowedly responsible therefor, or unless there appears upon such circular, poster or paper, in a conspicuous place, the names of at least two (2) officers of the political or other organization issuing the same, or the name of some duly registered elector with description of his election district, as responsible therefor, is guilty of a misdemeanor, and on conviction thereof, shall be sentenced to pay a fine not exceeding five hundred dollars ($500), or to undergo imprisonment not exceeding one (1) year, or both.

If the statements are untrue, the person so offending is also guilty of libel, and may be prosecuted in the civil or criminal courts, or both.

12 Sec. 1581. *Recovery of costs.*—In all actions upon the case for slanderous words, to be sued or prosecuted, by any person or persons, in any court, within this province, if the jury, upon trial of the issue in action, or the jury that shall inquire of the damages, do find or assess the damages under forty shillings, then the plaintiff or plaintiffs in such action shall have and recover only so much costs as the damages so given or assesses do amount unto, without any further increase of the same, any law or usage to the contrary notwithstanding.

12 Sec. 1582. *Justification may be pleaded in civil actions.*—In all civil actions for libel, the plea of justification shall be accepted as an adequate and complete defense, when it is pleaded, and proved to the satisfaction of the jury, under the direction of the court as in other cases, that the publication is substantially true and is proper for public information or investigation, and has not been maliciously or negligently made.

12 Sec. 1583. *Damages in civil actions.*—In all civil actions for libel, no damages shall be recovered unless it is established to the satisfaction of the jury, under the direction of the court as in other cases, that the publication has been maliciously or negligently made, but where malice or negligence appears such damages may be awarded as the jury shall deem proper.

23 Sec. 25. *Presentation of libel; contents; affidavit.*—Any

spouse may have his or her petition or libel in divorce presented to the court of common pleas when in session, or during vacation to a judge thereof at chambers. The petition or libel shall set forth therein, particularly and specifically, the cause of his or her complaint, and shall be accompanied with an affidavit, on oath or affirmation taken before one of the said judges or the prothonotary or clerk of the court of common pleas or any person in any county of the Commonwealth legally authorized to take acknowledgments, that the fact contained in said petition or libel are true to the best of his or her knowledge and belief, and that the said complaint is not made out of levity, or by collusion between the said husband and wife, and for the mere purpose of being freed and separated from each other, but in sincerity and truth for the causes mentioned.

In the case of any spouse on active duty in the armed service of the United States in time of war, the affidavit accompanying his or her libel in divorce may be taken within or without the Commonwealth before any officer commissioned in the armed forces of the United States authorized by law to take affidavits and acknowledgments.

In cases where the respondent is a hopeless lunatic, or non compos mentis, the fact of lunacy of the respondent, and such circumstances as may be sufficient to satisfy the mind of the court as to the truth of the allegation, shall be set forth in the petition or libel, and affidavit required by this section shall be taken by the petitioner.

In cases where the libellant is a minor, the libel shall be presented by a relative or next friend, and the affidavit thereto shall be taken by such minor libellant.

The court may allow any libel to be amended so as to include additional grounds or causes for divorce, including such as arose subsequent to the awarding to the subpoena. Notice of any such amendment shall be served on the respondent in such manner as the court may direct in its order allowing the amendment.

§1584a. *Burden of proof.*—

(1) In an action for defamation, the plaintiff has the burden

of proving, when the issue is properly raised:

(a) The defamatory character of the communication;

(b) Its publication by the defendant;

(c) Its application to the plaintiff;

(d) The recipient's understanding of its defamatory meaning;

(e) The recipient's understanding of it as intended to be applied to the plaintiff;

(f) Special harm resulting to the plaintiff from its publication;

(g) Abuse of a conditionally privileged occasion.

(2) In an action for defamation, the defendant has the burden of proving, when the issue is properly raised:

(a) The truth of the defamatory communication;

(b) The privileged character of the occasion on which it was published;

(c) The character of the subject matter of defamatory comment as of public concern. 1953, Aug. 21, P.L. 1291, §1.

§1585. *Exemption from liability when without power of censorship.*—Liability shall be denied and no recovery shall be allowed against the owners, licensees and operators of any visual or sound radio and television station or network of stations or against the agents, servants or employees of such owner, licensee or operator, for the publication, utterance or broadcasting of any defamatory matter, where the publication, utterance or broadcasting thereof is not subject to their censorship or control by reason of any Federal statute or any regulation, ruling or order of the Federal Communications Commission. 1953, Aug. 21, P.L. 1241, §1.

§1586. *Limitation of accrued actions.*—All actions for damages which have accrued in cases in which liability is denied, as set forth in section one of this act, shall be commenced within sixty days after the effective date of this act; and if not so commenced, shall thereafter be completely barred. 1953, Aug. 21, P.L. 1241, §2.

43 Sec. 206n. *Labor injunctions to have provision restraining employers.*—Every restraining order, temporary or perma-

nent injunction issued by a court of this Commonwealth in any case involving or growing out of a labor dispute, shall contain the following provision:

"That complainant and/or the employer and their or either of their agents or employes shall be enjoined from any and all acts or threats of violence, intimidation, coercion, molestation, libel or slander against the respondents or organizations engaged in the labor dispute."

48 Sec. 112. *Actions for slander or libel and recovery of separate property.*—Whensoever any husband shall have deserted or separated himself from his wife, or neglected or refused to support her, or she shall have been divorced from his bed and board, it shall be lawful for her to protect her reputation by an action for slander or libel, and she shall also have the right, by action, to recover her separate earnings or property: Provided, That if her husband be the defendant, the action shall be in the name of a next friend.

Constitution of Pennsylvania. Art. I, Sec. 7. *Freedom of the press; libel.*—The printing press shall be free to every person who may undertake to examine the proceedings of the Legislature or any branch of government, and no law shall ever be made to restrain the right thereof. The free communication of thoughts and opinions is one of the invaluable rights of man, and every citizen may freely speak, write and print on any subject, being responsible for the abuse of that liberty. No conviction shall be had in any prosecution for the publication of papers relating to the official conduct of officers or men in public capacity, or to any other matter proper for public investigation or information, where the fact that such publication was not maliciously or negligently made shall be established to the satisfaction of the jury; and in all indictments for libels the jury shall have the right to determine the law and the facts, under the direction of the court, as in other cases.

Limitations. 12 Sec. 31. *Personal actions, when to be brought.* —All actions of trespass quare clausum fregit, all actions of detinue, trover and replevin, for taking away goods and cattle, all actions upon account and upon the case (other than such accounts as concern the trade of merchandise between merchant and merchant, their factors or servants), all actions of debt grounded upon any lending, or contract without specialty, all actions of debt, for arrearages of rent, except the proprietaries' quit-rents, and all actions of trespass, of assault, menace, battery, wounding and imprisonment, or any of them, which shall be sued or brought at any time after the five and twentieth day of April, which shall be in the year of our Lord one thousand seven hundred and thirteen, shall be commenced and sued within the time and limitation hereafter expressed, and not after; that is to say, the said actions upon the case, other than for slander, and the said actions for account, and the said actions for trespass, debt, detinue and replevin, for goods or cattle, and the said actions of trespass quare clausum fregit within three years after the said five and twentieth day of April next, or within six years next after the cause of such actions or suit, and not after. And the said actions of trespass, of assault, menace, battery, wounding, imprisonment, or any of them, within one year next after the said five and twentieth day of April next, or within two years next after the cause of such actions or suit, and not after; and the said actions upon the case of words, within one year next after the words spoken, and not after.

12 Sec. 32. *Limitation in cases of slander and libel.*—The limitation provided in the last paragraph of the first section of the act entitled "An act for limitation of actions," passed March 27, 1713, to which this section is supplementary, in relation to words spoken, shall be held to extend to all cases of slander or libel, whether spoken, written or printed.

Puerto Rico

LAWS OF PUERTO RICO, 1956

33.§911. *Libel defined.*—A libel is a malicious defamation, expressed either by writing, printing, or by signs or pictures, or the like, tending to blacken the memory of one who is dead, or to impeach the honesty, integrity, virtue or reputation, or publish the natural or alleged defects of one who is alive, and thereby to expose him to public hatred, contempt, or ridicule. Penal Code, 1937, §243.132. §3144. Communications not held malicious; not presumed malicious. A publication or communication shall not be held or deemed malicious when made in any legislative or judicial proceeding or in any other proceeding authorized by law. A publication or communication shall not be presumed to be malicious when made:

First. In the proper discharge of an official duty.

Second. In a fair and true report of a judicial, legislative, official or other proceeding, or of anything said in the course thereof.

32.§3146. *Truth of charges as to public employee.*—If the plaintiff be a public employee and the libel refer to acts connected with his office, judgment shall be rendered for the defendant if he prove the truth of the charges.

32.§3148. *Publication of libel.*—To sustain the charge of publishing libel it is not needful that the words for which suit is brought should have been read by any person; it is enough and sufficient evidence if the accused knowingly parted with the immediate custody of the libel or exposed the same to view under circumstances which allowed it to be read by any other person.

33·§914. *Truth as a defense.*—In all criminal prosecutions for libel, the truth may be given in evidence to the court or jury, and if it appears to the court or jury that the matter charged as libelous is true, and was published with good motives and for justifiable ends, the party shall be acquitted. The jury have the right to determine the law and the facts. (Penal Code 1937, §246)

33·§916. *Author, editor, and proprietor chargeable.*—Each author, editor, and proprietor of any book, newspaper, or serial publication, is chargeable with the publication of any words contained in any part of such book or number of such newspaper or serial. (Penal Code, 1937, §248)

33·§912. *Punishment for libel.*—Every person who wilfully publishes or procures to be published any libel, or distributes or causes to be distributed any libelous matter in the form of leaflets, cards, or any other manner whatsoever, either printed or written, posting or causing them to be posted in any place, is punishable by fine not exceeding five thousand dollars, or imprisonment in jail for a term not exceeding two years, or both such fine and imprisonment, and also the costs of the action, in the discretion of the court. (Penal Code 1937, §244)

33·§233. *Limitations, Misdemeanors.*—The prosecution for any misdemeanor must be commenced within one year after the commission, except in cases of violation of the Internal Revenue Laws, when prosecution may be commenced within three years after the commission.

Rhode Island

GENERAL LAWS OF RHODE ISLAND, 1938, 1956

Basic Statutes. Constitution of Rhode Island. Art. I, Sec. 20. The liberty of the press being essential to the security of freedom in a state, any person may publish his sentiments on any subject, being responsible for the abuse of that liberty; and in all trials for libel, both civil and criminal, the truth, unless published for malicious motives, shall be sufficient defense to the person charged.

Chap. 289, Sec. 11. If the director or the commissioner or any authorized representative of the commissioner has reason to believe that any employer is not observing the provisions of any order made by him under Sec. 9 of this chapter, the director or the commissioner may, on 15 days' notice, summon such employer to appear before the director or the commissioner to show cause why the name of such employer should not be published as having failed to observe the provisions of such order. After such hearing and the finding by the director or the commissioner of nonobservance, the director may cause to be published in a newspaper or newspapers circulating within this state or in such manner as the director may deem appropriate, the name of any such employer or employers as having failed in the respects stated to observe the provisions of the directory order of the director. Neither the director nor any authorized representative of the director, nor any newspaper publisher, proprietor, editor, nor employee thereof shall be liable to an action for damages for publishing the name of any employer as provided for in this chapter, unless guilty of some wilful misrepresentation.

9-6-9. *Truth as defense to libel or slander.*—In every action or proceeding, civil or criminal, for libel or slander, the defendant may, with his plea of not guilty, file a written notice that he will prove the truth of the publication charged as libelous, or of the words charged as slanderous, and in such case may, upon the trial, give the truth in evidence, without any special plea of justification; and the truth, unless published or uttered from malicious motives, shall be sufficient defense to the person charged.

Limitations. 9-1-14. Actions for words spoken shall be commenced and sued within one year next after the words spoken, and not after. Actions for injuries to the person shall be commenced and sued within 2 years next after the cause of action shall accrue, and not after.

South Carolina

CODE OF LAWS OF SOUTH CAROLINA, 1943, 1962

Basic Statutes. Constitution of South Carolina, Art. I, Sec. 4. *Religious Worship—Freedom of Speech, Assembly and Petition.* —The General Assembly shall make no law respecting an establishment of religion or prohibiting the free exercise thereof, or abridging the freedom of speech or of the press; or the right of the people peaceably to assemble and to petition the Government or any department thereof for a redress of grievances.

Art. I, Sec. 21. *Libel.*—In all indictments or prosecutions for libel, the truth of the alleged libel may be given in evidence, and the jury shall be the judges of the law and the facts.

43-52. *No jurisdiction in certain cases.*—No magistrate shall have cognizance of a civil action:
(1) In which the State is a party, excepting for penalties and not exceeding one hundred dollars, or

(2) Where the title to real property shall come in question, except as provided in article 6 of this chapter.

(3) Nor of a civil action for an assault, battery, false imprisonment, libel, slander, malicious prosecution, criminal conversation, or seduction, where the damages claimed exceed one hundred dollars.

Pleading 10-676. *Libel and slander—how stated in complaint.*—In an action for libel or slander, it shall not be necessary to state, in the complaint, any extrinsic facts, for the purpose of showing the application to the plaintiff of the defamatory matter out of which the cause of action arose; but it shall be sufficient to state generally that the defamatory matter was published or spoken concerning the plaintiff. If such allegation be controverted the plaintiff shall be bound to establish, on trial, that it was so published or spoken.

10-677. *Answer in such cases.*—In the action mentioned in section 10-676, the defendant may, in his answer, allege both the truth of the matter charged as defamatory, and any mitigating circumstances, to reduce the amount of damages; and, whether he prove the justification or not, he may give, in evidence, the mitigating circumstances.

Sec. 527-1. *Attachment in libel and slander against non-residents or foreign corporations.*—Any and all attachments issued, made or levied in any of the courts of this State of the property, goods or credits of any non-resident of this State, or of any foreign corporation in actions for libel or slander, if otherwise good and valid, shall stand as if the suit had been brought upon any other cause of action, mentioned in 10-901 or provided by the law.

Sec. 756. *Costs follow event of action, except in chancery cases when otherwise ordered.*—In every civil action commenced or prosecuted in the courts of record in this State (except cases in chancery) the attorneys of plaintiff or defendant shall be entitled to recover costs and disbursements of the adverse party, as prescribed in Sections 757, 758, and chapter 117, such costs to be allowed as of course to the attorneys of plaintiff or defendant, and all officers of the court thereto entitled, accordingly as the action may terminate, and to be inserted in the judgment against the losing party. In cases of chancery, the same rule as to costs shall prevail, unless otherwise ordered by the court: *provided,* that whenever, in action for assault, battery, false imprisonment, libel, slander, malicious prosecution, criminal conversation or seduction, or in any other action for damages for torts, the amount recovered shall be less than one hundred dollars, the total amount of costs and disbursements shall not exceed the amount so recovered in the action.

Sec. 16-161. *Slander and libel.*—Any person who shall with malicious intent originate, utter or circulate, or publish, any false statement or matter concerning another, the effect of which shall tend to injure such person in his character or reputation, shall be deemed guilty of a misdemeanor, and, upon conviction therefor, be subject to punishment by fine not to exceed five thousand dollars, or by imprisonment for a term not exceeding one year, or by both fine and imprisonment, in the discretion of the court: *provided,* that nothing herein shall be construed to abridge any right any person may have by way of an action for damages for libel or slander, or libel under the existing law.

8-108. *False statement concerning solvency of bank.*—Any person who shall falsely and wilfully and with intent to injure, circulate any report, or make any false oral statement as to the assets or liabilities of any bank in this state, or to its solvency or ability to meet its obligations, or as to its soundness, or who shall make any other false oral statement, calculated to affect the credit or standing of such a bank, or to cast suspicion upon its solvency, soundness or ability to meet its deposits or other obligations in due course, shall be guilty of a misdemeanor and upon conviction thereof shall be fined not less than one hundred ($100.00) dollars, nor more than five hundred ($500.00) dollars, or be imprisoned for not more than one year, or both, in the discretion of the court.

10-2591. *Imputing want of chastity—Liability without proof of special damage.*—If any person shall utter and publish, either by writing or verbally, any words of and concerning any female, imputing to her a want of chastity, the person so uttering and publishing such words, shall be liable for damages in a civil action brought by the said female of whom said words may be uttered and published, without proving any special damage; subject, nevertheless, to the rules of evidence at common law.

23-7. *Liability of broadcasting system for defamatory statement by candidate.*—The owner, licensee or operator of a visual or sound radio broadcasting station or network of stations and the agents or employees of any such owner, licensee or operator shall not be liable for any damages for any defamatory statement published or uttered in or as part of a visual or sound radio broadcast by a candidate for political office in those instances where, under the acts of Congress or the rules and regulations of the Federal Communications Commission, the broadcasting station or network of stations is prohibited from censoring the material broadcast by such candidate, provided the owner, licensee or operator shall cause to be made at the conclusion of the broadcast the following announcement in substance; "The broadcast you have just heard was not censored in accordance with the immunity from censorship extended legally qualified political candidates." (1952 (47) 1939)

Limitations. 10-145. *Within two years:*

(1) An action for libel, slander, assault, battery, or false imprisonment.

(2) An action upon a statute, for a forfeiture or penalty to the State.

South Dakota

SOUTH DAKOTA CODE OF 1939, 1960

Basic Statutes. Constitution of South Dakota, Art. VI, Sec. 5.–Every person may freely speak, write and publish on all subjects, being responsible for the abuse of that right. In all trials for libel, both civil and criminal, the truth, when published with good motives and for justifiable ends shall be a sufficient defense. The jury shall have the right to determine the fact and the law under the direction of the court.

47.0501. *Obligation to refrain from.*–Every person is obligated to refrain from infringing upon the right of others not to be defamed.

47.0502. *Defamation classified and defined.*–

(1) Libel; or

(2) Slander.

Libel is a false and unprivileged publication by writing, printing, picture, effigy, or other fixed representation to the eye which exposes any person to hatred, contempt, ridicule, or obloquy, or which causes him to be shunned or avoided, or which has a tendency to injure him in his occupation.

Slander is a false and unprivileged publication, other than libel, which:

(1) Charges any person with crime, or with having been indicted, convicted, or punished for crime;

(2) Imputes to him the present existence of an infectious, contagious, or loathsome disease;

(3) Tends directly to injure him in respect to his office, profession, trade, or business, either by imputing to him general disqualification in those respects which the office or other oc-

cupation peculiarly requires, or by imputing something with reference to his office, profession, trade, or business that has a natural tendency to lessen its profit;

(4) Imputes to him impotence or want of chastity; or

(5) Which, by natural consequence, cause actual damage.

47.0503. *Privileged communications.*—A privileged communication is one made:

(1) In the proper discharge of an official duty;

(2) In any legislative or judicial proceeding, or in any other official proceeding authorized by law;

(3) In a communication, without malice, to a person interested therein, by one who is also interested, or by one who stands in such relation to the person interested as to afford a reasonable ground for supposing the motive for the communication innocent, or who is requested by the person interested to give the information;

(4) By a fair and true report, without malice, of a judicial, legislative, or other public official proceeding or of anything said in the course thereof.

In the cases provided for in subdivision (3) and (4) of this section, malice is not inferred from the communication or publication.

47.0504. *Notice and demand before certain actions for libel.* —Before any action for libel can be brought against a newspaper or the publisher, editor, or manager thereof, other than a libel of or concerning a female, the party aggrieved must at least three days before the commencement of such action serve a notice on the person or persons against whom said action is to be brought specifying particularly the statement or statements claimed to be false and defamatory, and if on the trial it appears that such statement or statements were written or published in good faith and with the belief founded upon reasonable ground that the same were true, and a full and fair retraction of the erroneous matter correcting any and all misstatements of fact therein contained was published in the next issue of the paper, or in the case of a daily paper within three days after the mistake was brought to the attention of the publisher, editor, or manager in as conspicuous type as the original statement and the same position in the paper, the plaintiff will be entitled to recover no punitive damages. But if the libel is against a candidate for office the retraction must also be made editorially in the case of a daily paper at least three days and in the case of a weekly paper at least ten days before the election.

47.0505. *Retraction rebuts presumption of malice.*—The publication of a full and fair retraction of the alleged defamatory statement as provided by section 47.0504 of this Code shall, on the trial of an action for such libel, be held and considered a rebuttal of any and all presumption of malice attached to and growing out of such alleged libel.

(Supplement to South Dakota Code of 1939) 47.0506. *Exemptions: radio stations; exceptions of failure to exercise due care.*—The owner, licensee or operator of a visual or sound radio broadcasting station or network of stations, and the agents or employees of any such owner, licensee or operator shall not be liable for any damages for any defamatory statement published or uttered in or as part of a visual or sound radio broadcast, by one other than such owner, licensee or operator, or agent or employee thereof, unless it shall be alleged and proved by the complaining party, that such owner, licensee, operator, such agent or employee, has failed to exercise due care to prevent the publication or utterance of such statement in such broadcast.

Limitations. 33.0232. *Limitation of time of commencement of actions other than for recovery of real property: general provisions: general exception.*—Except where, in special cases, a different limitation is prescribed by statute, civil actions other than for the recovery of real property can be commenced only within the following specified periods of time after the cause of action shall have accrued:

(6) Within Two Years:

(a) An action for libel, slander, assault, battery, or false imprisonment.

Tennessee

TENNESSEE CODE, 1943, 1956

Basic Statutes. *Freedom of speech and press.*—Constitution c Tennessee, Art. I, Sec. 19. That the printing presses shall b free to every person to examine the proceedings of the Legi lature, or of any branch or officer of the Government; and n law shall ever be made to restrain the right thereof. The fre communication of thoughts and opinions is one of the invalu able rights of man, and every citizen may freely speak, writ and print on any subject, being responsible for the abuse of th liberty. But in prosecutions for the publication of papers i vestigating the official conduct of officers or men in publi capacity, the truth thereof may be given in evidence; and i all indictments for libel the jury shall have a right to dete mine the law and the facts, under the direction of the cour as in other criminal cases.

39-2701. *Libel.*—A libel is the malicious defamation of person, made public by any printing, sign, picture, represent tion, or effigy, intending to provoke him to wrath, or expos him to public hatred, contempt, or ridicule, or to deprive hi of the benefits of public confidence and social intercourse; c any malicious defamation made public as aforesaid, designed t blacken and vilify the memory of one who is dead, and tendin to scandalize or provoke his surviving relatives or friends.

39-2702. *Necessity, what constitutes.*—No printing, wri ing, or other thing is a libel without publication; but the d livering, selling, reading, or otherwise communicating a libe or causing the same to be delivered, sold, read, or otherwise communicated to one or more persons, or to the party libeled, is a publication thereof.

39-2703. *Jury.*—Such libel shall be a misdemeanor, and in all indictments or prosecutions for same, the jury has a right to determine the law and the facts, under the direction of the court as in other criminal cases.

39-2704. *Truth may be given in evidence under a plea of not guilty.*—The truth of the matter charged in the indictment may be given in evidence by the person charged, under the plea of not guilty, with every advantage that could be had under a plea of justification in actions for libel.

19-301. *Civil Cases.*—The jurisdiction of justice of the peace, in civil cases, extends:
In all cases for the recovery of property, and in all cases of damages, except libel and slander, arising from either tort or contract, where the value of the property sued for, or the damages demanded, do not exceed 2500 dollars.

9310 5155 (3400). *Charge of adultery or fornication.*—Any words written, spoken, or printed of a person, wrongfully and maliciously imputing to such person the commission of adultery or fornication, are actionable, without special damage.

23-2603. *Truth under plea of general issue.*—In all civil actions for slander or libel the truth of the words spoken or written and the circumstances under which they were spoken or written may be given in evidence under the general issue in mitigation of damages.

Limitations. 28-304. *Personal tort actions—Statutory penalties.*—Actions for libel, for injuries to the person, false imprisonment, malicious prosecution, criminal conversation, seduction, breach of marriage promise, and statutory penalties shall be commenced within one year after cause of action accrued.

Texas

STATUTES OF THE STATE OF TEXAS
1940, 1953, 1954, 1957, 1959

Basic Statutes. *Freedom of speech and press; libel.* Constitution of Texas, Art. I, Sec. 8.–Every person shall be at liberty to speak, write or publish his opinions on any subject, being responsible for the abuse of that privilege; and no law shall ever be passed curtailing the liberty of speech or of the press. In prosecutions for the publication of papers, investigating the conduct of officers, or men in public capacity, or when the matter published is proper for public information, the truth thereof may be given in evidence. And in all indictments for libels, the jury shall have the right to determine the law and the facts, under the direction of the court, as in other cases.

CCP 13. *Liberty of speech and press.*–Every person shall be at liberty to speak, write or publish his opinion on any subject, being liable for the abuse of that privilege; and no law shall ever be passed curtailing the liberty of speech or of the press. In prosecutions for the publication of papers investigating the conduct of officers or men in public capacity, or when the matter published is proper tor public information, the truth thereof may be given in evidence. In all indictments for libels, the jury shall have the right to determine the law and the facts, under the direction of the court, as in other cases.

CCP 88. *Bond of person charged with libel.*–If any person shall make oath, and shall convince the magistrate that he has good reason to believe that another is about to publish, sell or circulate, or is continuing to sell, publish or circulate any libel against him, or any such publication as is made an offense by the penal law of the State, the person accused of such intended publication may be required to enter into bond with security not to sell, publish or circulate such libelous publication, and the same proceedings be had as in the cases before enumerated in this chapter.

CCP 89. *Destruction of libel.*—On conviction for making, writing, printing, publishing, selling or circulating a libel, the court may, if it be shown that there are in the hands of defendant or another copies of such libel intended for publication, sale or distribution, order all such copies to be seized and destroyed by the sheriff or other proper officer.

PC 1269. *Definition.*—He is guilty of "libel" who, with intent to injure, makes, writes, prints, publishes, sells or circulates any malicious statement affecting the reputation of another in respect to any matter or thing pointed out in this chapter.

PC 1269a. *Libel on banks.*—Any person who shall knowingly make, utter, circulate, or transmit to another, or others, any statement untrue in fact, derogatory to the financial condition of any bank, banking house, banking company, trust company, in the State, with intent to injure any such financial institution; or who shall counsel, aid, procure, or induce another to originate, make, utter, transmit, or circulate any such statement or rumor, with like intent, shall be guilty of an offense and upon conviction shall be punished by a fine of not more than five thousand ($5,000) dollars or confined in the State Penitentiary not more than five (5) years or both.

PC 1270. *Punishment.*—If any person be guilty of libel he shall be fined not less than one hundred nor more than two thousand dollars, or be imprisoned in jail not exceeding two years; and the court may enter up judgment and issue an order thereupon directing the sheriff to seize and destroy all the publications, prints, paintings or engravings constituting the libel as charged in the indictments.

PC 1271. *Forged writing.*—If any person with intent to injure the reputation of another shall without lawful authority make, publish or circulate a writing purporting to be the act of some other person, and which comes within the definition of libel, as given in this chapter, he shall be punished in the same manner as if the act purported to be his own; and the rules with respect to libel apply also to the making and circulation of such false writing.

PC 1272. *"Maker."*—He is the maker of a libel who originally contrived and either executed it himself by writing, printing, engraving or painting, or dictated or caused it to be done by others.

PC 1273. *"Publisher."*—He is the publisher of a libel, who, either of his own will or by the persuasion or dictation of another, executes the same in any of the modes pointed out as constituting a libel; but if any one by force or threats is compelled to execute such libel he is guilty of no offense.

PC 1274. *"Circulating."*—He is guilty of circulating a libel, who, knowing its contents, either sells, distributes or gives, or who, with malicious design, reads or exhibits it to others.

PC 1275. *The ideas the statement must convey.*—The written, printed or published statement, to come within the definition of libel, must convey the idea either:

1. That the person to whom it refers has been guilty of some penal offense; or

2. That he has been guilty of some act or omission which, though not a penal offense, is disgraceful to him as a member of society, and the natural consequence of which is to bring him into contempt among honorable persons; or

3. That he has some moral vice, or physical or mental defect or disease, which renders him unfit for intercourse with respectable society, and such as should cause him to be generally avoided; or

4. That he is notoriously of bad or infamous character; or

5. That any person in office or a candidate therefor is dishonest and therefore unworthy of such office or that while in office he has been guilty of some malfeasance rendering him unworthy of the place.

PC 1276. *Mode of publication.*—A libel may be either written, printed, engraved, etched, or painted, but no verbal defamation comes within the meaning thereof; and whenever a defendant is accused of libel by means of a painting, engraving, or caricature, it must clearly appear therefrom that the person said to be defamed was, in fact, intended to be represented by such painting, engraving, or caricature.

PC 1277. *A manuscript must be circulated.*—In order to render any manuscript a libel, it must be circulated or posted up in some public place.

PC 1278. *Editor, etc., prima facie guilty.*—If the libel be in printed form, and issues or is sold in any office or shop where a public newspaper is conducted, or where books or other printed works are sold or printed, the editor, publisher and proprietor of such newspaper, or any one of them, or the owner of such shop, is to be deemed guilty of making or circulating such libel until the contrary is made on the trial to appear.

PC 1279. *Editor, etc. may avoid responsibility.*—The editor, publisher, or proprietor of a public newspaper may avoid the responsibility of making or publishing a libel by giving the true author of the same, provided such author be a resident of this State and a person of good character except in cases where it is shown that such editor, publisher, or proprietor caused the libel to be published with malicious design.

PC 1281. *Actual injury not necessary.*—It is sufficient to constitute the offense of libel if the natural consequence of the publication of the same is to injure the person defamed, although no actual injury to his reputation has been sustained.

PC 1282. *Intent to injure presumed.*—The intent to injure is to be presumed if such would be the natural consequence of the libel, although no actual proof be made that the defendant had such design.

PC 1283. *The offense relates to persons.*—To constitute libel, there must be some injury intended to the reputation of persons, and no publication as to the government, or any of the branches thereof as such is an offense under the name of seditious writings or any other name.

PC 1284. *Not libelous.*—It is no libel:

1. To make any publication respecting a body politic or corporate as such.

2. To make publications respecting the merits or doctrines

of any particular religion, system of morals or politics, or of any particular form of government.

3. To publish any statement respecting any legislative or judicial proceedings, whether in fact true or not, unless in such statement a charge or corruption is made against some person acting in a legislative or judicial capacity.

4. To publish any criticism or examination of any work of literature, science or art or any opinion as to the qualifications or merits of the author of such work.

5. To publish true statements of fact as to the qualifications of any person for any occupation, profession or trade.

6. To make true statements of fact or express opinions as to the integrity or other qualifications of a candidate for any office or public place or appointment.

PC 1285. *Recorder of minutes not liable.*—Where any person by virtue of his office is required to record the proceedings of any department of the government or of any body corporate or politic, or of any association organized for purposes of business or as a religious, moral, benevolent, literary, or scientific institution, he cannot be charged with libel for any entry upon the minutes or records of such department, body, or association, made in the course of his official duties.

PC 1286. *Members who assent.*—If any false statement be entered upon the minutes or record of proceedings of any corporate body or association included within the meaning of the preceding article, which would be libel if written, printed, published, or circulated by an individual, according to the previous articles of this chapter, the members of such body or association who assent to and direct such libelous statement to be made, are guilty of libel under the same rules as if the false statement had been written, published, or circulated in any other manner than as a part of the record of proceedings of such body or association, subject, however, to the restrictions contained in the succeeding article.

PC 1288. *"Malicious."*—The word "malicious" is used to signify an act done with evil or mischievous design, and it is not necessary to prove any special facts showing ill feeling on the part of the person who is concerned in making, printing, publishing, or circulating a libelous statement against the person injured thereby.

PC 1289. *Statement in legislative or judicial proceeding.*—No statement made in the course of a legislative or judicial proceeding, whether true or false, although made with intent to injure and from malicious purposes, comes within the definition of libel.

PC 1290. *Truth of statement may be shown, when.*—In the following cases the truth of any statement charged as libel may be shown in justification of the defendant:

1. Where the publication purports to be an investigation of the official conduct of officers or men in a public capacity.

2. Where it is stated in the libel that a person has been guilty of some penal offense, and the time, place and nature of the offense is specified in the publication.

3. Where it is stated in the libel that a person is of notoriously bad or infamous character.

4. Where the publication charges any person in office, or a candidate therefor, with a want of honesty, or of having been guilty of some malfeasance in office rendering him unworthy of the place. In other cases the truth of the facts stated in the libel cannot be inquired into.

PC 1291. *Province of Jury.*—The jury in every case of libel are not only the judges of the facts and of the law under the direction of the court in accordance with the constitution, but they are judges of the intent with which a libel may have been published or circulated, subject to the rules prescribed in this chapter.

PC 1292. *Scope of title.*—This title regulates the law with regard to libel when prosecuted as a penal offense, and is not intended to affect civil remedies for the recovery of damages.

5431. *5596 Mitigation of damages.*—In any action for libel, in determining the extent and source of actual damage and in mitigation of exemplary or punitive damage, the defendant may give in evidence, if specially pleaded, all material facts and circumstances under which the libelous publication was made, and any public apology, correction or retraction made and published by him of the libel complained of, and may also give in evidence, if specially pleaded in mitigation of exemplary or punitive damage, the intention with which the libelous publication was made. The truth of the statement, or statements, in such publication shall be a defense to such action.

5432. 5597 *Privileged Matters.*—The publication of the following matters by any newspaper or periodical shall be deemed privileged and shall not be made the basis of any action for libel:

1. A fair, true and impartial account of the proceedings in a court of justice, unless the court prohibits the publication of same when in the judgment of the court the ends of justice demand that the same should not be published and the court so orders, or any other official proceedings authorized by law in in the administration of the law.

2. A fair, true and impartial account of all executive and legislative proceedings, including all reports of and proceedings in or before legislative committees and before each and all such committees heretofore appointed by the Legislature or either branch of the Legislature or hereafter to be appointed by such bodies or either of them and of any debate or statement in or before the Legislature or either branch thereof or any of its committees, and including also all reports of and proceedings in or before the managing boards of educational and eleemosynary institutions supported from the public revenue, of city councils or other governing bodies of cities and towns, of the commissioners' court of any county, and of the board of trustees of the public schools of any district, city or county, and of any debate or statement in or before any such body.

3. A fair, true and impartial account of the proceedings of public meetings, dealing with public purposes, including a fair, true and impartial account of statements and discussion in such meetings, and of other matters of public concern, transpiring and uttered at such public meetings.

4. A reasonable and fair comment or criticism of the official acts of public officials and of other matters of public concern

published for general information.

5. The privilege provided under Sections 1, 2, 3, and 4, of this article shall extend to any first publication of such privileged matter by any newspaper or periodical, and to subsequent publication thereof by it when published as a matter of public concern for general information; but any republication of such privileged matter, after the same has ceased to be a matter of such public concern, shall not be deemed privileged, and may be made the basis of an action for libel, upon proof that such matter had ceased to be of such public concern, and that same was published with actual malice.

5433. *Construction.*—Nothing in this title shall be construed to amend or repeal any penal law on the subject of libel, not to take away any now or at any time heretofore existing defense to a civil action for libel, either at common law or otherwise, but all such defenses are hereby expressly preserved.

5525. *Survival of cause of action.*—All cause of action upon which suit has been or may hereafter be brought for personal injuries, or for injuries resulting in death, whether such injuries be to the health or to the reputation, or to the person of the injured party, shall not abate by reason of the death of the person against whom such cause of action shall have accrued, nor by reason of the death of such injured person, but, in the case of the death of either or both, all such cause of action shall survive to and in favor of the heirs and legal representatives and estate of such injured party and against the person or persons liable for such injuries and his or their legal representatives, and may be instituted and prosecuted as if such person or persons against whom same accrued were alive.

5206. *Statement of cause of discharge.*—Any written statement of cause of discharge, if true, when made by such agent, company or corporation, shall never be used as the cause of an action for libel, either civil or criminal, against the agent, company or corporation so furnishing same.

Texas. 1957. Art. 5433a. *Radio or broadcasting station or network; limitations of liability.*—The owner, licensee or operator of a radio or television broadcasting station or network of stations, and the agent or employees of any such owner, licensee or operator shall not be liable for any damages for any defamatory statement published or uttered in or as part of a radio or television broadcast, by one other than such owner, licensee or operator, or agent or employee thereof, unless it shall be alleged and proved by the complaining party, that such owner, licensee, operator or such agent or employee has failed to exercise due care to prevent the publication or utterance of such statement in such broadcast.

Limitations. 5524. 5685, 3353, 3202. *Actions be commenced in one year.*—There shall be commenced and prosecuted within one year after the cause of action shall have accrued; and not afterward, all actions or suits in courts of the following description:

1. Actions for malicious prosecution or for injuries done to the character or reputation of another by libel or slander.

Utah

THE UTAH CODE, REPLACEMENT, 1951, 1953

Basic Statutes. 76-40-1. *Libel Defined.*—A libel is a malicious defamation, expressed either by printing or by signs or pictures or the like, tending to blacken the memory of one who is dead, or to impeach the honesty, integrity, virtue or reputation, or publish the natural defects, of one who is alive, and thereby to expose him to public hatred, contempt or ridicule.

State Constitution. Art. 1§15. *Freedom of speech and of the press—libel.*—No law shall be passed to abridge or restrain the freedom of speech or of the press. In all criminal prosecutions for libel the truth may be given in evidence to the jury, and if it shall appear to the jury that the matter charged as libelous is true, and was published with good motives, and for justifiable ends, the party shall be acquitted: and the jury shall have the right to determine the law and the fact.

Code of Criminal Procedure. 77-21-35. *Libel.*—(1) No information or indictment for libel shall be invalid or insufficient for the reason that it does not set forth extrinsic facts for the purpose of showing the application to the party alleged to be libelled of the defamatory matter on which the indictment is founded; but it shall be sufficient to state generally that the same was published concerning him. (2) The facts showing the application of the defamatory matter to the party libelled must be established on the trial.

76-40-2. *Penalty.*—Every person who wilfully and with a malicious intent to injure another publishes or procures to be published any libel is punishable by fine not exceeding $1,000 or by imprisonment in the county jail not exceeding one year.

76-40-3. *When Malice Presumed.*—An injurious publication is presumed to have been malicious if no justifiable motive for making it is shown.

76-40-4. *Need Not Be Seen or Read, if Exposed.*—To sustain a charge of publishing a libel it is not essential that the words or things complained of should have been read or seen by another. It is enough that the accused knowingly parted with the immediate custody of the libel under circumstances which exposed it to be read or seen by any other person than himself.

76-40-5. *Liability of Authors of Publications.*—Each author, editor and proprietor of any newspaper or serial publication is chargeable with the publication of any words contained in any part of such book or number of such newspaper or serial.

76-40-6. *Privilege—Fair Report Governmental Proceedings.*—No reporter, editor or proprietor of any newspaper is liable to any prosecution for a fair and true report of any judicial, legislative or other public official proceedings, or of any statement, speech, argument or debate in course of same, except upon proof of malice in making such report, which shall not be implied from the mere fact of publication.

76-40-7. *Id. Does Not Extend to Libelous Matter.*—Libelous remarks or comments connected with matter privileged by the next preceding section receive no privilege by reason of their being so connected.

76-40-8. *Id. Communications Between Persons Interested Therein.*—A communication made to a person interested in the communication by one who is also interested, or who stands in such relation to the former as to afford a reasonable ground for supposing his motive innocent, is not presumed to be malicious, and is a privileged communication.

76-40-11. *Conveying False Information to Newspapers.*—Any person who wilfully states, conveys, delivers or transmits, by any means whatsoever, to the manager, editor, publisher or reporter of any newspaper, magazine, periodical or serial for publication therein, any false or libelous statement concerning any person, and thereby secures publication of same, is guilty of a misdemeanor.

76-19-7. *Id. By Threatening to Publish Libel.*—Every person who threatens another to publish a libel concerning him, or concerning any parent, husband, wife, or child of such person, or member of his family; and every person who offers to prevent the publication of any libel upon another person, with intent to extort any money or other valuable consideration from any person, is guilty of a misdemeanor.

Rules 9-j-l. *Libel and Slander—Pleading Defamatory Matter.*—It is not necessary in an action for libel or slander to set forth any extrinsic facts showing the application to the plaintiff of the defamatory matter out of which the action arose; but it is sufficient to state, generally that the same was published or spoken concerning the plaintiff. If such allegation is controverted, the party alleging such defamatory matter must establish on the trial that it was so published or spoken.

Rules 9-j-2. *Pleading Defense.*—In answer to an action for libel or slander the defendant may allege both the truth of the matter charged as defamatory and any mitigating circumstances to reduce the amount of damages, and, whether he proves the justification or not, he may give in evidence the mitigating circumstances.

77-31-30. *Libel.—Truth May Be Given in Evidence—Jury to Determine Law and Fact.*—In all criminal prosecutions for libel, the truth may be given in evidence to the jury, and, if it appears to they jury that the matter charged as libelous is true, and was published with good motives and for justifiable ends, the defendant shall be acquitted. The jury shall have the right to determine the law and the fact.

45-2-1. *Retraction by Newspapers—Limit of Recovery.*—If it shall appear on the trial of any action brought for the publication of any alleged libel in any newspaper published in this state that the alleged libel was published in good faith, that the publication thereof was due to mistake or misapprehension of the facts, and that a full and fair retraction of any statement therein alleged to be erroneous was published in the same type and in the same position on the same page as was the article complained of as libelous, in the next regular issue of such newspaper, or in case of a daily paper within three days, after service upon the publisher of such newspaper, of a written notice specifying the statement alleged to be erroneous, or in case such notice is not served in the issue or within the time above specified after the filing of the complaint and service of the summons in said action, then the plaintiff shall recover only actual damages, *provided,* that if such libel was published in a Sunday edition, the publication of the retraction must have been in a Sunday edition within two weeks after the times above specified: *provided further,* that this section shall not apply in the case of any libel against any candidate for a public office at any election or primary, or any avowed candidate for nomination to any office before any political convention, unless the retraction of the charge was made editorially in a conspicuous manner at least five days before the holding of such election, primary or political convention in case such libelous article was published in a daily paper, or if published in a weekly paper, at least three days before the holding therof, which editorial retraction shall be in lieu of another retraction herein provided for.

45-2-3. *Privileged Publication Defined.*—A privileged publication which shall not be considered as libelous per se, is one made:

(1) In the proper discharge of an official duty.

(2) In any publication of or any statement made in any legislative or judicial proceeding, or in any other official proceeding authorized by law.

(3) In a communication without malice, to a person interested therein, by one who is also interested, or by one who stands in such relation to the person interested as to afford a reasonable ground for supposing the motive for the communication innocent, or who is requested by the person interested to give the information.

(4) By a fair and true report, without malice of a judicial, legislative, or of a charge or complaint made by any person to a public official, upon which a warrant shall have been issued or an arrest made.

(5) By a fair and true report without malice of the proceedings of a public meeting, if such meeting was lawfully convened for a lawful purpose and open to the public, or the publication of the matter complained of was for public benefit.

45-2-5. *Radio or television broadcasting station or network of stations.*—No person, firm, or corporation owning or operating a radio or television broadcasting station or network of stations shall be liable under the laws of libel, slander or defamation on account of having made its broadcasting facilities or network available to any person, whether a candidate for public office or any other person, or on account of having originated or broadcast a program for discussion of controversial or any other subjects, in the absence of proof of actual malice on the part of such owner or operator. In no event, however, shall any such owner or operator be held liable for any damages for any defamatory statement uttered over the facilities of such station or network by or on behalf of any candidate for public office.

45-2-6. *Right of station to require submission of matter intended to be broadcast.*—Any person, firm, or corporation owning or operating a radio or television broadcasting station shall have the right, but shall not be compelled, to require the submission and permanent filing, in such station, of a copy of the complete address, script, or other form of expression, intended to be broadcast over such station before the time of the intended broadcast thereof.

45-2-7. *Limitations and restrictions upon immunity from liability—Failure to exercise due care.*—Nothing in this act contained shall be construed to relieve any person broadcasting over a radio or television station from liability under the law of libel, slander, or defamation. Nor shall anything in this act be construed to relieve any person, firm, or corporation owning or operating a radio or television broadcasting station or network from liability under the law of libel, slander, or defamation on account of any broadcast prepared or made by any such person, firm, or corporation or by any officer or employee thereof in the course of his employment. In no event, however, shall any such person, firm, or corporaion be liable for any damages for any defamatory statement or act published or uttered in or as a part of a visual or sound broadcast unless it shall be alleged and proved by the complaining party that such person, firm, or corporation has failed to exercise due care to prevent the publicity or utterance of such statement or act in such broadcast. Bona fide compliance with any federal law or the regulation of any federal regulatory agency shall be deemed to constitute such due care as hereinabove mentioned.

45-2-8. *Liability in case of joint operation.*—In any case where liability shall exist on account of any broadcast where two or more broadcasting or television stations were connected together simultaneously or by transcription, film, metal tape, or other approved or adapted use for joint operation, in the making of such broadcast, such liability shall be confined and limited solely to the person, firm, or corporation owning or operating the radio or television station which originated such broadcast.

45-2-10. *Privileged broadcasts.*—A privileged broadcast which shall not be considered as libelous, slanderous, or defamatory per se, is one made:

1. In the proper discharge of an official duty.

2. In any broadcast of or any statement made in any legislative or judicial proceeding, or in any other official proceeding authorized by law.

3. By a fair and true report, without malice of a judicial, legislative or other public official proceeding, or of anything said in the course thereof, or of a charge or complaint made by any person to a public official, upon which a warrant shall have been issued or an arrest made.

4. By a fair and true report, without malice, of the proceedings of a public meeting, if such meeting was lawfully convened, for a lawful purpose and open to the public or the broadcast of the matter complained of was for the public benefit.

Limitations. 78-12-29. *Within one year:*—

(4) An action for libel, slander, assault, battery, false imprisonment or seduction.

Vermont

THE PUBLIC LAWS OF VERMONT, 1957, 1958

Basic Statutes. Constitution of Vermont: Chapter I;

Article 13th. That the people have a right to freedom of speech, and of writing and publishing their sentiments, concerning the transactions of government, and therefore the freedom of the press ought not to be restrained.

Article 14th. The freedom of deliberation, speech, and debate, in the Legislature, is so essential to the rights of the people, that it cannot be the foundation of any accusation or prosecution, action or complaint, in any other court or place whatsoever.

Title 13 §6560. *Truth as defense in prosecution for libel.*—If a person is prosecuted by information or indictment for uttering and publishing a libel, or for defaming the civil authority of the state, he may, under a plea of not guilty, give in evidence to the jury the truth of the words contained in such supposed libel, as set forth in the information or indictment; and if he proves their truth to the satisfaction of the jury, it shall in its verdict find the respondent not guilty.

Limitations. Title 12 §512. Actions for the following causes shall be commenced within three years after the cause of action accrues, and not after: . . .

(3) Slander and libel.

Virginia

VIRGINIA CODE OF 1942, 1950, 1957 REPLACEMENT

Basic Statutes. Constitution of Virginia. Sec. 12.—*Freedom of the press and of speech.*—That the freedom of the press is one of the great bulwarks of liberty, and can never be restrained but by despotic governments; and any citizen may freely speak, write and publish his sentiments on all subjects, being responsible for the abuse of that right.

Sec. 8.632 *Evidence in mitigation in actions for libel or defamation.*—In any civil action against the publisher, owner, editor, reporter or employee of any newspaper, magazine or periodical under §8.630, or for libel or for defamation, because of any article, statement or other matter contained in any such newspaper, magazine or periodical, the defendant, whether punitive damages be sought or not, may introduce in evidence in mitigation of general and punitive damages, or either, but not of actual pecuniary damages, all the circumstances of the publication, including the source of the information, its character as affording reasonable ground of reliance, any prior publication elsewhere of similar purport, the lack of negligence or malice on the part of the defendant, the good faith of the defendant in such publication; and that apology or retraction, if any, was made with reasonable promptness and fairness; provided that the defendant may introduce in evidence only such circumstances and to the extent set forth in his or its grounds of defense.

Sec. 18.1-255. *Punishment for using abusive language to another.*—If any person shall, in the presence or hearing of another, curse or abuse such person, or use any violent abusive language to such person concerning himself or any of his female relations, under circumstances reasonably calculated to provoke a breach of peace, he shall be guilty of a misdemeanor, and on conviction fined in any sum not less than two dollars and fifty cents nor more than five hundred dollars, in the discretion of the jury or the justice trying the case without a jury.

Sec. 18.1-256. *Slander and libel.*—If any person shall falsely utter and speak, or falsely write and publish, of and concerning any female of chaste character, any words derogatory of said female's character for virtue and chastity, or imputing to said female acts not virtuous and chaste, he shall be deemed guilty of a misdemeanor, and on conviction shall be fined not less than twenty-five dollars, nor more than five hundred dollars, or imprisoned in jail not more than six months, or both such fine and imprisonment. And if any person shall falsely utter and speak, or falsely write and publish, of and concerning another person any words which from their usual construction and common acceptation are construed as insults and tend to violence and breach of peace or shall use grossly insulting language to any female of good character or reputation, he shall be deemed guilty of a misdemeanor, and on conviction, shall be fined not less than five dollars, nor more than one hundred dollars, or imprisoned in the county jail not exceeding sixty days, either or both.

The defendant shall be entitled to prove upon trial in mitigation of the punishment, the provocation which induced the libelous or slanderous words, or any other fact or circumstance tending to disprove malice, or lessen the criminality of the offense.

Sec. 8.630. *For insulting words.*—All words which, from their usual construction and common acceptation, are construed as insults and tend to violence and breach of the peace, shall be actionable.

Sec. 18.1-407 *False publications.*—Any person who knowingly and wilfully states, delivers, or transmits by any means whatever to any publisher, or employee of a publisher, of any newspaper, magazine, or other publication, any false and untrue statement concerning any person or corporation, with intent that the same shall be published, shall be guilty of a misdemeanor.

Sec. 6–132. *Making derogatory statements affecting bank.*—Any person who shall wilfully and maliciously make, circulate or transmit to another or others, any statement, rumor or suggestion, written, printed or by word of mouth, which is directly or by reference derogatory to the financial condition or affects the solvency or financial standing of any bank, savings bank, banking institution or trust company doing business in this State, or who shall counsel, aid, procure or induce another to start, transmit or circulate any such statement or rumor, shall be guilty of a misdemeanor, and upon conviction thereof, shall be sentenced to pay a fine of not more than one thousand dollars, or to be confined in jail not more than one year, or both.

Sec. 54-4. *Lawyers not liable in action for words in proceedings concerning conduct.*—No lawyer, or association, or corporation composed of lawyers, shall be held liable in any civil action for words, written or spoken in any proceeding concerning, or investigation of, the professional conduct of any member of the bar of Virginia before any bar association or committee thereof, unless it be proved by the plaintiff that such words were used with actual malice, were false, and were used without reasonable or probable cause.

Sec. 30-9. *Privilege of members for words spoken or written.*—No member or former member of the General Assembly shall be arrested or imprisoned for or on account of any words spoken or written, or any proceedings had in either house; but nothing herein contained shall in any respect restrict the power which each house of the General Assembly now has over its respective members.

§8-632.1. *Defamatory statements in radio broadcast.*—The owner, licensee or operator of a visual or sound radio broadcasting station, or network of stations, and the agents or employees of any such owner, licensee or operator, shall not be liable for any damages for any defamatory statement published or uttered in or as part of a visual or sound radio broadcast, by one other than such owner, licensee or operator, or agent or employee thereof, unless it shall be alleged and proved by the complaining party, that such owner, licensee, operator, such agent or employee, failed to exercise due care to prevent the publication or utterance of such statement in such broadcast; provided, however, that in no event shall any owner, licensee or operator, or the agents or employees of any such owner, licensee or operator of such a station or network of stations be held liable for damages for any defamatory statement broadcast over the facilities of such station or network by or on behalf of any candidate for public office. (1948, p. 56; Michie Suppl. 1948, §5796б).

Sec. 8-24. *Of actions not before specified.*—Every personal action, for which no limitation is otherwise prescribed, shall be brought within five years next after the right to bring the same shall have accrued, if it be for a matter of such nature that in case a party die it can be brought by or against his representative; and, if it be for a matter not of such nature, shall be brought within one year next after the right to bring the same shall have accrued.

Virgin Islands

VIRGIN ISLANDS CODE, 1957

§1171. *Libel defined.*—A malicious publication by writing, printing, picture, effigy, sign or otherwise than by mere speech, which exposes any living person or the memory of any deceased person to hatred, contempt, ridicule or obloquy, or which causes or tends to cause any person to be shunned or avoided, or which has a tendency to injure any person in his or their business or occupation, is a libel.

§1172. *Punishment for libel.*—Fined not more than $500 or imprisoned not more than 1 year, or both.

§1174. *Truth as a defense.*—In all criminal prosecutions for libel, the truth may be given in evidence, and if it appears to the court that the matter charged as libelous is true, and was published with good motives and for justifiable ends, the party shall be acquitted.

§31. *Time for commencement of various actions.*

Two years.

5. A. An action for libel, slander, assault, battery . . .

Washington

REVISED STATUTES OF WASHINGTON, 1935, 1952, 1961, 1962

Basic Statutes. Constitution of State of Washington. Art. I, Sec. 5. *Freedom of Speech.*—Every person may freely speak, write, and publish on all subjects, being responsible for the abuse of that right.

Art. II, Sec. 17. *Freedom of Debate.*—No member of the legislature shall be liable in any civil action or criminal prosecution whatever forwords spoken in debate.

Sec. 4.36.130. *Answer in justification and mitigation.*—In an action mentioned in RCW 4.36.120, the defendant may, in his answer, allege both the truth of the matter charged as defamatory, and any mitigating circumstances to reduce the amount of damages; and whether he prove the justification or not, he may give in evidence the mitigating circumstances.

19.64.010 *Liability of owner or operator.*—Where the owner, licensee, or operator of a radio or television broadcasting station, or the agents or employees thereof, has required a person speaking over said station to submit a written copy of his script prior to such broadcast and has cut such speaker off the air as soon as reasonably possible in the event such speaker deviates from such written script, said owner, licensee, or operator, or the agents or employees thereof, shall not be liable for any damages, for any defamatory statement published or uttered by such person in or as a part of such radio or television broadcast unless such defamatory statements are contained in said written script.

4-36-120. *Libel or slander, how pleaded.*—In an action for

libel or slander, it shall not be necessary to state in the complaint any intrinsic facts, for the purpose of showing the application to the plaintiff, of the defamatory matter out of which the cause arose, but it shall be sufficient to state generally, that the same was published or spoken concerning the plaintiff, and if such allegation be controverted, the plaintiff shall be bound to establish on trial, that it was so published or spoken.

Sec. 2372. *Criminal contempt.*—Every person who shall commit a contempt of court of any one of the following kinds shall be guilty of a misdemeanor:

Sec. 2373 (7).

(7) Publication of a false or grossly inaccurate report of its proceedings;

9.58.01. *Libel, what constitutes.*—Every malicious publication by writing, printing, picture, effigy, sign, radio broadcasting or which shall in any other manner transmit the human voice or reproduce the same from records or other appliances or means, which shall tend:—

(1) To expose any living person to hatred, contempt, ridicule or obloquy, or to deprive him of the benefit of public confidence or social intercourse; or

(2) To expose the memory of one deceased to hatred, contempt, ridicule or obloquy; or

(3) To injure any person, corporation or association of persons in his or their business or occupation, shall be libel. Every person who publishes libel shall be guilty of a gross misdemeanor.

9.58.020. *How justified or excused—Malice, when presumed.* —Every publication having the tendency or effect mentioned in RCW 9.58.010 shall be deemed malicious unless justified or excused. Such publication is justified whenever the matter charged as libelous charges the commission of a crime, is a true and fair statement, and was published with good motives and for justifiable ends. It is excused when honestly made in belief of its truth and fairness and upon reasonable grounds for such belief, and consists of fair comments upon the conduct of any person in respect of public affairs, made after a fair and impartial investigation.

Sec. 9.58.030 *Publication, defined.*—Any method by which matter charged as libelous may be communicated to another shall be deemed a publication thereof.

Sec. 9.58.040 *Liabilities of editors and others.*—Every editor or proprietor of a book, newspaper or serial, and every manager of a copartnership or corporation by which any book, newspaper or serial is issued, is chargeable with the publication of any matter contained in any such book, newspaper or serial, and every owner, operator, proprietor or person exercising control over any broadcasting station or reproducing records of human voice or who broadcasts over the radio or reproduces the human voice or aids or abets either directly or indirectly in such broadcast or reproduction shall be chargeable with the publication of any matter so disseminated: *Provided,* That in any prosecution or action for libel it shall be an absolute defense if the defendant shows that the matter complained of was published without his knowledge or fault and against his wishes by another who had no authority from him to make such publication and was promptly retracted by the defendant with an equal degree of publicity upon written request of the complainant.

Sec. 9.58.050 *Report of proceedings privileged.*—No prosecution for libel shall be maintained against a reporter, editor, proprietor, or publisher of a newspaper for the publication therein of a fair and true report of any judicial, legislative or other public and official proceeding, or of any statement, speech, argument or debate in the course of same, without proving actual malice in making the report. The editor or proprietor of a book, newspaper or serial shall be proceeded against in the county where such book, newspaper or serial is published.

Sec. 9.58.070 *Privileged communications.*—Every communication made to a person entitled to or concerned in such communication, by one also concerned in or entitled to make it, or who stood in such relation to the former as to offer a reasonable ground for supposing his motive to be innocent, shall be presumed not to be malicious, and shall be termed a privileged communication.

Sec. 9.58.080 *Furnishing libelous information.*—Every person who shall wilfully state, deliver or transmit by any means whatever, to any manager, editor, publisher, reporter or other employee of a publisher of any newspaper, magazine, publication, periodical or serial, any statement concerning any person or corporation, which, if published therein, would be a libel, shall be guilty of a misdemeanor.

Sec. 9.58.090 *Threatening to publish libel.*—Every person who shall threaten another with the publication of a libel concerning that latter, or his spouse, parent, child, or other member of his family, and every person who offers to prevent the publication of a libel upon another person upon condition of the payment of, or with intent to extort money or other valuable consideration from any person, shall be guilty of a gross misdemeanor.

Sec. 9.44.040 *Forgery—Second degree.*—Every person who, with intent to injure or defraud shall—

(1) Make any false entry in any public or private record or account; or

(2) Fail to make a true entry of any material matter in any public or private record or account; or

(3) Forge any letter or written communication or copy or purported copy thereof, or send or deliver, or connive at the sending or delivery of any false or fictitious telegraph message or copy or purported copy thereof, whereby or wherein the sentiments, opinions, conduct, character, purpose, property, interest or rights of any person shall be misrepresented or may be injuriously affected, or, knowing any such letter, communication or message or any copy or purported copy thereof to be false, shall utter or publish the same or any copy or purported copy thereof as true, shall be guilty of forgery in the second degree, and shall be punished by imprisonment in the state penitentiary for not more than five years, or by a fine of not more than five thousand dollars.

Sec. 9.33.010 *Extortion.*—Every person, who under circumstances not amounting to robbery, shall extort or gain any money, property or advantage, or shall induce or compel another to make, subscribe, execute, alter or destroy any valuable security or instrument or writing affecting or intended to affect any cause of action or defense, or any property, by means of force or any threat, either—

(3) To publish or connive at publishing any libel; or

Sec. 49.44.010 *"Blacklisting" prohibited—Penalty.*—Every person in this state who shall wilfully and maliciously, send or deliver, or make, or cause to be made, for the purpose of being delivered or sent, or part with the possession of any paper, letter or writing, with or without name signed thereto, or signed with a fictitious name, or with any letter, mark or other designation, or publish or cause to be published any statement for the purpose of preventing any other person from obtaining employment in this state or elsewhere, and every person who shall wilfully and maliciously "blacklist" or cause to be "blacklisted" any person or persons, by writing, printing or publishing, or causing the same to be done, the name, or mark, or designation representing the name of any person in any paper, pamphlet, circular or book, together with any statement concerning persons so named, or publish or cause to be published that any person is a member of any secret organization, for the purpose of preventing such person from securing employment, or who shall wilfully and maliciously make or issue any statement or paper that will tend to influence or prejudice the mind of any employer against the person of such person seeking employment, or any person who shall do any of the things mentioned in this section for the purpose of causing the discharge of any person employed by any railroad or other company, corporation, individual or individuals, shall, on conviction thereof, be adjudged guilty of misdemeanor and punished by a fine of not less than one hundred dollars nor more than one thousand dollars, or by imprisonment in the county jail for not less than ninety days nor more than one year, or by both such fine and imprisonment.

19.64.010. *Liability of owner or operator limited.*—When the owner, licensee, or operator of a radio or television broadcasting station, or the agents or employees thereof, has required a person speaking over said station to submit a written copy of his script prior to such broadcast and has cut such speaker off the air as soon as reasonably possible in the event such speaker deviates from such written script, said owner, licensee, or operator, or the agents or employees thereof, shall not be liable for any damages, for any defamatory statement published or uttered by such person in or as a part of such radio or television broadcast unless such defamatory statements are contained in said written script.

19.64.020. *Speaker or sponsor liability not limited.*—Nothing contained shall be construed as limiting the liability of any speaker or his sponsor or sponsors for defamatory statements made by such speaker in or as a part of any such broadcast.

Limitations. 4.16.100. Action limited to two years.

1. An action for libel, slander, assault, assault and battery, and false imprisonment;

West Virginia

WEST VIRGINIA CODE OF 1943, 1961

Basic Statutes. Constitution of West Virginia. Art. III, Sec. 7. No law abridging the freedom of speech, or of the press, shall be passed; but the Legislature may by suitable penalties, restrain the publication or sale of obscene books, paper, or pictures, and provide for the punishment of libel, and defamation of character, and for the recovery, in civil actions, by the aggrieved party, of suitable damages for such libel, or defamation.

Art. III, Sec. 8. In prosecutions and civil suits for libel, the truth may be given in evidence; and if it shall appear to the jury, that the matter charged as libelous, is true, and was published with good motives, and for justifiable ends, the verdict shall be for the defendant.

Sec. 5725 (4). *Evidence in Mitigation of Damages in Actions for Defamation; Truth a Justification.*—In any action for defamation, the defendant may justify by alleging and proving that the words spoken or written were true, and after notice in writing of his intention to do so (given to the plaintiff at the time of, or for, pleading to such action) may give in evidence in mitigation of damages that he made or offered an apology to the plaintiff for such defamation before the commencement of the action, or as soon afterwards as he had an opportunity of doing so, in case action shall have been commenced before there was an opportunity of making or offering such apology.

Sec. 5471 (2). *Insulting Words.*—All words which, from their usual construction and common acceptation, are construed as insults and tend to violence and breach of the peace, shall be actionable. No demurrer shall preclude a jury from passing thereon.

Sec. 3164(32). *Wilfully Making, Circulating, etc., False Statement as to Financial Condition of Association.*—Whoever directly or indirectly, wilfully and knowingly, makes or transmits to another or circulates or counsels, aids, procures, or induces another to make, transmit, or circulate any false or untrue statement, rumor, or suggestion derogatory to the financial condition, solvency, or financial standing of any building and loan association, including any foreign building and loan association, doing business in this State, or with intent to depress the value of the shares, bonds or securities of any such association, directly or indirectly, wilfully and knowingly, makes or transmits to another, circulates or counsels, aids, procures, or induces another to make, transmit, or circulate any false or untrue statement, rumor, or suggestion derogatory to the financial standing or condition or with respect to the earnings or management of the business of any building and loan association, or resorts to any fraudulent means with intent to depress in value the shares, bonds, or securities of any building and loan association, shall be guilty of a misdemeanor, and upon conviction thereof, each offender shall be fined not more than one thousand dollars or imprisoned for not more than one year, or in the discretion of the court be both fined and imprisoned.

5482(1). *Liability of visual or sound broadcasting stations in libel cases.*—The owner, licensee or operator of a visual or sound radio broadcasting station or network of stations, and the agents or employees of any such owner, licensee or operator, shall not be liable for any damages for any defamatory statement published or uttered in or as part of a visual or sound radio broadcast, by one other than such owner, licensee or operator, or the agent or employee thereof, unless it shall be alleged and proved by the complaining party that such owner, licensee, operator or such agent or employee, has failed to exercise due care to prevent the publication or utterance of any such statement in such broadcast.

In no event, however, shall any owner, licensee or operator for the agents or employees of any such owner, licensee or operator of such a station or network of stations be held liable for any damages for any defamatory statement uttered over the facilities of such station or network by any legally qualified candidate for public office.

Limitations. *Libel and Slander.* §5404. (One Year.)

Wisconsin

WISCONSIN STATUTES, 1943, 1957

Basic Statutes. Wisconsin Constitution. Art. 1, s. 3. *Free Speech; Libel.*—Every person may freely speak, write and publish his sentiments on all subjects, being responsible for the abuse of that right, and no laws shall be passed to restrain or abridge the liberty of speech or of the press. In all criminal prosecutions or indictments for libel, the truth may be given in evidence, and if it shall appear to the jury that the matter charged as libelous be true, and was published with good motives and for justifiable ends, the party shall be acquitted; and the jury shall have the right to determine the law and the fact.

263.37. *Libel and slander, how pleaded.*—In an action for libel or slander it shall not be necessary to state in the complaint any extrinsic facts for the purpose of showing the application to the plaintiff of the defamatory matter out of which the cause of action arose: but it shall be sufficient to state generally that the same was published or spoken concerning the plaintiff, and if such allegation be controverted the plaintiff shall be bound to establish on the trial that it was so published or spoken.

263.38. *Answer in libel and slander.*—In an action for libel or slander the defendant may in his answer allege both the truth of the matter charged as defamatory and any mitigating circumstances to reduce the amount of damages; and whether he prove the justification or not he may give in evidence the mitigating circumstances. (1935 c. 541 s. 39.)

348.41. *Criminal libel and slander.*—

(1) Any person guilty of libel shall be punished by imprison-

ment in the county jail not more than one year or by fine not exceeding two hundred and fifty dollars.

(2) Every person who, in the presence and hearing of another, other than the person slandered whether he be present or not, shall maliciously speak of or concerning any person, any false or defamatory words or language which shall injure or impair the reputation of such person for virtue or chastity or which shall expose him to hatred, contempt, or ridicule shall be guilty of a misdemeanor for which said person shall be punished as heretofore provided in subsection (1). Every slander herein mentioned shall be deemed malicious if no justification therefor be shown and shall be justified when the language charged as slanderous, false, or defamatory was true and was spoken with good motives and for justifiable ends.

(3) No conviction shall be had under the provisions of subsection (2) upon the testimony of the person slandered unsupported by other evidence, but must be proved by the evidence of at least two persons other than such person who heard and understood the language charged as slanderous or by admission of the defendant.

348.411. *Slandering commercial or financial standing.*—Any person who shall wilfully and maliciously make, circulate or transmit to another or others, any false statement, rumor or suggestion, written, printed or by word of mouth, which is directly or by inference derogatory to the financial condition or affects the solvency or financial standing of any bank, savings bank, banking institution, building and loan association or trust company doing business in this state, or co-operative association organized under chapter 185, or any domestic mutual insurance company, including town mutuals, lawfully entitled to transact in this state the business of writing fire or casualty or workmen's compensation insurance, or who shall counsel, aid, procure or induce another to start, transmit or circulate any such statement or rumor, shall be punished by a fine of not more than $1,000 or by imprisonment for a term of not more than one year, or both. (1931 c. 18, 459; 1943 c. 553 s. 40.)

347.16. *Liability of editors and others.*—Every editor or proprietor of a book, newspaper or serial and every manager of a partnership or incorporated association by which a book, newspaper, or serial is issued, is chargeable with the publication of any matter contained in such book, newspaper, or serial. But in every prosecution therefor, the defendant may show in his defense that the matter complained of was published without his knowledge or fault and against his wishes, by another who had no authority from him to make the publication and whose act was disavowed by him as soon as known.

331.052. *Defamation by radio and television.*—The owner, licensee or operator of a visual or sound radio broadcasting station or network of stations, and the agents or employees of any such owner, licensee or operator, shall not be liable for damages for any defamatory statement published or uttered in, or as part of, a visual or sound broadcast by a candidate for political office in those instances in which, under the acts of Congress or the rules and regulations of the Federal Communications Commission, the broadcasting station or network is prohibited from censoring the script of the broadcast.

331.05. *Damages in actions for libel.*—

(1) The proprietor, publisher, editor, writer or reporter upon any newspaper published in this state shall not be liable in any civil action for libel for the publication in such newspaper of a true and fair report of any judicial, legislative or other public official proceeding authorized by law or of any public statement, speech, argument or debate in the course of such proceeding. This section shall not be construed to exempt any such proprietor, publisher, editor, writer or reporter from liability for any libelous matter contained in any headline or headings to any such report, or to libelous remarks or comments added or interpolated in any such report or made and published concerning the same, which remarks or comments were not uttered by the person libeled or spoken concerning him in the course of such proceeding by some other person.

(2) Before any civil action shall be commenced on account of any libelous publication in any newspaper, magazine or

periodical, the libeled person shall first give those alleged to be responsible or liable for the publication a reasonable opportunity to correct the libelous matter. . . . To the extent that the true facts are, with reasonable diligence, ascertainable with definiteness and certainty, only a retraction shall constitute a correction; . . . A correction, timely published, without comment in a position and type as prominent as the alleged libel, shall constitute a defense against the recovery of any damages except actual damages, as well as being competent and material in mitigation of actual damages to the extent the correction published does so mitigate them.

328.33. *Proof of malice in slander and libel.*—If the defendant in any action for slander or libel shall set up in his answer that the words spoken or published were true, such answer shall not be proof of the malice alleged in the complaint.

206.51. *False pretenses, libel.*—

(1) No life insurance company, and no officer or agent thereof, shall issue or circulate, or permit to be issued or circulated, any estimate, illustration, circular or statement misrepresenting the terms of any policy issued by it, or advantages promised thereby, or the dividends or share of surplus to be received thereon, or shall use any title of any policy or class of policies, misrepresenting the true nature thereof; or shall issue or circulate or permit to be issued or circulated, any statement, wilfully misrepresenting any other company, the nature or terms of its policies, its premium charge or dividends allowed or returned by such other company.

(2) No figures used in any statement or illustration of future dividends or of future net cost shall be issued or used by any company or agent, unless the same shall be a mathematical calculation based upon assumptions of the policy and dividend scale in actual use, nor unless each edition thereof shall be numbered serially and a copy thereof has been filed with the commissioner.

(4) This section shall apply to mutual benefit societies.

(5) Any officer or agent or deputy violating any of the pro-

visions of this section shall be fined not less than twenty-five dollars nor more than three hundred dollars, or be imprisoned not exceeding six months.

Limitations. 330.21. *Within two years:—*

(2) An action to recover damages for libel, slander, assault, battery or false imprisonment.

Wyoming

WYOMING REVISED STATUTES, 1931
WYOMING SUPPLEMENT, 1940
WYOMING STATUTES, 1957

Basic Statutes. Constitution of Wyoming, Art. I, Sec. 20. *Freedom of speech and press; libel; truth as a defense—Libel.*— Every person may freely speak, write and publish on all subjects, being responsible for the abuse of that right; and in all trials for libel, both civil and criminal, the truth, when published with good intent and for justifiable ends, shall be sufficient defense, the jury having the right to determine the facts and the law, under direction of the court.

89-412. *Libel, slander, assault, breach of promise, etc.—Statutory penalties.*—Within one year an action for libel, slander, assault, battery, malicious prosecution, breach of promise of marriage, or false imprisonment; an action upon a statute for a penalty or forfeiture; but where a different limitation is prescribed in the statute, by which the remedy is given, the action shall be brought within the period so limited.

§6-117. *Libel.*—Whoever makes, composes, dictates, prints or writes a libel to be published; or procures the same to be done; and whoever publishes or knowingly aids in publishing or communicating a libel, is guilty of libel, and shall be fined not more than one thousand dollars, to which may be added imprisonment in the county jail for not more than three months.

§7-147. *Justification of libel.*—In all prosecutions for libel the truth, when published with good intent and for justifiable ends, shall be sufficient defense, the jury having the right to determine the facts under the direction of the court.

§1-29. 7. *Abatement of actions by death.*—Except as otherwise provided, no action or proceeding pending in any court shall abate by the death of either or both of the parties thereto except an action for libel, slander, malicious prosecution, assault, or assault and battery, for a nuisance or against a justice of the peace for misconduct in office, which shall abate by the death of either party.

§1-2210. *When plaintiff shall not recover costs.*—When the judgment is less than one hundred dollars, unless the recovery be reduced below that sum by counter-claim or set-off, each party shall pay his own costs; and in all actions for libel, slander, malicious prosecution, assault and battery, false imprisonment, criminal conversation or seduction, action for nuisance, or against a justice of the peace for misconduct in office, when the damages assessed is under five dollars, the plaintiff shall not recover costs.

§1-872. *Radio and television stations—Liability of owner, agent, etc. generally.*—The owner, licensee, or operator of a visual or sound radio broadcasting station or network of stations, and the agents or employees of any such owner, licensee or operator, shall not be liable for any damages for any defamatory statement published or uttered in or as a part of a visual or sound radio broadcast, by one other than such owner, licensee or operator, or agent or employee thereof, unless it shall be alleged and proved by the complaining party, that such owner, licensee, operator, such agent or employee, has failed to exercise due care to prevent the publication of such statement in such broadcast. (Laws, 1947, ch. 37, §1)

§1-873. Same—*Liability for statements made by political candidates.*—In no event, however, shall any owner, licensee or operator, or the agents or employees of any such owner, licensee or operator of such a station or network of stations be held liable for any damages for any defamatory statement uttered over the facilities of such station or network by any candidate for public office. (Laws 1947, Ch. 37, §2)

Limitations. §1-19. *Libel and Slander.* (One Year.)

CASES

A. *Libel Against a Candidate for Public Office.*—Knapp *vs.* Post Co. (Colorado. 111 Colo. 492. No. 15,070. October 11, 1943).

This case well illustrates the principle that a candidate for public office must expose himself to far more criticism than one not running for public office, and that such criticism enjoys wide latitude. The Colorado court held that to say of any candidate that he "is not qualified for the public office to which he aspires, is not actionable per se. . . . One who is a candidate for an office at the hands of the people invites consideration of his qualifications, and tenders, as an issue to be tried out publicly before the people, his honesty, integrity and fitness for the office to be filled."

No. 15,070.

KNAPP *vs.* POST PRINTING AND PUBLISHING COMPANY, ET AL.

(144 P. [2d] 981)

Decided October 11, 1943. Rehearing denied January 10, 1944.

A suit for damages for libel. Judgment of dismissal.

Affirmed.

Error to the District Court of the City and County of Denver, Hon. Robert W. Steele, Judge.

Mr. GEORGE J. KNAPP, pro se.

Messrs. SMITH, BROCK, AKOLT & CAMPBELL, Mr. J. H. SHEPHERD, for defendants in error.

En Banc.

Mr. Justice Goudy delivered the opinion of the court.

This proceeding is here on writ of error for review of a judgment of the district court of the City and County of Denver dismissing the complaint of plaintiff in error, to whom we hereinafter refer as plaintiff.

December 6, 1940, plaintiff filed his complaint, pro se, against defendants in error, defendants below, hereinafter designated as defendants, for damages in a large amount arising out of their alleged libelous publication of certain statements regarding him in an issue of the Denver Post of September 9, 1940, plaintiff at that time being a candidate for nomination for governor of Colorado at the primary election to be held September 10, 1940.

After motions of defendants to strike and to make the complaint more specific, definite and certain, had been granted in part and denied in part, plaintiff filed a bill of particulars. Thereafter defendants filed their demurrer, based upon the grounds, inter alia, that the complaint did not contain or set forth facts sufficient to constitute a cause of action against them, or any of them; that the words alleged to be libelous were published on a privileged occasion; that the alleged libelous language is expressive only of the opinions of the defendants, and cannot be made the basis of a libel suit by innuendo or otherwise; that the alleged libelous publication is not actionable per se, and will not permit of the recovery of general damages in any event, and no element of special damage is alleged in the complaint; that the words alleged to be libelous must be interpreted according to their natural, ordinary and commonly-accepted meaning, and, so interpreted, they are harmless and impute no defamation of plaintiff, and such meaning cannot be changed by innuendo.

March 17, 1941, the trial court entered an order sustaining the demurrer, and it was further ordered that "leave to amend the complaint will not be granted." Judgment of dismissal followed in due course.

Our Code of Civil Procedure was still in effect March 17, 1941, and section 79 thereof provided, inter alia: "After the demurrer and before the trial of the issue of law therein, the pleadings demurred to may be amended as of course, and without costs, by filing the same as amended, and serving a copy thereof on the adverse party, or his attorney, within ten days, * * *." Construing this section, we stated in *Barnard vs. Moore,* 71 Colo. 401, 207 Pac. 332: "We are of the opinion that under the Code, §§79 and 81, the plaintiff, after demurrer sustained, had a right to amend without leave." In the instant case plaintiff waived his right to amend as of course by failing to file an amendment, and serve a copy thereof on the adverse party. *McDonald vs. Hallicy,* 1 Colo. App. 303, 29 Pac. 24.

The published article of which complaint is made is:

"Be sure to vote Tuesday—here are marked ballots to help you.

"These marked ballots are published for the convenience of the voters in Tuesday's primary election. Cut out the ballot of your party and take it to the polls with you. It will help you in eliminating the worst * * * and in selecting the best candidates. In publishing these marked ballots The Denver Post is not trying to tell anybody how to vote. It is merely passing on to the voters the results of its investigation of the merits of the various candidates. Few voters know personally all the candidates. Few have an opportunity to check up for themselves on all the candidates. As a public service, the Post has investigated carefully the candidates on both Democratic and Republican tickets. For the convenience of the voting public, The Post's conclusions are presented in the form of these marked ballots:

"For Governor (Vote for one)		"Mark in this Column
George E. Saunders John A. Carroll	Both Qualified	

George J. Knapp—Not Qualified"

Plaintiff was the only candidate for nomination on either the Democratic or Republican tickets who was designated by the publication as not qualified, but other choices were shown by marking a cross after the preferred candidates.

Plaintiff complains of the orders of the district court on defendants' motion to strike and motion to make more definite and certain, but a review of the complaint and these motions and orders does not convince us that plaintiff was prejudiced by the rulings of the trial judge, nor that this complaint is weakened in the slightest degree thereby. It is unnecessary, however, to give any further consideration to assignments of error thereon, as the judgment is being affirmed on other grounds, and it would make no difference in this opinion had the complaint appeared here in its original form.

A definition of libel which has received general acceptance and approbation is to be found in 33 American Jurisprudence, page 38, section 3. It reads: "A libel is a malicious publication, expressed either in printing or writing, or by signs and pictures, tending either to blacken the memory of one who is dead, or the reputation of one who is alive, and expose him to public hatred, contempt, or ridicule." See, also, 36 C.J., p. 1143, §3. Criminal libel in Colorado is defined in section 199, chapter 48, '35 C.S.A., in almost identical words, as follows: "A libel is a malicious defamation expressed either by printing, or by signs, or pictures or the like, tending to blacken the memory of one who is dead, or to impeach the honesty, integrity, virtue or reputation, or publish the natural defects of one who is alive, and thereby to expose him or her to public hatred, contempt or ridicule."

"Words may be actionable per se, that is, in themselves, or they may be actionable per quod, that is, only on allegation and proof of special damage." 33 Am. Jur., p. 39, §5. It is difficult to ascertain from plaintiff's brief what his position is. In some places he contends that the words are libelous per se, in others that they are libelous per quod. In his complaint he has attempted to allege innuendos which are unnecessary, if the words are libelous per se. "Words which are libelous per se do not need an innuendo, and, conversely, words which need an innuendo are not libelous per se." 33 Am. Jur., p. 40, §5.

In *Rocky Mountain News Printing Co. vs. Fridborn,* 46 Colo. 440, 104 Pac. 956, we said:

"Every false article is not an actionable libel, just as every untruth is not a lie. To be an actionable libel the elements to make it such must be present in the article itself, or fairly implied therefrom and the circumstances surrounding its publication. So if the elements that constitute libel are clearly expressed in the article, it is actionable per se, and becomes conclusive upon the publisher, unless, under the circumstances, the words used were fairly capable of being understood in a special sense, rendering them not defamatory, and that they were so understood.

"The intent of the publisher and the effect of the publication, must be gathered from the words and circumstances under which they were uttered, and the publisher is, prima facie, presumed to have used them in the sense which their use is calculated to convey to the minds of the readers of the publication. When so construed the words may be defamatory on their face, in which case the action may be maintained, unless the defendant can, and does, allege and prove, that, under the circumstances, they were fairly capable of being understood in a special sense, rendering them not defamatory, and that they were so understood. Or they may not be defamatory on their face, in which case the action cannot be maintained, unless the plaintiff can, and does, show that they were, under the particular circumstances, fairly capable of a special meaning rendering them defamatory and that they were so understood.

"We find in vol. 2, Current Law, p. 707, note, the law applicable to this case stated as follows:

" 'If the words, when construed according to their natural and ordinary meaning, are defamatory on their face, which, as we have seen, is a question of law for the court, the action may be maintained unless the defendant, and the burden is on him, can and does show that they were capable of a special meaning rendering them not defamatory, and that they were so understood. *Peake vs. Oldham,* Cowp. 275; Bigelow's Cas. 122; Bigelow's Lead. Cas. 73'."

In *Morley vs. Post Printing and Publishing Co.,* 84 Colo. 41, 268 Pac. 540, our court said: "To constitute libel, it is not necessary that a publication shall impute to a person the commission of a crime; it is sufficient if it tends to impeach his honesty, integrity, virtue or reputation. In *Republican Pub. Co. vs. Mosman,* 15 Colo. 399, 24 Pac. 1051, we held that any false and malicious writing published of another is libelous per se when its tendency is to render him contemptible or ridiculous in public estimation, or to expose him to public hatred or contempt, or to hinder virtuous men from associating with him. It is not necessary that the publication shall produce those results; it is sufficient if it has a tendency to produce any one of them. A newspaper publication must be measured by its natural and probable effect upon the mind of the average lay reader. *Dusabek vs. Martz,* 121 Okl. 241, 249 Pac. 145, 49 A.L.R. 253. 'In determining whether words are libelous, they are to be given their ordinary and popular meaning; and if they are susceptible of two meanings, one libelous and the other innocent, the former is not to be adopted and the latter rejected as a matter of course, but it must be left to the jury to determine in what sense they are used.' *Black vs. State Co.,* 93 S.C. 467, 77 S.E. 51, Ann. Cas. 1914 C, 989. 'It is generally held to be the function of the court to determine, as a question of law, whether a published statement is libelous per se, and if the words are unambiguous and admit of but one sense, the question whether they are defamatory is one which the court must decide, * * *'."

Testing the publication in question by the above definitions, we have no hesitation in pronouncing it not libelous per se. The words are not defamatory on their face, and cannot have the special meaning which plaintiff attempts to ascribe to them.

As the complaint contains no allegation of special damages, it is insufficient to state a cause of action on the words as libelous per quod. But it contains many innuendoes, and in fact, would have little value as a complaint if the innuendoes were stricken; so that plaintiff apparently cannot be alleging the words as libelous per se. Yet his brief so contends, and he has cited a large number of authorities thereon which he contends are pertinent. It seems to us that the only question for determination here is the one resolved by the trial judge—that is, that the words "worst" and "not qualified," as applied to plaintiff, and considered in the light of the entire publication, were not libelous per se.

Considering the complaint in the light of the alleged facts set forth by way of innuendo, we do not find the words "worst," and "not qualified," fairly capable of the meaning which plaintiff ascribes to them, or of any meaning which is defamatory. In construing words alleged to be libelous we cannot travel into the realm of conjecture, but must confine ourselves to the natural, ordinary and commonly-accepted meaning of the words themselves, considered in connection with the other facts alleged in the complaint. The expression of the opinion of representatives of the Post, that plaintiff is not qualified for the public office to which he aspires, is not actionable per se. The word "worst" is a relative term, and did not refer to the plaintiff alone; but even if it did, it would not carry the meanings which plaintiff by his allegations attempts to ascribe to it.

Webster's New International Dictionary (2d ed.) defines "qualified" as, "Possessed of certain qualities or capacities, especially good qualities; fitted by accomplishments or endowments for certain purposes; competent; fit." Also, "Having complied with the specific requirements or precedent conditions for an office, appointment, employment, etc." The synonyms are: fitted, capable; the antonyms are: incompetent, unfit.

A newspaper may state of a candidate for public office that he has no qualifications for the place, and this statement contains no possible reflection upon the plaintiff's personal or professional character, but, being confined to a criticism of his fitness for the place sought, is clearly permissible. *Walsh vs. Pulitzer Publishing Co.,* 250 Mo. 142, 157 S.W. 326.

One who is a candidate for an office at the hands of the people invites consideration of his qualifications, and tenders, as an issue to be tried out publicly before the people, his honesty, integrity and fitness for the office to be filled. *Coleman vs. MacLennan,* 78 Kan. 711, 98 Pac. 281, 130 A.S.R. 390; *Schull vs.*

Hopkins, 26 S.D. 21, 127 N.W. 550, 29 L.R.A. (N.S.) 691; 17 R.C.L., p. 353, §101.

Liberty of the press must remain an undefined term, and while certain boundaries within which it must be exercised are discernible, precise rules to govern it on particular occasions cannot be formulated in advance. It implies a right to freely publish whatever the citizen may please, and to be protected against responsibility therefor, unless such publication is a public offense because of blasphemy, obscenity or scandalous character, or, because of falsehood and malice, it injuriously affects the standing, reputation or pecuniary interests of individuals. Cooley, Const. Lim. (7th ed.) 603, 604; *Coleman vs. MacLennan, supra.*

It is one of the hazards which a candidate for public favor must face that he is exposed to critical, and perhaps unjust, comments, but these, unless they transcend the bounds of what the law permits, must be borne for the sake of maintaining a free press. Where actions for libel based upon such criticism have been sustained, the words used have been adjudged to contain a charge of positive misconduct. *Sillers vs. Collier,* 151 Mass. 50, 23 N.E. 723, 6 L.R.A. 680. There is authority which places candidates for public office in the same situation as other private individuals and denies the application of any doctrine of privilege in publishing matters concerning such candidates. 17 R.C.L., p. 354, §101. We do not believe that such a rule is compatible with a free press.

Finding no error which justifies reversal, the judgment is affirmed.

B. *Libel Against an Incumbent Public Official.*—Williams *vs.* Standard-Examiner Pub. Co. *et al.* (83 Utah 31. No. 5106. November 28, 1933).

This case involves a commissioner of a waterworks department who sued a newspaper that made grave charges against him pertaining to his responsibility for the spread of typhoid fever. The Supreme Court of Utah made light of the serious charges: "A public officer who is guilty of dereliction of a duty which may, and there is probable cause to believe does, result in the loss of human life, may not be heard to complain merely because plain and severe language is used to condemn his failure to perform his duty." The courts in all the states are jealous of the rights of the press to criticize public officials. This Utah case examines nearly all the relevant problems involved.

WILLIAMS *vs.* STANDARD-EXAMINER PUB. CO. *et al.*

No. 5106. Decided November 28, 1933. [27 P. (2d) 1.]

Appeal from District Court, Second District, Weber County; *Geo. S. Barker,* Judge.

Action by Fred E. Williams against Standard-Examiner Publishing Company and others. From an adverse judgment, named defendant appeals.

REVERSED AND REMANDED, WITH DIRECTION.

George C. Buckle, of Ogden, for appellant.

Stuart P. Dobbs, of Ogden, for respondent.

ELIAS HANSEN, J.

This action was brought by the plaintiff to recover from the defendants damages because of the alleged false and defamatory publication on July 14, 1929, of an article in a newspaper, known as the Standard-Examiner, owned by the defendant Standard-Examiner Publishing Company, a corporation. The trial resulted in the plaintiff securing a verdict and judgment against the defendant corporation for the sum of $3,000. A verdict of no cause of action was returned by the jury as to the defendants Abraham L. Glasmann, Joseph U. Eldredge, Jr., and James P. Casey. The defendant corporation appeals. Its assignments of error attack the judgment appealed from upon the following grounds: That the evidence does not support the verdict and judgment; that the trial court erred in the reception and rejection of evidence; in the instructions given to the jury; in refusing to give certain of appellant's requested instructions; and that the court erred in refusing to grant appellant a new trial. The insufficiency of the evidence to support a verdict for the plaintiff was raised in the court below by a motion for a nonsuit at the conclusion of plaintiff's evidence in chief and by a motion for a directed verdict for the defendants and each of them at the conclusion of all of the evidence. The motions were based upon defendants' claim that the publication complained of was shown by the evidence to be a qualifiedly or conditionally privileged communication and as such required proof of actual malice on the part of the defendants and that no such proof was offered, and upon the further ground that the evidence showed that the facts stated in the publication were true, and that the comments and criticisms appearing in the publication were fair and proper. Both motions were denied. Appellant assigns such rulings as error.

In the main the pleadings of the parties and the evidence given in support thereof agree upon the facts which occasioned the publication concerning which plaintiff complains. The following facts are either alleged and admitted in the pleadings or established by uncontradicted evidence: The defendant Standard-Examiner Publishing Company is a Utah corporation. For many years past it has printed and published a daily newspaper at Ogden, Utah. The paper, known as the Ogden Standard-Examiner, had an extensive circulation in Ogden City and Weber county, Utah. A few papers were sent to other parts of the state and neighboring states. The defendants Joseph U. Eldredge, Jr., James P. Casey, and Abraham L. Glasmann were, at the time mentioned in the complaint and at the time of the trial, the general manager, the associate general manager, and the editor, respectively, of the defendant corporation. During the years 1928 and 1929 plaintiff was one of the duly elected, qualified, and acting members of the board of commissioners of Ogden City, Utah. Soon after he qualified as a city commissioner he was assigned to the duty of supervising the waterworks department of the city. He continued in charge of that department up to the time of the trial of this action. Ogden City secured its water supply for domestic, culinary, and other purposes from forty-two artesian wells and three small streams located in the Ogden river watershed. The streams were known as Wheeler creek, Warm Water spring, and Cold Water creek. The artesian well water was conveyed from the wells by means of a pipe line into two distributing reservoirs. Wheeler creek, after flowing approximately two miles in an open stream, was (when the water supply from other sources was insufficient to supply the needs of the city) diverted into the pipe line which connected with the pipe line which conveyed the water from the artesian wells. The Wheeler creek water was thus commingled with the water from the artesian wells. A distributing system of pipes carried the water from the distributing reservoirs to the inhabitants of Ogden City. The Wheeler creek water had, for a number of years prior to 1928, been used to supplement the water secured from the artesian wells, Warm Water spring, and Cold Water creek whenever the water from those sources was insufficient to supply the needs of the city. During the summer of 1928 the Utah state board of health made an investigation and report of the Ogden City water supply. The report so made reads as follows:

"The supply is derived from forty-three wells and from three small creeks located on the Ogden River watershed, and is delivered by two distributing reservoirs to the city distribution system.

"Wells: The wells are located near where the Forks of the Ogden River converge in a natural gravel basin. The average flow from the wells is 9,500,000 gallons per day, which may be increased to 16,000,000 gallons per day. However, there is no meter or measuring device to determine the amount of water supplied by the wells. The State Water Engineer has measured the flow from time to time but other than his measurements the city has no way of knowing accurately how much water is supplied by the wells. The average depth of the wells is approximately 140 ft., some being as shallow as 90 ft. At the time of the investigation eight wells were being operated by the use of air pressure. Twenty-two of the wells are connected to air pumps. The water from the wells passes through three miles of 36 in. wood stave pipe to a collection box near the mouth of Wheeler Canyon. The water from Wheeler Canyon enters the box and together it is conveyed through two lines, a 34 in. wood stave pipe and a 24 in. Kalemein pipe down the canyon, a distance of five miles, passing over the hill through a steel pipe and to the distributing reservoirs through a 35 in. wood stave pipe.

"Wheeler Creek: The Wheeler Canyon intake is located approximately one-fourth mile above the Pine View Lodge and Summer Resort. The flow is diverted by a concrete dam into two 8 in. wood stave pipes, which converge in a collection box below resort and the remaining distance of 1,500 ft. to the point where Wheeler's Canyon supply enters the well supply is a 12 in. kalamein pipe. The water from the springs in Wheeler Canyon flows in an open stream for possibly two miles before it is diverted into the pipe line.

"The water shed above the intake is subject to serious potential contamination from day camping and picnicking parties. A sign near diversion dam warns people not to contaminate their culinary supply, but no signs were posted along the stream above the intake. A beaten trail leads up this canyon, which is often used by hiking parties. Cantaloupe rinds and empty cans caught on the grating of the intake were mute evidence of human contamination. Some cattle also graze on the upper watershed, which adds another source of pollution to the canyon supply.

"There are no means provided for accurately measuring this supply, but it is approximately 4 second ft., or roughly 2,500,000 gallons per day.

"Cold Water Creek: The water is diverted from the creek by a concrete dam, one-fourth mile from Ogden Canyon Highway, into a wood stave pipe line and enters the main supply line at the roadway. This canyon is a favorite haunt for picnics. The amount of water obtained from this supply is approximately 648,000 gallons per day.

"Warm Water Spring: The Warm Water Spring is about one-half mile below Cold Water Spring intake. Very little water is obtained from this source, estimated at ¼ second ft., or approximately 162,000 gallons per day.

"Contamination: During the summer months when the volume of available water from the streams is reduced, the number of visitors to the canyons is great, a goodly number of these are flagrantly careless from a sanitary standpoint, as proved by indications of contamination found near the streams. The danger of chance pollution by visitors on the drainage area is great. In this day few spots are so remote as not to attract the attention of visitors, many of whom dispose of their waste regardless of consequences.

"It is impractical to attempt to sanitate water sheds by adequately policing them. Wastes washed into stream water supplies during fall rains may lead to disastrous results in Ogden City. Drinking water from a surface source should be subjected to adequate storage and treatment.

"The bacteriological analyses from the Ogden supply during the summer months substantiate the sanitary survey findings of the pollution of the city water supply. The finding of the Bacillus Coli, an inhabitant of the intestinal tract, in a water is a certain indication of contamination with animal or human excreta. Since there are typhoid carriers at large, and also people convalescing from the disease, but still harboring the bacilli, the possibility of contaminating the water with typhoid organisms is very great.

"When there is reasonable possibility of a disease outbreak due to a polluted water supply it behooves the responsible city authorities to take all necessary measures to protect the people.

"Consumption: There are no records of consumption. The maximum consumption is 15,100,548 gallons per day, and the minimum, 7,724,781 gallons per day. The estimated consumption per capita is 350 gallons per day, which exceeds any reasonable requirements. At the present time the city is divided into districts, each of which is allowed to use water for sprinkling purposes for two hours in the morning and two hours in the evening. Only about 8% of the city is metered, including the commercial and industrial districts. Large quantities of water are evidently wasted by a defective distribution system. A pitometer survey made in 1924 showed that 587,000 gallons per day were wasted on account of defective plumbing, and 2,500,000 gallons per day wasted on account of neglectful use and defective lines.

"Storage Capacity: Two rectangular reservoirs lined with concrete containing 21,500,000 gallons of water furnish the only storage supply. The reservoirs are supplied by individual branches and supply the distribution system through two 20 in. lines. Either of the reservoirs may be by-passed. Recently the city has had some difficulty with Sea Gulls lighting upon the water during the molting season and contaminating it.

"The water passes over a sharp crested weir, with no end contractions as it enters the reservoirs. A recorder determines the amount of water passing over the weir. At the time of the investigation there was .97 ft., or 19.086 cu. ft. per second, or 12,335,604 gallons per twenty-four hours. The weir is so located and arranged that when the reservoir fills up the water backs up into weir house, giving a false and inaccurate reading on the automatic registering device. This occurred on the night of July 12th. There is no venturi meter or other device to record consumption on outlet from the reservoirs.

"Dead Ends: Gridironing is quite complete in the closely built up sections of the city, but in outlying districts dead ends are numerous. Approximately 10% of the total amount of pipe is in dead ends. Complaints were made that whenever the pressure is low those living on dead ends receive turbid water from sediment which had collected in the dead end lines.

"Distribution System: Much of the distribution system is in poor condition. As many as two leaks a day occur in some parts of the city. The old Matheson Steel Joint Pipe has been repaired, but much of it should be replaced with a more permanent and durable pipe line. The feeders to the distribution system are inadequate. The main arteries are well arranged and of good size, but additional supply mains and secondary feeders are needed to give adequate pressure in some parts of the city. There is too much 2 in. pipe in the system, especially is this true in certain sections of the city. The dead ends could be eliminated by inexpensive extensions and the quality of the water would be greatly improved.

"Recommendations: The establishment of a good waterworks system which is self-supporting is the first step in civic progress, and demands the attention of the city officials.

"The most satisfactory and fair way of adjusting water rates is by a meter system. It has been proved that people use twice as much water wastefully when not on meter system. We recommend a comprehensive plan of installing several hundred meters each year.

"In view of the fact that the Wheeler Canyon supply is the largest stream supply, and inasmuch as this supply will be subject to human contamination with its increase in popularity in the future, we recommend that the supply be chlorinated during the summer months from May 25th to October 15th, and longer if necessary. A method of treatment is desirable which can provide water free from disease organisms; can be satisfactorily operated by intelligent but not necessarily expert waterworks attendants; is dependable and subject to strict control at all times; is economical in first cost and in operation. Such a method is sterilization by liquid chlorine. The amount of chlorine used to treat the Wheeler Canyon Supply would be so small as not to be detectible in the city supply.

"The lower temperatures allow the typhoid bacilli to exist much longer than the higher temperatures. The concentration of bacteria in a stream flowing 5 second ft. will be greater than in one flowing 50 second ft. For this reason all trespassing in Cold Water Canyon and Warm Water Spring Canyon should be strictly prohibited. Signs should be posted near the intake warning people not to trespass above intakes. The supply in Cold Water and Warm Water Springs is very limited and pollution after rains is very evident.

"The present storage capacity should be increased to give the city adequate fire protection, as well as an adequate and safe culinary supply.

"It is valuable information for the city to know the amount of water flowing from the wells and from the creeks each season. It can only be accurately measured by installing weirs or other measuring devices, in order to determine the amount of water lost in transportation.

"The reservoir outlets should be equipped with venturi meters to determine the amount of water delivered to the distributing system.

"It is needless to say that to permit water to enter the system at any place from the Ogden or Weber Rivers is very dangerous and may be disastrous to the city.

"The use of cross connections between a safe water supply and a questionable supply should be prohibited by city ordinance.

"It is important that the present worn-out pipe be replaced with permanent pipe, and that all replacements and enlargements be made in accordance with an engineering plan.

"The dead ends should be eliminated as soon as possible by a more closely gridironed system.

"The distribution system is also far from adequate. It is in this respect that town officials are most liable to underestimate future needs. This is often a costly and serious error. Pipe lines that are outgrown and are leaking badly will so consume the pressure as to render the supply practically useless in case of a fire. It often costs five or ten times as much to tear up and replace outgrown pipe later as to install pipe of ample size in the beginning.

"Feeders to the system should be of sufficient size and be looped so that no district will depend upon a single feeder. It is important that foresight be used in determining the size of pipe necessary. Pipe should be sufficient size to provide for ordinary domestic consumption plus the fire flow without causing excessive pressure loss, which is prevalent in many of our city systems today.

"The court has ruled that 'water is a necessity of life' and one who undertakes to trade in it and supply customers stands in no different position to those with whom he deals than does a dealer in food stuffs. He is bound to use reasonable care that whatever is supplied for food or drink shall be ordinarily pure and wholesome.

"An adequate and safe water supply is a city's greatest asset, and we suggest that the city administration give the water system their first attention.

"We trust this information may be of value to the administration in conducting the waterworks system efficiently and economically, and assure you our support if we can be of service."

Copies of the foregoing report, together with copies of bacteriological tests made by the bacteriologist of the state of Utah, were forwarded to and received by the board of commissioners and the board of health of Ogden City. Most of the tests of

Wheeler creek water made by the state board of health during the year 1928 showed that the water of that creek contained colon bacilli to such an extent that it was unsafe for culinary uses. During the late summer, fall, and winter of 1928 considerable correspondence was had between the Utah state health department and the plaintiff city commissioner in charge of the waterworks system of Ogden with respect to the city water supply, especially as to the water of Wheeler creek. It appears that passenger trains engaged in interstate commerce when passing through Ogden were using water from the Ogden City water system. It also appears that the bureau of public health service of the United States, in order to insure a proper water supply for interstate passenger trains, relied upon the Utah state board of health for information as to the water which was supplied to such trains. After it was determined that the water of Wheeler creek was contaminated, the health department of Utah informed the commissioners of Ogden City that it would no longer certify that the water of Ogden was safe for culinary and domestic purposes unless the water from Wheeler creek was kept out of the water system of Ogden or something was done to purify that water. A meeting was finally called to discuss and if possible agree upon what should be done in the matter. The meeting was held in the latter part of the year 1928. There were present at that meeting the plaintiff and the mayor of Ogden City, Dr. T. B. Beatty, health commissioner of Utah, and representatives of the Ogden Union Depot & Railway Company. An agreement was finally reached whereby the plaintiff and the mayor of Ogden City promised that the water from Wheeler creek would not again be turned into the mains of the city until the city had constructed and put in operation a chlorinator for the chlorination of the water of Wheeler creek. In reliance upon the promise so made by the commissioners of the city, the Utah state board of health certified to the United States public health authorities the use of Ogden City water upon trains engaged in interstate commerce. In the budget for the expenses of Ogden City for the year 1929, an item was included for the purchase and installment of a chlorinator for use on Wheeler creek. Early in the year 1929 a chlorinator was purchased and later a contract was let for the construction of a building in which to place a chlorinator, but the same was not installed until after the occurrence of the matters involved in this controversy. On June 14, 1929, the water of Wheeler creek was turned into the water system of Ogden. On June 16th a heavy rain fell on the watershed of Wheeler creek. Soon after the rain began to fall the water of Wheeler creek was turned out of the city water system because when it rained the water of that creek became turbid. The water of Wheeler creek was again turned back into the Ogden City water system about a week or ten days after it had been turned out.

The plaintiff was absent from Ogden City in Portland, Or., from June 14th to July 6th. Early in July, 1929, samples of water from the Ogden City water system were taken and tested in the laboratory of the state board of health. Some of the samples so taken and tested showed a high number of coli bacillus. The laboratory tests were made on July 5, 1929. On the next day, July 6th, T. B. Beatty, state health commissioner, called the mayor of Ogden on the telephone and informed him of what he had ascertained about the presence of coli bacillus in the water supply of Ogden and that evidently Wheeler creek water was again being turned into the city mains without being chlorinated. The mayor requested Dr. Beatty to write him a letter about the matter. Accordingly, on the same day Dr. Beatty wrote and mailed a letter to the mayor and the city commissioner of Ogden wherein the doctor stated:

"You are advised that the report of the Laboratory examination of sample of water taken from the Ogden City Water Supply July 1st shows a high degree of contamination. (Copy of report enclosed.) I am informed that the Wheeler Canyon Water had been turned into the water system, which doubtless accounts for the contamination, as a separate test of the water taken from the wells was Negative.

"You will recall that you were requested by the State Board of Health last year to discontinue the use of the Wheeler Canyon water until chlorination apparatus should be installed and operated for the purpose of sterilizing the water, which was proved to be dangerously impure.

"I understand that the city has purchased the apparatus but has neglected to have it installed. The Board of Health must insist that this shall be done immediately and that the Wheeler Canyon supply shall be turned off until the chlorinator is in operation.

"The Board has certified the water supply to the United States Public Health Service for use on trains, with the understanding that it should be sterilized and we shall be obliged to withdraw such certification unless the above requests are complied with."

The foregoing letter was delivered to plaintiff on July 8th. As soon as the letter was read by plaintiff, he ordered the water of Wheeler creek turned out of the water system and the Wheeler creek water was accordingly turned out on July 8, 1929, and was not again turned back into the water system until the chlorinator was installed and in operation. In the latter part of June and early in July a number of inhabitants of Ogden City became sick from what later was determined to be typhoid fever. There is some evidence that one or two of the persons who had typhoid fever had symptoms of that disease early in June of that year. On July 11, 1929, Dr. Savage, the city health officer of Ogden City, called Dr. Beatty on the telephone and informed him that considerable sickness had developed in Ogden and that the nature of the sickness was rather obscure; that no diagnosis of the disease had been made. After some conversation as to the nature of the disease, Dr. Beatty asked why Dr. Savage did not suspect typhoid fever. On the following day, July 12, 1929, Dr. Beatty went to Ogden, where he consulted with the city commissioners and the city health officer of Ogden City, regarding the water situation and the disease which had broken out in that city. He was also interviewed by a representative of the defendant corporation. In that interview the doctor informed appellant's representative that the water of Wheeler creek was under suspicion and that the state board of health would make an investigation; that the city commissioners had failed to keep their promise not to turn the water of Wheeler creek into the water system of Ogden until it was chlorinated; that the people of Ogden should be advised not to drink the water of Ogden City until it was boiled. The representative of appellant stated that if they published anything derogatory to the water supply of Ogden they would get hell, to which the doctor responded that they might get hell but that they would save human lives. It was further stated in that interview by Dr. Beatty in substance that in this age of sanitation it is manslaughter to permit a water supply to become contaminated with typhoid in a city the size of Ogden, and that he was advised the courts have so held.

In the evening issue of July 12th the defendant corporation published an article wherein the citizens of Ogden were urged to boil the water taken from the Ogden City water supply. The article stated that Dr. Beatty, state health commissioner, and Dr. Savage, city physician of Ogden, had determined that the mysterious malady of which there were six cases in Ogden was typhoid fever and that there were several other patients with symptoms which indicated they had typhoid fever. Suspicion, the article stated, pointed to the source of the disease as being water from Wheeler creek. The article reported the views of Dr. Beatty and Dr. Savage and some other physician as to the source of the threatened typhoid epidemic. Plaintiff makes no complaint of that article. On July 13th at the suggestion of the Ogden Commercial Club two meetings were held at which were present representatives of the commercial club. The mayor and both commissioners of Ogden City were present at the forenoon meeting and the mayor and plaintiff attended the afternoon meeting. City Physician Dr. Savage attended the meetings, as did also representatives of the defendant corporation. Fred Packard, superintendent of the Ogden City waterworks, attended the afternoon meeting. At the forenoon meeting the president of the commercial club stated that pursuant to public demand the club desired to assist the city commissioners in every way possible to clear up the water and typhoid situation which existed in Ogden. Mr. Williams was questioned at some length as to why it was the Wheeler creek was turned into the water system, especially in view of the fact that a promise had been made by the commission that the water of that creek would not be used until it was chlorinated. Mr. Williams stated that he, as head of the waterworks department, assumed the responsibility for turning the Wheeler creek water into the Ogden water system; that his shoulders were broad enough to carry that responsibility; that he did not believe the Wheeler creek water was responsible for the typhoid fever; that the water of Wheeler creek had been used to supplement the city water supply for many years; that the city had purchased a chlorinator for the chlorination of water from Wheeler creek, but the same had not been installed; that the water of Wheeler creek had been turned into the city water system while he was away on his vacation; that immediately upon the receipt of the letter of July 6th from Dr. Beatty the water of Wheeler creek was turned out; that the air pumps on the artesian wells were started soon after the water from Wheeler creek was turned out; that the people of Ogden were using an excessive amount of water; that if the residents of Ogden would not waste water there would be sufficient without the use of the pumps on the wells to supply all legitimate demands; that upon the suggestion being made that the drinking fountains of the city be turned off, it was stated by some of those present that it would be a great detriment to the reputation of Ogden water supply if the newspapers were to publish a condemnation thereof. City Physician Dr. Savage stated an investigation was being made to ascertain the source of typhoid infection, but that no common source had been found except the water supply.

At the afternoon meeting Mr. Packard, superintendent of the city waterworks, was questioned concerning the city water supply and why it was that Wheeler creek water had been turned into the system. He stated that the Wheeler creek water was turned into the system when the supply became low the same as had been done in other years; that no one had told him not to turn the water in; that he had never heard of an agreement whereby the water of Wheeler creek was not to be used until chlorinated; that he did not believe the typhoid epidemic was caused by the water from Wheeler creek because a number of families were living in Ogden Canyon and using Wheeler creek water, but none of the members of those families had contracted the disease; that since the water of Wheeler creek had been turned out of the system the city reservoir had fallen; that Wheeler creek was turned out on July 11th; that with the use of the pumps on the wells there was a sufficient water supply if the people of Ogden would cease wasting water. It was agreed at that meeting that the water in the dead ends of the city water mains would be cleaned out and that an effort would be made by the city water department to prevent unnecessary waste of water. In the evening issue of July 13th of appellant's paper, a report of the forenoon meeting of that day was published, as was also a news item stating that two persons had died of typhoid fever and that many others were ill of that disease. There was also published a copy of the letter which has heretofore been quoted in this opinion written by Dr. Beatty to the city commission under date of July 6, 1929. Notice was also given that the state board of health had arranged for a free source of serum for inoculation against typhoid fever, and that every one was advised to take that treatment. Dr. Beatty was quoted as having said that, "Typhoid is manslaughter in these days of modern sanitation." No complaint was made of the publication of July 13th.

In the issue of the appellant's newspaper of Sunday morning, July 14th, appeared the publication of which plaintiff complains. Some of the language complained of appeared in an editorial, some in an article under the heading, "Blame Placed in Water Pollution, Williams Avers He's Responsible for Bad Supply," and some in an article under the heading, "Boil Your Water, Don't Drink From Fountains." The complaint alleges:

"That on the 14th day of July, 1929, the said defendants, intending to injure, malign, and defame the plaintiff, maliciously published of and concerning the plaintiff, as an individual and in his said official capacity, in the regular issue and Sunday edition of said newspaper, on said day, on prominent pages thereof, where the same would be most readily seen and read, the following libelous and defamatory words:

" 'Blame Placed in Water Pollution'

" 'Ogden is facing an epidemic of typhoid fever due to criminal carelessness on the part of the City Water Department in polluting the water supply. Defying the written order of the state board of health, the waters of Wheeler Canyon were turned into the City mains. The Water Department made the promise that it would install a chlorinator to purify this water, but now after the damage has been done, Fred Williams, the water commissioner, admits that the chlorinator was never used.

" 'A typhoid epidemic in a city the size of Ogden is nothing short of manslaughter. Better men than those responsible for this situation are wearing stripes for lesser crimes. Two citizens have died from typhoid within twenty-four hours. Many others are ill with the disease, and the number of cases is increasing daily.'

" 'Williams Avers He's Responsible For Bad Supply.'

" 'Commissioner Fred E. Williams of the Waterworks Department admitted yesterday that if there was any blame to be placed for the use of the Wheeler Creek water, he would accept responsibility. Further, he asserted, my shoulders are broad enough to carry it.'

" 'Typhoid Fever Is Manslaughter.'

" 'The present epidemic of typhoid fever in Ogden is nothing short of manslaughter and the responsibility for the crime rests squarely on the shoulders of the city commission. Two citizens have died from the disease within 24 hours and several others are critically ill, while the number of cases is increasing daily.

" 'The city commission and a few of their weak-kneed friends are sending up the howl that it is giving Ogden a bad name to put the real situation before the public and thereby giving the residents of this city an opportunity to protect themselves and their families from the ravages of this disease. A newspaper that would withhold this news from the public or in any way shield the bunglers who perpetrated this crime would not be worthy of its name as a purveyor of news and furthermore it would become an accessory after the fact. So the city commission and the public at large may take notice here and now that The Standard-Examiner's first duty is to the citizens of Ogden and the whole dirty deal will be exposed in the interests of public health and with the hope that a repetition of the crime may be forestalled in the future.

" 'Fred E. Williams, water commissioner, says the polluted waters of Wheeler Canyon were turned into the city mains last summer. This was done in secrecy over the written protest of the state board of health and without giving water users an opportunity to protect themselves. Again this year the crime was repeated. However, Mr. Williams made a public statement saying he would install a chlorinator. He was forced to admit yesterday that he lied—the chlorinator was never installed, but the pipe line from Wheeler creek was running full.

" 'The commission has been transferring about $75,000 a year from the waterworks department to the general fund—money that should be used to increase the water supply and improve the service. Yet they could not afford to pay $300 to install a chlorinator and they could not start the pumps at the wells until public opinion put the thumb screws on them. The chamber of commerce has just completed a drive for $29,000 to advertise Ogden as a good place to live. It would take several times that sum to restore two lives already lost and bring back to health those who are critically ill because of this criminal blunder of the waterworks department.

" 'Talk about giving Ogden a bad name by warning the citizens to protect their health against such vicious incompetency. It will take heroic and combined efforts of all citizens who have backbones instead of wishbones to restore the bad name painted on the city's door by these czars of the city hall.

" 'If Mr. Williams as head of the waterworks department is solely responsible for this crime the public should demand his immediate resignation. If he refuses to resign he should be impeached. If the responsibility is divided among the three commissioners as it should be, they should all resign or be impeached. Ogden must make it impossible for such crimes to be repeated. When the water supply is deliberately polluted and a deadly disease turned loose upon the community there is no time for quibbling, evasions and excuses. Such incompetency cannot be neutralized.

" 'This tragedy must be corrected and it is the duty of every citizen interested in his home and the future growth of the city to lend a hand. We must let the world know that the city of Ogden is able to protect the health and life of all who come. Typhoid fever is manslaughter. Who is responsible?' "

Other articles published in appellant's newspaper after the publication of July 14th were received in evidence upon the theory that they may have a bearing on both the questions of malice and the amount of damage, if any, that should be awarded by the jury. In the issue of July 15th there appeared two articles, one under the heading, "Contiue to Boil Water," and the other under the heading: "Packard Resigns As First 'Goat' in City Scandal. Commissioner Williams declares full charge of running department was left to Packard and he has accepted responsibility; Coldwater Canyon water warning issued; Police guard at Williams' home; M. E. Wilcox says Wheeler was turned in early in June." In the issue of July 16th two articles were published, one an editorial entitled, "Citizens of Ogden, Demand The Resignation of Williams," and one under the heading: "Danger Passing; City Water Soon to Become Safe. Doctor Beatty Reports Samples are Negative and Williams Reports Dead Ends Are Being Flushed; Inspectors Catch Water Wasters; Dr. Ezra C. Rich Issues Statement on Situation, Saying Wheeler Creek is Contaminated and Should Not Be Used." In the issue of July 17th two articles were published, one an editorial entitled, "Peery's 'Yes' Man Changes His Mind To Suit Occasion," and the other entitled: "Progress Is Made In Clearing Up Ogden City Water. Only Hundred Per Cent Pure Artesian Supply Is Pouring Into Reservoir and Pressure by Standard-Examiner and Chamber of Commerce Has Brought About Flushing of Dead Ends to Remove Suspicious Remnants; One New Case of Typhoid in Hospital." We quote such portions of the articles as might have a bearing on the issues involved in this controversy. In the issue of July 15th it was said:

"Mr. Williams said that when he declared he assumed responsibility for the turning of Wheeler creek water into the city mains, he assumed that responsibility as head of the waterworks department.

"'I gave Mr. Packard, who knows more about the waterworks department than any other man, full responsibility of caring for the details of the operation of the system,' he said, 'I left it all up to him. While I feel the responsibility of my department, as its head, I do not feel that I was to blame for the turning of Wheeler creek into the system.

"'As true as there is a God above, I'm telling you, I don't know Wheeler creek was in the city mains. I gave Packard the responsibility of running the system. He told me this morning, when he offered his resignation, that he turned Wheeler creek into the system late in June, while I was on my vacation.

"'Packard led me to believe that the wells were throwing plenty of water. When I received Dr. Beatty's letter telling me he thought Wheeler creek was being used I called Mr. Packard. This was on about July 6. I asked Packard if Wheeler creek was in the system. He told me it was and I ordered him to cut it out at once. * * *

" 'Mr. Packard tendered his resignation to me this morning and accepted full and sole responsibility for Wheeler creek having been used. I will move to the commission that the resignation be accepted immediately. Mayor Francis and Commissioner Peery can then vote on it.' "

The editorial published on July 16th had this to say:

"Citizens of Ogden, the present status of your water supply is a shame and a disgrace to the community and a menace to life and health. Three deaths from typhoid fever have occurred in as many days and many others are gravely ill with the disease. During all the time this has been occurring the city commission has put in its time manufacturing alibis and passing the buck.

"Fred E. Williams, water commissioner, in full charge of the department and with power of attorney, from the other two commissioners, according to their own admission, to handle the department as he pleases has proven himself absolutely incompetent for the job. On last Saturday he stated that he would assume all responsibility for turning the polluted waters of Wheeler canyon into the city mains. Yesterday he called God to witness that he knew nothing of what was going on in his department and attempts to shift the blame to Fred Packard, a paid employe of the department. It is a rank admission of ignorance and incompetency on the part of Mr. Williams as well as an attempt to seek cover.

"Williams has proven conclusively that he should be summarily removed as head of the water department in the interest of the life and health of the citizens of Ogden. To let him continue would be to encourage manslaughter. More innocent victims will fall before his defiance of law and his ignorance of the job he holds by the gift of the people.

"This water situation can be cleared up and that quickly and the good name of Ogden restored, but it cannot be done with Fred Williams on the job. He has made no effort to chlorinate the polluted waters turned into the city mains. He has been forced by the chamber of commerce to start cleaning out the 'dead ends' in the city mains which are a lurking place for messengers of death. As Harman Peery's 'yes' man he has sat around the city hall charging politics and trying to figure out alibis to stay on the city payroll regardless of the consequences to the public.

"The directors of the chamber of commerce after repeated insults and rebuffs from Williams and Peery are attempting to clean up the nasty situation. The Standard-Examiner as the representative of the public at large will continue to keep its readers fully informed on this tragedy visited on the city by the water department. This newspaper is receiving letters and telephone calls from every part of the city commending it for its efforts to check the typhoid epidemic and expose those responsible for it. However, the situation demands more than verbal and written commendation.

"It demands immediate and decisive action and that action must come from the taxpayers and citizens of Ogden.

"Citizens of Ogden, this crisis calls for leadership. It calls for men and women of courage who will organize and see to it that Fred Williams resigns as head of the water department or failing in that, see that he is impeached for gross incompetency on his own admission. Do not be fooled by his plea of economy. The water department is transferring $75,000 a year into the general fund and there is no economy in sacrificing the lives and health of the community. The same commissioners preached economy when they were licensing bootleggers at $100 per month to sell whisky.

"Men and women of Ogden, it is your duty to see that Mr. Williams leaves the water department at once. You can't leave all the work to the chamber of commerce and The Standard-Examiner, but as long as he is there you will have no assurance that your water supply will be properly safeguarded, for he has proven himself unfit and unsafe for the job. Your lives and your health must no longer rest in his incompetent hands. Demand his resignation and see that it comes. This typhoid epidemic must not occur again. Your life, your health and the good name of Ogden must be protected." . . .

The other articles which were published subsequent to July 14th in appellant's newspaper contain statements of facts which are not in dispute, and which facts in the main have heretofore been recited in this opinion. Other facts which were established by the uncontradicted evidence are: That Ogden City had transferred about $75,000 per year from the revenue derived from the water department into the general fund; that there were fourteen known cases of typhoid fever during the summer of 1929, and three or four others who probably had typhoid fever. Five died as a result of the disease. The usual period that elapses from the time typhoid germs are taken into the system until the symptoms of the disease develop is from a week or ten days to three weeks. The period may be shorter or longer. Coli bacilli is found in the excrement of human beings and warm-blooded animals. The presence of coli bacilli in water is indicative of but does not necessarily mean that the germs of typhoid fever are present. Water which shows an excessive amount of coli bacilli is unfit for culinary use unless it is boiled or chlorinated before being used. Mr. Packard continued to act as assistant superintendent of the Ogden City water system up to the time this action was tried. The record is silent as to whether or not his resignation was presented to the board of commissioners, and if so what action, if any, was taken thereon by the commission. The publication complained of was written by the defendant James P. Casey. Mr. Casey testified that he wrote the article with the sole purpose of protecting the citizens of Ogden from the threatened typhoid epidemic and that he had no ill will or desire to injure the plaintiff. Plaintiff testified that when he was elected to the office of city commissioner, Mr. Eldredge, one of the defendants, called him into his (Eldredge's) office and stated that Fred Packard had to go because he had insulted Mayor Francis, who was a former editor of defendant's newspaper; that Mr. Eldredge further stated there were other men who should not be retained in the employ of the city; that plaintiff had been elected with Mayor Francis and not with Peery. Plaintiff, according to his testimony, refused to follow the request. Mr. Eldredge was not called as a witness. Mr. Peery, the other commissioner, testified that both the chamber of commerce and the defendants' corporation were after both of us (meaning himself and Williams) because we would not play with them and listen to their dictations about city affairs; that he never thought there was anything wrong with the water and that he didn't think so now; that the attack of the Standard-Examiner was just one of those attacks which it was in the habit of staging about every six months; that there had been feelings for years between the Standard-Examiner and the city commissioners. About 75 per cent. of typhoid epidemics are caused by the use of contaminated water. There is a conflict in the evidence as to these facts. Plaintiff testified that he told Mr. Packard in the summer of 1928 not to turn the water of Wheeler creek into the Ogden City water supply until it was chlorinated. A number of witnesses testified that Mr. Packard stated at the meeting held on July 13th that he turned the Wheeler creek water into the water system because that had been the custom for years; that no one had told him not to turn the water of Wheeler creek into the system; that he had never heard of an agreement whereby the city commissioners had promised not [to?] use Wheeler creek until it was chlorinated; that the water of Wheeler creek was turned out on July 11th. Mr. Packard testified in the cause but did not deny that he made the foregoing statements or that such statements were contrary to the facts, except that when he stated the water of Wheeler creek was turned out on July 11th he was confused about the date; that the water was turned out on July 8th. Defendant claims that there is evidence which shows that Wheeler creek was running in the reservoir early in June of 1929. There was offered in evidence the records kept at the city distributing reservoirs during the month of June, 1929. Those records showed that water, in addition to the artesian well water, was flowing into the distributing reservoirs. Plaintiff's evidence, however, tends to show that the additional water came from Warm spring and Cold Water, and not from Wheeler creek, prior to June 14, 1929, when admittedly the water from Wheeler creek was turned in. There is a sharp conflict in the evidence of the expert witnesses as to the cause of the outbreak of typhoid fever in Ogden in the summer of 1929. Numerous witnesses were examined touching that question. The state board of health made an investigation, as did also Dr. L. L. Daines, professor and head of the department of bacteriology and pathology at the University of Utah, and Dr. J. E. Greaves, professor of bacteriology in the agricultural college of Utah. The city commission employed Drs. Daines and Greaves to make their investigation and report. The conflict in the testimony as to the source of the typhoid outbreak may be illustrated by the written reports rendered by the state health department and by Drs. Daines and Greaves. The last report rendered by the state health department reads as follows:

"The following report of the investigation of the State Board of

Health of the recent typhoid outbreak in Ogden is supplemental to the preliminary report submitted July 23rd:

"Further investigation has furnished evidence which forces the conclusion that the contaminated water from Wheeler Creek, which had been turned into the water system during the month of June, was responsible for the typhoid cases.

"As stated in the preliminary report, the water from Wheeler Creek, an open stream frequented by campers, had been proved by numerous laboratory tests to be dangerously contaminated, and its use for culinary purposes had been condemned by the State Board of Health. The Board did not possess the legal power to compel the purification of the water or the discontinuance of its use until purified, but after long continued effort had in 1928 secured the agreement of city authorities to turn out the Wheeler Creek water from the system until after the installation of chlorination apparatus. Notwithstanding this agreement and the proved impurity of the water, it was turned into the water system during the month of June and was not disconnected until July 8th, after the receipt of a demand from the State Board of Health dated July 5th that such action should be taken. The demand was made upon the discovery that the water supply was grossly contaminated and that Wheeler Creek water was entering the system.

"Cases of sickness began to appear in Ogden following June 20th which were for the first time called to the attention of the State Board of Health July 20th. The sickness proved to be typhoid fever of which fourteen cases were reported resulting in five deaths. The symptoms of the last cases began prior to July 7th, since which date no further cases have been reported in Ogden.

"The weather bureau reports show that on June 10th and June 16th rains had occurred in Wheeler Creek, flushing into the stream surface impurities which might, and may now be stated without reasonable doubt did, include excreta deposited by a typhoid carrier. The typhoid cases occurred in two series sharply defined and separated, one beginning ten days to two weeks following the first rain, the usual incubation period of the disease, and the other a like period following the second rain. There were no cases in Ogden prior to the expiration of the first incubation period and no cases occurred after the incubation period dating from the second rain.

"Under such conditions the presumption that the infection originated in the water supply could only be set aside or controverted by definite and positive proof of some other cause. After a careful investigation and analysis of all possible factors, no evidence in substantiation of such cause has been discovered.

"Any possibility of milk as a cause was immediately ruled out by the fact that different milk supplies were consumed in each case. The alleged theory that the infection was contracted at certain restaurants can be wholly discarded. Four different restaurants have been mentioned as having been patronized by some of the cases. Others had not eaten at a restaurant. No typhoid carrier has been discovered serving food at any of the restaurants. It has been established that no foods that were open to suspicion to typhoid contamination have been dispensed by any of the restaurants.

"It is proper to assume that all of the cases reported had a common origin. The only substance consumed by all of them was the water from the public water supply. Any connection of the disease with the restaurants is further negatived by the fact that although the restaurants had been operating and serving hundreds of people before and after the sudden outbreak, no case of typhoid was contracted except during the few days covering the presence in the water system of the contaminated Wheeler Creek water following the rains. Even if such proof of water contamination had not been established as a potential cause of the infection, it is impossible by the utmost stretch of imagination to conceive of circumstances that could suddenly convert the restaurants into typhoid 'depots' on the two separate and brief occasions which would be necessary in order to check with the periods of incubation of the two series of cases. It is to be deplored that on no more evidence than the fact that victims of typhoid had eaten at certain restaurants, the business of the restaurants, according to information received, has been seriously injured by alleged efforts to fix upon them responsibility for the disease. The aim and purpose of an investigation as to the cause of a typhoid outbreak should be solely to establish if possible the facts, in order that justice may be rendered to all concerned and to prevent a repetition of the misfortune.

"The possible connection with the disease of contaminated food products from the farming area west of Ogden was carefully studied. While the use for irrigation purposes in that section of water contaminated with Ogden sewage is an unsafe practice, both to the farmers and to persons consuming vegetables produced under such conditions, a fact which the State Board of Health has repeatedly called to the attention of the City and County officials and the farming community, there is nothing to show that it had any connection with the typhoid situation in Ogden.

"Of the two cases reported at Plain City, situated in the area in question, the first symptoms in one began July 10th, which was later than any of the cases that occurred in Ogden, and the history showed that the patient had drunk water from an irrigation ditch ten days before. As was pointed out in the recent communication from the State Board of Health to the Ogden City Commission, the danger to those living in the area using irrigation water contaminated by Ogden sewage has been greatly aggravated by discharges from the typhoid cases, and its use was ordered discontinued by the State Board of Health. Steps should be taken before another season to purify this sewage if its use for irrigation purposes is permitted. The other case at Plain City contracted the disease at the same time as the later cases in Ogden and may have been infected in Ogden, which he visited daily, or at his home in Plain City from sewage contaminated water.

"In brief it may be repeated that all possible channels through which the typhoid infection might have been transmitted have been analyzed, and the final conclusion has been reached that the contaminated water supply was the cause of the outbreak.

"Chlorination of Wheeler Creek water, provision for which has now been made, will if properly operated hereafter insure the purity and safety of that source of supply. The major supply taken from the artesian wells has always been proved by tests to be pure and may be relied upon to continue to be an ideal supply if the further precautions recommended by the State Board of Health and the Engineer of the United States Public Health Service to safeguard its purity are carried out.

"If the recent lesson of the consequences of neglect of essential public health precautions is given serious consideration by the citizens of Ogden, and the employment of competent and reliable persons as guardians of the water supply is hereafter insisted upon, there need be no fear of future menace to the public health from that source. . . ."

In the foregoing statement of the evidence we have attempted to confine ourselves to such portions thereof as we deem necessary to serve as a background of our discussion and determination of the questions of law which are presented on this appeal. To recite even the substance of all of the evidence offered and received at the trial would extend this opinion beyond reasonable limits and would serve no useful purpose.

Appellant concedes, as well it may, that the publication complained of was libelous if it was false and not privileged. It is quite generally held that the truth of matters charged as defamatory exempts the publisher thereof from civil liability.

Plaintiff makes no claim the law is otherwise. It is only in the event that defendant has published concerning plaintiff defamatory matter which is untrue that recourse need be had to the doctrine applicable to communications which are privileged. Privileged communications are of two classes: (1) Absolute privilege, and (2) qualified or conditional privilege. In the case of absolutely privileged communications the utterances or publication, although both false and malicious, does not give rise to a cause of action. In the case of a qualifiedly or conditionally privileged communication the law raises merely a prima facie presumption in favor of the occasion. Both classes of privileged communications rest upon grounds of public policy,—the necessity of the individual to surrender his personal rights for the common welfare. A qualifiedly privileged communication "extends to all communications made bona fide upon any subject-matter in which a party communicating has an interest, or in reference to which he has a duty to a person having a corresponding interest or duty; and the privilege embraces cases where the duty is not a legal one, but where it is of a moral or social character, of imperfect obligation." Newell, Slander and Libel (4th Ed.) § 341, pp. 380, 381, and cases there cited; *Spielberg vs. A. Kuhn & Brother,* 39 Utah 276, 116 P. 1027. The publication here in question clearly falls within that class of communications which are qualifiedly or conditionally privileged. When the publication was made, two residents of Ogden City had died from typhoid fever and others were seriously sick with that disease. There was grave danger that the disease would spread. That appellant and the residents of Ogden City had a common interest in the threatened typhoid epidemic, in its source, and in the prevention of its spread, is not open to question. It is equally clear that appellant and the inhabitants of Ogden had a common interest in fixing, if possible, the responsibility for the outbreak of the disease, and in taking such steps as might be necessary to check its spread and prevent its recurrence. Information concerning the manner in which plaintiff as city commissioner in charge of the waterworks department of the city had been and was handling the city culinary water supply was likewise a matter of common interest to appellant and the citizens of Ogden. 36 C. J. 1284, § 291, and cases there cited; *People vs. Glassman,* 12 Utah 238, 42 P. 956. Appellant by informing its readers upon such matters was performing a duty which falls within that class mentioned in the rule as "of a moral or social character of imperfect obligation." Such were the views entertained by the trial court. The jury was instructed that the publication complained of was qualifiedly privileged. Respondent has not assigned the giving of such instruction as error.

When, as in the instant case, the publication was qualifiedly privileged, the burden of proving malice in fact or actual malice, as distinguished from malice in law or implied malice, was cast upon the plaintiff. *Spielberg vs. A. Kuhn & Brother,* supra. The doctrine announced by this court in that case is in accord with the weight of judicial authority. Cases which support the majority rule, as well as those to the contrary, will be found annotated in 54 A. L. R. beginning at page 1143.

Whether appellant's motion for a nonsuit should or should not have been granted depends upon how the following questions are answered: Were the statements of facts contained in the publication true? If not true, was the publication made in good faith, without actual malice, and with reasonable or probable grounds for believing it to be true? Were the comments and criticisms contained in the publication declared on concerning the manner in which respondent conducted the waterworks system, and how he should be dealt with because of his conduct in such respect, reasonable and fair, in the light of the facts and circumstances that existed or appeared to exist at the time such comments and criticisms were published? As heretofore stated, most of the statements made in the publications declared on are true. While there was a conflict in the evidence at the trial as to the probable source of the typhoid epidemic, such conflict was based upon investigations made after the publication of the matters complained of. On July 14th, when the article was published, the facts then available pointed to the water of Wheeler creek as the source of the disease. Such were the expressed views of the state health commissioner, of the Ogden city physician, and of other doctors familiar with the available facts. Such remained the views of the state health department after making a thorough investigation of the facts. The expert witnesses, who were called by plaintiff, while expressing the opinion that the outbreak of the typhoid epidemic was not the city water supply, were none the less agreed that it was a serious mistake to turn water containing an excessive amount of coli bacilli into the water supply of Ogden City and "that it cannot be too strongly stressed that this should never be permitted to occur again." Upon this record the only conclusion permissible is that at the time appellant published the various articles which were received in evidence there was probable cause for believing that the typhoid epidemic which occurred in Ogden in the summer of 1929 was caused by the water of Wheeler creek being turned into the city water supply. In this connection it should be noted that if appellant was to perform any service to the citizens of Ogden by way of preventing a further spread of the disease, it was necessary that they be warned of the danger at once. To have waited for an investigation before informing them of the threatened danger might well have cost the lives of more of the residents of that community.

Respondent contends that the publication declared on expressly charged him with the commission of the crime of manslaughter and that in no event is such a charge permissible unless it is true. Cases dealing with that question will be found collected in 17 R. C. L. page 355, § 103. The language used in the publication falls short of charging the plaintiff with manslaughter or any other crime. Most of the language declared on does not purport to be a statement of the facts but is in the nature of comment upon the facts and a criticism of the acts of respondent and those in charge of the waterworks department. Under the heading quoted in the complaint, "Williams Avers He's Responsible For Bad Supply. Commissioner Fred E. Williams of the Waterworks Department admitted yesterday that if there was any blame to be placed for the use of the Wheeler Creek water, he would accept responsibility. Further he asserted, my shoulders are broad enough to carry it," was published a full, fair, and substantially true statement of the history of the controversy about the Wheeler creek water, of what occurred at the meeting held the day before, of the views of the state health commissioner, of the Ogden City physician, and of other physicians with respect to the cause of the typhoid epidemic. It also contained an accurate account of an interview had by a representative of appellant with the respondent. All the remainder of the language set out in the complaint is quoted from two articles, one entitled, "Boil Your Water, Don't Drink From Fountains," and the other an editorial published in the editorial column under the heading "Typhoid Fever is Manslaughter." If appellant is to be held liable in this case, it is because of its comments and criticisms contained in the two articles just referred to, rather than because it misstated the facts which formed the basis of such comments and criticisms. The law applicable to what may and what may not lawfully be said by way of comment and criticism is thus stated in Newell on Slander and Libel (4th Ed.), beginning on page 520:

Sec. 481. "Criticism differs from defamation in the following particulars.

"1. Criticism deals only with such things as invite public attention or call for public comment. It does not follow a public man into his private life or pry into his domestic concerns.

"2. It never attacks the individual, but only his work. Such work may be either the policy of a government, the action of a member of a legislative body, a public entertainment, a book published or a picture exhibited. In every case the attack is on a man's acts, or on some thing, and not upon the man himself. A true critic never indulges in personalities, but confines himself to the merits of the subject-matter.

"3. It never imputes or insinuates dishonorable motives unless justice absolutely requires it, and then only on the clearest proofs.

"4. The critic never takes advantage of the occasion to gratify private malice or to attain any other object beyond the fair discussion of matters of public interest, and the judicious guidance of the public taste. He carefully examines the matter, and then honestly and fearlessly states his true opinion of it."

Sec. 482. "Every person has a right to publish such fair and candid criticism, although the author may suffer loss from it. Such a loss the law does not consider as an injury, because it is a loss which the party ought to sustain. It is, in short, the loss of fame and profits to which he was never entitled. Reflection upon personal character is another thing. Liberty of criticism must be allowed or we should neither have purity of taste nor of morals. Fair discussion is essentially necessary to the truth of history and the advancement of science. A publication, therefore, which has for its object, not to injure the reputation of any individual, but to correct misrepresentations of fact, to refute sophistical reasoning, to expose a vicious taste in literature, or to censure what is hostile to morality, is not actionable. The critic must confine himself to criticism and not make it the veil for personal censure, nor allow himself to run into reckless and unfair attacks merely from the love of exercising his power of denunciation."

Sec. 483. "Criticism and comment on well-known or admitted facts are very different things from the assertion of unsubstantiated facts. A fair and bona fide comment on a matter of public interest is an excuse of what would otherwise be a defamatory publication. The statement of this rule assumes the matter of fact commented upon to be somehow ascertained. It does not mean that a man may invent facts, and comment on the facts so invented in what would be a fair and bona fide manner on the supposition that the facts were true. If the facts as a comment upon which the publication is sought to be excused do not exist, the foundation fails. There is no doubt that the public acts of a public man may lawfully be made the subject of fair comment or criticism, not only by the press, but by all members of the public. But the distinction cannot be too clearly borne in mind between comment or criticism and allegations of fact, such as that disgraceful acts have been committed, or discreditable language used. It is one thing to comment upon or criticize, even with severity, the acknowledged or proved acts of a public man, and quite another to assert that he has been guilty of particular acts of misconduct. To state matters which are libelous is not comment or criticism."

In 36 C. J., beginning on page 1282, it is said:

Sec. 285. "Comment or criticism consists of opinions or inferences from facts assumed to be true. An allegation of fact may be justified by its being an inference from other facts truly stated; but if the opinion or inference is not stated as such, but as facts, its truth must be established; and there is no immunity if there is no foundation in fact for the inference or opinion. The right of comment is not restricted to a restatement of the naked facts. As a general rule it may include the right to draw inferences or express opinions from facts established. The soundness of the inferences or opinions is immaterial whether they are right or wrong, provided they are made in good faith and based upon the truth. So comment or criticism may include the inference of motives for conduct in fact exhibited if there is foundation for the inference."

Sec. 286. "While there are dicta to the effect that if the comment or criticism is true and made bona fide, immunity from civil liability therefor exists whether it is reasonable or unreasonable, it is generally held that the comment or criticism in order to receive immunity from civil liability, or to be privileged, must be reasonable and fair."

Sec. 287. "The criticism may be severe, harsh, bitter, or sarcastic. Mere exaggeration, ridicule, or even gross exaggeration does not of itself make the comment or criticism so unfair as to destroy the immunity. It is generally held that such comment may be caustic or severe if the facts warrant it."

Sec. 288. "It is generally held that express malice defeats the defense of comment and criticism, whether it is viewed as a separate defense or an instance of qualified privilege. On the other hand it has also been held that the motive of the commentator, or critic, if he keeps within the bounds of comment or criticism, is immaterial."

In the instant case the trial court instructed the jury that:

"You are instructed that manslaughter, under the laws of this state, is the unlawful killing of a human being without malice, and is of two kinds: Voluntary and involuntary.

"Involuntary manslaughter is the unlawful killing of a human being without malice in the commission of a lawful act which might produce death in an unlawful manner, or without due caution and circumspection.

"You are instructed that carelessly or without due caution and circumspection to permit impure or polluted water carrying indications of typhoid fever infection to flow into the waters and water mains furnishing water to the inhabitants of Ogden City might constitute the crime of involuntary manslaughter. That is to say, if the plaintiff, as the city commissioner of Ogden City having direct charge of the water works department, during the times alleged in plaintiff's complaint herein, with knowledge or in the exercise of due care and circumspection might have acquired knowledge that such polluted water was flowing into such water mains, negligently and without due caution and circumspection allowed unchlorinated water to be served from an impure source of supply through city water mains to the inhabitants of Ogden City, and that a typhoid fever epidemic resulted therefrom, causing the death of one or more persons from such disease, that such conduct on the part of the plaintiff would constitute the crime of manslaughter of the grade of involuntary manslaughter under the law."

Upon this appeal respondent makes no complaint of the foregoing instruction. If there was any inaccuracy in that statement of the law it has not been pointed out. We repeat the facts which tend to support each of the elements necessary to establish the crime of involuntary manslaughter as defined in the foregoing court's instructions to the jury: The water of Wheeler creek was polluted with such an amount of coli bacilli in 1928 that it was unsafe for use. The city commissioners knew such facts and agreed not to use the water of that creek until it was chlorinated. It was turned into the water system of Ogden without being chlorinated and without any attempt being made to ascertain whether or not the water of that creek was safe for use. A typhoid fever epidemic broke out in Ogden City which might well have been caused by the use of the water from Wheeler creek. Two persons had died from that disease at the time the publication was made. Plaintiff stated that he as commissioner of the waterworks department assumed the responsibility for turning the Wheeler creek water into the water system of Ogden. If established facts bespeak a crime has been committed, civil liability does not attach to one who charges such facts as a crime. *Klinck vs. Colby,* 46 N. Y. 427, 7 Am. Rep. 360. To conclude from the facts disclosed by this record that the one responsible for the turning of the Wheeler creek water into the Ogden City water system was guilty of manslaughter, as defined in the trial court's instruction to the jury, may not be said to be unreasonable. That respondent was derelict in his duties if he failed to take measures to see that Wheeler creek water was not turned into the water system during 1929 unless it was chlorinated is not open to question. Much of the evidence tends to show that he did not perform that duty. He did testify at the trial that he informed Mr. Packard in 1928 not to turn the water of Wheeler creek into the city water system, but he made no such claim as far as appears prior to the time of the publication declared on. The dereliction to perform such duty upon a matter so vital to the health and lives of those who were using the water of Ogden City may justly call for the expression of honest indignation. A public officer who is guilty of dereliction of a duty which may, and there is probable cause to believe does, result in the loss of human life, may not be heard to complain merely because plain and severe language is used to condemn his failure to perform his duty. One who makes malicious charges of a defamatory character of a public officer without probable cause for believing such charge to be true is not shielded against liability; but, on the other hand, a public officer who fails to perform his duty to the public is not shielded from criticism honestly made even though the language of such criticism of a public officer who has apparently been derelict in the performance of the duties of his office. The comments and criticisms declared on may not be said to give rise to civil liability in the absence of proof that they were published with malice in fact or actual malice. There is some judicial authority which seems to be to the effect that no civil liability attaches to the publication of a qualifiedly privileged communication where it is made to appear there was probable cause for believing the publication to be true. Those authorities seem to proceed upon the theory that the law of malicious prosecution is applicable to slander and libel—the latter being but a form of the former. It is quite generally held in actions for malicious prosecution that the existence of probable cause defeats the action. If actions for slander and libel are a species of actions for malicious prosecution, it would seem to follow that as the latter action is defeated by the presence of probable cause the same rule should be applied to the former actions. However, the great weight of judicial authority as well as the text-writers support the view that the presence of probable cause does not defeat an action founded upon a qualifiedly privileged communication if the defamatory matter was uttered or published with actual malice. It is quite generally held that a defendant who publishes or utters a qualifiedly privileged communication containing defamatory matter with the intent or motive of injuring the plaintiff is not protected by the privilege even though there was probable cause for believing the utterances or publication to be true. The authorities, however, are all to the effect that the presence of probable cause for believing the truth of a qualifiedly privileged communication is important as evidence of good faith and of the absence of malice in fact. At the outset of our examination of whether or not there was sufficient evidence to go to the jury on the question of the motive or intent of appellant in publishing the matters complained of, we are confronted with the rule of law which casts the burden on the plaintiff to establish actual malice, and with the fact that the publication here involved was either true or there was probable cause to believe it to be true. The evidence which respondent claims supports the burden cast upon him is: (1) That Joseph U. Eldredge, Jr., general manager of the appellant about eighteen or twenty months before the time of the publication declared on, stated to plaintiff that the superintendent of Ogden City waterworks must be discharged and that other changes must be made in the personnel of the city employees, but plaintiff refused to comply with the request: (2) the testimony of Mr. Peery, the other commissioner, to the effect that for a number of years prior to the date of the publication an ill feeling existed between the appellant on the one hand and plaintiff and himself on the other; (3) that the language of the publication declared on and the language of some of the comments and criticisms published thereafter contained such intemperate and exaggerated statements as to indicate the writer thereof was prompted by ulterior motives. The question of whether a qualifiedly privileged article is written or published with malicious motive or otherwise is, generally speaking, a question of fact to be determined by the jury. However, in the absence of proof that such communication was published with actual malice, it is within the power and duty of the courts to say as a matter of law that the motive of the publication was without malice. The fact that plaintiff and general manager of appellant had a disagreement some eighteen or twenty months before the time in question as to who should be appointed to one or more of the city offices can have but little, if any, probative value in determining the motive which prompted the publication of the article in question. Disagreements are common and of everyday occurrences between the best of friends as well as between enemies. Ill will may or may not be engendered by disagreement. It is rare indeed that ill will is nourished for a period of eighteen or twenty months and then manifests itself in a slander or libel. The testimony of Commissioner Peery is likewise of little probative value. While his testimony was to the effect that defendant was in the habit of saying unpleasant things about himself and plaintiff about every six months, he does not advise us of the nature thereof or whether they were true or false. As we view this record, the only evidence offered by plaintiff which has any substantial bearing upon the motive which he claims prompted the publication of the articles in question is the publication itself and the articles which were published thereafter. It is true that some of the language used in the articles by way of criticizing plaintiff was severe, but that alone, as we have heretofore indicated, is not sufficient to support a finding that the motive which prompted the writing of the article declared on was actual malice. The occasion was such as to merit criticism, and the language of those articles is not inconsistent with honest indignation in the light of the established facts and circumstances surrounding the occurrence. It is such language as might well be expected from one who honestly believed that the typhoid epidemic with its suffering and loss of human life was caused by the failure of those in charge of the waterworks department to perform their plain duty. To say that the writer and publisher of the articles here in question was motivated by a desire to injure plaintiff rather than for the purpose of promoting the public weal would be a mere guess. Upon this record a finding that the article declared on was published with malice in fact is without any substantial evidence to support it. There is an abundance of evidence tending to show that the articles were published with a proper motive.

We are of the opinion that the court below was in error in

refusing to grant the motion for a nonsuit and the motion for a directed verdict.

Appellant also complained because the court below by its instructions permitted the jury to award plaintiff punitive damages. In the view we take it was error to submit the question of general damages to the jury, and therefore it follows that it was likewise error to permit the jury to award exemplary damages. So also does appellant complain because the jury was by the court permitted to consider a subsequent publication, not only as bearing upon the question of malice, but also as bearing upon the question of aggravation of damages. The evidence being insufficient to sustain a judgment for general damages, the subsequent publication could not aggravate damages to which plaintiff was not entitled.

In its motion for a new trial appellant contended that the jury having found for the defendants Joseph U. Eldredge, Jr., Abraham L. Glasmann, and James P. Casey, it follows as a matter of law that the verdict against the defendant corporation cannot stand. The argument is made that if there were an absence of malice in fact on the part of the personal defendants who wrote and published the article complained of there could be no malice in fact on the part of the appellant corporation. Having reached the conclusion that a new trial must be granted because of a failure of proof of malice in fact on the part of any one connected with the publication declared on, it becomes unnecessary to further consider that phase of the case.

The wife of plaintiff was permitted to testify concerning certain communications she had over the telephone. She made no claim that she informed the plaintiff of those conversations. At the conclusion of her evidence appellant moved to strike all of her testimony with respect to such communications. The motion was denied. Error is assigned because of that ruling. We are of the opinion that the motion should have been granted. However, the matters concerning which Mrs. Williams testified were not of sufficient moment, standing alone, to justify a disturbance of the verdict and judgment.

For the reasons stated the judgment is reversed. This cause is remanded to the district court of Weber county, with directions to grant a new trial. Appellant has printed a very voluminous abstract of the evidence. It contains a verbatim copy of nearly all the questions asked and the answers given by the various witnesses who testified at the trial. The evidence could have been condensed so as to require about one-half the space actually used. Because of that fact appellant should not be awarded costs for the printing of the entire abstract. Appellant is awarded its costs, but in computing the same respondent should be required to pay for only one-half of the abstract. Such is the order.

FOLLAND, EPHRAIM HANSON, AND MOFFAT, JJ., concur.

STRAUP, Chief Justice (concurring).

I fully concur in the result. I, however, disagree with the statement in the opinion that there was a "sharp conflict in the evidence of the cause of the outbreak of typhoid fever." I think there was no substantial conflict. There is no conflict in the evidence that during the period in question the waters of Wheeler creek turned in the water system were, by laboratory tests and examinations, found to carry colon bacilli, that the waters were so dangerously contaminated as to cause typhoid fever, and that about 75 per cent of such diseases were due to drinking or using such or similar contaminated and polluted waters. By the testimony of officers both of the state and local health departments, as well as by other physicians having personal knowledge of such contaminated and polluted conditions of the waters, and of the diseases, and their cause, it was shown that the cause and spread of the disease of typhoid was due to such contaminated and polluted conditions. We thus have positive and direct evidence of witnesses with personal knowledge of the facts and of records as to the cause of such disease and the spread of it.

As against that we have nothing but speculation, conjecture, and argument of several biologists, who had made no test or examination of the waters in question, who in no particular disputed the polluted and contaminated condition of such waters, and who admitted that about 75 per cent of typhoid diseases were due to such conditions. They in effect testified and admitted that the report made by them and filed with the city commissioners and put in evidence was not based on matters of which they had personal knowledge, but on information given them by others, some of which was shown to have been unfounded in fact. They reported that all the individuals who contracted the disease "ate at lunch stands" which had a common milk supply. Such statement was based merely on heresay. No evidence was given to show that such milk supply or food furnished at any of such places carried typhoid germs or was in any particular contaminated, polluted, or impure. They further reported that the first individual to contract the disease was a waiter "at one of these lunch counters." There is no evidence whether such was the case or not. They further say that such individual had typhoid fever 45 years previously and that during the latter part of May or the first part of June, 1929, "he was ill"; that he recently gave a certain positive Weidal test for typhoid "which indicates his recent illness *may have been typhoid fever,* but in a mild form due to immunity carried over from the previous attack or due to his being a carrier"; and thus they further reported that it was "highly probable that this waiter in the early stages of his recent illness or due to his being a carrier contaminated food which was the cause of the typhoid outbreaking." In other words, the illness of the waiter may have been "typhoid"; ergo, if he had typhoid, he may have contaminated milk or food at lunch counters where others ate, without a showing that any such supply or food was contaminated. When the biologists were advised that the individual referred to was not a waiter at any of the lunch counters until after the illness of those suffering from typhoid, they answered that he might have been about there and become a carrier by shaking hands or the like with those at or about the lunch counter. But no evidence was given to show that the waiter did so, or that those who ate at the lunch counter even touched the hem of his garment. In giving their testimony, the biologists did not say, as indicated by their report, "highly probable," but that "it was possible," that the epidemic was due to eating contaminated food by those suffering from the disease or by coming in contact with others carrying germs of the disease. Further argument was made by them that if the polluted and contaminated waters were the sole cause of the epidemic they would expect a much larger number of cases of typhoid than was reported. And since the spread of the disease caused from contaminated foods is not likely to be so great or extensive as when caused by a common supply of contaminated drinking water; ergo, the cause of the epidemic in question was from contaminated foods and not from the common supply of admitted and indisputable contaminated and polluted waters. Further, they reported and testified that they talked with divers persons who drank water from Wheeler creek and from the waterworks system and learned that none of those had contracted the disease; ergo, the admitted contaminated waters were not the cause of the epidemic, or that the epidemic was equally attributable to other causes. As well say Jane and Mary slept with the maid who admittedly had the itch, and in due course they broke out with the disease; others slept with the maid and did not contract the disease; ergo, Jane and Mary must have contracted the disease elsewhere without any showing that it was so contracted except argument that it "might have been," that it was "possible," that it could have been contracted elsewhere, for we all may get the itch without sleeping with maids.

On the record no one may successfully, no one does, controvert that there is sufficient positive and direct evidence to justify a finding that the contaminated and polluted waters were the immediate and consequential cause of the epidemic. On the contrary, a finding that the epidemic was due to contaminated food, or to a cause other than the contaminated waters, would on the record have no support other than by mere argument and conjecture without evidence to justify either. Thus on the record the only natural and consequential cause of the epidemic was due to the contaminated and polluted waters. To argue that it might have been caused from food eaten or milk drunk at the lunch counter, without any evidence that such food or milk supply was in any particular impure or contaminated, argues nothing.

C. *Libel by a Religious Organization*—Moyle *vs.* Franz (N.Y. Second Dept. 267 App. Div. 423. March 6, 1944).

Can a member or a former member of a religious organization be libeled by it? Does a religious organization enjoy absolute privilege or qualified privilege? This recent New York case, which concerns a publication of Jehovah's Witnesses, takes in all the major problems involved. The majority of the court held that a religious organization's privilege to publish is not absolute but qualified. "The qualified privilege of a religious society to publish matters of interest to its members may be destroyed by showing excessive publication or other evidence of malice." The long and vigorous dissent by a minority of the court digs deep into some aspects of the principle of religious freedom.

OLIN R. MOYLE, RESPONDENT, *vs.* FRED W. FRANZ et al., Appellants. (Appeal No. 1.)
Second Department, March 6, 1944.

APPEAL from a judgment of the Supreme Court, Kings County, entered June 30, 1943, in favor of plaintiff upon a verdict rendered at a Trial Term (UGHETTA, J.), bringing up for review an order of the trial court which denied a motion by defendants for a directed verdict.

Hayden C. Covington and *Ernest P. Seelman* for appellants.

Walter Bruchhausen, William G. Fennell and *John H. Van Surdam* for respondent.

Per Curiam. Upon a prior appeal in this libel action this court affirmed an order denying a motion to dismiss the complaint under rule 106 of the Rules of Civil Practice. (*Moyle vs. Rutherford,* 261 App. Div. 968.)

The action is predicated upon the publication by defendants in *The Watchtower,* a semi-monthly magazine, of two defamatory articles concerning the plaintiff. At the close of the case a motion to dismiss the second cause of action as against the individual defendants was granted upon the ground that they were not shown to have been connected with the publication of the article "Snares." The jury returned a verdict against all the defendants on the first cause of action for $5,000 in actual damages and $10,000 in punitive damages; and against the corporate defendants on the second cause of action for an additional $5,000 in actual damages and an additional $10,000 in punitive damages.

The trial court charged the jury that it was the law of the case that the statements sued upon were libelous. No exception was taken to the court's charge in that respect and no request was made to have the trial court charge otherwise. Upon this appeal the appellants have restricted their arguments to the defenses which they urged upon the trial. They claim that the evidence proved the truth of the defamatory statements; that the statements were qualifiedly privileged and made without malice; and that the awards of actual and punitive damages were excessive.

In considering the merits of the appellants' arguments, we have been guided by their express disclaimer of any desire to obtain a new trial by reason of any errors that may have been committed by the trial court. In part the disclaimer reads: "If defendants have not disproved these charges and established their defenses as a matter of law, they do not desire a new trial."

We are unable to agree with either alternative of the appellants' various contentions that each of their defenses is sustained by the "undisputed evidence or overwhelming preponderance of evidence." As to damages, we find that there was sufficient proof from which malice could be inferred and upon which an award of punitive damages could be based.

In the dissenting opinion dismissal of the complaint is recommended upon the ground that the statements were absolutely privileged and that the jury, in effect, decided upon the propriety of the language used by a religious society in characterizing what it considered misconduct by one of its members. We do not intend to detract from the right of a duly constituted religious or ecclesiastical tribunal to deal with matters subject to its jurisdiction, nor from its privilege to publish the results of its proceedings in an official organ. The jury in this case was instructed that a religious organization had the privilege of publishing such matters in its official magazine. The privilege is, however, not absolute but qualified. The jury was so instructed. Neither upon the trial nor before this court have the appellants contended that their publications were absolutely privileged. In their requests for special findings and in their requests to charge they specifically described their defense as one of qualified privilege. The qualified privilege of a religious society to publish matters of interest to its members may be destroyed by showing excessive publication or other evidence of malice. (*Pecue vs. West,* 233 N. Y. 316, 321-322; 33 Am. Jur., Libel and Slander, § 188, p. 179; 17 R. C. L., Libel and Slander, § 90, p. 344; and see *Murray vs. Brancato,* 290 N. Y. 52, 58.) Evidence was adduced from which the jury could have found that there was excessive publication. It was testified that *The Watchtower* was distributed to all persons willing to pay its subscription price and not merely to persons interested in the affairs of the appellants' organization. The jury could, therefore, have inferred that *The Watchtower* was a magazine of general circulation rather than one restricted to persons having a mutual interest in the statements published. The jury was also entitled to infer malice from the tenor of the articles, from the fact that several defamatory statements had been published, and from the evidence that without knowledge, or with only fragmentary knowledge of the incidents to which their signed statement related, most of the individual defendants had acquiesced in defamation of the plaintiff. It is, therefore, impossible to hold as a matter of law that the defendants acted in good faith and without malice. Nor do we find these propositions established by the "undisputed evidence or overwhelming preponderance of evidence."

The jury's verdict, however, was grossly excessive, and should be reduced to $7,500 on each cause of action.

The judgment should be reversed on the facts and a new trial granted, with costs to abide the event, unless within ten days from the entry of the order hereon the plaintiff stipulate to reduce the amount of the verdict on the first cause of action from $15,000 to $7,500, and the amount of the verdict on the second cause of action from $15,000 to $7,500, in which event the judgment as so reduced is affirmed, without costs. The order denying defendants' motion for a directed verdict should be affirmed, without costs.

CARSWELL, J. (dissenting). This litigation had its genesis in a letter written by Moyle, the plaintiff, to Rutherford, the head of a religious society. It was followed by disciplinary action or expulsion of the plaintiff from the Society. The letter and rejoinders thereto were published and this action for libel eventuated. Plaintiff has recovered heavy compensatory and punitive damages. Defendants appeal from the judgment therefor.

The contentions of the defendants are clothed in legal terminology commingled with a distinctive type of religious vernacular. They do not stress a principle that should be determinative of this litigation. It is that all matters arising out of ecclesiastical relations or the administration of the affairs of a spiritual or religious group are to be determined solely by the governing authority in the religious group. To insure unimpaired the integrity of this principle, courts will not inquire into or concern themselves, directly or indirectly, with conflicting contentions relating to the practice or to the administration of the doctrinal affairs of religious groups, or the merits of or grounds for the imposition of discipline for claimed violations of duties owing to a religious group by a member thereof. This principle was enforced against a minister in *Connitt vs. R. P. D. C. of N. Prospect* (54 N. Y. 551); against a priest in *Baxter vs. McDonnell* (155 N. Y. 83); against a nun in *Noonan vs. Gibbons* (253 App. Div. 837); and in support of a rabbinical adjudication in *S. S. & B. L. P. Corp. vs. Kashruth Assn. of G. N. Y., Inc.* (158 Misc. 358). To be sure, courts will enforce civil rights possessed by those in ecclesiastical relationships, but they are not astute to perceive such rights when they are claimed to emerge from conflicts between a member of a spiritual or religious group and its governing authority in respect of practices, doctrine or dogma, or conduct claimed to be in violation thereof. This course recognizes the impropriety of courts by their action impinging upon religious doctrine, or administration relating thereto, or disputes germinating therefrom. Any other course would be productive of public mischief and bring obloquy to all religion by the parading of criminations and recriminations which should be disposed of *in camera* by duly constituted officials.

The applicability of this principle became manifest on the first day of the trial when plaintiff put in evidence a publication of defendants of September 1, 1939, of which no mention is made in his complaint. It revealed that plaintiff had been actually ousted (not merely recommended for ouster) from the Society upon a final adjudication of "unfaithfulness." The subject matter of the publications of which plaintiff complains was unfaithfulness. One merely gave some of the details of the basis of the disciplinary action.

The defendants might well have directed the court's attention to the significance of this September 1, 1939, exhibit, and the court might have *sua sponte,* or on request, exercised its inherent power to control the order of proof and limit the evidence to this primary and controlling factor. This would have obviated, as irrelevant, the adducing of evidence during many days of the trial as to the truth or untruth of plaintiff's letter and defendants' publications, and avoided the public mischief attendant upon such a spectacle. The course pursued resulted in a jury, in effect, passing judgment upon unfamiliar religious doctrine, religious administration, and discipline relating thereto. The jury, in effect, determined the propriety of the conduct of the affairs, spiritual and internal, of a religious society and the right of a religious society to use Scriptural terms to characterize misconduct relating to its religious practices, doctrine or administration, which, in the judgment of its duly constituted authorities, merited discipline.

Defendants are entitled to the full benefit of this pertinent principle even though some of their ideas meet with disfavor and their conduct toward some members of the community is irritating and exasperating. We are not concerned with this latter phase so long as they merely exercise fundamental rights under the law and keep their conduct within prescribed legal limits. The benefit of this principle should not be denied to them because they are inept in invoking it or because they function in a manner different from other conventionally organized or orthodox groups. This principle is indispensable to the independence of all religious groups.

We need only concern ourselves here with certain unchallenged facts. The individual defendants belong to and are directors of a society known as Jehovah's Witnesses. They follow a primitive form of practice and profession of Christianity under theocratic auspices. They disclaim being a sect or a cult. Each member of the Society becomes a "minister" or a "Witness." By joining it he or she voluntarily agrees to submit himself or herself to the existing government thereof. The Society divides itself into groups, each of which is referred to as a "family," with a distinctive name. Each member, or as he is called, each "Witness," foregoes pecuniary gain and dedicates all his native and acquired earthly skills to the religious society as part of his all-inclusive duty to advance the "kingdom interests" as a "Witness" or a "minister." One of these groups located in Brooklyn is known as the Bethel Family.

Plaintiff as a Jehovah's Witness, an ordained minister, and a lawyer, became a member of the Bethel Family. He was assigned to legal work for the group. An incident relating to a certain court proceeding occurred, which, with seeming justification, subjected him to reproach. Legal work was not his exclusive field, as he at all times acted as a "minister" or a "Witness" like the others. He decided to cease to be a member of the Bethel Family as of September 1, 1939, and on July 21, 1939, wrote a long letter to Rutherford, the head of the Society, who is since deceased. In that letter he criticized and slurred the conduct of Rutherford and other members of that family group. He had the letter delivered to Rutherford and immediately left on a vacation. On about sixteen occasions between July 21, 1939, and September 1, 1939, he distributed the letter or the substance thereof to various members of this religious society throughout the country. Meanwhile, on August 8, 1939, Rutherford called a meeting of the Board of Directors at the Bethel Family. The delay in so doing was due to certain members being on vacation.

Plaintiff was invited and attended the meeting. The letter of plaintiff was read at that meeting. Plaintiff was asked to justify his animadversions. The meeting became a sort of trial of plaintiff respecting his assertions in the letter and his conduct as a "Witness" acting for other "Witnesses" in certain court proceedings. During the meeting a resolution was adopted by the Board recommending the expulsion of plaintiff. Rutherford, the head of the Society, adopted the recommendation and directed plaintiff to leave the Bethel Home at once. He did so. As the letter referred to conduct of the entire Bethel Family, it was then read to the entire group, which numbered more than two hundred, and they were informed of the disposition made in respect of plaintiff.

In a magazine called *The Watchtower,* published by a nonstock corporate defendant owned by this religious society, the defendants, on September 1, 1939, published a notice, which stated that plaintiff was no longer with the Society and that this was due to "his unfaithfulness to the kingdom interests, *and to those who serve the kingdom.*" It also stated *inter alia* that the Board of Directors by unanimous vote on August 8, 1939, had recommended that the president sever plaintiff's connection with the Society *and that this had been done.*

Up to this point the defendants' conduct was clearly within their legal rights under the doctrine above stated. It was further sanctioned by well-settled authority respecting the propriety of publication of the severance of such relations and the reasons therefor in the exercise of absolute privilege. (*Barrows vs. Bell,* 73 Mass. 301; *Fairchild vs. Adams,* 65 Mass. 549; *Farnsworth vs. Storrs,* 59 Mass. 412; *Cranfill vs. Hayden,* 22 Tex. Civ. App. 656.) If this right did not exist, an unfaithful minister or priest would be able to do untold damage to the religious group or church that ousted him. The only way mischievous activities of such an adjudged recreant can be frustrated or neutralized is by publishing, to those to whom his disrupting or unauthorized activities are directed, the reasons for his ouster, so that they may evaluate his representations or his claimed authority to speak on behalf of or to the church or group, in the light of findings of unfaithfulness made by the duly authorized body or official.

After September 1, 1939, plaintiff appeared at various meetings in the West of members of this religious society and publicized his reasons for leaving the Bethel Family. His explanations reflected unfavorably upon the conduct thereof and after September 1, 1939, he circulated fifty or more copies of his July 21, 1939, letter to members of various congregations of the defendant religious society who requested it, and to about eighteen who apparently made no request therefor. This conduct evidently precipitated a meeting of the defendants on September 21, 1939, at which an article prepared by Rutherford was read and signed by the individual defendants. It was entitled "Information" and it was later, on October 15, 1939, published in the defendants' magazine called *The Watchtower.* This article restates *part* of what had been done on August 8, 1939, in reference to the plaintiff's July 21, 1939, communication and also refers to plaintiff's conduct in circulating that letter (which was referred to as a libel), and asserts that plaintiff, who had been entrusted with confidential matters of the Society, "assaults and maligns those who trusted him" (having reference to his July 21, 1939, letter) just as Judas had proved his unfaithfulness to Christ Jesus. It makes no mention of plaintiff as a lawyer. This article, in substance, adds nothing to the ultimate effect of the publication of September 1, 1939, of which plaintiff did not complain, because that article stated that plaintiff had been ousted by reason of "unfaithfulness to the kingdom interests, *and to those who serve the kingdom,*" meaning the Society and the "Witnesses."

When plaintiff became a member of this religious Society he voluntarily obligated himself to submit to and abide by the government thereof, and to devote all his talents, native and acquired, not only as a "Witness" or ordained minister but also his incidental or acquired skill as a lawyer, to the faithful service and welfare of the Society and his associate "Witnesses." When the authorized body of the Society, exercising unquestioned jurisdiction, found him guilty of unfaithfulness, it made an adjudication upon him as an ordained minister or as a "Witness," and included as a part thereof was an adjudication of unfaithfulness to his obligations and duties as a lawyer to his associate "Witnesses," that is to "those who serve the kingdom." The September 1, 1939, publication and findings based on the August 8, 1939, meeting referred to in the October 15, 1939, publication, were that plaintiff was ousted because of "his unfaithfulness to the kingdom interests [that is, the Society of which he was a member], and to those who serve the kingdom," that is, as a "Witness" and lawyer to his associate "Witnesses." This determination of the Society is conclusive upon the courts, since no recognized vitiating element is invoked. It was a conclusive adjudication against plaintiff in respect of the July 21, 1939, letter and the unfaithful character of his conduct generally as a "Witness."

By widespread circulation of the July 21, 1939, letter plaintiff precipitated on October 15, 1939, a republication of part of the decision of the governing body published September 1, 1939. This republication, in amplified form, in no wise added in substance to the effect of the original publication or findings of the governing body. In fact this later publication was milder than was the one of September 1, 1939. It left unsaid that he had been expelled. It merely indicated that his expulsion had been recommended. It repeated in different language that he had been "unfaithful," by the use of the term "Judas," which is merely a synonym for "unfaithfulness," or the personification of that quality. To say, in effect, that he was like Judas is merely to say in a more colorful way, or with the use of a Scriptural term, what had been said in a prosaic way, in the unchallenged September 1, 1939, decision and publication—that he had been unfaithful to the kingdom and to those who serve the kingdom. The original publication of September 1, 1939, was absolutely privileged under the authorities. The absolute privilege which permitted the first publication stems from the same reason which accords absolute privilege to the republication. That the republication of a part of the basis of the September 1, 1939, article was likewise absolutely privileged became clear when plaintiff's proof relating to the September 1, 1939, article showed that his expulsion had occurred because of the facts stated in the October 15, 1939, article. It was first made known in plaintiff's proof, on the first day of the trial, that there was this September 1, 1939, publication not mentioned in the complaint.

Plaintiff's conduct necessitated the detailed and clarified republication. He professed to be desirous of not creating dissension in this religious Society. His pretensions in this regard are not borne out by the undisputed fact that he circulated the July 21, 1939, letter or the substance thereof, both before and after the publications of September 1 and October 15, 1939. He was seeking co-operation of a rival group which was formerly part of the defendant Society. He was, during these periods, with his July 21, 1939, letter sowing the seeds of distrust, dissension and disunion among other groups in the defendant Society. To explain or neutralize his activities, defendants were entitled, under the cases cited (*supra*), to have recourse to a clarified publication of the official basis of the decision resulting in plaintiff's ouster.

This analysis of the pertinent undisputed activities of these individuals may make unnecessary a decision as to whether or not, apart from absolute privilege, there was an actionable libel in the article of October 15, 1939. The fact that no libel was seasonably asserted by suit in respect of the article of September 1, 1939, supports the view that the publication of October 15, 1939, was not a libel since it is a mere amplification of a phase or basis of the earlier publication. It is my view, without reference to the September 1, 1939, article, that the October 15, 1939, article is absolutely privileged. When considering this phase, an observation of Lord Cockburn in a kindred situation (*Koenig vs. Ritchie,* 3 F. & F. 413) has pertinency: "I own I cannot feel much sympathy for a man, who, having been the first to make an appeal to public opinion, when he is answered in the same manner by a counter appeal, changes the tribunal which he has himself selected, and invokes the arm of the law."

Plaintiff continued his activities after October 15, 1939, in spreading his July 21, 1939, letter and Rutherford wrote and had published on November 15, 1939, in defendants' *The Watchtower* another article entitled "Snares." It is a homily, permeated with the distinctive didactic vernacular of this Society. It makes no mention of or reference to plaintiff. It might properly be read as an admonition to other "Witnesses" doing legal work. In another setting it would not attract attention. In the abstract it reproves any person who, while consecrated as a "Witness," acts as a lawyer for another "Witness" in a fashion which indicates "unfaithfulness to the kingdom." It merely declares the propriety of a finding of unfaithfulness against any person who, as a "Witness," is unfaithful in his incidental conduct as a lawyer while functioning as a "Witness" on behalf of another consecrated person or "Witness." There is no case which authorizes a court or a jury or a nonmember of this Society to pass judgment on the propriety of a pronouncement of abstract doctrine of this Society, or any other religious group, in its official organ, which makes no mention of plaintiff. Even if the observations be heretical or unsound or in bad taste (none of which here appears) in the eyes of nonmembers, the right to publish them is absolute, and no private right of action may be founded thereon. The writing of the article may have been inspired by plaintiff's conduct, but that has no legal significance. From the earliest times, general or abstract religious and philosophical meditations and observations have been inspired by particular instances of conduct. It has never been considered a proper function of courts to police abstract theological polemics.

If the article be deemed applicable only to plaintiff because he thinks it accurately describes his conduct, it adds nothing to the publications of September 1, 1939, and October 15, 1939. Those publications concretely referred to plaintiff and involved an adjudication of his unfaithfulness to the religious Society of which he was a part. This November 15, 1939, article merely dealt in the abstract with the same type of unfaithfulness. It did so with no mention of the plaintiff, who had been the subject of a permissible publication with reference to him as a "Witness," under a decision by the Board of a religious Society and the action of its President.

We need not consider plaintiff's circulation after the November 15, 1939, publication, of over 1,500 copies of his July 21, 1939, letter, or the extent it illumines his claimed lack of desire to disrupt the Society.

The benefit of the above principles was saved by the defendants and may be accorded to them for two reasons:

(a) On their motion to dismiss at the close of the plaintiff's case, and on the motion at the close of the entire case they asserted that the articles were "privileged," without limitation by the use of the terms "absolute" or "qualified," even though the motion was not supported by the arguments given above. "In our review we are confined to the *questions* raised or argued at the trial but not to the arguments there presented. 'Nor is it material whether the case was well presented to the court below, in the arguments addressed to it. * * *.' (*Oneida Bank vs. Ontario Bank,* 21 N. Y. 490, 504.)" (*Persky vs. Bank of America Nat. Assn.,* 261 N. Y. 212, 218.) Here the question of "privilege" was raised and the foregoing determinative principles rest on absolute privilege. Moreover, the defendants were entitled to the benefit of this plea of absolute privilege even without an allegation thereof in their answer. Privilege is usually a matter of defense but if it appears in the plaintiff's evidence or pleading, the defendants may have the advantage of it without setting it up in an answer. (*Tierney vs. Ruppert,* 150 App. Div. 863, 867; *Chapman vs. Dick,* 197 App. Div. 551, 554; 33 Am. Jur., Libel and Slander, § 251; 37 C. J., Libel and Slander, § 403.) Here the facts establishing absolute privilege first appeared in plaintiff's case when he put the September 1, 1939, publication in evidence and it then became apparent that the October 15, 1939, publication was a mere paraphrase of a phase thereof and had been the basis of a binding adjudication according to the theretofore unmentioned September 1, 1939, publication.

(b) The defendants duly excepted, but even in the absence of such exception in the interest of justice the defendants would be entitled to the benefit of the authorities relating to absolute privilege, under section 583 of the Civil Practice Act, and sections 105 and 584, the successor sections to section 1317 of the

Code of Civil Procedure. Under section 583, to prevent manifest injustice an appellate court may review a prejudicial ruling that was not acquiesced in affirmatively by the defendants, or a refusal to grant a motion of such parties. In the instant case there was a failure to grant defendants' motions to dismiss the complaint or to direct a verdict. Section 583 reinforces what was said in the *Persky* case (*supra,* p. 218): " 'It was the duty of the judges to ascertain and declare the whole law upon the undisputed facts spread before them; and it is our duty now to give such a judgment as they ought to have given.' (*Oneida Bank vs. Ontario Bank,* 21 N. Y. 490, 504)," even if the case was not " 'well presented to the court below, in the arguments addressed to it.' " This doctrine is applicable as these arguments involve the entire controversy. Their acceptance completely eliminates liability and they may be advanced on appeal even though not specifically referred to upon the trial, provided the facts, as here, upon which the question of absolute privilege rests, appear in the record. (*Oneida Bank vs. Ontario Bank,* 21 N. Y. 490; *Cook vs. Whipple,* 55 N. Y. 150; *Wright vs. Wright,* 226 N. Y. 578, 579.)

These views make it unnecessary to pass upon whether the defense of qualified privilege was established as a matter of law. There is a basis for so holding, as the rejoinders by the defendants were confined in their publication to a medium that was distributed only to "Witnesses" and the like, who were the ones to whom, directly or indirectly, plaintiff was publishing and distributing his letter of July 21, 1939.

The judgment should be reversed on the law and the facts, with costs, and the complaint dismissed on the law, with costs. The appeal from the order should be dismissed, without costs.

CLOSE, P. J., HAGARTY and LEWIS, JJ., concur in *Per Curiam* opinion; CARSWELL, J., dissents and votes to reverse the judgment on the law and the facts, with costs, to dismiss the complaint on the law, with costs, and to dismiss the appeal from the order denying defendants' motion for a directed verdict, without costs, an opinion in which JOHNSTON, J., concurs.

Judgment reversed on the facts and a new trial granted, with costs to abide the event, unless within ten days from the entry of the order hereon plaintiff stipulate to reduce the amount of the verdict on the first cause of action from $15,000 to $7,500, and the verdict on the second cause of action from $15,000 to $7,500, in which event the judgment as so reduced is affirmed, without costs.

The order denying defendants' motion for a directed verdict is affirmed, without costs.

D. *Libel and Unchastity in a Woman*—Morey *vs.* Barnes. (212 Minnesota 153. No. 33,080. February 27, 1942).

Calling a woman a prostitute and her home a brothel is generally libelous per se, but the defamation must be clear and direct. If the defamation is vague and indirect, a complaint of libel is of dubious validity—how dubious it can be is made clear by this case.

DOROTHY S. MOREY *vs.* C. W. BARNES.
February 27, 1942.
No. 33,080.

Action for libel in the district court for Watonwan county, tried before Harry A. Johnson, Judge, and a jury. After verdict for defendant, plaintiff appealed from an order denying her motion for a new trial. Affirmed.

W. E. Hottinger, for appellant.

Willard Crowley and *John V. Bumby,* for respondent.

GALLAGHER, CHIEF JUSTICE.

Suit for libel, in which defendant had a verdict. Plaintiff appeals from an order denying her motion for new trial.

Plaintiff and her husband, Tony Morey, lived in rooms over a beer parlor and restaurant known as "Tony's Cafe" in Butterfield, Minnesota. The evidence is conflicting as to whether at the time here involved the cafe was owned and operated by plaintiff or her husband, or whether it was jointly owned and operated by them. It appears that plaintiff worked in the cafe with her husband and did all of the cooking.

Defendant owned and published the *Butterfield Advocate,* a weekly newspaper having a circulation of about 600 copies in and around Butterfield. On August 15, 1940, the *Advocate* published a contributed article in its "Open Forum" column which read:

"Butterfield, Minn.,
"August 13, 1940.

"Editor of the Butterfield Advocate.

"Dear Sir:

"Don't you think that it is time that Butterfield people cleaned up their town?

"On Wednesday night at the Farmers Day celebration three of the saloons had gambling games going full blast. In one of the brothels there was a dispute over the gambling which started a fight and a young farm hand was thrown out into the street by the proprietor and struck and knocked down with some kind of a weapon made of steel or iron which fits around the fingers. The young fellow laid there for half an hour with a fractured skull until some good soul happened along and called a doctor. The boy was taken to a hospital at St. James and he is still there. He did not regain consciousness until several hours after the affair and even now he does not know what is going on about him.

"A special policeman is said to have been there when this was taking place and that he did nothing about it. Also it is said that a member of the council who has been in office a long time, calls at one of the brothels every morning and gets a free half pint of liquor to sustain him during the day and this is his pay for protecting law evaders.

"None of the members of our family has ever been in any of these brothels but we hear from neighbors that one of them is known as the "Murder House," one is called "The Hole," and the other, the "Pest House." These are good names for such un-Godly places. Decent farmers should keep away from Butterfield until these places are closed and their proprietors jailed for long terms. It is even believed now that one of these hell-hole owners may not be a citizen of these United States. If it is found that this is true he ought to be deported.

"If your town must have saloons you should get men to run them who will observe the laws and who will not serve beer to school children and who will not have school children as bartenders.

"This is a matter for the county sheriff to look into and he also should attend to his business better than he is doing now. Your paper can be of tremendous good in your community and we hope you will help out by publishing this letter.

"A Farm Family."

Shortly after the publication of the article plaintiff served upon defendant a notice to retract, and defendant published a retraction in its edition of September 26, 1940.

It is conceded that Tony's Cafe is one of the places referred to in the article and that the fight took place in front of it. Defendant admits that he knew that Mrs. Morey lived in the building, but contends that the published article did not refer to her but to Tony's Cafe. It appears that Tony was convicted for participation in the fight on the occasion referred to in the article and that he had been convicted of liquor violations during prohibition days. There was testimony that the reputation of Tony's Cafe was bad and that the village council, after the incident in question, refused to issue a license for the sale of beer in the place. There was no testimony indicating that plaintiff was not a person of good character and reputation. At the close of the testimony plaintiff moved for a directed verdict, claiming that the use of the word "brothel" made the article libelous *per se* and that the only issue for the jury was the amount of damages. The trial court denied the motion and submitted to the jury under appropriate instructions the issues (1) whether the article imputed that plaintiff was an unchaste woman, and (2) the amount of damages, if any, to which plaintiff was entitled. There was no exception to the instructions and no request for other or additional instructions.

The only point urged here is that the published article was libelous *per se* and that the trial court should have granted plaintiff's motion for a directed verdict. It is contended that the use of the word "brothel" designated plaintiff's home as a house of prostitution and thus imputed unchastity to her.

It is only where a publication clearly defames a person that the court should instruct the jury that it is libelous as a matter of law. Sharpe *vs.* Larson, 67 Minn. 428, 70 N. W. 1, 554; Alwin *vs.* Liesch, 86 Minn. 281, 90 N. W. 404; Moore *vs.* Francis, 121 N. Y. 199, 23 N. E. 1127, 8 L. R. A. 214, 18 A. S. R. 810. To be libelous *per se,* words must be of such a nature that the court can say, as a matter of law, that they will tend to disgrace and degrade the party defamed or hold him up to public hatred, contempt, or ridicule, or cause him to be shunned or avoided. Herringer *vs.* Ingberg, 91 Minn. 71, 97 N. W. 460. If an article is not obviously defamatory but is reasonably susceptible of an innocent meaning, the question of libel or no libel is for the jury to decide under proper instructions. Odgers, Libel and Slander (6 ed.) p. 94; Sharpe *vs.* Larson, *supra.* In deciding whether words will bear an innocent meaning, a writing must be construed as a whole without taking any word or phrase out of context, or placing undue emphasis upon any one part. Tawney *vs.* Simonson, Whitcomb & Hurley Co. 109 Minn. 341, 124 N. W. 229, 27 L.R.A.(N.S.) 1035; Prosser, Torts, § 91, p. 790; Odgers, Libel and Slander (6 ed.) p. 97. The words must be construed with other parts of the published matter. Johnson *vs.* Force, 80 Minn. 315, 83 N. W. 182.

"Brothel" is defined as a "house of lewdness or ill fame; a house frequented by prostitutes"; or a "bawdyhouse." Webster's New International Dictionary (2 ed.) 1934. But words are not always used in their correct sense. Some persons, in a forced attempt at colorful expression, indulge in ill-advised use of inaccurate terminology; and an article written in that manner may or may not be libelous, depending on the occasion and circumstances and how it is understood by those reading it. This is well established in Australia Newspaper Co. Ltd. *vs.* Bennett

[1894] A. C. p. 284, an English case decided by the House of Lords. It was argued in that case that the use of the word "Ananias" necessarily imputed to the plaintiff willful and deliberate falsehood. Lord Herschell, L. C., said:

"Even admitting that the natural effect of the use of the word 'Ananias' standing alone would be to convey the imputation suggested, the learned judge appears to their Lordships, with all respect, to have lost sight of the fact that people not unfrequently use words, and are understood to use words, not in their natural sense, or as conveying the imputation which, in ordinary circumstances, and apart from their surroundings, they would convey, but extravagantly, and in a manner which would be understood by those who hear or read them as not conveying the grave imputation suggested by a mere consideration of the words themselves. Whether a word is, in any particular instance, used, and would be understood as being used, for the purpose of conveying an imputation upon character must be for the jury."

Flanagan *vs.* Nicholson Pub. Co. 137 La. 588, 68 So. 964, L. R. A. 1917E, 510, Ann. Cas. 1917B, 402; Yakavicze *vs.* Valentukevicious, 84 Conn. 350, 80 A. 94, Ann. Cas. 1912 C, 1264; Fawsett *vs.* Clark, 48 Md. 494, 30 Am. R. 481; Norton *vs.* Ladd, 5 N. H. 203, 20 Am. D. 573.

The article in this case, although couched in loose phraseology, is directed at certain specific evils. It protests the gambling, drinking, and fighting allowed to prevail in the taverns of Butterfield. It criticizes the laxity of the law enforcement officials, and gives particular attention to a fight which occurred in the street outside Tony's Cafe. But it does not seem to regard prostitution as one of the evil conditions existing in Butterfield. Certainly it does not give that condition the treatment its relative seriousness would seem to deserve. The word "brothel" hardly fits into the general tenor of the article. Whether those reading it would understand it as imputing that plaintiff was a woman of unchaste character was properly for the jury.

The order appealed from is affirmed.

E. *Libel by Imputation of Illness*—Kassowitz *vs.* Sentinel Co. (226 Wisconsin 468. January 11, 1938).

Is it libelous to say that someone has suffered from tuberculosis? The Supreme Court of Wisconsin says no: "It may be unfortunate, but it is no disgrace to be tubercular. Contracting the disease is not due, as in some cases of disease, to any immorality." A charge of tuberculosis, then, is not libelous per se, but special damages may be pleaded. In the absence of such a plea there is no case.

KASSOWITZ, Appellant, *vs.* SENTINEL COMPANY, Respondent.
December 7, 1937—January 11, 1938.

APPEAL from an order of the circuit court for Milwaukee county: OTTO H. BREIDENBACH, Circuit Judge. *Affirmed.*

Action for a libel commenced May 22, 1937. Defendant demurred to the complaint for the reason that "it appears upon the face of said complaint that the same does not state facts sufficient to constitute a cause of action." From an order sustaining the demurrer, plaintiff appeals. The news item containing the alleged libel published by the defendant in the Milwaukee Sentinel, on April 22, 1937, is, in full, as follows:

"COUNTY URGED TO DISCHARGE TUBERCULARS.
"O'Boyle Issues Warning; Coffey Will Make Survey.

"Removal from the county service of all employees with a previous record of tuberculosis was recommended yesterday by Oliver L. O'Boyle corporation counsel, who warned of probable 'heavy financial damage' to the county if the step was not taken.

"It could not be immediately learned how many employees would be involved. William L. Coffey, manager of county institutions, to whom O'Boyle's advice was addressed, said he would make a study of the situation. If he follows the recommendation he will file charges of physical disability with the civil service commission.

"O'Boyle's action was prompted by the recent case of Miss Doris Strathmann, who was given employment at Muirdale, the county tuberculosis sanitarium, as an arrested case of the disease. When the disease became active again she filed a claim against the county, which will aggregate $15,000 over a period of years.

"Others File Claims.

"An industrial commission examiner denied the claim on the ground it had not been established that her labors for the county caused recurrence of the disease, but the commission overruled him and the supreme court upheld the commission.

"Immediately after the final ruling in the Strathmann case two similar claims were filed, one by Caroline Halverson, formerly an employee at the county hospital for the chronic insane, the other by August Serkowski, formerly employed at the county general hospital. These two claims are now awaiting adjudication.

"O'Boyle pointed out that Miss Strathmann was given a job at Muirdale under the prevalent medical theory that persons with a prior record of tuberculosis can best care for themselves when so employed and thus run fewer chances of a recurrence of the disease than when engaged in private industry.

"That theory is in practice at Muirdale, Coffey said, and there are a number of persons employed there, including part-time doctors, who are so-called arrested cases of tuberculosis. In the Strathmann case, however, the industrial commission blamed the county for the recurrence.

"To Protect County.

" 'Since the commission takes this attitude in these cases, which is contrary to the best medical opinion,' O'Boyle wrote, 'it is incumbent upon the county, we feel, to protect itself.

" 'Since there is no reason to believe the commission will reverse its policy as established in the Strathmann case, much as we regret depriving needy persons of employment, we believe it incumbent upon yourself and the board of trustees to forthwith separate from the county service all employees with a previous record of tuberculosis.'

"He also urged Coffey to have all institutional employees, particularly at Muirdale, subjected immediately to chest examinations and X-rays, and to repeat such examinations periodically 'so that there may, if possible, be a cessation of this type of claim.'

"These tuberculosis claims and other demands upon the county for workmen's compensation have recently increased to such an extent that O'Boyle last week requested the county board to create a new position of investigator in his office. The judiciary and finance committee yesterday authorized him to make a temporary ninety-day appointment pending a civil service examination."

The trial court held that:

"To say of one that he is suffering with tuberculosis, however, is not stating that he has a loathsome disease;" that the words were not libelous *per se;* and that the complaint did not state special damages. The court further held:

"Inasmuch as the complaint is insufficient to state a cause of action for the reasons just discussed, it is unnecessary to determine whether or not the language of the alleged libelous statement is so inclusive as to identify all of the part-time doctors, thus permitting any one of them to bring suit."

The cause was submitted for the appellant on the brief of *Gold & McCann* of Milwaukee, and for the respondent on that of *Lines, Spooner & Quarles,* attorneys, and *Charles B. Quarles* of counsel, all of Milwaukee.

MARTIN, J. The following paragraph contains the alleged libel:

"That theory is in practice at Muirdale, Coffey said, and there are a number of persons employed there, including part-time doctors, who are so-called arrested cases of tuberculosis. . . ."

The appellant's first contention is that the article, above quoted, sufficiently identifies the plaintiff to permit him to maintain the action. It is alleged in the complaint that at the time of the publication, there were, including plaintiff, four part-time doctors employed at the Muirdale sanitarium. The article states: "There are a number of persons employed there, including part-time doctors, who are so-called arrested cases of tuberculosis." The trial court did not reach the question whether or not the language of the alleged libelous statement is so inclusive as to identify all the part-time doctors, thus permitting any one of them to bring suit. This court in recent years has on several occasions passed upon the sufficiency of identification in libel actions. In *Helmicks vs. Stevlingson,* 212 Wis. 614, 615, 250 N. W. 402, the court said:

" 'It is well settled that defamatory words must refer to some ascertained or ascertainable person and that person must be the particular plaintiff. Statements are not libelous unless they refer to some ascertained or ascertainable person.' *Schoenfeld vs. Journal Co.* 204 Wis. 132, 136, 235 N. W. 442; *Williams vs. Journal Co.* 211 Wis. 362, 247 N. W. 435, 439."

"In every action for defamation, two things are necessary:

"(1) A defamation apparent from the words themselves, for no innuendo can alter the sense.

"(2) Certainty as to the person who is defamed, for no innuendo can render certain that which is uncertain." Newell, Slander and Libel (4th ed.), § 200. (On Sufficiency of Identification, see Annotation, 91 A. L. R. p. 1161.)

In *Williams vs. Journal Co.* 211 Wis. 362, 367, 247 N. W. 435, the defendant newspaper published the following:

" 'Our attention has been called to instances where a member of the city attorney's staff has, while so employed, accepted retainers from a local carrier. . . . We believe this to be bad in principle—opens a wide field of temptation—raises grave question of positive damage in case of future conflict of interest.' "

In this case, Mr. Williams was at the time an assistant city attorney. The court said:

"In the article complained of in the fifth cause of action the plaintiff is not mentioned by name. Neither from that article nor the extraneous facts, which are alleged in the complaint by way of inducement, can it be ascertained that the plaintiff was the particular person to whom the statements in that article related. The nearest approach in that article to an identification of any person is the statement that 'a member of the city attorney's staff has accepted such retainers from a local carrier.' That, however, does not identify the plaintiff as the particular member of that staff to whom that statement is intended to refer. Although it is alleged in the complaint by way of inducement that the plaintiff is the only attorney rendering professional services to the city who was known as the special assistant city attorney, and that he accepted employment from the Chicago, Milwaukee & St. Paul Railroad Company to condemn a freight depot site, it is not alleged and it does not otherwise appear that there were not also other members of the city attorney's staff who also accepted retainers from a local carrier, and to whom consequently that article was equally applicable and was intended to refer. Because the statements complained of in the article upon which the fifth cause of action is based do not refer to some ascertained and ascertainable person, they are not libelous."

The city attorney's staff at the time consisted of not more than four or five assistant city attorneys. In the instant case, there were only four part-time doctors employed at the Muirdale sanitarium. The lack of sufficient identification, as held in the *Williams Case,* is applicable to the facts in the case at bar. The alleged libelous article does not state that all of the part-time doctors are arrested cases of tuberculosis. The ones referred to may have been any of the four and not necessarily this plaintiff. This branch of the case is ruled by *Schoenfeld vs. Journal Co.* 204 Wis. 132, 235 N. W. 442, 444; *Williams vs. Journal Co., supra; Helmicks vs. Stevlingson, supra.*

Though the conclusion reached results in an affirmance of the order sustaining the demurrer, we will consider whether the article is libelous *per se.* Appellant cites *Kirby vs. Smith,* 54 S. D. 608, 609, 224 N. W. 230, 231, an action for slander under the Revised Code, section 98, subdivisions 2, 3. The complaint, in substance, alleged:

"That plaintiff was eighteen years of age, by trade or profession a clerk, and until the time complained of was engaged in clerical work in business houses in Rapid City, where she was a resident and had an extensive acquaintance. That in the month of February, 1927, the defendant, in conversation with numerous persons in Rapid City, did speak of and concerning the plaintiff the following words: 'That the plaintiff was then afflicted with tuberculosis (and did thereby impute to her the existence of an infectious and contagious disease), and that plaintiff was physically unfit to be employed in any capacity in said city wherein she must meet or deal with the public, and that her condition of health was such that any person dealing with her or transacting any business or coming in contact with her was likely to become afflicted with said infectious and contagious disease.' "

The South Dakota Code, section 98, so far as applicable to the case, defines "slander" as follows:

"Slander is a false and unprivileged publication, other than libel, which: . . .

"2. Imputes to him the present existence of an infectious, contagious, or loathsome disease;

"3. Tends directly to injure him in respect to his office, profession, trade, or business, either by imputing to him general disqualification in those respects which the office or other occupation peculiarly requires, or by imputing something with reference to his office, profession, trade, or business that has a natural tendency to lessen its profit."

The trial court sustained an objection to the introduction of any evidence, directed a verdict for defendant, and entered judgment dismissing the action. The plaintiff appealed. In reversing the judgment, the supreme court said (p. 611):

"The complaint in the present case alleges that the defendant published of and concerning the plaintiff that she was afflicted with tuberculosis to an extent that any person dealing with her or transacting any business or coming in contact with her was likely to become afflicted and infected with tuberculosis. It seems to us that this would have a tendency to make some people avoid her.

"It is further alleged that defendant said her condition was such that she was physically unfit to be employed in any capacity where she must meet or deal with the public. We think that this would tend to injure her in respect to her profession or business. It imputes to her a general disqualification in respect to the occupation of a clerk, and the language alleged to have been spoken by the defendant of and concerning the plaintiff would certainly have a tendency to prevent her from procuring employment."

In 36 C. J. p. 1167, § 33, it is said:

"To charge one falsely in writing with having any repulsive disease or condition which would necessarily cause him to be shunned or avoided is libelous *per se*."

We have carefully examined the other cases cited by appellant, and do not find any in point. We do not regard the decision in *Kirby vs. Smith, supra,* as applicable to the facts at bar. The alleged slanderous statements in that case came clearly within the inhibition of the state code defining slander. In 17 R. C. L. p. 294, § 33, it is said:

"It is a rule of the common law that an action will lie, without proof of special damage, for speaking words of another which impute that he has a loathsome or contagious disease, at the time of publication, it being obvious that such charges would, if believed, wholly or partially exclude such person from good society. To come within the rule, however, the disease charged must be either leprosy, plague, or a venereal disease. . . ."

We have been unable to find any case directly in point. It may be unfortunate, but it is no disgrace to be tubercular. Contracting the disease is not due, as in some cases of disease, to any immorality.

The alleged libelous statement in the instant case refers to so-called "arrested cases of tuberculosis." The words, "arrested case," may be defined in a medical way, or may be interpreted in the much looser terms of the layman, to whom it may mean an individual well enough to leave a sanitarium and resume his usual existence. It may mean that the person afflicted has so far recovered that he would not communicate the disease to others. We take the following medical definition from the Official Diagnostic Standards (10th ed., 1935), of the National Tuberculosis

Association. Therein the definition of an arrested case is as follows:

"All constitutional symptoms absent; sputum, if any, microscopically negative for tubercle bacilli; X-ray findings compatible with a stationary or retrogressive lesion. These conditions shall have existed for a period of six months, during the last two of which the patient has been taking one hour's walking exercise twice daily or its equivalent."

Webster's New International Dictionary gives the following medical definition of the word "arrest:"

"To bring to a standstill or state of inactivity; as, arrested tuberculosis."

We have no hesitancy in holding that the alleged libelous words are not actionable *per se.* The plaintiff resorts to an innuendo to allege that an "arrested case of tuberculosis" is loathsome and a contagious disease, and that the phrase "an arrested case of tuberculosis" is understood by the general public and by the readers of the defendant's papers to mean an individual who is still tubercular and subject to the same hazards of relapse and spread of disease as is common in cases of clinical and manifest tuberculosis.

"Words which are defamatory *per se* do not need an innuendo, and, conversely, words which do need an innuendo are not defamatory *per se.*" 36 C. J. p. 1151, § 17; *Shaw C. & D. vs. Des Moines Dress Club,* 215 Iowa, 1130, 245 N. W. 231, 86 A. L. R. 839 (see Annotation commencing at page 848); Newell, Slander and Libel (4th ed.), § 200; *Helmicks vs. Stevlingson, supra; Schoenfeld vs. Journal Co., supra.*

"The general effect of the innuendo is only to explain matter which has been already sufficiently expressed before; the import of the words used it cannot enlarge, extend, or change. It has also been held that in determining whether a publication is libelous *per se,* the court is confined to the language employed in the publication and cannot look to the innuendo alleged in the petition. . . . The innuendo cannot aver a fact, or do anything more than refer back to some facts stated in the inducement, and if the inducement is wanting the deficiency cannot be supplied by the statement of the facts in the innuendo." 17 R. C. L. p. 396, § 151.

It is well settled that, in matters not libelous *per se,* special damages must be pleaded. No special damages are alleged. The published matter not being libelous *per se,* no cause of action is stated. *Judevine vs. Benzies-Montanye Fuel & Whse. Co.* 222 Wis. 512, 517, 269 N. W. 295.

By the Court.—Order affirmed.

F. *Libel in a Charge of Suicide*—Hughes *vs.* New England Newspaper Publishing Company. (312 Massachusetts 178. September 9, 1942).

Can a wife sue for libel a newspaper that falsely stated that her husband committed suicide? The Supreme Judicial Court of Massachusetts says that she cannot: "The general rule is that a libel upon the memory of a deceased person that does not directly cast any personal reflection upon his relatives does not give them any right of action, although they may have thereby suffered mental anguish or sustained an impairment of their social standing among a considerable class of respectable people of the community in which they live by the disclosure that they were related to the deceased. . . . A wife has no cause of action for libel on account of a publication that did nothing more than state that her husband took his own life."

ELAINE HUGHES *vs.* THE NEW ENGLAND NEWSPAPER PUBLISHING COMPANY.

Suffolk. April 10, 13, 1942.—September 9, 1942.

Present: FIELD, C.J., DONAHUE, DOLAN, COX, & RONAN, J.J.

Libel and Slander. Actionable Tort.

TORT. Writ in the Superior Court dated June 10, 1941.

A demurrer was sustained by *Collins,* J. The plaintiff appealed.

T. L. Mackin, for the plaintiff.

H. M. Leen, (*T. H. Bilodeau* with him,) for the defendant.

RONAN, J. This is an action of tort for libel. The plaintiff alleges in the first count, which is the only count with which we are now concerned, that the defendant maliciously and falsely published in its newspaper an article stating that her husband, John S. Hughes, pursuant to an arrangement with two of his business associates, committed suicide, and that Hughes had recently moved from Needham to Main Street, in Medfield, where he resided with his wife and two children. Although the article made no other reference to the plaintiff, the declaration further alleged that this article was "false, defamatory and libelous to the plaintiff personally and as the widow of said John S. Hughes insofar" as it stated that he had committed suicide. The case is here on appeal from an order of the Superior Court sustaining a demurrer.

A false statement that Hughes ended his own life charged him with the commission of a crime, for self destruction is a criminal offence in this Commonwealth. *Commonwealth vs. Mink,* 123 Mass. 422. *State vs. Carney,* 40 Vroom, 478. The publication of that statement gave the plaintiff no cause of action. One who defames the memory of the dead, whatever his responsibility may be under the criminal law, *Commonwealth vs. Clap,* 4 Mass. 163; *The King vs. Topham,* 4 T. R. 126; *State vs. Haffer,* 94 Wash. 136, is not liable civilly to the estate of the decedent or to his relatives. The general rule is that a libel upon the memory of a deceased person that does not directly cast any personal reflection upon his relatives does not give them any right of action, although they may have thereby suffered mental anguish or sustained an impairment of their social standing among a considerable class of respectable people of the community in which they live by the disclosure that they were related to the deceased. *Security Sales Agency vs. A. S. Abell Co.* 205 Fed. 941. *Turner vs. Crime Detective,* 34 Fed. Sup. 8. *Skrocki vs. Stahl,* 14 Cal. App. 1. *Saucer vs. Giroux,* 54 Cal. App. 732. *Hurst vs. Goodwin,* 114 Ga. 585. *Bradt vs. New Nonpareil Co.* 108 Iowa, 449. *Fleagle vs. Downing,* 183 Iowa, 1300. *Pattison vs. Gulf Bag Co. Ltd.* 116 La. 963. *Child vs. Emerson,* 102 Mich. 38. *Rose vs. Daily Mirror, Inc.* 284 N. Y. 335. *Wellman vs. Sun Printing & Publishing Association,* 66 Hun, 331. *Sorensen vs. Balaban,* 11 App. Div. (N. Y.) 164. *Benton vs.*

Knoxville News-Sentinel Co. 174 Tenn. 661. *Houston vs. Interstate Circuit, Inc.* 132 S. W. (2d) (Texas) 903. *Renfro Drug Co. vs. Lawson,* 144 S. W. (2d) (Texas) 417. Am. Law Inst. Restatement: Torts, § 560.

The false statement that Hughes committed suicide and left a widow did not constitute a libel on the latter. That statement, which was entirely directed against Hughes, charged him with having committed suicide in accordance with an agreement with his business associates, and clearly implied that no one else had any connection with his death. His widow was not charged with any wrongdoing or with any connection with her husband's act. There are instances where the publication of a written statement concerning one person is of such a nature that it imports misconduct upon the part of another. To publish that a third person is an illegitimate child or that he is the husband of a faithless wife or that a married man is single and about to be married imputes immorality to the mother or wife. *Vicars vs. Worth,* 1 Stra. 471. *Cassidy vs. Daily Mirror Newspapers, Ltd.* [1929] 2 K. B. 331. *Shelby vs. Sun Printing & Publishing Association,* 38 Hun, 474. *Hall vs. Huffman,* 159 Ky. 72. *McDavid vs. Houston Chronicle Printing Co.* 146 S. W. (Texas) 252. Am. Law Inst. Restatement: Torts, § 564, comment e. This principle is not applicable where, as here, the natural effect of the mere statement that the husband took his own life would not cast any aspersion upon his widow.

The plaintiff, however, contends that she is the person referred to as the widow and that this reference to her, considered with the rest of the article, was a defamation upon her. If the publication was directed against her and tended to expose her to public hatred, contempt and ridicule and to induce an evil opinion of her among a considerable class of right thinking persons or to cause her to be deprived of their confidence and social intercourse, then it would result in injuring her reputation and entitle her to damages. *Lyman vs. New England Newspaper Publishing Co.* 286 Mass. 258. *Fahy vs. Melrose Free Press Inc.* 298 Mass. 267. *Ingalls vs. Hastings & Sons Publishing Co.* 304

Mass. 31. *Themo vs. New England Newspaper Publishing Co.* 306 Mass. 54.

A copy of the article is incorporated in the declaration and the question raised by the demurrer is whether the words published, taken in their usual and ordinary sense, could be reasonably understood by those who read them as disparaging the plaintiff's reputation. *Twombly vs. Monroe,* 136 Mass. 464. *Fay vs. Harrington,* 176 Mass. 270. *Riceman vs. Union Indemnity Co.* 278 Mass. 149.

The residence of Hughes was given in the article as Main Street, Medfield, to which, it was stated, he had recently moved "from Needham with his wife and two children." This is no more than a statement that Hughes was a married man living with his family which consisted of his wife and two children. It was descriptive of Hughes and not of those who comprised his household. The mention of them was incidental, for the subject matter of the publication was Hughes and not his family. Although the plaintiff was not named, the mention of her as the wife of Hughes could be found to be sufficient to identify the plaintiff as the person so referred to in the article. *Robinson vs. Coulter,* 215 Mass. 566. *Brown vs. Journal Newspaper Co.* 219 Mass. 486. *Northrop vs. Tibbles,* 215 Fed. 99. *Watson vs. Detroit Journal Co.* 143 Mich. 430. *Gross vs. Cantor,* 270 N. Y. 93. *Burkhart vs. North American Co.* 214 Penn. St. 39. *Schoenfeld vs. Journal Co.* 204 Wis. 132. Other than this reference to the plaintiff as the wife of Hughes, nothing further was said of her. The article no doubt focused public attention upon the plaintiff and caused her some embarrassment and mental anguish, and while these may be taken into account where the plaintiff has a cause of action, they do not alone furnish any foundation for recovery, because the only basis upon which an action for defamation may be grounded is damage to one's reputation. *Kimmerle vs. New York Evening Journal, Inc.* 262 N. Y. 99. *Themo vs. New England Newspaper Publishing Co.* 306 Mass. 54, 57. The only harm that the plaintiff sustained from the publication arose entirely from the statements about her deceased husband

and not from anything published concerning her. At most it disclosed merely her marital relationship to one who was falsely accused of having committed suicide. A wife has no cause of action for libel on account of a publication that did nothing more than state that her husband took his own life. *Skrocki vs. Stahl,* 14 Cal. App. 1. *Sorensen vs. Balaban,* 11 App. Div. (N. Y.) 164. *Brown vs. Tribune Association,* 74 App. Div. (N. Y.) 359. *Goldwasser vs. Jewish Press Publishing Co.* 157 App. Div. (N. Y.) 908. *Birmingham vs. Daily Mirror, Inc.* 175 Misc. (N. Y.) 372. See *Hargrove vs. Oklahoma Press Publishing Co.* 130 Okla. 76. Compare *Bradley vs. Cramer,* 59 Wis. 309.

This case is not ruled by *Merrill vs. Post Publishing Co.* 197 Mass. 185. The publication in that case was to the effect that the plaintiff was the postmaster in charge of a post office where his sister was employed; that his sister had been arrested for larceny from the mails; and that there were those who believed that she stole in order "that she might help others." Page 193. It was held that the article could be found to have been directed against the plaintiff and his sister; and that to write that one was a brother of a person who had been arrested for larceny might tend to lower his standing in his community. The plaintiff in the case cited was in charge of the post office where the theft occurred by a clerk who was employed there. In the case at bar the article was not aimed at the plaintiff and it did not state, nor was it averred in the declaration, that she had any connection whatever with the death of her husband. Furthermore, it is at least doubtful from the reasoning of the opinion in the *Merrill* case, whether, if the article had stated merely that the clerk had been arrested for larceny and that she had a brother, the latter would have a cause of action. No question was there presented as to the right of a relative to recover for defamation of a deceased person, and the remark in the opinion that a man's standing may be affected by a publication that his parents or ancestors were criminals was unnecessary to the decision. The case has never been cited by this court or, as far as we are aware, by the majority opinion of any court as authority for the proposition that defamation of the memory of a deceased person gives a cause of action to his relatives. The almost unanimous trend of judicial thought is that such a proposition is unsound. Many of the cases are collected in 132 Am. L. R. 888. Compare *Huot vs. Noiseux,* 2 Queb. Q. B. 521; *Chiniquy vs. Bégin,* 24 Queb. K. B. 294. The *Merrill* case cannot be employed to extend liability into a field whose boundaries can hardly be defined with any fair degree of certainty and permit the recovery of damages by relatives, friends and business associates who have been injured by a publication that at most did no more than blacken the memory of a deceased person.

The order sustaining the demurrer is affirmed and judgment must be entered for the defendant. *Keljikian vs. Star Brewing Co.* 303 Mass. 53. *Swinton vs. Whitinsville Savings Bank,* 311 Mass. 677.

So ordered.

G. *Libel Against a Deceased*—Benton *vs.* Knoxville News-Sentinel Co. (174 Tennessee 658. July 1, 1939).

In libeling a dead person or one who has died since the libelous act, does one ipso facto libel the dead person's surviving relatives? The answer, as this case shows, is generally no. A relative can sue only if he or she can prove special damages.

BENTON, ADMRX., *vs.* KNOXVILLE NEWS-SENTINEL CO.
(*Knoxville,* September Term, 1938.)
Opinion filed July 1, 1939.

Error to Circuit Court of Knox County.—HON. HAMILTON S. BURNETT, Judge.

Action by Mrs. Caroline Jordan Benton, administratrix of the estate of Fred D. Benton, deceased, against the Knoxville News-Sentinel Company to recover damages for the wrongful death of Fred D. Benton. To review a judgment sustaining defendant's demurrer to the declaration, plaintiff brings error. Affirmed.

GRAHAM & DAVIS, of Knoxville, for plaintiff in error.

FRANK B. CREEKMORE, of Knoxville, for defendant in error.

Mr. Justice Cook delivered the opinion of the Court.

This is an action of damages for the wrongful death of Fred D. Benton. It is charged in the declaration that as a result of the publication by defendant of a defamatory article on July 5, 1938, affecting the character of Fred D. Benton, he worried to the point of distraction, suffered great mental anguish, fell into a decline in physical health, and that the worry and mental anguish finally affected his heart and caused his death on August 6, 1938.

The trial judge sustained defendant's demurrer to the declaration, and the plaintiff appealed. The appellant says that the principal question presented by the appeal is whether or not an action lies for injury produced by mental anguish, emotion, worry, and fear, that resulted from publication of the libel.

(1-5) Mental anguish, worry, fear, and loss of health are the several results of the one wrongful act, namely, the libel, and when the cause of action for that wrongful act was abated by death of the person libelled, the consequences of the wrongful act cannot be made the basis of a new cause of action. By the common law, actions for personal injury abated upon the death of the person injured. The survival statute, Code, section 8694, does not preserve causes of action for libel and other actions affecting the character of the injured person. *Akers vs. Akers,* 84 Tenn. (16 Lea), 7, 57 Am. Rep., 207. The damages recoverable under the survival statute are such as the deceased could have recovered if he had lived. *Loague vs. Railroad,* 91 Tenn., 458, 19 S. W., 430. Inasmuch as Code, section 8694, creates no new and independent cause of action, but merely preserves the cause of action that belonged to the person injured (*Whaley vs. Catlett,* 103 Tenn., 347, 53 S. W., 131), and because the statute does not preserve the right of action in cases of libel, this cause of action abated upon the death of Fred D. Benton. When it abated, the consequences that followed the cause of action as elements of damage could not be made the basis of a new action by the widow and next of kin.

We find no error in the judgment of the trial court.

Affirmed.

BENTON *vs.* KNOXVILLE NEWS-SENTINEL CO.
(*Knoxville,* September Term, 1938.)
Opinion filed July 1, 1939.

Error to Circuit Court of Knox County.—HON. HAMILTON S. BURNETT, Judge.

Action by Mrs. Caroline Jordan Benton against the Knoxville News-Sentinel Company to recover damages for alleged injuries resulting from an article published by defendant concerning plaintiff's husband who died subsequent to the publication. To review a judgment sustaining defendant's demurrer to the declaration and dismissing the action, plaintiff brings error. Affirmed.

GRAHAM & DAVIS, of Knoxville, for plaintiff in error.

FRANK B. CREEKMORE, of Knoxville, for defendant in error.

MR. JUSTICE DEHAVEN delivered the opinion of the Court.

This case is before the court on plaintiff's appeal from the judgment of the trial court sustaining defendant's demurrer to the declaration and dismissing the suit.

Plaintiff brought her action to recover $50,000 damages for alleged injuries to her reputation and character as the result of an article published by defendant of and concerning her husband, Fred D. Benton, who died subsequent to such publication. The article complained of was as follows:

"Sent Car—It was Wrecked

"Frank Hampton, 23, of 615 South Broadway, was charged with the larceny of an automobile. The owner, Fred Benton, 705 Market Street, testified he became sick and asked Hampton to drive him home. Then, he said, Hampton took the car keys from his pocket while he was asleep, drove his car to Jefferson City and wrecked it.

"Hampton said Benton was drunk and gave him permission to 'take his car out and get some girls and have a good time.'

" 'He was drunk and I drove him to his apartment, then out to places to buy more whisky,' he said. 'He gave me the keys and told me to go have a good time.'

"Judge MYNATT altered the charge to criminal trespassing and fined Hampton $50."

Plaintiff alleged in her declaration that the above article was wholly false insofar as statements contained therein attributed to her husband was concerned. She further alleged as follows:

". . . because of her legal connection and relation with the said Fred D. Benton, now deceased, her said husband, the said parties being as one in fact as well as in legal contemplation, that irreparable injury and damage has been done to her character and that her reputation has been diminished as a result of said deliberately false, malicious and defamatory article, published of and concerning the head of her family as a result of which both before and after the death of her said husband on or about the – of —, 1938, she has been held up to the scorn and ridicule of her neighbors and acquaintances, her name has been tarnished and her standing and position in the community and the church lowered and degraded.

"Said false and defamatory statements made of and concerning the said Fred D. Benton, her deceased husband, has caused her great mental anguish, loss of prestige among her religious associates and friends, has held her up to ridicule, ignominy and contempt of her social and religious associates."

It was further alleged that the libelous publication caused her husband loss of prestige in his business, thereby "jeopardizing her security and happiness through its effects upon the family income."

Defendant demurred to the declaration upon the grounds, in substance, (1) that the action for libel on account of said publication could only be maintained by Fred D. Benton; (2) that the cause of action for the alleged libel abated by the death of Fred D. Benton; (3) that no special damages to plaintiff is alleged in the declaration; (4) that the declaration wholly fails to state a cause of action.

The trial judge sustained the demurrer and dismissed the suit.

(1) The cause of action that Fred D. Benton had on account of the libelous article abated with his death. Code, section 8694;

Mrs. Caroline Jordan Benton, Administratrix, vs. Knoxville News-Sentinel Company, 174 Tenn., 658, 130 S. W. (2d), 105, this day decided, Opinion by Cook, J.

(2, 3) The proper party to sue as plaintiff in an action for libel is the person directly defamed. 17 R. C. L., 374. It is alleged in the declaration that the article complained of was published of and concerning Fred D. Benton. Plaintiff was not mentioned in the article, directly or indirectly. As wife, she has no cause of action because of the libel of her deceased husband. That cause of action ceased to exist with the death of Fred D. Benton. Family relationship with the deceased does not save the cause of action. In *Bradt vs. New Nonpareil Co.,* 108 Iowa, 449, 79 N. W., 122, 45 L. R. A., 681, it was held that a mother cannot recover damages for a libelous publication about her deceased son. The court said in that case:

"There was nothing in the article which tended in any manner to reflect on the plaintiff, and her sufferings were of the same kind as that produced by publication upon any of the other relatives or close friends of deceased. To permit a recovery in this case would allow the mother of any person libel to bring suit in her own name for the consequential damages done to her feelings, and the death of the person libeled would be a wholly irrelevant matter; for the suffering is in kind the same whether the person libeled be living or dead. We have not been cited to an authority, and, after a diligent search, we have been unable to find one, which authorizes a recovery in such a case. On the other hand, the following cases hold such action will not lie: *Sorenson vs. Balaban* [11 App. Div., 164], (Sup.), 42 N. Y. S., 654; *Wellman vs. Sun Printing & Pub. Asso.,* 66 Hun, 331, 21 N. Y. S., 577."

In *Hurst vs. Goodwin,* 114 Ga., 585, 40 S. E., 764, 765, 88 Am. St. Rep., 43, it was held that an action for slander of a child was properly brought by her next friend on her behalf. The court said: "As a general rule, the parent does not sustain damage from the defamation of his child's character, whether that defamation be oral or written; and ordinarily, therefore, the parent cannot maintain an action for slander or libel against the defamer of his minor child's character." To like effect is the case of *Pattison vs. Gulf Bag Co., Ltd.,* 116 La., 963, 41 So., 224, 114 Am. St. Rep., 570.

In Gatley on Libel and Slander (3 Ed.), at page 424, it is stated:

"A cannot bring an action of libel or slander against B for words defamatory of C, . . . But if A has sustained special damage as the direct and natural result of a libel or slander published of C, he may be able to maintain an action on the case in respect of such damage."

(4) To support such an action on the case special damage must be alleged, for it is an action which only lies in respect to such damage as has actually occurred. Gatley on Libel and Slander (3 Ed.), 152.

(5-9) Plaintiff alleged no special damage. The fact that the publication was libelous *per se* as to Fred D. Benton, and would entitle him, were he suing, to damages in some amount as a matter of law, cannot be held to relieve plaintiff from the necessity of alleging special damages, which alone she would be entitled to recover in an action on the case. A husband may maintain an action to recover damages suffered by him as the result of the libel of his wife. This on the theory of loss of society and services of the wife. *Garrison vs. Sun Printing & Pub. Ass'n,* 207 N. Y., 1, 100 N. E., 430, 45 L. R. A. (N. S.), 766, Ann. Cas., 1914C, 288. But, whether he sues jointly with his wife or separately, he can recover only for any special damage that may have accrued to him. *Butler vs. Stites,* 7 Tenn. App., 482; Odgers, Libel and Slander (5 Ed.), 567. The legal principle upon which the husband may sue for damages suffered by him as the result of a libel of the wife—loss of consortium—does not, of course, exist in the case of the wife. Nevertheless, if the wife suffers special damages by reason of the libel of the husband, she may maintain a suit to recover the same. But, such special damages must be pleaded with particularity so that the defendant may be able to contradict it if untrue. Special damages are not pleaded by the general averments in plaintiff's declaration. *Fry vs. McCord Bros.,* 95 Tenn., 678, 33 S. W., 568.

The trial judge properly sustained the demurrer to the declaration and the judgment dismissing the suit is affirmed. Appellant will pay the costs of the appeal.

H. *Libel by Mistaken Identity*—Roth *vs.* News Co. (217 North Carolina 13. February 2, 1940).

Newspapers sometimes make an honest mistake in imputing a wrongful deed to the wrong person, but, in the words of the North Carolina Supreme Court, "An honest mistake will not protect the defendant."

HARRY ROTH *VS.* GREENSBORO NEWS COMPANY.
(Filed 2 February, 1940.)

APPEAL by defendant from *Erwin, Special Judge,* at May Term, 1939, of GUILFORD. No error.

Civil action to recover damages resulting from the publication of a libel.

The defendant is a corporation which publishes and circulates *The Greensboro Daily News* and *The Greensboro Record,* two daily newspapers published in the city of Greensboro. On 30 August, 1937, it published in *The Greensboro Daily News* an Associated Press dispatch from Atlantic City, N. J., under date of 29 August, reciting the round-up and arrest of alleged members of a vice ring which was operating in several cities of the United States. It stated that Harry L. Roth, who was arrested in New York, was listed by the Assistant U. S. District Attorney as a principal defendant; that Roth was released from the Federal Penitentiary 9 February after serving two years on a Mann Act conviction and that his record showed arrests in New York, Philadelphia and Detroit on Mann Act and other charges. On 31 August, 1937, it carried another Associated Press dispatch in which, among other things, it was stated that "Harry Roth 42 year old New Yorker who was linked to Luciano by J. Edgar Hoover, Chief of the Federal Bureau of Investigation, was committed to Mercer County Jail today in default of $25,000 bail." It was stated that "Roth was charged with transporting a girl identified as Teddy Blaine from Philadelphia to Atlantic City for immoral purposes."

This article repeated that Roth was charged with transporting a girl from one State to another for immoral purposes and that the raids were part of the concerted drive by the F. B. I. to stamp out the White Slave Traffic.

The Greensboro Record, in its edition of 30 August, 1937, carried an Associated Press dispatch under Trenton, N. J., date line, containing, among other things, the statement that "Federal agents plan to bring here from New York for questioning today a man identified by Hoover as Harry Roth who he said was reputedly a member of the Charles (Lucky) Luciano Gang."

This article quoted the Federal Agent as stating that 37 prisoners arrested were "principals, procurers and madames."

On the night of 31 August, one Morgan, F. B. I. agent stationed at Greensboro, telephoned J. N. Benton, engaged by the defendant as a newspaper reporter on *The Record,* and told him that he, Morgan, had just returned from Newark where he had engaged in the raids and that he thought there was a local story in connection with this raid in Jersey City and surrounding New York and that one of the men referred to in the Associated Press dispatch carried that morning was named Harry Roth and that he understood that Roth was formerly in Greensboro; that Roth had been tried here (Greensboro) some two or three years previous on a white slavery charge similar to the one he had just been arrested for and that he (Benton) could check up on it and get a local story probably. Benton, whose duty it was in part to prepare the column of the events of 10, 20 and 30 years ago carried by *The Record,* was aware of the fact that Roth Brothers had purchased the Palace Theatre in Greensboro in 1927. He mentioned that fact to Morgan and Morgan in reply stated that he understood that Roth, who was arrested in New York, "had been in the entertainment business."

The next morning Benton examined the Greensboro City Directory. In the 1928 directory he found listed, "Harry Roth, Palace Theatre, residence Y. M. C. A."; in each of the 1929 and 1930 directories he found. "Harry Roth (Palace Theatre) r

Asheville, N. C." The name Harry Roth did not appear in either the 1931 or 1932 directory. Benton then went to the office of the Clerk of the United States District Court where he ascertained that one Harry Roth was tried at the June Term, 1935, under the Mann Act and sentenced to three years imprisonment.

Thereupon, without any investigation at the Palace Theatre or at the Y. M. C. A. and without any further inquiry, Benton wrote for publication and the defendant published in its *Greensboro Record,* on 1 September, 1937, under the large type headlines, "VICE RING MAN IS KNOWN HERE" the following article: "Harry Roth One of Men Taken at Atlantic City in Roundup, Once Lived Here. The recent raid of the federal investigators in Atlantic City, N. J., and other cities that resulted in the arrest of Harry Roth on Monday night, is of local interest as Roth formerly resided in Greensboro. He is now under $25,000 bond, being charged with complicity in gigantic vice operations in violation of the Mann White Slave Law. Between 125 and 150 men were taken into custody as a result of the drive, headed by J. Edgar Hoover. Roth is regarded as one of the higher-ups in the conspiracy.

"Roth, 42, listed as a resident of New York, was for a time connected with the Palace Theatre in Greensboro, it is understood. In June, 1935, he was tried in United States Court for violation of the Mann White Slave Act and given two years in Atlanta on each of four counts, the sentences to run concurrently. It will be recalled that he was arrested in San Francisco, Calif., after federal officers had traced him to various parts of the country. He was specifically charged with inducing young women to go from Greensboro to New York, promising employment. Arriving in the metropolis, it was brought out during the trial, the true motive of the journey was revealed and several girls testified to their experiences after making the trip to New York on the promise of employment.

"After Roth was arrested in San Francisco it was necessary to have one of the prosecuting witnesses taken to the Pacific coast city for purpose of identification, the prisoner resisting removal.

"R. L. Morgan, of the Greensboro office of the F. B. I., was among the number summoned to New York and Atlantic City to assist in the vice gang roundup. He returned home Tuesday."

On the afternoon of 1 September, after the issue of *The Record* containing said article was put in circulation, Max Zager, who operates the Palace Theatre in Greensboro under lease from plaintiff and his brother, after reading the article, called *The Greensboro Record* and asked them how they knew it was the Harry Roth that was formerly connected with the Palace Theatre. Defendant's agent in answer advised him that the information they got was from the F. B. I. man who told him he was; that the F. B. I. man had questioned this man and he told them he formerly lived in Greensboro and he operated the Palace Theatre. Zager then advised the defendant through its agent that the Roth who was formerly connected with the Palace Theatre was much younger than 42 years of age, that he was a man of good character and good habits and that he was sure that he was not linked up in that affair. The agent of the defendant then advised Zager that that was the information they received from the F. B. I. man. Zager then called plaintiff's brother at Harrisburg, Va., and inquired if the report was true. He was advised that it was not, that plaintiff resided in Suffolk, Va. On the same afternoon Mr. Stern likewise phoned the defendant relative to the article and advised the defendant that it had made a mistake.

Upon receiving the information from Zager and Stern, Benton advised the managing editor of the *News* of the mistake and suggested that the article be not published in the morning edition of the *News*. Thereafter, there was no further publication in either *The Greensboro News* or *The Greensboro Record* in anywise referring to plaintiff except that *The Greensboro Record* in its issue of 2 September, carried the following article:

"ANOTHER HARRY ROTH FIGURES IN AFFAIR.

"*The Greensboro Record* was informed Wednesday afternoon that the Harry Roth, arrested in the vice raids in Atlantic City and other northern cities Monday night, was not the Harry

Roth who some years ago was connected with the Palace Theatre, as was stated in the article in Wednesday's *Record*. The Harry Roth who was engaged in business here was a much younger man, it was said, and he was a young man of exemplary habits and character, according to citizens who were personally acquainted with him.

"The statement in Wednesday's paper was based on informa- that the prisoner, following arrest in New Jersey, had indicated to officers he was at one time in the movie business in Greensboro."

On 11 September, 1937, plaintiff wrote *The Greensboro Record* calling attention to the article of 1 September and its contents and demanding a retraction in the following language:

"Said statements as appeared in your paper are false and untrue and I hereby demand a full and fair correction, apology and retraction published in your paper and in as conspicuous a place and type as was the article published by you on September 1, 1937." The letter was received by the managing editor of defendant and he, in reply, in behalf of *The Greensboro Record,* wrote the plaintiff enclosing a copy of the article which appeared in *The Greensboro Record* of 2 September and requested that if said article did not meet with plaintiff's approval he so inform *The Greensboro Record*. The defendant received no reply, published no retraction and took no further action in respect thereto.

Plaintiff instituted this action 20 October, 1937, to recover damages, both compensatory and punitive.

In answer to appropriate issues submitted, the jury found that the article published by defendant 1 September, 1937, was published of and concerning the plaintiff Harry Roth and assessed compensatory damages, but answered the issue as to punitive damages in the negative. There was judgment on the verdict and the defendant excepted and appealed.

Stern & Stern for plaintiff, appellee.

Douglass & Douglass, Hobgood & Ward, and Chas. M. Ivey, Jr., for defendant, appellant.

Barnhill, J. On this appeal the defendant presents a number

of questions for determination: (1) Did the court err in overruling the defendant's motion for judgment as of nonsuit on plaintiff's first cause of action for compensatory damages? (2) Did the court err in overruling defendant's motion for judgment as of nonsuit on plaintiff's second cause of action for punitive damages? (3) Was it error for the court to admit evidence of defendant's financial worth? (4) Did the court err in refusing to charge the jury that it would be warranted in awarding only nominal damages as prayed by the defendant? And, (5) Did the court err in failing to give the defendant's special prayer for instructions to the effect that the jury should answer the first issue "No"?

The article not only states that Roth was arrested on a charge of violating the White Slave Act and with imprisonment in default of bond but it likewise attributes to him conduct of such vile baseness and depravity as to indicate a total lack of any sense of the social duty that a man owes to his fellow man and to society. If it had reference to the plaintiff it was false. This is conceded by the defendant. Being false it is a libel *per se. Flake vs. News Co.,* 212 N. C., 780, 195 S. E., 55. The court below so instructed the jury, to which there is no exception.

On the defendant's motion to nonsuit on the first cause of action and its prayer for a directed verdict, on the first issue then, the only question to be determined is as to whether there was sufficient evidence that the publication was "of and concerning the plaintiff."

The testimony of the witness Benton clearly indicates that he wrote the article because of its supposed local interest and concerning the Roth who formerly operated the Palace Theatre and resided at the Y. M. C. A. It was so understood by the witness Zager and by Mr. Stern and by others who accosted and joked the plaintiff in respect thereto. After receiving a phone call from Zager, Benton informed the managing editor that there had been a mistake. The managing editor wrote the plaintiff that the information was obtained from the Federal investigator Morgan stating "Investigator Morgan told this newspaper that Roth stated he has been connected with the Palace Theatre in

Greensboro." In the publication attempting to correct the false impression made the defendant stated that: "Another Harry Roth Figures in Affair;" and that it was informed "That the Harry Roth arrested in the vice raids in Atlantic City and other northern cities Monday night was not the Harry Roth who some years ago was connected with the Palace Theatre." Benton likewise testified that when he wrote the article "he was under the impression that the man referred to therein was formerly connected with the Palace Theatre."

It would seem, therefore, that the article was not only understood by those who read it as being of and concerning the plaintiff but that the defendant, by mistake of fact, so intended it. In any event, the evidence raises an issue of fact which was properly submitted to the jury. On the issue so submitted the court charged the jury fully in the language of special instructions prepared by learned counsel for the defendant. Naturally the charge on this aspect of the case was as favorable to the defendant as the law would permit. At least there is no exception thereto.

Under the view we take of the evidence the second and third questions may be treated as one.

When the allegations of the complaint are sufficient to support a demand for punitive damages, and there is testimony tending to support the allegations, evidence of the pecuniary circumstances and wealth of the defendant is competent on the issue thereby raised. *Adcock vs. Marsh,* 30 N. C., 360; *Reeves vs. Winn,* 97 N. C., 246, 1 S. E., 448; *Baker vs. Winslow,* 184 N. C., 1, 113 S. E., 570, and authorities therein cited at p. 10.

In some jurisdictions it is held that where malice exists exemplary damages may be given, and that it is immaterial whether the malice is actual or such as is implied in law for the publication of a libel *per se.* 25 Cyc., 536, *et seq.* In this jurisdiction punitive damages may not be awarded on a showing of implied malice only. To support an award of vindictive damages it must appear that the publication was prompted by actual malice (as contra-distinguished from imputed malice, or malice implied by the law from intentionally doing that which in its natural tendency is injurious), or that the defamation was recklessly or carelessly published. *Baker vs. Winslow, supra; Gilreath vs. Allen,* 32 N. C., 67; *Bowden vs. Bailes,* 101 N. C., 612; *Upchurch vs. Robertson,* 127 N. C., 127. Such damages may be awarded when there is evidence of oppression, or gross and willful wrong; *Reeves vs. Winn, supra;* or a wanton and reckless disregard of the plaintiff's right; *Fields vs. Bynum,* 156 N. C., 413, 72 S. E., 449; or of gross indifference; *Woody vs. Bank,* 194 N. C., 549, 140 S. E., 150; or reckless and criminal indifference to plaintiff's rights; *Hall vs. Hall,* 179 N. C., 571, 103 S. E., 136.

The F. B. I. agent stated to the defendant's news agent that he understood the Roth arrested "was formerly in Greensboro and had been tried in Greensboro," and that "he had been in the entertainment business." He did not state that he was formerly a resident of Greensboro or that he had ever been connected with the Palace Theatre. The reporter ascertained a man by the name of Roth had been for an undisclosed length of time, in Greensboro pursuing his vocation as a professional pimp and had been arrested and tried in the United States District Court. He further ascertained that Roth, the plaintiff, formerly resided in Greensboro at the Y. M. C. A. and was connected with the Palace Theatre. He published the article without investigation either at the place of employment or at the place of residence of the Roth about whom he wrote when such an investigation before the publication would have disclosed the true facts. The managing editor stated to Zager that the F. B. I. agent had told him that the Roth who was arrested was a man who formerly lived in Greensboro and operated the Palace Theatre. The record fails to disclose that such information was received from the F. B. I. agent.

"A good name is rather to be chosen than great riches." A good reputation, when based on sound character, is a man's most precious possession. No publication, the tendency of which is to seriously impair or destroy a good name, should be permitted without most careful investigation. The failure to go to a known and easily available source of information, coupled with other facts and circumstances which appear in this record and considered in connection with the presumption of legal malice arising from the publication of a libelous article, constitutes more than a scintilla of evidence tending to show that in publishing the article the defendant acted with reckless disregard of plaintiff's rights and is sufficient to support the submission of an issue of punitive damages. This is all we are required to determine.

A consideration of the whole record leads to the conclusion that the defendant acted through an honest mistake. The jury accepted that view of the evidence and answered the issue on punitive damages in the negative. But, an honest mistake will not protect the defendant. *Washington Post vs. Kennedy,* 3 F. (3d), 207, 41 A. L. R., 483; also see Anno. 26 A. L. R., 464, *et seq.*

As there is sufficient evidence to be submitted to the jury on the issue of punitive damages there was no error in the admission of testimony relating to the defendant's financial condition.

Nor is the defendant protected by its publication of 2 September in which it corrects, on information, the publication of 1 September. The plaintiff duly served notice on the defendant by letter, the receipt of which is admitted, demanding a retraction as provided by ch. 557, Public Laws 1901; C. S., 2430. If the defendant desired to avail itself of the provisions of this statute it was its duty to publish an apology and retraction as prescribed by statute. This it did not do.

While the statute, C. S., 2430, does not require the retraction to be in any particular form or couched in any particular language, it does require "a full and fair correction, apology and retraction" which must clearly refer to and admit the publishing of the article complained of and directly, fully and fairly, without any uncertainty, evasion or subterfuge, retract and recall the alleged false and defamatory statements and apologize therefor. *Oray vs. Times Co.* (Minn.), 77 N. W., 204. The alleged correction falls far short of this requirement. It neither retracts nor apologizes therefor, but merely states that the defendant is then in possession of information *contra* that contained in the original publication. See *Osborn vs. Leach,* 135 N. C., 627; *Paul vs. Auction Co.,* 181 N. C., 1, 105 S. E., 881.

The demand for the apology gave the defendant the election of complying therewith or risking the consequence of noncompliance. It was not the duty of the plaintiff to approve or disapprove the article already published. Failure to do so does not exculpate the defendant or protect it against the submission of any issue of punitive damages on a proper showing.

It may be noted that under express terms of C. S., 2430, the publication of the apology and retraction standing alone is not sufficient. It must be made to appear further in the trial that "said article was published in good faith, that its falsity was due to an honest mistake of fact, and that there were reasonable grounds for believing that the statements in said article were true."

While the court declined to charge the jury in substance that it would be warranted in awarding only nominal damages as prayed by the defendant, it did charge the jury on the issue of damages that "if the plaintiff would recover more than nominal damages under the second issue, he must satisfy you by the greater weight of the evidence in this case that he is entitled to recover actual damages of the defendant . . . your award of damages to plaintiff under the second issue will be confined to nominal damages unless the plaintiff establishes by the greater weight of the evidence that he has suffered actual damages as the direct and proximate result of the wrongful acts and conduct of the defendant." If there was any error in this charge it was favorable to the defendant.

When an unauthorized publication is libelous *per se,* malice and damage are presumed from the fact of publication and no proof is required as to any resulting injury. The law presumes that general damages actually, proximately and necessarily result from an unauthorized publication which is libelous *per se* and they are not required to be proved by evidence since they arise by inference of law, and are allowed whenever the immediate tendency of the publication is to impair plaintiff's reputation, although no actual pecuniary loss has in fact resulted.

Flake vs. News Co., supra; Bowden vs. Bailes, supra; Fields vs. Bynum, supra; Hamilton vs. Nance, 159 N. C., 56, 74 S. E., 627; *Barringer vs. Deal,* 164 N. C., 246, 80 S. E., 161; *Paul vs. Auction Co., supra; Baker vs. Winslow, supra; Jones vs. Brinkley,* 174 N. C., 23, 93 S. E., 372; *N. Y. Evening Post Co. vs. Chaloner,* 265 F., 204, 36 C. J., 1150; *Oates vs. Trust Co.,* 205 N. C., 14, 168 S. E., 869.

In the *Bowden case, supra,* a charge that "the plaintiff is entitled to some damages" resulting from a slander *per se* was affirmed. In the *Barringer case, supra,* citing the *Hamilton* and *Fields cases, supra,* it was held that on a slander *per se* compensatory damages which embrace compensation for those injuries which the law will presume must naturally, proximately and necessarily result, including injuries to the feelings and mental suffering endured in consequence, should be awarded; and that it is not required that the plaintiff introduce evidence that he has suffered special damage. In the *Fields case, supra,* the court declined to charge the jury "It is incumbent on the plaintiff to show to the jury evidence that he has suffered damage before he can ask you to award any to him." This Court held that the refusal to give the requested instruction was proper. The other cited cases are to like effect.

"Where the facts and nature of the action so warrant, actual damages include pecuniary loss, physical pain, and mental suffering . . . compensatory damages include all other damages than punitive, thus embracing not only special damages as direct pecuniary loss but injury to feelings, mental anguish, etc." *Baker vs. Winslow, supra.* "Compensatory damages include (1) pecuniary loss direct or indirect, *i.e.,* special damages; (2) damages for physical pain and inconvenience; (3) damages for mental sufferings; and (4) damages for injury to reputation." *Osborn vs. Leach, supra; Fields vs. Bynum, supra; Barringer vs. Deal, supra.*

However, the fact that the law presumes that general damages result from the publication of a libel *per se* does not preclude the plaintiff from offering evidence of damages both general and special.

The plaintiff testified in substance that he had suffered mental anguish, humiliation and embarrassment as a result of the publication complained of. This evidence, together with the presumption of general damages resulting from the publication of the libel, entitled the plaintiff to the award of some damages, the amount of which it was the duty of the jury to determine.

A careful examination of the record and the briefs filed leads us to the conclusion that the exceptive assignments of error are without substantial merit.

No error.

I. *Libel by Mistaken Identity, and the Matter of Damages for Such Libel*—Behrendt *vs.* Times-Mirror Co. (Vol. 96, California Appellate Decisions, 3. Civil No. 11907. Second Appellate District. Division Two. December 21, 1938).

This case of libel by mistaken identity is somewhat more extensive and more inclusive of problems of libel in this area of defamation than the preceding North Carolina case. It shows how careful newspaper reporters must be if they would spare their papers prosecutions for libel, it shows how little avail it is to an offending paper to point out that other papers printed the same alleged libel and were not prosecuted, and it shows what great power a jury in a libel case has in assessing damages. It also shows that the printing of a retraction is worth only what the jury thinks it's worth—nothing at all or a slight reduction in damages. On the matter of damages the California court was very clear: "To justify interference by an appellate court with a verdict in a libel action it must appear that the amount awarded is so grossly excessive as to shock the moral sense and raise a reasonable presumption that the jury was under the influence of passion or prejudice. . . . In actions for libel or slander the amount of damages recoverable is peculiarly within the discretion of the jury, for there can be no fixed or mathematical rule on the subject."

Civil No. 11907. Second Appellate District, Division Two. December 21, 1938.

R. ALLEN BEHRENDT, Plaintiff and Respondent, *vs.* THE TIMES-MIRROR COMPANY, Defendant and Appellant.

Appeal by defendant from a judgment of the Superior Court of Los Angeles County, Harry R. Archbald, Judge, in an action for damages for libel. *Affirmed*. McComb, J., *dissents*.

For Appellant—Cosgrove & O'Neil, F. B. Yoakum, Jr.

For Respondent—Raymond L. Haight, Arthur L. Syvertson, Lyle C. Newcomer, Jr., of Haight, Trippet & Syvertson; Harvey A. Harkness, John W. Lehners, Harkness & Lehners, of Counsel.

This is an action for damages for libel. A jury returned a verdict in favor of plaintiff in the sum of $10,000 as compensatory damages and the further sum of $15,000 as punitive damages and judgment was accordingly entered. Thereafter upon motion for a new trial the trial court made an order that a new trial would be granted unless plaintiff should reduce "the judgment entered to the sum of $10,000 and costs, the amount of the compensatory damages awarded". In accordance with the conditional order of the court plaintiff remitted that part of the judgment over and above the sum of $10,000 awarded as compensatory damages.

The libel which is the basis of the action was published by the defendant in its newspaper, "Los Angeles Times", on May 24, 1937. The libelous matter was published in three separate editions of the newspaper and each edition is made the basis of a separate count. It was published of and concerning plaintiff that he had been arrested, charged with the theft of narcotics and had himself used the stolen narcotics as an addict until his health had become destroyed; that he could not be arraigned on the charge because of his physical condition. The statements were entirely untrue. At the time of the publication plaintiff was a physician and surgeon of the age of 32 years. He was a graduate of Rush Medical College and had been established for several months as a practitioner in an office in Los Angeles. He was well and favorably known in Los Angeles and had previously attained prominence as a football player at the University of Southern California. He was engaged to be married and the date of the marriage had been set for May 25, 1937.

Ralph A. Behrend, who on Friday, May 21, 1937, was resident physician at the Metropolitan Water District Hospital at Banning, was on that date arrested on the charge of stealing narcotics and was brought to Los Angeles by police officers. He was taken by the officers to the home of Dr. Carey, the chief of the medical staff of the Metropolitan Water District. He was unmanageable and Dr. Carey and the officers took him to the Hollywood police station and the next morning he was taken to Riverside County Hospital for confinement and treatment. It will be noticed that the name of the plaintiff, R. Allen Behrendt, is similar to that of the party arrested, Ralph A. Behrend, the initials being the same. An interesting fact to be noted is that the plaintiff had been resident physician at the Metropolitan Water District Hospital at Banning before this position was held by Ralph A. Behrend.

On Sunday afternoon, May 23, a Times reporter was told by one of the officers at the Hollywood police station that he had missed a story concerning the doctor who had been in the station on Friday afternoon and who was being detained in Riverside. The reporter saw the records in the Hollywood station where the name "R. A. Behrend" appeared, together with a notation that he had been taken to Riverside. The reporter telephoned to the editorial rooms of the Times with the suggestion that if the man involved was the one who had been a football player at the University of Southern California it would make a good story. One of the Times staff telephoned to the office of the sheriff of Riverside and made inquiries concerning the identity of the man who had been taken to the Riverside County Hospital. Without here setting forth the details of the evidence concerning the efforts of the staff of the Times to investigate the identity of the person under arrest it is sufficient to say that the plaintiff claims that the publication was made without reasonable investigation and that the defendant claims that the publication was made "after investigation of the facts stated and upon dependable and reliable information".

The defendant voluntarily published in the Times of May 25, 1937, a retraction of the statements made concerning plaintiff and explained the reasons why the mistake in identity had been made. The retraction was accompanied by a photograph of plaintiff and was printed in several editions on that date. On June 10, 1937, plaintiff served upon defendant a demand for a retraction in accordance with the provisions of section 48a of the Civil Code. On June 18, 1937, defendant printed a retraction which it claims was published, "in as conspicuous a place and type" as were the statements which formed the basis of the litigation. The plaintiff claims that the retraction was not printed in as conspicuous a place and type as were the articles of which complaint is made.

It is contended on behalf of defendant that the trial court erred in refusing to allow the introduction of evidence to the effect that other newspapers in the city of Los Angeles had on May 24, 1937, printed statements similar to those printed in the Times. It is particularly urged that the jury should have received this evidence in mitigation of the amount of compensatory damages. In *Wilson vs. Fitch,* 41 Cal. 363, a situation was presented similar to the one now before us and it was held that the evidence of other publications was inadmissible. In that case the article complained of was published in the *Bulletin.* The defendant sought to show that a similar article had been published three days earlier in the *Call.* The particular point now raised by the defendant was not discussed but it is pointed out in the opinion that the publication in the *Call* could be "treated in no other or more favorable light than as a printed rumor". The point presented by defendant has been directly passed upon in *Palmer vs. New York News Pub. Co.,* 52 N. Y. Supp. 539, and also in *Hagener vs. Pulitzer Pub. Co.,* [Kan.] 158 S. W. 54. In both of these cases it was held that publications of similar libels in other newspapers may not be shown for the purpose of reducing the amount of the compensatory damages. The theory upon which the evidence is held inadmissible is sound and is aptly expressed in *Palmer vs. New York etc. Co.,* supra: "Each libel is a separate and distinct tort, and each person who sees fit to publish it is separately liable to the plaintiff for whatever damages may be fairly said to accrue. If 100 persons at 100 different places make 100 separate publications of a libel in 100 different newspapers, the fact that this simultaneous action of all of them has ruined the plaintiff's character is no reason why 1 of them, when sued for it, should shelter himself behind the acts of the other 99, and say that 99/100 of the plaintiff's character was ruined by the others, and therefore he is liable for only 1/100 part of the damage. The true rule is, and must be, that whoever publishes a libel publishes it at his peril, and he cannot mitigate his damages because some other reckless or evil-disposed person has incurred the same liability that he has for the same story."

Complaint is made of the ruling of the trial court receiving in evidence testimony that plaintiff was not a user of narcotics. It was admitted by the pleadings that plaintiff was not a user of narcotics but we know of no rule which prevents plaintiff from presenting testimony concerning the facts, even though they be stipulated by both parties. (*Davis vs. Hearst,* 160 Cal. 143, 187.) It was within the discretion of the trial court to permit plaintiff to prove the allegations which had been conceded. As pointed out in *Martin vs. Pacific Gas & Electric Co.,* 203 Cal. 291, 299, "a naked admission might have the effect to rob the evidence of much of its fair and legitimate weight".

Complaint is also made of the ruling of the court by which plaintiff was permitted to testify concerning his condition of mind resulting from the publication of the libel. Defendant particularly criticizes the form of some of the questions. In one instance plaintiff was asked, "In your own mind, Doctor, what did you think about your own professional career?" The witness answered, "I thought my—in as far as the practice of medicine in this community, it was finished on my own part". It was proper for plaintiff to prove that his feelings had been injured and that he believed that the libels had affected his standing in the community and the happiness of members of his family. These matters could be presented as tending to prove injury to his feelings. (*Earl vs. Times-Mirror Co.,* 185 Cal. 165, 171.) Although some of the questions might have been improved upon, the answers given concerned the feelings and state of mind of plaintiff and were proper for presentation to the jury. Defendant has not been prejudiced by the ruling.

The defendant contends that the court erred in receiving evidence of the physical suffering of plaintiff and in later instructing the jury on the subject of compensatory damages that they might "take into consideration the physical pain and suffering, if any, inflicted on plaintiff by the publication of the articles". It was established that plaintiff suffered frequent urination and other symptoms of extreme nervous shock beginning immediately after the publication. Dr. Bennetts, a witness called by plaintiff, testified concerning the passage of a stone from plaintiff's kidney to the bladder several months after the date of the publication. He testified that an extreme nervous shock would aggravate the symptoms of the condition which he described; that "the condition may have been aggravated or precipitated by such anguish or such mental shock". The witness was cross-examined at great length concerning the passage of the kidney stone and he explained to the jury the nature of the ailment and the probable effects upon plaintiff's condition of the nervous shock which he had received. The jury was not misled by the ruling admitting this testimony for they were carefully instructed by the court that the damages allowable were such as would "compensate the plaintiff for the injury he has actually sustained as the natural and probable consequence of the libelous publication".

Although there is some conflict in the authorities, the better reasoned cases hold that damages may be awarded for physical suffering as well as mental anguish. (*Sweet vs. Post Pub. Co.*, 215 Mass. 450, 102 N. E. 660; *Burt vs. McBain,* 29 Mich. 260; *Garrison vs. Sun Printing & Publishing Co. Ass'n,* 207 N. Y. 1, 100 N. E. 430; *Osborne vs. Leach,* 135 N. C. 628, 66 L. R. A. 648; *Hatt vs. Evening News,* 94 Mich. 119; *Warner vs. Press Pub. Co.,* 132 N. Y. 181, 30 N. E. 393.) No sound reason can be advanced why damages should not be awarded for physical suffering as well as mental anguish provided of course that the physical suffering be caused by the libel and be a natural and probable result of its publication.

Further conflict appears in the authorities on the question whether it is necessary to specifically plead physical injury or suffering. In *Sweet vs. Post Pub. Co.*, supra, it was urged on appeal that the trial court had erred in admitting evidence of illness suffered by the plaintiff in consequence of the libel. In the complaint plaintiff had alleged that he was an attorney at law and that the publication of the libel had caused him loss in his business and greatly injured his feelings and his reputation in his profession. In sustaining the judgment the reviewing court held that "under these counts the plaintiff was entitled to recover for mental suffering and distress and for illness suffered by him in consequence of the libel". In *Burt vs. McBain,* supra, an action for slander, the appellant urged that the trial court had erred in receiving evidence that the plaintiff's health had been affected. The reviewing court thus disposed of the point: "Another error assigned is, that plaintiff was permitted, although the declaration did not claim special damages, to show that in consequence of the slander she was excluded from the society in which she formerly moved, and was affected in mind and health. But these results are the natural, and we might also say the inevitable results of such a slander of a virtuous young woman, and they might be shown without setting them out in the declaration". In *Hatt vs. Evening News,* supra, under a general allegation of damages, the plaintiff introduced evidence that he was rendered sick and unfit to work. In disposing of the contention that the injury should have been specially pleaded the court held that "under a declaration which sets out a libel which is actionable per se, it is not necessary, in order to introduce evidence of so-called special damages, to show that the results which naturally flow from the publication did in fact appear". Plaintiff's complaint contains the following allegation: "As a direct and proximate consequence of the publication of said articles, including their headlines and captions, the plaintiff has been caused to suffer a severe nervous shock and great mental anguish and humiliation . . .". In accordance with those decisions which hold that physical suffering must be specially pleaded as well as under the decisions to which reference has just been made, this allegation must be held sufficient to justify the reception in evidence of plaintiff's testimony concerning his physical suffering. Since the neural system is an important part of the human body, a severe shock to the neural system, causing suffering, can properly be said to occasion physical suffering.

The record discloses an additional reason why defendant may not complain of the ruling of the trial court on the subject of physical suffering. Plaintiff testified in detail concerning the effect of the libel upon him physically. No objection was interposed and defendant cross-examined at length on the point. Plaintiff was asked to describe his "physical reaction". He was also asked this question: "What was the situation with reference to your physical condition a week later?" On cross-examination counsel asked: "With reference to the mental anguish that you have referred to in your testimony that resulted from a reading of this article by yourself, I would like to ask a few questions, and the physical suffering that you also explained. Did this suffering result in loss of weight?" To this question plaintiff answered, "Yes, it did at the time". At one point the judge remarked: "I just thought I would inquire as to what the purpose of it is". Thereupon the attorney for the defendant stated: "Yes. I want to show just the condition of the man in so far as any nervous shock or any physical condition that is a result of reading this article and any mental anxiety, that is most likely to occur at that time". During the examination of plaintiff there was considerable discussion between counsel on the admissibility of testimony and counsel for defendant stated, substantially, that testimony concerning the physical suffering and condition of plaintiff was proper. Reference might be made to one example. Counsel for plaintiff asked the witness what was the effect of the publication upon his professional work. In objecting to this question counsel for defendant stated, "but as I understand the law, it must be the effect on him, it must be the result of mental anguish. He has been explaining it here at some considerable length, and the physical effect, and the effect on him mentally, emotionally, of reading the article, and we think it should be confined to that". Having taken the position at the opening of the trial that testimony concerning physical suffering was proper, having permitted such testimony without objection and having cross-examined the witness at length on the point, defendant is not now in position to claim that it has been prejudiced by the ruling of the court in receiving the testimony and in instructing the jury that it should be taken into consideration. (*Jackson vs. Snow,* 62 Cal. App. 56.)

A number of criticisms are leveled at the court's rulings in instructing the jury. Defendant requested the court to instruct the jury that punitive damages could not be awarded. The court did not give this instruction but did instruct the jury: "Should you find that the defendant published the articles in question here wantonly, recklessly, and in utter disregard of plaintiff's good name and reputation and with wanton and reckless disregard for the truth or falsity of the statements made therein concerning plaintiff, you may from such evidence infer that the defendant acted maliciously and award exemplary damages to the plaintiff in such sum as you may deem just in view of all the circumstances revealed by the evidence." The court very elaborately and accurately instructed the jury on the subject of compensatory damages. As heretofore stated the jury returned a verdict for $15,000 exemplary damages but the trial court required plaintiff to remit the exemplary damages as a condition of the denial of the motion for a new trial. It must be presumed that the jury weighed the evidence and awarded compensatory damages in accordance with the instructions of the court. The judgment for which plaintiff seeks an affirmance is for compensatory damages only. Questions concerning exemplary damages have become moot. Our conclusion that defendant was not prejudiced by the giving of the instruction is in harmony with the decision in *Lightner Mining Co. vs. Lane*, 161 Cal. 689, a case in which the jury awarded $27,000 compensatory damages and an additional $27,000 as exemplary damages. The Supreme Court ruled that the evidence was insufficient to justify exemplary damages and held that the giving of an instruction on the subject of exemplary damages "could be prejudicial only with regard to punitive damages included in the verdict, and the error can be sufficiently cured by reducing the judgment to the amount of damages allowed as compensation".

The defendant requested the court to instruct the jury that "the evidence in this case discloses that the retraction published by the defendant is a full, fair and complete retraction of the article of which the plaintiff complains". In place of the requested instruction the court gave instruction No. 22 as follows: "The plaintiff alleges in his complaint that on June 10, 1937, he served upon the defendant a notice specifying the libelous statements and requested that the same be withdrawn. The defendant admits that this request for a retraction was served upon it and alleges that it has in fact published a retraction in as conspicuous a place and type in The Los Angeles Times as were the statements complained of, and within two weeks after the date of the service upon it of the notice and demand, to wit: on June 18, 1937. The written request for a retraction and the articles published by The Los Angeles Times thereafter on June 18, 1937, have been presented to you in evidence. You are to determine from this evidence whether or not the articles published by the defendant on June 18, 1937, constitute a retraction or a correction of the libelous publications in as conspicuous a place and type in The Los Angeles Times as were the statements complained of. If you find from the evidence that a retraction or correction was not published pursuant to the written notice of plaintiff of June 10, 1937, in as conspicuous a place and type as were the statements complained of, then you may award to the plaintiff and against the defendant exemplary damages in such sum as you may deem just, unless you believe from the evidence that the libelous publication was made in good faith, without malice, and under a mistake as to the facts."

The defendant is not in position to complain of the ruling of the court in giving this instruction. Under the provisions of section 48a of the Civil Code it might have been made more favorable to plaintiff. The jury had before it the various libels which were the basis of the action and the various retractions printed by defendant. The retractions were not printed in the same locations in the newspapers as were printed the libelous articles. The headlines were clearly different in kind. One of the libels was printed under a heading in bold type which ran across the top of the newspaper. It was the duty of the jury to determine whether the retractions were fair and complete and to what extent they mitigated the damages suffered by plaintiff. (*Lawrence vs. Herald Pub. Co.,* 158 Minn. 455, 122 N. W. 1084.) In *Turner vs. Hearst,* 115 Cal. 394, 404, the court in referring to a retraction published by a newspaper, stated: "The question of the sufficiency or insufficiency is peculiarly a question of fact, and, therefore, peculiarly for the determination of the jury."

It is argued that by giving instruction No. 22, above quoted, the court in effect told the jury that the retractions printed on May 25, 1937, were of no force and effect as retractions. We see no merit in this contention. The jury was instructed in three separate instructions that the retractions printed on both dates should be considered on the point of compensatory damages.

The defendant contends that plaintiff's counsel was guilty of prejudicial misconduct. On several occasions counsel for defendant cited certain remarks of plaintiff's counsel as misconduct. We set forth the incidents concerning one of the assignments of misconduct, one which if not typical, is as serious as any of them. The record discloses: "Q. By Mr. Haight: Who was present at the time that you saw this story in the paper? Mr. Cosgrove: That is objected to on the ground it is incompetent, irrelevant and immaterial, it has no tendency to prove any of the issues of the case. The Court: I will sustain the objection at this time. Q. By Mr. Haight: Now, I suppose you got up and got dressed? A. Yes, sir. Q. And what was the next thing you did, Dr. Behrendt? Mr. Cosgrave: That is objected to on the ground it is incompetent, irrelevant and immaterial, and has no tendency to prove any of the issues of the case. I realize, in making that objection, it may or it may not be relevant, but it is entirely indefinite, and it may or may not refer to this particular matter. I think the question should be made more definite than that. I think counsel should undertake to state the subject-matter, of what it is he is proceeding to. Mr. Haight: I can appreciate the desperation with which he wants to keep that out of the record—— Mr. Cosgrove: I object to that statement, if the Court please, on the ground—— The Court: The jury is instructed to disregard the statement of counsel. Statements of counsel are not evidence, or any statement that the Court makes is not evidence."

The various remarks which are assigned as misconduct were made at various intervals during the trial which lasted eight days and which is called "intense" in one of the briefs. In several instances the trial court properly instructed the jury to disregard the remarks of counsel. In its motion for a new trial defendant urged misconduct of counsel as one of the grounds for its motion, but the trial court held that there was not prejudicial misconduct. The trial judge is in a better position than an appellate court to determine whether a verdict in a given case is probably due to alleged misconduct. The conclusion reached by the trial judge should not be disturbed unless it is plainly wrong. (*Lafargue vs. The United Railroads,* 183 Cal. 720, 724.) In view of all the circumstances of the present case we cannot hold that the conclusion of the trial court was wrong.

It is contended on behalf of defendant that the verdict of $10,000 as compensatory damages is excessive. To justify interference by an appellate court with a verdict in a libel action it must appear that the amount awarded is so grossly excessive as to shock the moral sense and raise a reasonable presumption that the jury was under the influence of passion or prejudice. (*Wilson vs. Fitch,* supra.) In actions for libel or slander the amount of damages recoverable is peculiarly within the discretion of the jury, for there can be no fixed or mathematical rule on the subject. Questions concerning the amount of the verdict are directed primarily to the discretion of the trial court, which has the power to weigh the evidence in order to determine whether the verdict is correct in view of all the testimony in the case. The trial court has the power to set aside the verdict if it is considered to be unjust. This power is not vested in a reviewing court. (*Scott vs. Times-Mirror,* 181 Cal. 345.) The trial court found no occasion to interfere with the verdict and we find no occasion to interfere with its conclusion.

Many cases have been reviewed in the briefs. In some of these large amounts have been sustained by the reviewing courts and in others the jury awards have been held to be excessive. It would prolong this discussion unnecessarily to review many of these cases. However, the case of *Scott vs. Times-Mirror,* supra, has been cited by both parties and reference to it might be helpful. In that case the jury awarded the plaintiff $7,500 as compensatory damages and $30,000 as exemplary damages. Mr. Scott, the plaintiff, had practiced law over twenty years in his community and had achieved an enviable reputation. In his complaint he had alleged that the defendant had published a libel concerning his actions in conducting a divorce case in the courts. In *Broughton vs. McGrew,* 39 Fed. 672, the court instructed the jury that they could consider that there was less likelihood of a slander hurting a man of established character, whereas, "if he was a new man starting in the effort to build up a reputation, the same slander might well cause more harm". In the case under consideration Dr. Behrendt was a young professional man who was endeavoring to build up a practice in the community. He had not established an enviable reputation in his profession after a long period of practice. The jury doubtless took into consideration the fact that the libels were more likely to injure him than if he had been practicing his profession for many years.

The Scott case was decided in 1919. Since that time radical changes have taken place in conditions affecting the cost of living. This fact has been recognized by the courts in passing upon the amounts of verdicts. In *O'Meara vs. Haiden,* 204 Cal. 354, 367, the court quoted with approval from *Quinn vs. Chicago, M. & St. P. Ry. Co.,* 162 Minn. 87, 202 N. W. 275, in which it is stated that the courts approve of verdicts which would have been unhesitatingly set aside as excessive ten or fifteen years earlier.

The judgment is affirmed.

WOOD, J.

I concur:

CRAIL, P. J.

I dissent:

McCOMB, J.

J. *Libel in a Headline*—Norfolk Post Corp. *vs.* Wright. (140 Virginia 735. December 18, 1924).

This case brings up points covered in previous cases, especially that of similar allegedly libelous publications in other newspapers, but it is reprinted here because it contains a ruling on the matter of libel in headlines: "Unsupported headlines may be in themselves libellous."

NORFOLK POST CORPORATION, A CORPORATION, *vs.* MILTON T. WRIGHT.

December 18, 1924.

Error to a judgment of the Court of Law and Chancery of the city of Norfolk, in an action for libel. Judgment for plaintiff. Defendant assigns error.

Affirmed.

The opinion states the case.

Wolcott, Wolcott & Lankford and *W. L. Devany, Jr.,* for the plaintiff in error.

Alfred Anderson, for the defendant in error.

HOLT, J., delivered the opinion of the court.

Milton T. Wright was arrested in Norfolk on July 14, 1922. The circumstances attendant upon this arrest so far as they are relevant are as follows:

Just preceding this date there had been a series of burglaries in Colonial Place and Riverview, residential sections of Norfolk lying just south of Lafayette river near each other but not contiguous.

Several special officers were detailed to cope with this outbreak of lawlessness, one of them was detective Leon Nowitzky. To him had been reported the recent looting of the home of P. W. Powell, east 39th street, in Riverview. While on this special detail his attention was directed to plaintiff and to a companion of his, Overton; these men he stopped and questioned. They told him that they were working for the Dixie Motor Car Company, and were making a house to house canvass in an effort to sell automobiles. Nowitzky called up that company over the telephone and verified this information. He then, possibly with some reluctance, permitted them to go about their business. All of this took place in Riverview and on July the 13th. That afternoon he received some additional information tending to confirm his suspicion as to Wright and on the following day, in company with a fellow officer, Williams, went to Wright's place of business and brought him and Overton to the police station where he was identified by a Mrs. Smallwood, the mother of Mrs. P. W. Powell, as the man seen at her daughter's home. Thereupon a warrant of arrest was sued out formally charging him with that crime. It is not entirely clear that an arrest was made at the Dixie Motor Car Company's place of business. There is evidence tending to show that these men came voluntarily to the police station and were first arrested there on said warrant. In any event a formal warrant then issued. They were held on it, bailed and discharged after a preliminary hearing. At that trial or preliminary hearing nothing was said about Colonial Place robberies, the investigation was limited to the offense charged in the warrant of arrest. Plaintiff appears to have been a man of excellent reputation.

The defendant corporation publishes an afternoon paper in the city of Norfolk, and on the day of this arrest published an account of this incident. It is that publication which is the basis of this action and which contains the alleged libel. It is:

"Suspect nabbed.

"Man held in Colonial Place robberies.

"Milton T. Wright, twenty-five, Portsmouth, was arrested shortly before noon today by detectives Nowitzky and Williams on Jamestown avenue, in connection with the burglary of numerous houses in Colonial Place recently." On this action was brought and there was a verdict and judgment for the plaintiff, which we are asked to set aside.

There are three assignments of error. The first, because the court refused to set aside the verdict as being without evidence to support it; the second, because of instructions given, while the third is based upon the refusal of the court to admit certain evidence claimed to be proper.

Defendant says there was no libel, but that the facts stated in this publication are substantially true. When Nowitzky halted and examined the plaintiff in Riverview, on 39th street, on July the 13th, the crime then immediately in his mind was the Powell robbery in Riverview and it was upon new evidence connected therewith that he brought Wright to the police station on the following day, where, after further examination, a warrant was issued which reads in part as follows:

"Whereas, officer L. Nowitzky, No.................street, has this day made complaint and information on oath before me, William T. Anderson, a justice of said city, that on the 11th day of July, 1922, at said city, Milton T. Wright, No. ....street, did unlawfully and feloniously break and enter the home of P. W. Powell, 268 east 39th street, in the day time, and did take, steal and carry away from therefrom, etc."

[1] Mr. Chase, the reporter who was the author of the article, testified that it but restates and accurately states information the detectives gave him. The correctness of this information was a risk assumed. *Stevens vs. Commercial-News Co.,* 164 Ill. App. 6.

On the face of the record Wright was not "held in Colonial Place robberies." He was arrested and held for house breaking in Riverview.

[2] The article itself substantially supports the headlines, but if it did not, the law is that unsupported headlines may be in themselves libellous. In an extended note to *McAllister vs. Detroit Free Press Co.,* 15 Am. St. Rep. 347, it is said:

"The headline of an article or paragraph, being so conspicuous as to attract the attention of persons who look casually over a paper without reading all its contents, may itself inflict very serious injury upon a person, both because it may be the only part of the article which is read, and because it may cast a graver imputation than all the other words following it. There is no doubt that in publications concerning private persons, as well as in all other publications which are claimed to be libellous, the headlines directing attention to the publication may be considered as a part of it, and may even justify a court or jury in regarding the publication as libellous when the body of the article is not necessarily so."

[3] It could have been, and doubtless was, argued with great force that "Colonial Place robberies" was a generic term and covered the series of crimes lately perpetrated in a particular section of Norfolk. And the jury might have believed that "Colonial Place" and "Riverview" were comprehensive and interchangeable terms used to designate a general residential section of that city harassed by a persistent thief. So also it was proper to argue that to publish one as suspected of robbing "A" when he was in fact suspected of robbing "B" could do no damage beyond what a statement literally correct would have done. All of this may be true, but it was not true as a matter of law, and if it was true as a matter of fact, it was for the jury to say. These offenses might have differed in degree and the damage might have been nominal or substantial; this, too, was for the jury. 25 Cyc. 463.

That the statement made is not in exact accord with the facts admits of no dispute. Wright was arrested for housebreaking in Riverview. He was held for that crime and at his trial Colonial Place was not even mentioned. The character of the charge was a matter of public record and had the reporter seen fit to examine it rather than to rely upon the statement of the detectives this litigation could never have arisen. The verdict is not without evidence to support it and so this assignment is overruled.

The next assignment of error is predicated upon the proposition that the article was true; and that it was therefore error to give any instructions based upon the theory that it was not, or under which a recovery could be had. It follows from what has just been said that this assignment is without merit.

[4] And lastly, exception is taken to the refusal of the court to permit Wright, on cross-examination, to be asked if the same statement published by the defendant had been published by

the Ledger-Dispatch, another afternoon Norfolk paper. These publications bear a common date. The claim being that this should have been admitted in mitigation of damages.

In support of this we are referred to 17 R. C. L. page 414, where it is said:

"Evidence showing that similar charges have been made by others has generally been held inadmissible to prove the truth of the defamatory words, but in an action of libel against the publisher of a newspaper for charging that the jury perjured themselves in rendering a verdict, evidence that other newspapers, published in the place where the verdict was rendered, severely criticized the action of the jury as extraordinary, has been held admissible in justification." To sustain the latter proposition *Welch vs. Tribune Pub. Co.,* 83 Mich. 661, 47 N. W. 562, 11 L. R. A. 233, 21 Am. St. Rep. 629, is cited. It will be noted that the authority just quoted states that this testimony was competent to establish justification and not mitigation of damages. In the Michigan case it appears that "the verdict was characterized as extraordinary, and the testimony (other publications) tended to show that the public regarded it as such." That is to say the court was dealing with proof to establish the libel rather than with evidence in mitigation thereof. That the article in the instant case was a libel unless true, admits of no doubt. Next is cited 17 R. C. L. 449, note 5. It is there said: "According to many authorities, the defendant in an action for libel or slander may show other publications, made prior to his own and to the same effect, in mitigation of damages, the ground being that such evidence tends to show want of actual malice or bad faith in many instances. Thus it has been held that a newspaper publisher, when sued for libel, may show, in mitigation of damages, that prior to publishing the alleged libel he had seen the same matter in other newspapers. Some authorities, however, have denied the right to show other publications in mitigation of damages in action for libel, and slander."

Hoboken Printing Co. vs. Kahn, 59 N. J. L. 218, 35 A. 1053, 59 Am. St. Rep. 585, is also relied upon. That case shows that the defendant but restated a rumor already in wide circulation.

The distinction above made is not always followed. Judge Holmes, now Mr. Justice Holmes, in *Burt vs. Advertising News Co.*, 154 Mass. 238, 28 N. E. 1, 13 L. R. A. 97, said: "As a general proposition the defendant cannot show that the plaintiff's damages are less than they otherwise would have been because the charge had been made and published before."

To the same effect see *Sun Printing and Publishing Association vs. Schenck,* 40 C. C. A. 163, 98 Fed. 925, which holds: "No one can say which of many defamations has destroyed or materially impaired a reputation; or whether, but for the last, the earlier ones would have made any grave impression upon the opinion of the public. It would be idle to submit such an inquiry to a jury."

See also *Gray vs. Publishing Co.*, 35 App. Div. 286, 55 N. Y. S. 35, and *Smith vs. Sun Printing Association,* 5 C. C. A. 91, 55 Fed. 240. In *McDuff vs. Detroit Evening Journal Co.*, 84 Mich. 1, 47 N. W. 671, 22 Am. St. Rep. 673, the court said: "In an action of libel founded on a newspaper article an editorial in any other paper upon the same subject matter as that in suit, but not shown to be the basis therefor, was inadmissible." And so also *Dorn & McGinty vs. Cooper,* 139 Iowa, 742, 117 N. W. 1, 118 N. W. 35, 16 Ann. Cas. 744; and *Folwell vs. Providence Journal Co.*, 19 R. I. 551, 37 Atl. 6.

[5] Authorities might be multiplied, but it is not necessary. The substance of them is that such evidence is sometimes admitted in mitigation of damages when it but repeats reports theretofore published, particularly when this appears upon the face of the libel. But it is not admitted when the publications are simultaneous and in no wise connected.

The verdict is not without evidence to support it.

The instructions are good.

The evidence excluded should have been excluded.

The verdict was approved by the learned judge who presided at the trial and heard the evidence, and we, under the facts as they are detailed in the record, and under settled rules of law, have no power to interfere with it.

It follows that the verdict of the jury and the judgment of the court in confirmation thereof must be affirmed.

Affirmed.

K. *Libel Against a City*—City of Chicago *vs.* Tribune Co. (307 Ill. 595. No. 15202. April 18, 1923).

Can a city maintain an action for libel? The City of Chicago sued the Chicago *Tribune* for allegedly libeling its credit in the bond market and because as a result of the publication in question the city's other assets as a functioning municipality were injured. A lower court held that a city could not be libeled and the higher court upheld it in a vigorous opinion. The appellate court pointed out that "no court of last resort in this country has ever held, or even suggested, that prosecutions for libel on government have any place in the American system of jurisprudence." Then it went on thus: "By its demurrer appellee admits it published malicious and false statements regarding the City of Chicago with intent to destroy its credit and financial standing, and assuming that there was a temporary damage to the city and a resultant increase in taxes, it is better than an occasional individual or newspaper that is so perverted in judgment and so misguided in his or its civic duty should go free than that all of the citizens should be put in jeopardy of imprisonment or economic subjugation if they venture to criticise an inefficient or corrupt government."

(No. 15202.—Judgment affirmed.)
THE CITY OF CHICAGO, Appellant, *vs.* THE TRIBUNE COMPANY, Appellee.
Opinion filed April 18, 1923.

APPEAL from the Circuit Court of Cook county; the Hon. HARRY M. FISHER, Judge, presiding.

SAMUEL A. ETTELSON, Corporation Counsel, (CHESTER E. CLEVELAND, OTTO W. ULRICH, and EDWARD C. HIGGINS, of counsel,) for appellant.

MCCORMICK, KIRKLAND, PATTERSON & FLEMING, (WEYMOUTH KIRKLAND, HOWARD ELLIS, and ROBERT R. MCCORMICK, of counsel,) for appellee.

Mr. Chief Justice Thompson delivered the opinion of the court:

The city of Chicago, a municipal corporation, brought in the circuit court of Cook county its action of trespass on the case for libel against the Tribune Company, a corporation publishing a newspaper circulating in the city of Chicago and surrounding territory, alleging damages of $10,000,000. The declaration consists of twelve counts. It avers that the city has a population of about 3,000,000 people; that it owns property, consisting of public buildings, public parks, public streets and bridges, public hospitals, a waterworks system, police and fire equipment, and other property, of the value of $350,000,000; that exclusive of amounts required for school purposes it spends each year for materials, labor and supplies about $50,000,000; that it purchases each year new property valued at approximately $7,000,000; that it is obliged to purchase most of this property, materials and supplies through competitive bidding; that it is necessary, in order to advantageously purchase such property, materials and supplies, to have good credit; that the city must from time to time issue bonds for public purposes and that the market value of these bonds depends upon the financial standing of the city; that the Tribune Company in its newspaper maliciously published concerning the city false, scandalous and defamatory matter; that in various articles appearing from time to time in 1920 it charged that the city was "broke;" that it "owes millions of 1921 funds;" that "bankruptcy is just around the corner from the city of Chicago;" that its "credit is shot to pieces;" that "the city is headed for bankruptcy unless it makes immediate retrenchments;" that "the city's financial affairs are in a serious way;" that "it is the issue between this Tammany government, which has bankrupted the treasury of the city of Chicago, which is in default to the city creditors;" that the city administration "having busted the city and having reduced it to such insolvency that it is issuing Villa script to pay its bills, is reaching out for the State;" that the administration "is paying city debts with city hall script, and we have just begun to feel the effects of being busted;" that "Chicago is drifting into a receivership;" that "the city is hurrying on to bankruptcy and is threatened with a receivership for its revenue;" that the city "is bankrupt and the banks of the city have refused it credit;" that "the city government has run on the rocks;" that "the city cannot pay its debts,—it is bankrupt, the bankers have refused it credit," and divers other similar false and defamatory statements; that while the city was deprived of $7,000,000 theretofore derived from saloon licenses, and that while it was obliged to meet the current high cost of labor, supplies, materials and property, in consequence of which the corporate fund was depleted and there was not enough actual cash to meet the current obligations of the city, there was at all times abundant cash in each of the other funds, to-wit, special assessment fund, waterworks fund, bond fund, traction fund and other special funds, but the false publications made by the Tribune Company were general in their nature and applied indiscriminately to these several funds, thereby injuriously affecting the credit and financial standing of the city; that each and all of said publications were false and were published maliciously and in reckless disregard of the rights of the city; that none of said statements were published with good motives or for justifiable ends; that said statements were published to promote the political and financial interests of the Tribune Company, its political friends and the public utility corporations associated and acting in co-operation with it; that said statements were published with the intent and purpose to impair the credit and financial standing of the city and to give the impression to its readers and to the public that the management of the administrative and governmental affairs of the city was incompetent and corrupt, that the city was unworthy of credit and could not pay its obligations, and that it would be dangerous for persons or firms to invest in bonds issued by the city and to enter into contracts with the city for the sale of property, materials and supplies; that by reason of said publications many persons and firms that would otherwise have been ready, able and willing to sell and furnish property, material and supplies to the city neglected to file their bids, by reason whereof competition was stifled and the city was compelled to pay, and did pay, higher prices than it otherwise would have been obliged to pay, by reason of which it lost $5,000,000; that by reason of said publications certain persons who would otherwise have bid for the city's bonds refused to bid for them, in consequence of which the bonds sold for less amount than would otherwise have been realized, whereby the city lost $2,500,000; and that by reason of said publications, and in consequence of the resulting injury to the city's credit and financial standing, it was unable to conduct its business on an economical basis, thereby suffering a further loss of $2,500,000. A demurrer filed to this declaration was sustained, and this appeal followed.

The articles were published in the summer of 1920 during the progress of the campaign between rival candidates for the republican nomination for Governor of the State. One of the two leading candidates was supported by the Tribune Company and the other by the administration of the city of Chicago. Many of the publications are quotations from speeches of the candidate supported by the newspaper and of his political friends. The Tribune Company claims it was within its rights guaranteed by section 4 of article 2 of the constitution, which declares: "Every person may freely speak, write and publish on all subjects, being responsible for the abuse of that liberty;" and further, that it is a fundamental principle of the American system of government that any person may criticise the government with impunity so long as he does not advocate the violation of existing law or the overthrow of the existing government by unlawful means. The city contends that the constitutional privilege extends only to the publication of "the truth when published with good motives and for justifiable ends," and that a city, as any other corporation, may be libeled with respect to its private enterprises. Many procedural questions have been argued, but we shall consider only the substantive question, Can a city maintain an action for libel?

The struggle for freedom of speech has marched hand in hand

in the advance of civilization with the struggle for other great human liberties. History teaches that human liberty cannot be secured unless there is freedom to express grievances. As civilization advanced and as the means for expressing grievances multiplied, the struggle between the people and their despotic rulers became more bitter. With the opening of the seventeenth century the people began to publish newspapers, and history begins to record unspeakable prosecutions of the editors. For one hundred years the crown forbade the publication of a newspaper without a license. As the seventeenth century drew to a close the right to publish without a license was recognized, and from that time to this no English government has claimed or practiced the royal prerogative of licensing the press. Licensing of the press was never effective in the American colonies. The last attempt to enforce this common law right of the crown in the American colonies failed in 1725, and so for more than fifty years prior to the adoption of the Federal constitution, and for nearly one hundred years prior to the adoption of our first State constitution, licensing of the press was completely abolished in America. While this right of the crown went out with the seventeenth century, freedom of speech had not yet been established and the restriction of this fundamental right then took the form of subsequent punishments. Political prosecutions by the government were vigorously used to silence opposition. Truth was no defense, because the despotic governments declared that "the greater the truth the greater the libel." The names of martyrs to the cause of freedom of speech became household words in England and in America. To obtain freedom from this oppression of the crown was one of the many reasons why the American colonists revolted.

It is interesting to follow the viewpoint of the writers of different periods in their discussion of the right of the citizen to criticise his government. Holt, an early English author, says in his Law of Libel, (1st Am. ed. p. 92): "If it be the highest crime known to our laws to attempt to subvert by force the constitution and State, it is certainly a crime, though of inferior magnitude yet of great enormity, to endeavor to despoil it of its best support,—the veneration, esteem and affection of the people. It is therefore a maxim of the law of England, flowing by natural consequence and easy deduction from the great principle of self-defense, to consider as libels and misdemeanors every species of attack, by speaking or writing, the object of which is wantonly to defame or indecorously to calumniate that economy, order and constitution of things which make up the general system of the law and government of the country. Opinion is strength, and the good fame of government is necessary to maintain this opinion. The distance is not very great between contempt of the laws and open resistance to them." And again, on page 102 he says: "Our courts of justice considered all abuse and invective against the king and his court officers, all slander which interfered with the government of the nation, and all libels which reflected upon the conduct and management of State affairs, as little short of treason and concerted designs for the subversion of the government itself. It is no wonder, therefore, if in those times [prior to James I] we should find such words and writings charged as acts of treason which in our age of improved learning and mildness in the administration of the law pass only for libels,—the overflowings of seditions gall and the resentments of disorderly and petulant spirits." Note the change when Stephen, in his History of Criminal Law of England, written in 1883, says: "In one word, nothing short of direct incitement to disorder and violence is a seditious libel. * * * It is enough to say that in this country and in this generation the time for prosecuting political libels has passed and does not seem likely to return within any definable period." (2 Stephen, pp. 375, 376.) Odgers, another English writer, says: "The test whether the statement is a seditious libel is not either the truth of the language or the innocence of the motive with which the statement is published, but is this: Is the language used calculated to promote public disorder or physical force or violence, or violence in a matter of State?" (Odgers on Libel and Slander,—5th ed.—p. 513.)

There were few prosecutions for libel on government in the American colonies, and no court of last resort in this country has ever held, or even suggested, that prosecutions for libel on government have any place in the American system of jurisprudence. The right of the government to prosecute its accusers was founded on the theory that the king could do no wrong. He was an hereditary monarch and was not responsible to the people. When the people became sovereign, as they did when our government was established under our constitution and the ministers became servants of the people, the right to discuss government followed as a natural sequence. When the sovereign power is vested in an hereditary monarch there is no occasion for discussing the government and exposing its inefficiency or corruption unless to advocate reformation by violence, because there can be no remedy except by revolution. It appears, therefore, that there was reasonable foundation for prosecuting the government's critics in the days of "divine rights" of kings, but since the people are sovereign and since the magistrates are servants of the people the magistrates can do wrong, and the people have a fundamental right to criticise them and to expose their inefficiency and corruption so that they may be displaced. It is one of the fundamental principles, therefore, of the American system of government, that the people have the right to discuss their government without fear of being called to account in the courts for their expressions of opinion. Cooley says: "The English common law rule which made libels on the constitution or the government indictable, as it was administered by the courts, seems to us unsuited to the conditions and circumstances of the people of America and therefore to have never been adopted in the several States. If we are correct in this, it would not be in the power of the State legislatures to pass laws which should make mere criticisms of the constitution or of the measures of government a crime, however sharp, unreasonable and intemperate it might be." (Cooley's Const. Lim. –7th ed.–614.) Stephen says: "There may, indeed, be breaches of the peace which may destroy or endanger life, limb or property, and there may be incitements to such offenses, but no imaginable censure of the government short of a censure which has an immediate tendency to produce such a breach of the peace ought to be regarded as criminal. * * * The change of public sentiment as to the free discussion of political affairs has practically rendered the law as to political libels unimportant, inasmuch as it has practically restricted prosecutions for libel to cases in which a libel amounts either to a direct incitement to crime or to false imputations upon an individual of disgraceful conduct in relation to either public or private affairs." (2 Stephen's History of Criminal Law, pp. 300, 301.) In the second volume of his Constitutional History of England (7th ed. p. 379,) May says: "Prosecutions for libel, like the censorship, have fallen out of our constitutional system. When the press errs it is by the press itself that its errors are corrected. Repression has ceased to be the policy of rulers, and statesmen have at length fully realized the wise maxim of Lord Bacon that 'the punishing of wits enhances their authority, and a forbidden writing is thought to be a certain spark of truth, that flies up in the faces of them that seek to tread it out.' "

Only once in the history of the United States has there ever been an attempt to transplant the English rule of libels on government to American soil. In 1798 Congress passed the infamous Sedition law, which punished false, scandalous and malicious writings against the government, either house of Congress or the President, if published with intent to defame any of them or to excite against them the contempt or hatred of the people. In so far as this law punished defamation of the President or any other person and in so far as it punished those who advocated resistance to law or rendered aid to a foreign foe, it was, of course, constitutional, but in so far as it sought to make criminal any defamation of the government or of the administration in power it has been generally considered to be unconstitutional. In discussing this act James Madison said: "Some degree of abuse is inseparable from the proper use of everything, and in no instance is this more true than in that of the press. It has accordingly been decided by the practice of the States that it is better to leave a few of its noxious branches to their luxuriant growth, than by pruning them away to injure the vigor of those yielding the proper fruits. And can the wisdom of this policy be doubted by anyone who reflects that to the press, alone, checkered, as it is, with abuses, the world is indebted for all the triumphs which have been gained by reason and humanity over error and oppression; who reflects that to the same beneficent source the United States owe much of the lights which conducted them to the rank of a free and independent nation and which have improved their political system into a shape so auspicious to their happiness? Had sedition acts forbidding every publication that might bring the constituted agents into contempt or disrepute, or that might excite the hatred of the people against the authors of unjust or pernicious measures, been uniformly enforced against the press, might not the United States have been languishing at this day under the infirmities of a sickly confederation? Might they not, possibly, be miserable colonies, groaning under a foreign yoke?" (4 Elliot's Debates on the Federal Constitution, 571.) Cooley says: "The Sedition law was passed during the administration of the elder Adams, when the fabric of government was still new and untried and when many men seemed to think that the breath of heated party discussions might tumble it about their heads. Its constitutionality was always disputed by a large party and its impolicy was beyond question. It had a direct tendency to produce the very state of things which it sought to repress. The prosecutions under it were instrumental, among other things, in the final overthrow and destruction of the party by which it was adopted, and it is impossible to conceive at the present time of any such state of things as would be likely to bring about its re-enactment or the passage of any similar repressive statute. * * * If any such principle of repression should ever be recognized in the common law of America, it might reasonably be anticipated that in times of high party excitement it would lead to prosecutions by the party in power to bolster up wrongs and sustain abuses and oppressions by crushing adverse criticism and discussion. The evil, indeed, could not be of long continuance, for, judging from experience, the reaction would be speedy, thorough and effectual; but it would be no less a serious evil while it lasted, the direct tendency of which would be to excite discontent and to breed a rebellious spirit. Repression of full and free discussion is dangerous in any government resting upon the will of the people." Cooley's Const. Lim.—7th ed.—pp. 613, 614.

There were a number of prosecutions under the Sedition act and many recalcitrant spirits were thrown into jail for expression of opinions contrary to those entertained by the administration in power. When Jefferson became President he remitted, with interest, the fines that had been levied against persons convicted under the act and pardoned all those who were sentenced to imprisonment. In answer to the criticism of his acts he replied: "I discharge every person under punishment or prosecution under the Sedition law because I considered, and now consider, that law to be a nullity as absolute and palpable as if Congress had ordered us to fall down and worship a golden image." The proponents of the Sedition act argued that true liberty of the press permitted only the truth to be published with good motives and for justifiable ends. To this Madison replied: "In the first place, where simple and naked facts, alone, are in question, there is sufficient difficulty in some cases, and sufficient trouble and vexation in all, in meeting a prosecution from the government with the full and formal proof necessary in a court of law. But in the next place, it must be obvious to the plainest minds that opinions and inferences and conjectural observations are not only in many cases inseparable from the facts, but may often be more the objects of the prosecution than the facts themselves; or may even be altogether abstracted from particular facts; and that opinion and inferences and conjectural observations cannot be subjects of that kind of proof which appertains to facts before a court of law. Again, it is no less obvious that the intent to defame or bring into contempt or disrepute or hatred, which is made a condition of the offense created by the act, cannot prevent its pernicious influence on the freedom of the press. For, omitting the inquiry how far the malice or the intent is an inference of the law from the mere publication, it is manifestly impossible to punish the intent to bring those who administer the government into disrepute or contempt without striking at the right of freely discussing public characters and measures, because those who engage in such discussions must expect and intend to excite these unfavorable sentiments so far as they may be thought to be deserved. To prohibit the intent to excite those unfavorable sentiments against those who administer the government is equivalent to a prohibition of the actual excitement of them; and to prohibit the actual excitement of them is equivalent to a prohibition of discussions having that tendency and effect; which, again, is equivalent to a protection of those who administer the government, if they should at any time deserve the contempt or hatred of the people, against being exposed to it, by free animadversions on their characters and conduct. Nor can there be a doubt, if those in public trust be shielded by penal laws from such strictures of the press as may expose them to contempt or disrepute or hatred where they may deserve it, that in exact proportion as they may deserve to be exposed will be the certainty and criminality of the intent to expose them and the vigilance of prosecuting and punishing it; nor a doubt that a government thus intrenched in penal statutes against the just and natural effects of a culpable administration will easily evade the responsibility which is essential to a faithful discharge of its duty." 4 Elliot's Debates on the Federal Constitution, 575.

The fundamental right of freedom of speech is involved in this litigation and not merely the right of liberty of the press. If this action can be maintained against a newspaper it can be maintained against every private citizen who ventures to criticise the ministers who are temporarily conducting the affairs of his government. Where any person by speech or writing seeks to persuade others to violate existing law or to overthrow by force or other unlawful means the existing government he may be punished, (*People vs. Lloyd,* 304 Ill. 23; *Gilbert vs. Minnesota,* 254 U. S. 325, 41 Sup. Ct. 125;) but all other utterances or publications against the government must be considered absolutely privileged.

While in the early history of the struggle for freedom of speech the restrictions were enforced by criminal prosecutions, it is clear that a civil action is as great, if not a greater, restriction than a criminal prosecution. If the right to criticise the government is a privilege which, with the exceptions above enumerated, cannot be restricted, then all civil as well as criminal actions are forbidden. A despotic or corrupt government can more easily stifle opposition by a series of civil actions than by criminal prosecutions, because (*a*) a civil action can be started without the filing of a complaint with leave of court and without the necessity of a grand jury investigation; (*b*) in a civil action the judge instructs the jury and the jury must follow his instructions on the law, while in a criminal prosecution the jury are the judges of the law as well as of the facts; (*c*) in civil actions the judge may grant new trials until the defendant is exhausted by expense or until a jury is found that will give judgment against him; (*d*) our statute limits the punishment in criminal cases to a $500 fine or jail imprisonment of one year, whereas in civil actions there is no limit to the amount of damages that may be sought; (*e*) in a civil action the government can recover by proving its case by a mere preponderance of the evidence, while in a criminal action it must prove its case beyond a reasonable doubt; (*f*) the defendant in a criminal action is presumed to be innocent until he is proven guilty, and no such presumption exists in a civil action; and (*g*) the government is required in a criminal prosecution to furnish to the defendant the names of the witnesses by whom it expects to sustain its charges, but in a civil action it may keep its proof a secret until it is revealed from the witness stand. It follows, therefore, that every citizen has a right to criticise an inefficient or corrupt government without fear of civil as well as criminal prosecution. This absolute privilege is founded on the principle that it is advantageous for the public interest that the citizen should not be in any way fettered in his statements, and where the public service or due administration of justice is involved he shall have the right to speak his mind freely.

The government consists of associated persons representing the sovereign, who make, interpret and enforce the laws. The American system of government is founded upon the fundamental principle that the citizen is the fountain of all authority. Under our system this sovereign citizen has conferred certain authority upon his servants,—officers of the law commissioned for a fixed time to discharge specific duties. In order to serve their needs the citizens of Illinois, acting through the State government erected by them, have authorized the organization of city governments. The persons living within the corporate limits of these cities select officers who constitute the city government. The activities of these governments are limited by the needs of the people. All organized governments own and operate more or less property, and certain proprietary rights have long been recognized as necessary for the welfare of the inhabitants of the municipality. Municipal corporations, however, exist primarily for governmental purposes, and they are permitted to enter the commercial field solely for the purpose of subserving the interests of the public which they represent. A city is no less a government because it owns and operates its own water system, its own gas and electric system and its own transportation system. In *Byrne vs. Chicago General Railway Co.* 169 Ill. 75, this court said: "The city is but an agency of the State, and governs, within its sphere, for the State. * * * The government exercised by the city is exercised as an agency of the whole public and for all the people of the State. A municipal corporation, like a State or county, is within its prescribed sphere a political power." In *City of Chicago vs. M. & M. Hotel Co.* 248 Ill. 264, we said: "The city of Chicago is organized under the statute known as the City and Village act. It may exercise only such powers as are expressly delegated to it by the legislature and such as are necessarily implied from those expressly given. All governmental powers primarily reside in the people. Some of these powers have been delegated to the Federal government by the constitution of the United States. All of the powers not thus delegated are reserved to the people of the several States and are exercised by the people through their representatives in the legislature and the other departments of the State government. * * * The legislature may delegate all or a part of its power to municipalities created by the legislature. * * * Counties, * * * cities, villages and other municipal and *quasi* municipal corporations are created under the authority of the legislature to better accomplish the purposes of local government." While for certain limited purposes it is often said that a municipality owns and operates its public utilities in its capacity as a private corporation and not in the exercise of its powers of local sovereignty, yet because of its proprietary rights it does not lose its governmental character. Its property is not subject to execution, (*City of Chicago vs. Hasley,* 25 Ill. 485,) nor to Federal taxation, (*Pollock vs. Farmers' Loan and Trust Co.* 157 U. S. 429, 584,) nor is the city subject to garnishment, (*Merwin vs. City of Chicago,* 45 Ill. 133,) and its so-called private property may, with exceptions, be taken from it by the State. (*Ward vs. Field Museum,* 241 Ill. 496.) It is manifest that the more so-called private property the people permit their governments to own and operate, the more important is the right to freely criticise the administration of the government. As the amount of property owned by the city and the amount of public business to be transacted by the city increase, so does the opportunity for inefficient and corrupt government increase and the greater will be the efforts of the administration to remain in control of such a political prize. The richer the city the greater the incentive to stifle opposition. In so far as the question before us is concerned, no distinction can be made with respect to the proprietary and governmental capacities of a city.

By its demurrer appellee admits it published malicious and false statements regarding the city of Chicago with intent to destroy its credit and financial standing, and assuming that there was a temporary damage to the city and a resultant increase in taxes, it is better that an occasional individual or newspaper that is so perverted in judgment and so misguided in his or its civic duty should go free than that all of the citizens should be put in jeopardy of imprisonment or economic subjugation if they venture to criticise an inefficient or corrupt government. We do not pass upon the truth or falsity of the publications nor the merits of the political controversy between the parties. We consider the question solely from the standpoint of public policy and fundamental principles of government. For the same reason that members of the legislature, judges of the courts and other persons engaged in certain fields of the public service or in the administration of justice are absolutely immune from actions, civil or criminal, for libel for words published in the discharge of such public duties, the individual citizen must be given a like privilege when he is acting in his sovereign capacity. This action is out of tune with the American spirit and has no place in American jurisprudence.

The judgment of the circuit court is affirmed.

Judgment affirmed.

L. *Libel in a Charge of Unwillingness to Pay a Debt*—Newton *vs.* Lewis Apparel Stores (N. Y., Third Dept. 267 App. Div. 728. May 10, 1944).

This case is of interest on two counts: it shows how a letter can be the subject of a libel, and it takes up the question of libel in the allegation of a person's unwillingness to pay a debt. A lower court held that there was not a sufficient case to constitute a cause of action and dismissed the complaint. But the appellate court held otherwise: "To publish of one that he is unwilling or refuses to pay his debts conveys the implication intended to be conveyed that the debtor is unworthy of credit. The effect of such a publication would impair the standing of an individual and bring him into disrepute with right thinking people in a community. . . . Certainly a question for a jury is presented. . . ."

ROBERT NEATON, Appellant, *vs.* LEWIS APPAREL STORES, INC., et al., Respondents.

Third Department, May 10, 1944.

APPEAL from a judgment of the Supreme Court, Albany County, in favor of defendants, entered November 9, 1942, upon an order of the court at Special Term (BERGAN, J.), held in Rensselaer County, which granted a motion by defendants for a dismissal of the complaint on the ground that it did not state facts sufficient to constitute a cause of action.

Glenn A. Frank, attorney for appellant.

Wiswall, Walton, Wood & MacAffer, attorneys (*Carl O. Olson* on the brief), for respondents.

HEFFERNAN, J. This action is for libel. Plaintiff has appealed from an order of the Rensselaer Special Term of the Supreme Court dismissing his complaint, under rule 106 of the Rules of Civil Practice, for failure to state facts sufficient to constitute a cause of action.

After alleging that plaintiff is a resident of Albany County, employed by A. & P. Food Stores; that the corporate defendant is a domestic corporation and that the individual defendant is its manager, the complaint charges: "4. That on or about September 24, 1941, the defendants maliciously published, concerning the plaintiff, by transmitting the same through the United States mails, to the plaintiff's employer, the A. & P. Food Stores, Broadway, Albany, New York, the following false and defamatory letter:

'THE LEWIS STORE — AMERICA'S LEADING CREDIT CLOTHIERS.

329 River St.,
Troy, N. Y.

September 24, 1941.

A. & P. WAREHOUSE
Broadway,
Albany, New York.

Re: Robert Neaton 16886
$20.96

GENTLEMEN:

We may have to garnishee the wages of one of your employees but before doing so, wish to ask your assistance in trying to liquidate a just debt.

This employee has been given every opportunity to pay the debt in small payments, without results, and as it is against our wishes to garnishee unless forced to do so. We ask you to be good enough to speak to this party if the above balance or installments on same cannot be paid at once. By so doing considerable annoyance and trouble can be avoided, also the employee will save the additional expense involved.

We certainly hope that you will not feel that we are making a collection agency of your firm, but only ask your assistance in the interest of good business and fair treatment. Thanking you, we are

Very truly yours,

LEWIS APPAREL STORES, INC.,

By R. BIGADI,

Mgr.' "

It is further alleged that the meaning of the quoted letter is that plaintiff did not pay his bills; that he was unworthy of credit and that defendants were the owners of a claim against him which was uncollectible, except by garnishee process; that plaintiff was not indebted to defendants in any amount whatsoever, nor had they secured a judgment against him and that the publication was wholly false with the result that plaintiff's credit was impaired and his financial standing injured.

For the purpose of this review we are bound to assume the truth of the allegations contained in the complaint. The court below has held, and it is the contention of respondents in this court, that because the publication does not affect plaintiff in his business or profession it is not libelous *per se*. This argument does not commend itself to us. "Any written or printed article is libelous or actionable without alleging special damages if it tends to expose the plaintiff to public contempt, ridicule, aversion or disgrace, or induce an evil opinion of him in the minds of right-thinking persons, and to deprive him of their friendly intercourse in society. (*Bennet vs. Commercial Advertiser Assn.*, 230 N. Y. 125; *Triggs vs. Sun Printing & Pub. Assn.*, 179 N. Y. 144.) A publication is libelous *per se* where its tendency is to disgrace the plaintiff, and bring him into ridicule and contempt. (*Morey vs. Morning Journal Assn.*, 123 N. Y. 207.)" (*Sydney vs. Macfadden Newspaper Pub. Corp.*, 242 N. Y. 208, 211-212.)

In construing this publication we are not restricted to a literal interpretation of the language used, disassociated from the purpose, intent and consequence that may follow from the thought expressed in the words used. If the publication is made maliciously and for the purpose and with the intent of injuring the plaintiff, and would, in its ordinary meaning and purpose, tend to expose one to public hatred, contempt or ridicule, or deprive him of public confidence or esteem, it is actionable *per se;* that is, if, upon the face of the publication, this would be the usual and ordinary effect upon the minds of other people to whom it comes, it must be presumed that it had that effect—the effect that it usually and ordinarily has upon the mind. It is the thought conveyed to the minds of others by the publication that distills the poison which defames the good name or character of the person assailed.

To publish of one that he is unwilling or refuses to pay his debts conveys the implication intended to be conveyed that the debtor is unworthy of credit. The effect of such a publication would impair the standing of an individual and bring him into disrepute with right thinking people in a community.

The meaning of the language used in the publication before us was not a question of law for the court. If the language is capable of two meanings, one of which would be libelous and actionable and the other not, it is for a jury to say, under all the circumstances surrounding its publication, including extraneous facts admissible in evidence, which of the two meanings would be attributed to it by those to whom it is addressed or by whom it may be read. (*Washington Post Co. vs. Chaloner,* 250 U. S. 290.) It is only when the court can say that the publication is not reasonably capable of any defamatory meanings, and cannot reasonably be understood in any defamatory sense, that the court can rule, as matter of law, that the publication is not libelous. (*Fahy vs. Melrose Free Press, Inc.,* 298 Mass. 267.)

In *Peck vs. Tribune Co.* (214 U. S. 185) plaintiff sued for libel on the ground that defendant published an advertisement which represented plaintiff as a nurse who praised Duffy's Pure Malt Whiskey. The trial court directed a verdict for defendant, and its action was sustained by the Circuit Court of Appeals (154 F.

330) but reversed by the United States Supreme Court. Speaking for a unanimous court, Mr. Justice HOLMES said: "The question, then, is whether the publication was a libel. It was held by the Circuit Court of Appeals not to be, or at most to entitle the plaintiff only to nominal damages, no special damage being alleged. It was pointed out that there was no general consensus of opinion that to drink whiskey is wrong or that to be a nurse is discreditable. It might have been added that very possibly giving a certificate and the use of one's portrait in aid of an advertisement would be regarded with irony, or a stronger feeling, only by a few. But it appears to us that such inquiries are beside the point. It may be that the action for libel is of little use, but while it is maintained it should be governed by the general principles of tort. If the advertisement obviously would hurt the plaintiff in the estimation of an important and respectable part of the community, liability is not a question of a majority vote.

"We know of no decision in which this matter is discussed upon principle. But obviously an unprivileged falsehood need not entail universal hatred to constitute a cause of action. No falsehood is thought about or even known by all the world. No conduct is hated by all. That it will be known by a large number and will lead an appreciable fraction of that number to regard the plaintiff with contempt is enough to do her practical harm. * * * It seems to us impossible to say that the obvious tendency of what is imputed to the plaintiff by this advertisement is not seriously to hurt her standing with a considerable and respectable class in the community. Therefore it was the plaintiff's right to prove her case and go to the jury."

In *Katapodis vs. Brooklyn Spectator, Inc.* (287 N. Y. 17) wherein it appeared that a newspaper article recited that the parents of a small boy who had been accidentally killed were in dire financial straits, and, if immediate financial aid was not forthcoming, had no alternative but to let their son be interred "in Potter's Field, burying ground of the homeless, friendless and penniless" the court held that it could not be said as matter of law that such an imputation necessarily did not hurt the plaintiffs. In writing for the court Judge LOUGHRAN said: "The false words portrayed them [plaintiffs] as being steeped in poverty to the very lips. We think it is not for us to say that the publication of such a piece of news did not hurt the plaintiffs by tending to deprive them of friendly association with a considerable number of respectable members of their community. We believe it is the right of the plaintiffs to have a jury say whether the false words did, in fact, so defame them."

"Communications are often defamatory because they tend to expose another to hatred, ridicule or contempt. A defamatory communication may tend to disparage another by reflecting unfavorably upon his personal morality or integrity or it may consist of imputations which, while not affecting another's personal reputation, tend to discredit his financial standing in the community, and this is so whether or not the other is engaged in business or industry." (Restatement of the Law, Torts, Vol. Ill, §559, Comment b.)

We are also satisfied that under the authority of *Keating vs. Conviser* (246 N. Y. 632) the complaint states a good cause of action.

With these authorities to guide us we conclude that the language in the publication before us might reasonably be construed by the average reader as a reflection on the character and standing of the plaintiff. Certainly a question for a jury is presented as to the meaning to be attributed to it and consequently the motion to dismiss the complaint should have been denied.

The order and judgment appealed from are reversed on the law, with costs, and the motion to dismiss the complaint is denied, with ten dollars costs, with leave to respondents to answer within twenty days after service of a copy of the order to be entered hereon.

BREWSTER, J. (dissenting). The complaint is in libel. It is founded upon a letter written by defendants to plaintiff's employer, charging in effect that plaintiff was in arrears in the payment of a single indebtedness. I agree with the Special Term that within the authorities there is nothing in the letter that, as pleaded, may be held to be libelous *per se*. To falsely so write as to a single account does not so expose one to obloquy, ridicule or disgrace or so cause one to be shunned, that general damage may be inferred.

In *Woodruff vs. Bradstreet Co.* (116 N. Y. 217) cited by the Special Term, the gravamen of the alleged libel was the publication of the recovery of a judgment for money. Such was held not to be libelous *per se*. The court there reasoned (p. 222) that the "* * * recovery of a judgment does not necessarily import conceded default in payment of a debt." And further "It is a matter of frequent observation that controversies, arising apparently out of an honest difference of opinion, go into the courts for determination. Litigation also not infrequently comes from causes in which is involved no personal credit or default. There is nothing in the defendant's report to indicate that the judgment was produced by any cause prejudicial to the credit of the plaintiff, and there is no presumption in that respect upon the subject in aid of the action." While in that case only the rendition of a money judgment was published, and the comment relative [to?] the absence of an import of conceded default is somewhat significant, still the weight of authority seems to be that falsely writing of one concerning or charging delinquency in the payment of a debt is not thus libelous, when the alleged debtor is not a merchant or so engaged that financial credit is a necessary factor in his trade or business. Such were the holdings in *Stannard vs. Wilcox & Gibbs* (118 Md. 151) and cases cited therein; *Windisch-Muhlhauser Brewing Co. vs. Bacom* (21 Ky. L. Rep. 928); *Harrison vs. Burger* (212 Ala. 670); *Fry vs. McCord Bros.* (95 Tenn. 678). The following excerpt from *Nichols vs. Daily Reporter Co.* (30 Utah 74, 79) seems in point, viz.: "To write and publish of one not a trader or merchant and not of or concerning his business affairs that he is indebted to another, and, though able to pay, has neglected or refused to do so, is that such an impeachment of honesty, or does it import such degradation of morals or character, or expose him to public hatred or ridicule, or tend to disgrace him, as a court can say its publication necessarily must, in fact, or, by a presumption of evidence, occasion damage and pecuniary loss to him, and, therefore, he was relieved from otherwise alleging or proving any? We think not. We are not saying that such language may not, as a natural and proximate consequence, occasion loss and damage; but the plaintiff, in order to recover, must allege and prove them." Since the complaint in question pleads no special damages and the alleged cause of action is so pleaded that its legal sufficiency must be based upon the matter counted upon being libelous *per se,* I therefore think the Special Term was correct in dismissing it on the motion made therefor.

However, for the reasons next stated, I think it proper to direct a modification of the order and judgment of dismissal by permitting plaintiff, on terms, to plead over or anew. I assume he would need this in order to do that, and that we have power to grant it under section 283 of the Civil Practice Act. Such appears to be an indulgence usually granted. (*Hehmeyer vs. Harper's Weekly Corporation,* 170 App. Div. 459, 463; *Fagan vs. New York Evening Journal Publishing Co.,* 129 App. Div. 28, 30; *Ellenborger vs. Slocum,* 123 N. Y. S. 342.) While the office of an innuendo may not be used to extend the alleged libel beyond its import it may be used "to explain the application of words by connection with such facts and circumstances as are alleged." (*Woodruff vs. Bradstreet Co., supra,* p. 221.) The defendants' letter characterized plaintiff's obligation as "a just debt" which he had "been given every opportunity to pay * * * in small payments, without results," and it asked assistance from plaintiff's employers "in the interest of * * * fair treatment." If by the pleading of extrinsic facts and special damages and the legitimate use of an innuendo, any or all of these may serve to state a cause of action, I think plaintiff should have that opportunity. I favor an affirmance of the order and judgment appealed from, with the modification aforesaid, contingent upon plaintiff's payment of costs in the court below and here.

HILL, P. J., and BLISS, J., concur with HEFFERNAN, J.; BREWSTER, J., dissents in opinion in which SCHENCK, J., concurs.

Judgment and order reversed on the law, with costs, and the motion to dismiss the complaint denied, with ten dollars costs, with leave to respondents to answer within twenty days after service of a copy of the order to be entered hereon. [See 268 App. Div. ——.]

M. *Libel by Advertisement*—Goss *vs.* The Needham Cooperative Bank (312 Massachusetts 309. October 28, 1942).

This brief case is interesting because it proves how easy it is even for a careful financial institution to slip into a libelous publication by way of an advertisement to "change a house into a home by owning it."

ARTHUR C. GOSS, JUNIOR, *vs.* THE NEEDHAM CO-OPERATIVE BANK.

Suffolk. October 7, 1942.—October 28, 1942.

Present: FIELD, C.J., LUMMUS, QUA, DOLAN, & COX, JJ.

Libel and Slander.

TORT. Writ in the Superior Court dated February 21, 1940.

The action was tried before *O'Connell,* J.

E. O. Proctor, for the defendant.

R. Clayton, for the plaintiff.

LUMMUS, J. This is an action for libel, based upon an advertisement inserted by the defendant in a newspaper called The Needham Chronicle, published in Needham, where the plaintiff lived. The advertisement consisted of a picture of the plaintiff's house, and beneath it these words: "An important question 'To rent or to own'—change a house into a home by owning it—we will help you decide how—The Needham Co-operative Bank. Amos H. Shepherdson, Treasurer." At the conclusion of the evidence, the judge denied the defendant's motion for a directed verdict, and the defendant excepted to such denial. The jury returned a verdict for the plaintiff. The case comes here on the defendant's exceptions to the denial of its motion, and to the denial of four requests presented by the defendant which raised no point not covered by the motion.

In *Ingalls vs. Hastings & Sons Publishing Co.* 304 Mass. 31, 33, it is pointed out that "a writing is a libel if, in view of all relevant circumstances, it discredits the plaintiff in the minds, not of the court . . . nor of wise, thoughtful and tolerant men, nor of ordinarily reasonable men, but of any 'considerable and respectable class in the community.'" *Fahy vs. Melrose Free Press Inc.* 298 Mass. 267. *Streeter vs. Eldridge,* 311 Mass. 180, 182. It is not essential to a libel that any wrongdoing or bad character be imputed to the plaintiff. *Themo vs. New England Newspaper Publishing Co.* 306 Mass. 54, 56, 57.

In the present case readers of the newspaper might well draw the inferences, as upon the evidence many of them could be found to have done, that the defendant was offering the house for sale and that it had acquired it upon a foreclosure due to the plaintiff's financial inability to perform his obligations. The plaintiff testified that the defendant had no mortgage upon the house. Although inability to meet one's obligations does not necessarily show want of good character, it may lower one in the estimation of the community. *Cox vs. Lee,* L. R. 4 Ex. 284, 288. *Katapodis vs. Brooklyn Spectator, Inc.* 287 N. Y. 17; 137 Am. L. R. 910, 913. There was no error in permitting the case to go to the jury.

Exceptions overruled.

N. *Libel and Humor and the Use of the Word "Nigger"*— Franklin *vs.* World Publishing Co. (183 Oklahoma 507. No. 28137. October 11, 1938).

Is it libelous to make fun of a lawyer? Is it libelous to call anyone a "nigger"? Apparently it is not libelous to do either in the South, as this Oklahoma case indicates.

FRANKLIN *vs.* WORLD PUBLISHING CO.

No. 28137. Oct. 11, 1938.

Appeal from District Court, Tulsa County; Prentiss E. Rowe, Judge.

Action by B. C. Franklin against the World Publishing Company for damages for libel. Judgment for defendant, and plaintiff appeals. Affirmed.

Amos T. Hall, P. A. Chappelle, and Primus C. Wade, for plaintiff in error.

M. A. Breckinridge, for defendant in error.

Davison, J. This is an appeal from a judgment of the district court of Tulsa county. The plaintiff, B. C. Franklin, brought this action against the World Publishing Company for damages based upon an alleged defamatory publication.

The defendant demurred to the plaintiff's petition. The demurrer was sustained, and the plaintiff has appealed.

The published article complained of, in so far as it refers to the plaintiff and is necessary to consider here, is as follows:

" 'Dire calamity circled over the Joe Louis Club like a hungry turkey buzzard Monday afternoon.

" 'Twice within recent months the club has been subjected to raids as a resort where gambling is illegally perpetrated and Judge Hatch's lips were straightened out in a thin, ominous line preparatory to exterminating the place altogether.

" 'Eleven ill-at-ease negro boys shifted uneasily from one foot to the other out in front of the judge and Uncle Ben Franklin, Greenwood's legal luminary, braced back on his hind legs, loosened up his supple tongue, and rallied to the defense of the beleaguered institution.

" ' "Jedge, that there Joe Louis club is a virtuous, charitable institution. Keeps pore colored nigger boys off'n the streets, gives 'em food and sustenance when they bellies whinnies fer food. Herbert Hill, the club managah, is addin' stahs to his crown in heben by runnin' the place. Please don't close it down."

" 'Uncle Ben went on to Herb Hill, dressing him in raiment of the snowiest white. Declared him as innocent as a new-born lamb—with a soul as white as the driven snow. He dragged out a halo and tenderly placed it above Herb's brow and he called attention to the sprouting of downy wings on the good man's shoulders. Of course, the halo was a bit shop-worn and considerably tarnished, and the white wings a bit bedraggled and moulting, but this was to be expected since Uncle Ben has been parading Herb around in these props for quite a spell now.

" ' "What I want to know," cut in Judge Hatch, who was surfeited with oratory, "is whether these 11 boys were gambling or not."

" ' "Now, jedge," placated the philosophical Ben, 'you knows that anywheres they's two, three nigger boys gits together, they's jes' simply gwine ter be a few li'l ole craps shot."

" ' "You knows and Ah knows," he finished in a resigned voice, "that eben ole St. Peter hisse'f is gonna have a hahd time keepin' these boys fum shootin' craps on the golden streets when they gets to heben." ' "

The plaintiff alleges in his petition that he is a member of the Negro race; that he is an attorney admitted to practice in the Supreme Court of Oklahoma and with good standing with the State Bar; that he had enjoyed the support, patronage, esteem, respect, and confidence of his neighbors and the people throughout the state; that his practice as an attorney was limited to menbers of his own race and that anything that tends to lower him in the estimation and esteem of the negroes in the city of Tulsa and elsewhere, by holding him up to scorn, ridicule, contempt, and hatred of negroes, is injurious to his profession as an attorney.

No special damages having been alleged, the petition was presented to the court upon the theory that the matter complained of was libelous per se.

The only contention presented is that the trial court erred in sustaining the demurrer to plaintiff's petition. If this contention is to be sustained, we must find that the publication complained of, shorn of the many innuendoes and inferences pleaded in the petition, was libelous per se and that it was unnecessary to allege any special damages. The words of the publication must, within themselves, be opprobrious.

Law writers have found much difficulty in defining libel. This court has generally adhered to statutory definition. In section 724, O. S. 1931, "libel" is thus defined:

"Libel is a false or malicious unprivileged publication by

writing, printing, picture, or effigy or other fixed representation to the eye, which exposes any person to public hatred, contempt, ridicule or obloquy, or which tends to deprive him of public confidence, or to injure him in his occupation, or any malicious publication as aforesaid, designed to blacken or vilify the memory of one who is dead, and tending to scandalize his surviving relatives or friends."

If the language in the article complained of did not expose the plaintiff to public hatred, contempt, ridicule, or obloquy, or did not tend to deprive him of public confidence, or to injure him in his occupation, we must conclude that it is not libelous in any event. Furthermore, if the article within itself and without reference to its relation, stripped of all insinuations, innuendo, colloquium, and explanatory circumstances, is not defamatory on its face, it cannot be said to be libelous per se. Tulsa Tribune Co. *vs.* Kight, 174 Okla. 359, 50 P.2d 350.

There is no fixed rule by which the court can determine whether or not a statement is libelous per se, and the statement alleged to be defamatory must be examined before it can be determined whether or not it is libelous per se. Fite *vs.* Oklahoma Publishing Company, 146 Okla. 150, 293 P. 1073. The trial court held that the published statement was not libelous per se. Whether or not the trial court committed error is the only question presented to this court.

Portions of the particular language upon which libel was based included the word "nigger," as ascribed to have been used by the plaintiff.

It is contended that the word "nigger" is detestable to the members of the negro race, and the use of the word in public as ascribed to have been used by the plaintiff held him up to scorn, hatred, ridicule, and contempt of the members of the negro race, and tended to deprive him of the public confidence, resulting in substantial injury to him as a lawyer.

Other language in the published article complained of as libelous contained the words: "Twice within recent months the club has been subjected to raids as a resort where gambling is illegally perpetrated." The further language relative to the plaintiff's praises of Herb Hill conclude with the words: "But this was to be expected since Uncle Ben has been parading Herb around in these props for quite a spell now."

The plaintiff contends that if the language here quoted were true, it would subject the plaintiff to disbarment proceedings or other disciplinary action at the hands of the court or State Bar of Oklahoma, since, if true, would show that plaintiff was engaged in shyster practice and in criminal conspiracy with the operation of a gambling house to keep it open to commit illegal operations. The plaintiff further contends that the use of such illiterate and ungrammatical language as used in the article ascribed to have been used by plaintiff, portrays him as being illiterate and lacking in the preparation, skill, ability, and training of an attorney.

It is seriously contended that the portion of the article referring to the Joe Louis Club as a virtuous, charitable institution contains language libelous per se, owing to the type of language used and the wrongful representation as to the use of certain words.

In Tulsa Tribune Co. *vs.* Kight, supra, this court held:

"Words used in any article alleged to be defamatory are to be construed by the most natural and obvious meaning, and in the sense that would be understood by those to whom they were addressed."

The published article complained of, as shown therein, represents a court trial proceeding upon gambling charges brought in an inferior court against a number of negro boys or men as offenders of the law.

The article appears to reflect upon the Joe Louis Club, the place where gambling seems to have been taking place. Repeated acts of such violation are referred to. The article, with considerable degree of jocularity, referred to the plaintiff, the legal defender of those charged. The acts and words attributed to the plaintiff in his defense of his clients are such as are commonly used by the more illiterate Southern Negro. The word "nigger," complained of, has been brought forward from the days of negro slavery and is today frequently used by both the white man and the negro in a friendly way without reflection or ill feeling. This practice, while not universal, is very common in the Southern states. At most, it is but an abbreviated or substituted form for the word "negro," and we are unable to see how the use of the word as generally used when referring to the negro casts any insult or reflection whatsoever. Many books have been written portraying the acts, habits, and language of the negro and written in negro dialect. These books are found in the public libraries of both races and are read with interest and appreciation.

The Chinaman is frequently referred to as a "Chink." The Northern man is often referred to as "Yankee" and the Southern man as "Rebel." The people of Oklahoma are referred to as "Sooners." The word "nigger" was nowhere used in the article to describe or to identify the plaintiff, but it was the ascribed use of the word by the plaintiff in his remarks before the court that is alleged to be offensive to the negro race and libelous in effect. It is contended that the type of language generally used in the article portrays the plaintiff as being illiterate and lacking in preparation, skill, and ability as an attorney.

The plaintiff has quoted in his brief from Phoenix Printing Co. *vs.* Robertson, 80 Okla. 191, 195 P. 487, wherein this court held:

"The fact that a publication may be unpleasant, and annoy or irk the subject thereof and may subject him to jest or banter, so as to affect his feelings, is not, standing alone, sufficient to make it libelous. In order to be libelous it must tend to lower him in the opinion of men whose standard of opinion the court can properly recognize or tend to induce them to entertain an ill opinion of him."

Following the reasoning therein set forth, we are unable to agree that the article complained of or any particular part of same is libelous per se when given to it that meaning which would naturally be ascribed thereto by those who would read the publication. We are unable to agree that the article, standing entirely alone, exposes the plaintiff to public hatred, contempt, or ridicule or tends to deprive him of public confidence or injure him in his profession as an attorney among his race, who are more or less familiar with his qualifications as an attorney and of his standing with the courts of his county and state. It therefore follows that the trial court commited no error in sustaining the defendant's demurrer to the plaintiff petition.

"Where a demurrer is interposed by the defendant to the petition of the plaintiff, the demurrer only admits the truth of the facts pleaded, but does not admit the truth of the inference of the pleader based on the facts pleaded, unless the facts themselves are sufficient to authorize such inferences." Hargrove *vs.* Oklahoma Press Publishing Co., 130 Okla. 76, 265 P. 635; Holway *vs.* World Publishing Co., 171 Okla. 306, 44 P.2d 881.

Judgment is affirmed.

OSBORN, C. J., and RILEY, PHELPS, and GIBSON, JJ., concur.

O. *Libel in Fiction*—Corrigan *vs.* Bobbs-Merrill Co. (228 N. Y. 58. January 27, 1920).

Libel in fiction is one of the most troublesome sections in the whole realm of libel. This case, dealing with libel in a novel, takes in most of the major problems in this department. The New York Court of Appeals held that "The appellant is chargeable with the publication of the libelous matter if it was spoken 'of and concerning' him, even though it was unaware of his existence or that it was written 'of and concerning' any existing person." Intent or lack of intent to injure anybody is irrelevant if it can be proven someone was injured. "Reputations may not be traduced with impunity, whether under the literary forms of a work of fiction, or in jest . . . or by inadvertence . . . or by the use of words with a double meaning."

JOSEPH E. CORRIGAN, Respondent, *vs.* THE BOBBS-MERRILL COMPANY, Appellant, Impleaded with Another.

(Argued January 12, 1920; decided January 27, 1920.)

APPEAL from a judgment of the Appellate Division of the Supreme Court in the first judicial department, entered March 21, 1918, modifying and affirming as modified a judgment in favor of plaintiff entered upon a verdict.

The nature of the action and the facts, so far as material, are stated in the opinion.

John L. Lockwood for appellant. The dismissal of defendant's first separate defense was error. (*White vs. Nichols,* 44 U. S. 266; *Morey vs. Morning Journal,* 123 N. Y. 207; *Cooper vs. Greeley,* 1 Den. 247; *Coxhead vs. Richards,* 2 Man., G. & S. 569; Code Civ. Pro. § 535; *Corr vs. Sun P. & P. Co.,* 177 N. Y. 131; *Stokes vs. Morning Journal,* 66 App. Div. 569; *People vs. Parr,* 42 Hun, 313; *Morrison vs. Smith,* 177 N. Y. 366; *Lewis vs. Chapman,* 16 N. Y. 369; *Samuels vs. Evening Mail,* 9 Hun, 288; 75 N. Y. 604.) No authority of Bernhardt was shown to act as agent of the Bobbs-Merrill Company so as to make proof of his knowledge or declarations admissible or binding upon the defendant, and the jury's finding that such authority existed is not merely contrary to the evidence, but without evidence to support it. (*Taylor vs. Comcl. Bank,* 174 N. Y. 187; *Foster vs. Bookwalter,* 152 N. Y. 166; *Peoples Bank vs. St. Anthony's R. C. Church,* 109 N. Y. 512; *Norton vs. Duke,* 120 App. Div. 1; *Nixon vs. Palmer,* 8 N. Y. 398; *Adair vs. Brimmer,* 74 N. Y. 539; *Whitney vs. Martini,* 88 N. Y. 535; *Baldwin vs. Burrows,* 47 N. Y. 199; *King vs. Mackellar,* 109 N. Y. 215; *Seymour vs. Wyckoff,* 10 N. Y. 213; *Trustees vs. Bowman,* 136 N. Y. 521, 526; *Prichard vs. Sigafus,* 103 App. Div. 535, 539; *Hogue vs. Simonson,* 94 App. Div. 139, 141.) The court erred in admitting testimony by the witnesses Johnson, Francis and Kingsley as to the knowledge and declarations of Carl Bernhardt concerning the libelous character of the book and Howard's malicious purpose in writing it, and in denying defendant's motions to strike out such testimony. (*Cobb vs. United Engineering Co.,* 191 N. Y. 475; *State Bank vs. Brocton F. J. Co.,* 208 N. Y. 492; *Peoples Bank vs. St. Anthony's R. C. Church,* 109 N. Y. 512; *Corn vs. Bergman,* 145 App. Div. 218; *Taylor vs. Comcl. Bank,* 174 N. Y. 181; *Bank of N. Y. N. B. Assn. vs. Am. D. & T. Co.,* 143 N. Y. 559; *White vs. Miller,* 71 N. Y. 118; *Goetz vs. Met. St. Ry. Co.,* 54 App. Div. 365; *Constant vs. University of Rochester,* 111 N. Y. 604; *Badger vs. Cook,* 117 App. Div. 328.) The court erred in refusing to charge the jury defendant's requests as to Carl Bernhardt and the evidence of his authority. (*Comey vs. Harris,* 133 App. Div. 686; *Badger vs. Cook,* 117 App. Div. 328; *Constant vs. University of Rochester,* 111 N. Y. 604; *Brigger vs. Mutual R. F. Life Assn.,* 75 App. Div. 149.)

Henry N. Arnold and *Cambridge Livingston* for respondent. The court was right in dismissing the pretended complete defense, denominated "a first separate defense to plaintiff's alleged cause of action." (*Holmes vs. Jones,* 147 N. Y. 59; *Broughton vs. McGraw,* 39 Fed. Rep. 672; *Town Topics Pub. Co. vs. Collier,* 144 App. Div. 191; *Brinkman vs. Taylor,* 103 Fed. Rep. 773; *Loftus vs. Bennett,* 68 App. Div. 128; *Kelly vs. Huffington,* Fed. Cas. No. 7671; *Grossman vs. Morning Journal,* 197 N. Y. 474; *Tillotson vs. Cheatham,* 3 Johns. 56; *Bingham vs. Gaynor,* 135 App. Div. 426; *Palmer vs. News,* 31 App. Div. 210.) The court having dismissed the pretended complete defense, correctly charged the jury concerning the immateriality of the publisher's actual intent under the general issue. (*Van Ingen vs. Mail & Express,* 156 N. Y. 376; *Stokes vs. Morning Journal,* 66 App. Div. 569.) The court committed no error in charging the jury or in refusing to charge as requested by defendant. (*Cohalan vs. Press Co.,* 212 N. Y. 344; *Smith vs. Matthews,* 152 N. Y. 152; *Crane vs. Bennett,* 177 N. Y. 106; *Brandt vs. Morning Journal Assn.,* 81 App. Div. 188; 177 N. Y. 544; *Carpenter vs. Evening Journal,* 111 App. Div. 266; *Palmer vs. Mahin,* 120 Fed. Rep. 737.)

POUND, J. The plaintiff, Joseph E. Corrigan, has recovered a judgment against appellant for $25,000 damages in an action for libel. He is a city magistrate of the city of New York, of good standing as a man and a judge. Defendant is an Indiana corporation having its place of business and principal office in Indianapolis. It publishes books of fiction and has a New York office. The defendant George Bronson Howard, a writer of stories and plays, who was not served and did not appear in the action, wrote a sensational novel entitled "God's Man," of which appellant published upwards of ten thousand copies in the regular course of its extensive book business. The novel depicts, somewhat realistically, the adventures of one Arnold

L'Hommedieu in New York's underworld and elsewhere and contains chapters entitled "Arnold's Adventures in Plunderland," "Sons of Subterranea" and the like. A chapter, which in the table of contents bears the caption "Justice—a la Corigan" but which in the body of the book is headed "Justice—a la Cornigan," brings the hero into Jefferson Market Court in the city of New York, a court in which plaintiff frequently sat as magistrate, and deals with the disposition of cases by the magistrate Cornigan. The inference from the unsavory details as related to the facts is unmistakably that the author Howard intended by this chapter deliberately and with personal malice to vilify plaintiff, under the barely fictitious name of Cornigan, in his official capacity and to expose him to hatred, contempt, ridicule and obloquy as being ignorant, brutal, hypocritical, corrupt, shunned by his fellows, bestial of countenance, unjust, dominated by political influences in making decisions and grossly unfit for his place. A paragraph in another chapter entitled "The Gay Life," of like import, portrays the man Cornigan even more offensively, as an associate of low and depraved characters. No attempt was made by defendant to establish the truth of these allegations or any of them, and the only question here is whether plaintiff properly proved his case.

Defendant's first separate defense is that it published a supposedly fictitious narrative in good faith; did not know plaintiff and had no intent to injure him. This is not a complete defense. Even the Massachusetts rule as laid down in *Smith vs. Ashley* (11 Metc. 367) holding the writer alone responsible in such a case, has been discredited by later decisions in that jurisdiction. (*Hanson vs. Globe Newspaper Co.*, 159 Mass. 293, 295.) The appellant is chargeable with the publication of the libelous matter if it was spoken "of and concerning" him, even though it was unaware of his existence or that it was written "of and concerning" any existing person. Apart from the question of express malice, proof that the chapter actually referred to plaintiff would sustain his cause of action.

"If the publication was libelous, the defendant took the risk. As was said of such matters by Lord MANSFIELD, 'Whatever a man publishes, he publishes at his peril.' " (HOLMES, J., in *Peck vs. Tribune Co.,* 214 U. S. 185, 189.)

The fact that the publisher has no actual intention to defame a particular man or indeed to injure any one, does not prevent recovery of compensatory damages by one who connects himself with the publication, at least, in the absence of some special reason for a positive belief that no one existed to whom the description answered. The question is not so much who was aimed at, as who was hit.

"The writing, according to the old form, must be malicious, and it must be of and concerning the plaintiff. Just as the defendant could not excuse himself from malice by proving that he wrote it in the most benevolent spirit, so he cannot shew that the libel was not of and concerning the plaintiff by proving that he never heard of the plaintiff. His intention in both respects equally is inferred from what he did. His remedy is to abstain from defamatory words." (Lord LOREBURN, L. C., in *Hulton vs. Jones,* 1910, A. C. 20, 24.)

This rule is unqualifiedly applied to publications in the newspaper press, and is no different when applied to those who issue books. Works of fiction not infrequently depict as imaginary, events in courts of justice or elsewhere actually drawn or distorted from real life. Dickens, in "Pickwick Papers" has a well-known court scene of which Mr. Serjeant Ballantine says in his "Experiences" that Mr. Justice Gaselee "has been delivered to posterity as having presided at the famous trial of *Bardell vs. Pickwick.* I just remember him and he certainly was deaf." Goldwin Smith, the distinguished historian and publicist, said of Disraeli's veiled attack upon him as "The Oxford Professor" in the novel "Lothair," that (Reminiscences, p. 171): "He afterwards pursued me across the Atlantic, and tried to brand me, under a perfectly transparent pseudonym, if 'Oxford Professor' could be called a pseudonym at all, as a 'social sycophant.' There is surely nothing more dastardly than this mode of stabbing a reputation." The power of Charles Reade's descriptions of prison life in "It's Never Too Late to Mend" and the abuses of private insane asylums in "Hard Cash" is undeniable, although the truth of some of his details was challenged. The novel of purpose, such as "Uncle Tom's Cabin," often deals with incidents and individuals not wholly imaginary. Reputations may not be traduced with impunity, whether under the literary forms of a work of fiction, or in jest (*Griggs vs. Sun Printing & Pub. Assn.,* 179 N. Y. 144), or by inadvertence (*Moore vs. Francis,* 121 N. Y. 199, 207), or by the use of words with a double meaning. (*Morrison vs. Smith,* 177 N. Y. 366; *First Nat. Bank of Waverly vs. Winters,* 225 N. Y. 47, 50.) Publishers cannot be so guileless as to be ignorant of the trade risk of injuring others by accidental libels.

The conventional way of putting the general rule is "that in a case of libelous publication, the law implies malice and infers some damage." (*Byam vs. Collins,* 111 N. Y. 143, 150.) Avoiding, for the nonce, the time-honored words "implied malice," which are a stumbling block for many, we may safely say that unless the judge rules that the occasion is privileged, the question of malice is never for the jury when compensatory damages alone are sought; the plaintiff recovers damages if he proves that the words apply to him and that his reputation has been injured, whether such injury is the result of defendant's evil disposition towards him or a mere concatenation of adventitious circumstances.

Plaintiff made out a cause of action for compensatory damages, but he did not rest his case on proof that the publication was "of and concerning" him and libelous. He went further and sought to prove something, not to be presumed as against appellant from the publication itself, that would justify the jury in giving him an additional sum by way of exemplary damages or smart money, based on an inference of actual malice or willingness to injure his reputation on the part of the appellant.

The distinction between the right to compensatory and punitive damages is clear. Actual injury to reputation must be paid for in all events. From an intent to injure, chargeable to defendant, follows the rule that exemplary damages, "a sort of hybrid between a display of ethical indignation and the imposition of a criminal fine" (*Haines vs. Schultz,* 50 N. J. Law, 481), may also be awarded. Malice may, in some cases, be implied from the publication itself, where the natural inference from the libel is that it was aimed directly at reputation, but where that inference does not flow naturally from the facts, adequate evidence of actual malice or its equivalent should be produced if punitive damages are sought.

Actual malice might be inferred as against the author from the falsity of the publication (*Cohalan vs. New York Press Co.*, 212 N. Y. 344), but not as against the mere publisher of a libel in a novel which on its face does not purport to be serious or bear the evidence of malice against an actual individual or against any one. (*Times Pub. Co. vs. Carlisle*, 94 Fed. Rep. 762.) The publisher in such a case is not liable to exemplary damages for the acts of the author upon mere proof of publication. If defendant had, in entire good faith, supposed that it was publishing a satire on courts of justice generally, which would hit no judge in particular, and which would be so understood by the readers of the book, and if its belief in that regard was justifiable, the circumstances not calling for some inquiry at the source, it could not be said to be inspired by malice in fact.

Of course, as the trial justice said, "malice is malice," but it, unfortunately, has two distinct meanings in the law of libel from which two distinct burdens are imposed on plaintiff. It may mean "either actual malice or such malice as by legal fiction is presumed for the purpose of reconciling certain other rules in the law of libel." (HISCOCK, Ch. J., in *Norske Ameriekalinje vs. Sun P. & P. Assn.*, 226 N. Y. 1, 9.) In order to recover punitive damages, plaintiff was bound to satisfy the jury by a fair preponderance of evidence that defendant (1) was animated, in such publication, by conscious ill will toward him, or (2) did not publish the Cornigan chapter of the book in good faith and in the honest belief that it was fiction, but was indifferent as to whether the violent and indecent abuse heaped upon the supposedly fictitious magistrate would injure some real party actually referred to by the author. Indifference as to the rights of others, such as might be found from the fact of publishing scurrilous comment without reasonable investigation, is the equivalent of the intentional violation of such rights.

Not content with resting his case upon the falsity of the publication and its obvious portrayal, with a venomous pen, of scenes, real or imaginary, before a magistrate in Jefferson Market Court—evidence from which a jury might, under the special circumstances of the case, have inferred indifference as to whether any one was injured or not (*Warner vs. Press Publishing Co.,* 132 N. Y. 181)—plaintiff sought to establish that officers and agents of defendant corporation, whose knowledge was chargeable to it, knew before publication that the purpose of the publication was to injure plaintiff. It may be remarked, parenthetically, as bearing on the question of damages, that as soon as defendant was informed that plaintiff was identified with the Corigan or Cornigan of the book, it suppressed the edition. It also offered to publish, but did not publish, a retraction and apology. It also alleged in its answer as a partial defense, but made no effort to prove, that plaintiff had secured the republication of the libel in the New York *American* in order to enhance his damages.

Evidence of a woman named Saville tends to connect Mr. Curtis, the defendant's vice-president, from whose New York office the advertising of the book was directed, with actual knowledge of a purpose to libel plaintiff, after he had read the book before publication. This witness recanted, and the best that can be said of her testimony, taken alone, is that it was unsatisfactory proof of knowledge on the part of Curtis of Howard's purpose.

Evidence of several witnesses connects intimately Bernhardt, the manager of defendant's dramatic department, with Howard and the book. If Bernhardt acquired knowledge as to the nature of the publication while acting within the scope of his authority, on behalf of defendant, for its benefit, the defendant is chargeable with his knowledge, otherwise not. (*Corporation of Glasgow vs. Lorimer,* 1911, A. C. 209.) Bernhardt had to do with sales and leases and other disposition of dramatic and moving picture rights for defendant based on its publications. His contract called on him to devote his "whole time, effort and attention" to the business of the dramatic department and to engage in no other employment whatever. He had a share in the net profits of his department and a personal interest in having books with dramatic possibilities published by defendant, with a view to their future use in his department, but it is not to be presumed that everything he did for Howard was done for defendant. He was not a manuscript reader for defendant. Others did that work for it. He aided Howard on the manuscript and galley proofs of the book not "during ordinary office hours" but at Howard's home in Port Jefferson on week end visits there. It does not appear that defendant ever intrusted him with that kind of work on its behalf. A jury might well infer that he knew that Howard was full of hate and bitterness toward plaintiff, due to his personal experience before the magistrate as defendant on a criminal charge. On one or more occasions, as witnesses testified, it was brought home to Bernhardt directly that Howard was getting even with plaintiff by means of his book, and that Bernhardt knew it was a serious libel but said that defendant was willing to take a chance for the sake of the publicity that might result. We fail to see how Bernhardt's acts, knowledge or declarations in this connection are chargeable to defendant. Publishing books or accepting or preparing books for publication, was not an incident of the defendant's dramatic department. It does not appear that anything that Bernhardt did or said in connection with the preparation and publication of Howard's book was within the scope of his employment. The relation of the book to dramatic purposes before publication was remote and speculative. His acts and declarations had no connection with any transaction then being conducted by him with authority for his principal. Authority cannot be inferred from what he said and did, from the mere fact that he was in defendant's employ in a different capacity, even if it appeared that defendant's general officers knew that he was helping Howard, unless it could be inferred that it was *as defendant's agent* that he was helping Howard. His knowledge was not acquired in defendant's business and therefore was not the knowledge of defendant. An employee of a publisher, not charged with reading manuscripts, might aid an author to prepare a libel and get it published and boast about his firm's connection with it without creating any reasonable inference that he was acting for his employer in that regard, so long as his knowledge was not communicated to his employer. While a corporation knows a fact only as its officers and agents know it, it does not know all that its agents know, but only what comes to them while acting for the corporation within the scope of their agency, when it is their duty to report their knowledge to the general officers or agents of the company, and it may be presumed that they have told the principal what they know. (*Weisser vs. Denison,* 10 N. Y. 68, 77; *Welsh vs. German American Bank,* 73 N. Y. 424; *Cragie vs. Hadley,* 99 N. Y. 131; *Casco Nat. Bank vs. Clark,* 139 N. Y. 307, 313, 314; *Taylor vs. Commercial Bank,* 174 N. Y. 181.) An inference may not be drawn as to the intention of defendant from the state of mind of Bernhardt, who had no part in accepting the novel or deciding on behalf of defendant what it should contain.

"To bring about this result two things must concur, viz., the possession by the agent of pertinent information and his personal participation in respect thereto on behalf of the corporation." (*Willard vs. Denise,* 50 N. J. Eq. 482, 484.) Thus, information as to the true state of health and physical condition of an applicant for life insurance, given to a soliciting agent of the company having no authority to effect insurance and issue policies is not the knowledge of the company, because "it is a fundamental principle in the law of agency that for information given an agent to be attributable to his principal the information must be imparted to the agent in the course of his agency." (Cullen, J., in *Butler vs. Michigan Mut. Life Ins. Co.,* 184 N. Y. 337, 340.)

Nor can it be said that defendant in any way consciously accepted the result of Bernhardt's assistance to Howard as having achieved anything that it sought to have accomplished, or from which it might have any benefit. What Bernhardt did for Howard was not done for defendant and was not for defendant's profit in any sense and was neither authorized nor ratified by it.

There can be no ratification without knowledge or notice of the facts. (*Smith vs. Kidd,* 68 N. Y. 130, 132). Bernhardt's knowledge was no more chargeable to defendant than would be the knowledge of the printer if Howard had taken him into his confidence.

Respondent urges that it is "past the bounds of belief" that Bernhardt had never reported his knowledge of Howard's purpose to appellant, or that appellant did not know that Bernhardt was working for it on the book. The inference that defendant was chargeable with such information is purely speculative and the jury may not thus bridge the gap between evidence and conjecture. (*Kelly vs. Nassau El. Ry. Co.,* 227 N. Y. 39.)

The evidence of Bernhardt's knowledge of Howard's purpose to defame plaintiff was properly excepted to and should not have been submitted to the jury. The nature of such evidence was to aggravate damages by bringing Howard's purpose directly home to defendant, thus making it an active and conscious participant in the libel. Howard was vindictive and if Bernhardt stood in defendant's shoes, defendant was chargeable with inexcusable malice, for it had not even the poor excuse of a personal grudge, and sought only financial gain. This line of evidence was dwelt upon at great length in the judge's charge and is given much importance on the trial and here. The trial justice fairly left the question to the jury to decide whether defendant was responsible for Bernhardt's knowledge, but the evidence was insufficient to present the question. (*Matter of Case,* 214 N. Y. 199, 203, 204.) Its admission cannot be said to be immaterial error. It appears, on the contrary, to be substantial error. It would be essentially unjust to attach such serious consequences to the knowledge of an agent who had no authority to acquire the knowledge for, and was under no duty to communicate it to, his employer. This court may not assume that the effect of the error was counteracted by the fact that the verdict was substantially reduced in the Appellate Division.

Another line of evidence must also be considered. The book is dedicated "to Hewitt Hansom Howland, The Second Father of this Book." The evidence which connects Howard and Howland must be carefully considered, for one may not assume the honor of parentage without some added responsibility for the offspring. Howland was defendant's literary editor and chief manuscript reader at Indianapolis, intimately familiar with the manuscript and in intimate correspondence with the author. What he knew, or should have known, of Howard's purpose was the knowledge of defendant. Although he was not authorized to accept a malicious libel for publication, if he did so in the course of his employment, intentionally or without proper inquiry, defendant is fully liable for his act. (*Citizens Life Ass. Co. vs. Brown,* 1904, A. C. 423.) He made no investigation or inquiry about the motive of the Corrigan chapter, although he had it in his possession and had been over every page several times before accepting it for publication. The tone and style of the libel were vituperative in the extreme. It was directed at the administration of criminal justice in a real court, in a manner tending to bring the court into disrepute without the slightest justification or excuse. Howland was indifferent as to that. The jury might be permitted to say that he was negligent and reckless in not at least seeking from Howard some information as to whether the author's diatribes were intended as mere generalizations or as offensive personalities, and, if the latter, whether they were fair criticism or malicious falsehool. (*Crane vs. Bennett,* 177 N. Y. 106, 114, 115.) That he knew of Howard's ill will toward plaintiff has no substantial foundation in the evidence. Although he knew, as the jury might have found, that Bernhardt was correcting the proof for Howard, Bernhardt's knowledge of Howard's motives was not imputable to him. On the other hand, the varnish of fiction was not so opaque as to conceal from the experienced manuscript reader the possibility that Howard was using bad language and abuse about a magistrate in Jefferson Market Court with more feeling than an author's license permitted. It may not be the duty of the publisher to check up all the author's villains to free himself from the imputation of malice, but the jury may say that Howland, the second father of the book, should, from the nature of things, have been on his guard in a case like this.

Certain exceptions to defendant's requests to charge are also urged as error. In substance the requests are to the effect that plaintiff must establish malice as above defined in order to recover punitive damages. These requests were not read in the presence of the jury. They might, without error, have been charged as requested, but the principal charge, considered in its entirety, except as it submits to the jury the question of defendant's participation in Howard's purpose, fairly presents the principles of law applicable to the case. The refusals to charge as requested having made no impression on the minds of the jury, may be regarded as mere abstractions on the record and cannot be said to have been prejudicial under the circumstances and "the letter and the spirit of section 1317 of the Code of Civil Procedure." (*Cohalan vs. New York Press Co., supra.*)

The judgment must, therefore, be reversed and a new trial granted, with costs to abide the event.

HISCOCK, Ch. J., COLLIN, MCLAUGHLIN and ELKUS, JJ., concur; HOGAN, J., votes for affirmance under provisions of section 1317, Code of Civil Procedure; ANDREWS, J., votes for affirmance.

Judgment reversed, etc.

P. *Libel of an Individual Through an Organization.*—Noral *vs.* Hearst. (102 California Appellate Decisions 403. Civil No. 12554. Second Appellate District, Division Two. August 9, 1940).

Is it possible to libel an individual by libelling a group to which he belongs? The California court held that you cannot "unless there be certainty as to the individuals concerned," and apparently that certainty must be very certain indeed.

Civil No. 12554. Second Appellate District, Division Two. August 9, 1940.

Alexander Noral, Plaintiff and Appellant, *vs.* Hearst Publications, Incorporated (a Corporation), Defendant and Respondent.

For Appellant—Gallagher, Wirin & Johnson.

For Respondent—Lawler, Felix & Hall; A. Laurence Mitchell.

Plaintiff's action having been dismissed after the general demurrer to his complaint as amended had been sustained, he takes this appeal.

In a lengthy complaint, plaintiff alleges in substance that he is the president and chief official of the Workers' Alliance of California; that he has conducted the affairs of his office in accordance with its constitution and by-laws and with honesty and fidelity; that there are only three paid officials in said organization and that $50 per week is the salary divided among the three; that on April 29, 1939, the said three officials presented before a committee of the state senate a factual statement, a copy of which is attached to the complaint; that about the same time said officials on behalf of the said Alliance sent an "open letter" contained in said "Exhibit A" to all California state legislators including Senator Metzger, chairman of said senate committee; that by reason of said open letter, said Metzger and the defendant knew that they were referring to said three paid officials of said Alliance when they referred to "officials of the Workers' Alliance"; that the defendant well knowing the premises and with the intent to hold him up to shame and public obloquy and to deprive him of the confidence and good repute of the members of the Alliance and of the public at large, and with the intent to impute to the plaintiff the crime of embezzlement or larceny, did publish, in defendant's newspaper words contained in a false and untrue article entitled "STATE MAY PROBE RED ACTIVITY HERE", purporting to be a quotation of statements, made May 30, 1939, at Los Angeles, by California State Senator Jack Metzger, chairman of the state senate committee investigating pressure groups;

"That said article contained among others, the following false and scandalous words which the readers of the paper read and understood to be about and concerning the plaintiff in his capacity as a paid official of the state organization of the Workers' Alliance, namely, State President of said Alliance, to-wit:

"*'Californians are rapidly becoming aroused to the folly of taxing citizens to finance Moscow propaganda.' This occurs under the present set up, he explained, because taxpayers pay the relief bill for the 31,000 Workers' Alliance members and their officials divert their membership dues to further Communist agitation under direct orders from the Third Internationale headquarters in Russia.*"

In subsequent paragraphs of the pleadings, plaintiff pleads matters of inducement and innuendo for the purpose of removing doubt as to whether or not the published article referred to plaintiff and for the purpose of emphasizing the defamatory sense in which the language was used by the defendant. We omit them from our discussion for the reason that they will play no part in the consideration of the problem presented to us.

The complaint must fail because the publication does not defame any ascertainable person. It appears from the exhibits attached to the complaint that the Workers' Alliance consists of 162 locals, besides county organizations. It must have at least 162 officials besides state officials and its board. Said exhibit declares that the activities must be performed by members and officers who serve in their spare time without compensation. In view of the fact that many of the officers serve without compensation, it is a reasonable inference that many of the offices of the Alliance are each held by a number of officials in the course of a year. This would enlarge the number of "officials of the Alliance". To say that "their officials divert membership dues" is an attack upon a large group of persons. An accusation such as that complained of cannot have the quality of a libel unless there be a certainty as to the individuals accused. There is nothing in the published article that makes a personal application to the plaintiff. He cannot by use of the colloquium make the language which is applicable to so large a group of persons be made specifically to refer to him. The reference to "their officials" who are accused of diverting membership dues to further Communist agitation applies no more to plaintiff than would a similar statement, accusing federal judges of encouraging violations of the import tax laws be made to apply to any one judge. It is no nearer a libel against plaintiff than it would libel the defendant by publishing a declaration that the metropolitan press of California is devoted to the corrupting of public life, lowering moral standards and debauching public officials. Certainly such general language against a class or group of people cannot constitute libel. Where a group is very large and nothing that is said applies in particular to the plaintiff, he cannot recover. (17 R. C. L. 375; *Times vs. Stivers,* 252 Ky. 843; 35 Cor. Jur. 1161.)

In the case of *Lynch vs. Kirby,* 74 Misc. 266, 131 N. Y. Supp. 680, the plaintiff as president of the International Typographical Union of North America sued the National Association of Manufacturers for libel when it caused the publication of its resolution accusing said union of "long continued, cowardly and recklessly illegal determination to destroy the business of the Los Angeles Times . . . and recognizes this act of destruction of life and property as in line with the general policy of criminal unionism", etc. It was held that there was nothing in the publication that would warrant the court in finding that plaintiff was the individual referred to in the resolution; that the mere allegation that the libel had reference to the plaintiff was not sufficient unless some fact were alleged to show that the article was intended to refer to the plaintiff; that, although the article "referred to the Union of which the plaintiff was an officer, and the mere fact that he was such officer could not be construed to mean that he fostered such organization for the purpose of committing the crime referred to in the resolution".

A political sermon charged that the actual sovereigns of the city were 73 saloon keepers and wholesale dealers and that "officials under its benumbing influence violated their oaths of office". Although the district attorney was the official properly chargeable with the enforcement of the law, the Supreme Court of Wisconsin held that "it does not refer to the district attorney nor to the plaintiff but to all officials who come under the benumbing influence of this deadly exhalation and under such influence violated their oaths of office. . . . If the words used really contain no reflection on any particular individual, no averment or innuendo can make them defamatory. . . . There is nothing to show that it points to the district attorney more than it does to any other officer, unless it be the innuendo which is not warranted by the context." (*Arnold vs. Ingram,* 151 Wis. 438, 138 N. W. 111.)

In a published article containing the headline "Parking Lot Racket Probe Ordered Here", it was charged that the parking lot owners in the city of Washington made a practice of moving cars from parking lots on to the streets in order to make room for parking more cars. Although the plaintiff showed that, in the downtown section of Washington, there were 20 or more lots operated by 10 or 12 owners and though he was the operator of 9 of the lots, it was held that no libel was alleged. "The article could not reasonably be said to concern more than the owners of downtown parking lots . . . as a class" and therefore there was no libel. *On the one hand is the social interest in free press discussion of matters of general concern* and on the other is the individual interest in reputation. *The courts have chosen not to limit freedom of public discussion except to prevent harm occasioned by defamatory statements reasonably susceptible of special application to a given individual.*" (*Service Parking Corp. vs. Washington Times,* 92 Fed. [2d] 505.)

Even where there is a small group involved and the language fails to indicate affirmatively that all members were involved in the charge, it was held that "defamatory words must refer to some ascertained or ascertainable person, and that that person must be the particular plaintiff". (*Helmicks vs. Stevlingson,* 212, Wis. 614, 615, 250 N. W. 402.)

"In every action for defamation, two things are necessary (1) A defamation apparent from the words themselves, for no innuendo can alter the sense. (2) Certainly as to the person who is defamed, for no innuendo can render certain that which is uncertain." (*Schoenfeld vs. Journal Co.,* 204 Wis. 132, 136, 235 N. W. 442.)

The fact that a number of the cases have authorized recovery by a member of a small group where it was clear that the defamation applied to all of the group does not detract from the doctrine above announced or from the force of the decisions above cited. If a published article of a defamatory nature were to charge that the entire board of supervisors of a particular community, consisting of five members, is corrupt and diverts the public funds to the maintenance of brothels, each member of that board could recover but if a similar article were to charge all of the supervisors of the state with corruption, it would not be libelous as against an individual supervisor because the group accused would be too numerous. (*Weston vs. Commercial Advertiser Assn.,* 184 N. Y. 479; *Barron vs. Smith,* 19 So. Dak. 50, 101 N. W. 1105.)

Charges of libel against a publication which has reported or commented upon matters involving public policy should be viewed with caution. It is in such matters that the freedom of the press is of paramount concern. Without such freedom, the march of progress might be stayed or the venom of alien cultures might stealthily undermine cherished landmarks. "It is far better for the public welfare that some occasional consequential injury to an individual, arising from general censure of his profession, his party, or his sect, should go without remedy, than that free discussion on the great questions of politics, or morals, or faith should be checked by the dread of embittered and boundless litigation." (*Tyckman vs. Delavan,* 25 Wend. [N. Y.] 186, 199.)

Plaintiff asserts that it is sufficient for him to allege that the published article referred to him and that it is a matter for investigation at the trial of the facts of the case to determine whether in fact his allegation be true. (Code Civ. Proc., sec. 460.) That section, in effect, declares that it is sufficient to state generally that the same was published or spoken concerning the plaintiff. But it appears to have been the intention of the legislature to establish a rule of pleading and not to assert a principle of substantive law. They could not have intended to declare what is not a libel is a libel by suggesting a form in which a pleader might frame his language to allege a libel.

The purpose of said section 460 is to allow the pleader to state his cause in general terms, not to enable him to reach the point of trial when he is unable to state a case. If the publication does "not in fact charge plaintiff with the things set forth in the innuendo, and when fairly read it appears that the plaintiff is not so charged, its meaning cannot be extended by innuendo to make it constitute a libel against him". (*Hays vs. American Defense Soc.,* 252 N. Y. 266, 169 N. E. 380.)

In view of the foregoing, it will be unnecessary to consider defendant's second contention, to-wit, that the matters alleged do not constitute a libel per se. Also, plaintiff's grievance that the trial court abused its discretion in not ordering further privilege of amending the complaint is disposed of by our holding that plaintiff cannot state a cause of action.

The judgment is affirmed.

MOORE, P. J.

I concur:

McCOMB, J.

Q. *Libel by Charging Membership in the Communist Party or the Harboring of Communist Sympathies.*—Sidney S. Grant *vs.* The Reader's Digest Association, Inc. (United States Circuit Court of Appeals for the Second Circuit. No. 46—October Term, 1945. Argued October 5, 1945. Decided November 2, 1945).

The terms "Communist," "fellow traveler," "Communist sympathiser," and such have become common epithets in current controversies regarding public affairs, and several courts have been asked to decide whether they are libelous or not. The issue apparently is still moot. Courts in the same state have often held opposing views. This case—involving a Boston, Mass., lawyer, and the Reader's Digest,—is the most recent one (at this writing) to come up for decision. It is here reprinted because it presents the problems clearly and because of the eminence of the court and especially of the judge who wrote the opinion of the court.

United States Circuit Court of Appeals for the Second Circuit.
Decided November 2, 1945.

SIDNEY S. GRANT, Appellant, against THE READER'S DIGEST ASSOCIATION, INC., Appellee.

Before:

L. HAND, SWAN, and CLARK

Circuit Judges.

Appeal from a judgment of the District Court for Southern District of New York dismissing a complaint in libel for insufficiency in law upon its face.

OSMOND K. FRAENKEL, for the appellant.

PATRICK H. SULLIVAN, for the appellee.

L. HAND, Circuit Judge:

This is an appeal from a judgment dismissing a complaint in libel for insufficiency in law upon its face. The complaint alleged that the plaintiff was a Massachusetts lawyer, living in that state; that the defendant, a New York corporation, published a periodical of general circulation, read by lawyers, judges and the general public; and that one issue of the periodical contained an article entitled "I Object to my Union in Politics," in which the following passage appeared:

"And another thing. In my state the Political Action Committee has hired as its legislative agent one, Sidney S. Grant, who but recently was a legislative representative for the Massachusetts Communist Party."

The innuendo then alleged that this passage charged the plaintiff with having represented the Communist Party in Massachusetts as its legislative agent, which was untrue and malicious. Two questions arise: (1) what meaning the jury might attribute to the words; (2) whether the meaning so attributed was libellous. So far as the wrong consisted of publishing the article in New York, the decisions of the courts of that state are authoritative for us under now familiar principles. As to publication in another state, a question might arise whether we should follow the decisions of that state or any decisions of New York which determined what effect in such cases the courts of New York give to the decisions of another state. No such question comes up upon this motion; and we leave it open. The innuendo added nothing to the meaning of the words, and indeed, could not. *Hays vs. American Defense Society,* 252 N.Y. 266. However, although the words did not say that the plaintiff was a member of the Communist Party, they did say that he acted on its behalf, and we think that a jury might in addition find that they implied that he was in general sympathy with its objects and methods. The last conclusion does indeed involve the assumption that the Comunist Party would not retain as its "legislative representative" a person who was not in general accord with its purposes; but that inference is reasonable and was pretty plainly what the author wished readers to draw from his words. The case therefore turns upon whether it is libelous in New York to write of a lawyer that he has acted as agent of the Communist Party, and is a believer in its aims and methods.

The interest at stake in all defamation is concededly the reputation of the person assailed. And any moral obliquity of the opinions of those in whose minds the words might lessen that reputation, would normally be relevant only in mitigation of damages. A man may value his reputation even among those who do not embrace the prevailing moral standards; and it would seem that the jury should be allowed to appraise how far he should be indemnified for the disesteem of such persons. That is the usual rule. *Peck vs. Chicago Tribune,* 214 U.S. 185; Restatement of Torts, §559. The New York decisions define libel, in accordance with the usual rubric, as consisting of utterances which arouse "hatred, contempt, scorn, obloquy or shame," and the like. . . . However, the opinions at times seem to make it a condition that to be actionable the words must be such as would so affect "right-thinking" people; and in *Kimmerle vs. New York Evening Journal, Inc.,* supra, 102, 103 (262 N.Y. 99) that was the turning point of the decision. The same limitation has apparently been recognized in England; (*Mycroft vs. Sleight,* 90 L.J.K.B. 883); and it is fairly plain that there must come a point where that is true. As was said in *Mawe vs.*

Piggott, Irish Rep. 4 Comm. Law, 54, 62; among those "who were themselves criminal or sympathized with crime," it would expose one "to great odium to represent him as an informer or prosecutor or otherwise aiding in the detection of crime"; yet certainly the words would not be actionable. Be that as it may, in New York if the exception covers more than such a case, it does not go far enough to excuse the utterance at bar. *Katapodis vs. Brooklyn Spectator, Inc.,* supra (226 N.Y. 17), following the old case of *Moffatt vs. Cauldwell,* 3 Hun 26, held that the imputation of extreme poverty might be actionable; although certainly "right thinking" people ought not shun, despise, or otherwise condemn one because he is poor. Indeed, the only declaration of the Court of Appeals (*Moore vs. Francis,* 121 N.Y. 199, 205, 206) leaves it still open whether it is not libellous to say that a man is insane. . . . We do not believe, therefore, that we need say whether "right-thinking" people would harbor similar feelings toward a lawyer, because he had been an agent for the Communist Party, or was a sympathizer with its aims and means. It is enough if there be some, as there certainly are, who would feel so, even though they would be "wrong-thinking" people if they did. . . .

The lower courts in New York have passed on almost the same question in three cases. In *Garriga vs. Richfield,* 174 Misc. 315, Pecora, J. held that it was not libellous to say that a man was a Communist. In the next year in *Levy vs. Gelber,* 175 Misc. 746, Hofstader, J. held otherwise. That perhaps left the answer open; but *Boudin vs. Tishman,* 264 App. Div. 842, was an unescapable ruling, although there was no opinion. Being the last decision of the state courts, it is conclusive upon us, unless there is a difference between saying that a man is a Communist and saying that he is an agent for the party or sympathizer with its objects and methods. Any difference is one of degree only: those who would take it ill of a lawyer that he was a member of the Party, might no doubt take it less so if he were only what is called a "fellow-traveler"; but, since the basis for the reproach ordinarily lies in some supposed threat to our institutions, those who fear that threat are not likely to believe that it is limited to party members. Indeed, it is not uncommon for them to feel less concern at avowed propaganda than at what they regard as the insidious spread of the dreaded doctrines by those who only dally and coquette with them, and have not the courage openly to proclaim themselves.

Judgment reversed; cause remanded.

R. *Libel of Public Officials.*—L. B. Sullivan *vs.* The New York Times. Decided by the United States Supreme Court, March 9, 1964.

This is perhaps the most important decision, so far, in the history of libel in so far as it relates to the discussion of public affairs and the conduct of such affairs by public officials. In the unanimous decision written by Mr. Justice William J. Brennan, Jr., the United States Supreme Court said the following: ". . . we consider this case against the background of a profound national commitment to the principle that debate on public issues should be uninhibited, robust, and wide open, and that it may well include vehement, caustic, and sometimes unpleasantly sharp attacks on government and public officials. . . . Criticism of their official conduct does not lose its constitutional protection merely because it is effective criticism and hence diminishes their official reputation." Mr. Justice Hugo Black, in a concurring opinion, went further. He asked for "granting the press an absolute immunity for criticism of the way public officials do their public duty."

UNITED STATES SUPREME COURT, 39, THE NEW YORK TIMES COMPANY, petr., *v.* L. B. SULLIVAN; and UNITED STATES SUPREME COURT, 40, RALPH D. ABERNATHY *et al.,* petrs., *v.* L. B. SULLIVAN.

Decided March 9, 1964.

Justice Brennan:

We are required for the first time in this case to determine the extent to which the constitutional protections for speech and press limit a state's power to award damages in a libel action brought by a public official against critics of his official conduct.

Respondent L. B. Sullivan is one of the three elected commissioners of the city of Montgomery, Ala. He testified that he was "Commissioner of Public Affairs and the duties are supervision of the Police Department, Fire Department, Department of Cemetery and Department of Scales." He brought this civil action against the four individual petitioners, who are Negroes and Alabama clergymen, and against petitioner The New York Times Company, a New York corporation which publishes The New York Times, a daily newspaper. A jury in the Circuit Court of Montgomery County awarded him damages of $500,000, the full amount claimed, against all the petitioners, and the Supreme Court of Alabama affirmed. 273 Ala.

Respondent's complaint alleged that he had been libeled by statements in a full-page advertisement that was carried in The New York Times on March 29, 1960. Entitled "Heed Their Rising Voices," the advertisement began by stating that "as the whole world knows by now, thousands of Southern Negro students are engaged in widespread nonviolent demonstrations in positive affirmation of the right to live in human dignity as guaranteed by the United States Constitution and the Bill of Rights." It went on to charge that "in their efforts to uphold these guarantees, they are being met by an unprecedented wave of terror by those who would deny and negate that document which the whole world looks upon as setting the pattern for modern freedom . . ." Succeeding paragraphs purported to illustrate the "wave of terror" by describing certain alleged events. The text concluded with an appeal for funds for three purposes: support of the student movement, "the struggle for the right-to-vote," and the legal defense of Dr. Martin Luther King Jr., leader of the movement, against a perjury indictment then pending in Montgomery.

Of the 10 paragraphs of text in the advertisement, the third and a portion of the sixth were the basis of respondent's claim of libel. They read as follows:

Third paragraph:

"In Montgomery, Ala., after students sang 'My Country, 'Tis of Thee' on the State Capitol steps, their leaders were expelled from school, and truckloads of police armed with shotguns and tear-gas ringed the Alabama State College campus. When the entire student body protested to state authorities by refusing to re-register, their dining hall was padlocked in an attempt to starve them into submission."

Sixth paragraph:

"Again and again the Southern violators have answered Dr. King's peaceful protests with intimidation and violence. They have bombed his home, almost killing his wife and child. They have assaulted his person. They have arrested him seven times —for 'speeding,' 'loitering' and similar offenses. And now they have charged him with 'perjury'—a felony under which they would imprison him for 10 years. . . ."

Although neither of these statements mentions respondent by name, he contended that the word "police" in the third paragraph referred to him as the Montgomery commissioner who supervised the Police Department, so that he was being accused of "ringing" the campus with police. He further claimed that the paragraph would be read as imputing to the police, and hence to him, the padlocking of the dining hall in order to starve the students in submission. As to the sixth paragraph, he contended that since arrests are ordinarily made by the police, the statement "they have arrested [Dr. King] seven times" would be read as referring to him in his capacity as commissioner.

It is uncontroverted that some of the statements contained in the two paragraphs were not accurate descriptions of events which occurred in Montgomery. Although Negro students staged a demonstration on the State Capitol steps, they sang the National Anthem and not "My Country, 'Tis of Thee." Although nine students were expelled by the State Board of Education, this was not for leading the demonstration at the Capitol, but for demanding service at a lunch counter in the Montgomery County Courthouse on another day. Not the entire student body, but most of it, had protested the expulsion, not by refusing to register, but by boycotting classes on a single day; virtually all the students did register for the ensuing semester. The campus dining hall was not padlocked on any occasion. And the only students who may have been barred from eating there were the few who had neither signed a preregistration application nor requested temporary meal tickets. Although the police were deployed near the campus in large numbers on three occasions, they did not at any time "ring" the campus, and they were not called to the campus in connection with the demonstration on the State Capitol steps, as the third paragraph implied. Dr. King had not been arrested seven times, but only four; and although he claimed to have been assaulted some years earlier in connection with his arrest for loitering outside a courtroom, one of the officers who made the arrest denied that there was such an assault.

On the premise that the charges in the sixth paragraph could be read as referring to him, respondent was allowed to prove that he had not participated in the events described. Although Dr. King's home had in fact been bombed twice when his wife and child were there, both of these occasions antedated respondent's tenure as commissioner, and the police were not only not implicated in the bombings, but had made every effort to apprehend those who were. Three of Dr. King's four arrests took place before respondent became commissioner. Although Dr. King had in fact been indicted (he was subsequently acquitted) on two counts of perjury, each of which carried a possible five-year sentence, respondent had nothing to do with procuring the indictment.

Respondent made no effort to prove that he suffered actual pecuniary loss as a result of the alleged libel. One of his witnesses, a former employer, testified that if he had believed the statements, he doubted whether he "would want to be associated with anybody who would be a party to such things as stated in that ad," and that he would not re-employ respondent if he believed "that he allowed the Police Department to do the things that the paper says he did." But neither this witness nor any of the others testified that he had actually believed the statements in their supposed reference to respondent.

The cost of the advertisement was approximately $4,800, and it was published by The Times upon an order from a New

York advertising agency acting for the signatory committee. The agency submitted the advertisement with a letter from A. Philip Randolph, chairman of the committee, certifying that the persons whose names appeared on the advertisement had given their permission. Mr. Randolph was known to The Times's advertising acceptability department as a responsible person, and in accepting the letter as sufficient proof of authorization it followed its established practice. There was testimony that the copy of the advertisement which accompanied the letter listed only the 64 names appearing in the text, and that the statement, "We in the South . . . warmly endorse this appeal" and the list of names thereunder, which included those of the individual petitioners, were subsequently added when the first proof of the advertisement was received. Each of the individual petitioners testified that he had not authorized the use of his name, and that he had been unaware of its use until receipt of respondent's demand for a retraction.

The manager of the advertising acceptability department testified that he had approved the advertisement for publication because he knew nothing to cause him to believe that anything in it was false, and because it bore the endorsement of "a number of people who are well known and whose reputation" he "had no reason to question." Neither he nor anyone else at The Times made an effort to confirm the accuracy of the advertisement, either by checking it against recent Times news stories relating to some of the described events or by some other means.

Alabama law denies a public officer recovery of punitive damages in a libel action brought on account of a publication concerning his official conduct unless he first makes a written demand for a public retraction and the defendant fails or refuses to comply. Alabama Code, Title 7, Section 914.

Respondent served such a demand upon each of the petitioners. None of the individual petitioners responded to the demand, primarily because each took the position that he had not authorized the use of his name on the advertisement and therefore had not published the statements that respondent alleged to have libeled him. The Times did not publish a retraction in response to the demand, but wrote respondent a letter that "We . . . are somewhat puzzled as to how you think the statements in any way reflect on you," and "You might, if you desire, let us know in what respect you claim that the statements in the advertisement reflect on you." Respondent filed this suit a few days later without answering the letter. The Times did, however, subsequently publish a retraction of the advertisement upon the demand of Gov. John Patterson of Alabama, who asserted that the publication charged him with "grave misconduct . . . and improper actions and omissions as Governor of Alabama and ex-officio chairman of the State Board of Education of Alabama. When asked to explain why there had been a retraction for the Governor but not for respondent, the secretary of The Times testified: "We did that because we didn't want anything that was published by The Times to be a reflection on the State of Alabama and the Governor was, as far as we could see, the embodiment of the State of Alabama and the proper representative of the state and, furthermore, we had by that time learned more of the actual facts which the ad purported to recite and, finally, the ad did refer to the action of the state authorities and the Board of Education, presumably of which the Governor is ex-officio chairman. . . ." On the other hand, he testified that he did not think that "any of the language in there referred to Mr. Sullivan."

The trial judge submitted the case to the jury under instructions that the statements in the advertisement were "libelous per se" and were not privileged, so that petitioners might be held liable if the jury found that they had published the advertisement and that the statements were made "of and concerning" respondent. The jury was instructed that, because the statements were libelous per se, "the law . . . implies legal injury from the bare fact of publication itself," "falsity and malice are presumed," "general damages need not be alleged or proved but are presumed," and "punitive damages may be awarded by the jury even though the amount of actual damages is neither found nor shown." An award of punitive damages—as distinguished from "general" damages, which are compensatory in nature—apparently requires proof of actual malice under Alabama law, and the judge charged that "mere negligence or carelessness is not evidence of actual malice or malice in fact, and does not justify an award of exemplary or punitive damages." He refused to charge, however, that the jury must be "convinced" of malice in the sense of "actual intent" to harm or "gross negligence and recklessness," to make such an award, and he also refused to require that a verdict for respondent differentiate between compensatory and punitive damages. The judge rejected petitioners' contention that his rulings abridged the freedoms of speech and of the press that are guaranteed by the First and 14th Amendments.

In affirming the judgment, the Supreme Court of Alabama sustained the trial judge's rulings and instructions in all respects. 273 Ala. 656, 144 So. 2d 25. It held that "where the words published tend to injure a person libeled by them in his reputation, profession, trade or business, or charge him with an indictable offense, or tend to bring the individual into public contempt," they are "libelous per se"; that "the matter complained of is, under the above doctrine, libelous per se, if it was published of and concerning the plaintiff"; and that was actionable without "proof of pecuniary injury . . . such injury being implied." Id., at 673, 676, 144, So. 2d, at 73, 41. It approved the trial court's ruling that the jury could find the statements to have been made of and concerning respondent, stating: "We think it common knowledge that the average person knows that municipal agents, such as police and firemen, and others, are under the control and direction of the city governing body, and more particularly under the direction and control of a single commissioner. In measuring the performance or deficiencies of such groups, praise or criticism is usually attached to the official in complete control of the body." Id., at 674-675; 144 So. 2d, at 39. In sustaining the trial court's determination that the verdict was not excessive, the court said that malice could be inferred from The Times "irresponsibility" in printing the advertisement while "The Times in its own files had articles already published which would have demonstrated the falsity of the allegations in the advertisement"; from The Times's failure to retract for respondent while retracting for the Governor, whereas the falsity of some of the allegations was then known to The Times and "the matter contained in the advertisement was equally false as to both parties"; and from the testimony of The Times's secretary that, apart from the statement that the dining hall was padlocked, he thought the two paragraphs were "substantially correct." Id., at 686-687; 144 So. 2d, at 50-51. The court reaffirmed a statement in an earlier opinion that "there is no legal measure of damages in cases of this character." Id., at 686; 144 So. 2d, at 50. It rejected petitioners' constitutional contentions with the brief statements that "the First Amendment of the United States Constitution does not protect libelous publications" and "the 14th Amendment is directed against state action and not private action." Id., at 676; 144 So. 2d, at 40.

Because of the importance of the constitutional issues involved, we granted the separate petitions for certiorari of the individual petitioners and of The Times. 371 U.S. 946. We reverse the judgment. We hold that the rule of law applied by the Alabama courts is constitutionally deficient for failure to provide the safeguards for freedom of speech and of the press that are required by the First and 14th Amendments in a libel action brought by a public official against critics of his official conduct. We further hold that under the proper safeguards the evidence presented in this case is constitutionally insufficient to support the judgment for respondent.

I

We may dispose at the outset of two grounds asserted to insulate the judgment of the Alabama courts from constitutional scrutiny. The first is the proposition relied on by the State Supreme Court—that "the 14th Amendment is directed against state action and not private action." That proposition has no application to this case. Although this is a civil lawsuit between private parties, the Alabama courts have applied a state rule of law which petitioners claim to impose invalid restrictions on their constitutional freedoms of speech and press. It matters not that that law has been applied in a civil action and that it is common law only, though supplemented by statute. See, e.g., Alabama Code, Title 7, Sections 908-917. The test is not the form in which state power has been applied but, whatever the form, whether such power has in fact been exercised. See Ex Parte Virginia, 100 U.S. 339, 346-347; American Federation of Labor v. Swing, 312 U.S. 321.

The second contention is that the constitutional guarantees of freedom of speech and of the press are inapplicable here, at least so far as The Times is concerned, because the allegedly libelous statements were published at part of a paid, "commercial" advertisement. The argument relies on Valentine v. Chrestensen, 316 U.S. 52, where the Court held that a city ordinance forbidding street distribution of commercial and business advertising matter did not abridge the First Amendment freedoms, even as applied to a handbill having a commercial message on one side but a protest against certain official action on the other. The reliance is wholly misplaced. The court in Chrestensen reaffirmed the constitutional protection for "the freedom of communicating information and disseminating opinion"; its holding was based upon the factual conclusions that the handbill was "purely commercial advertising" and that the protest against official action had been added only to evade the ordinance.

The publication here was not a "commercial" advertisement in the sense in which the word was used in Chrestensen. It communicated information, expressed opinion, recited grievances, protested claimed abuses and sought financial support on behalf of a movement whose existence and objectives are matters of the highest public interest and concern. See N.A.A.C.P. v. Button, 371 U.S. 415, 35.

That The Times was paid for publishing the advertisement is as immaterial in this connection as is the fact that newspapers and books are sold. Smith v. California, 631 U.S. 147, 150; cf. Bantam Books, Inc. v. Sullivan, 372 U.S. 58, 64, N. 6. Any other conclusion would discourage newspapers from carrying "editorial advertisements" of this type, and so might shut off an important outlet for the promulgation of information and ideas by persons who do not themselves have access to publishing facilities—who wish to exercise their freedom of speech even though they are not members of the press. C. Lovell v. Friffin, 303 U.S. 444, 452; Schneider v. State, 308 U.S. 147, 164. The effect would be to shackle the First Amendment in its attempt to secure "the widest possible dissemination of information from diverse and antagonistic sources." Association Press v. United States, 326 U.S. 1, 20. To avoid placing such a handicap upon the freedoms of expression, we hold that if the allegedly libelous statements would otherwise be constitutionally protected from the present judgment, they do not forfeit that protection because they were published in the form of a paid advertisement.

II

Under Alabama law as applied in this case, a publication is "libelous per se" if the words "tend to injure a person . . . in his reputation" or to "bring (him) into public contempt"; the trial court stated that the standard was met if the words are such as to "injure him in his public office, or impute misconduct to him in his office, or want of official integrity, or want of fidelity to a public trust. . . ." The jury must find that the words were published "of and concerning" the plaintiff, but where the plaintiff is a public official his place in the governmental hierarchy is sufficient evidence to support a finding that his reputation has been affected by statements that reflect upon the agency of which he is in charge. Once "libel per se" has been established, the defendant has no defense as to stated facts unless he can persuade the jury that they were true in all their particulars. Alabama Ride Co. v. Vance, 235 Ala. 263, 178 So. 438 (1938); Johnson Publishing Co. v. Davis, 271 Ala. 474, 494-495, 124 So. 2d 441, 457-458 (1960). His privilege of "fair comment" for expressions of opinion depends on the truth of the facts upon which the comment is based. Parsons v. Age-Herald Publishing Co., 181 Ala. 439, 450, So. 345, 350 (1913).

Unless he can discharge the burden of proving truth, general damages are presumed, and may be awarded without proof of pecuniary injury. A showing of actual malice is apparently a prerequisite to recovery of punitive damages, and the defendant may in any event forestall these by a retraction meeting the statutory requirements. Good motives and belief in truth do not negate an inference of malice, but are relevant only in mitigation of punitive damages if the jury chooses to accord them weight. Johnson Publishing Co. v. Davis, Supra, 271 Ala., at 495, 124, So. 2d, at 458.

The question before us is whether this rule of liability, as applied to an action brought by a public official against critics of his official conduct, abridges the freedom of speech and of the press that is guaranteed by the First and 14th Amendments.

Respondent relies heavily, as did the Alabama courts, on statements of this court to the effect that the Constitution does not protect libelous publications.

Those statements do not foreclose our inquiry here. None of the cases sustained the use of libel laws to impose sanctions upon expression critical of the official conduct of public officials. The dictum in Pennekamp v. Florida, 328 U.S. 331, 348-349, that "when the statements amount to defamation, a judge has such remedy in damages for libel as do other public servants," implied no view as to what remedy might constitutionally be afforded to public officials. In Beauharnais v. Illinois, 343 U.S. 250, the court sustained an Illinois criminal libel statute as applied to a publication held to be both defamatory of a racial group and "liable to cause violence and disorder." But the court was careful to note that it "retains and exercises authority to nullify action which encroaches on freedom of utterance under the guise of punishing libel"; for "public men are, as it were, public property," and "discussion cannot be denied and the right, as well as the duty, of criticism must not be stifled." Id., at 263-264, and N. 18. In the only previous case that did present the question of constitutional limitations upon the power to award damages for libel of a public official, the court was equally divided and the question was not decided. Schenectady Union Pub. Co. v. Sweeney, 316 U.S. 642. In deciding the question now, we are compelled by neither precedent nor policy to give any more weight to the epithet "libel" than we have to other "mere labels" of state law. N.A.A.C.P. v. Button, 371 U.S. 415, 429. Like "insurrection," contempt, advocacy of unlawful act, breach of the peace, obscenity, solicitation of legal business and the various other formulae for the repression of expression that have been challenged in this court, libel can claim no talismanic immunity from constitutional limitations. It must be measured by standards that satisfy the First Amendment.

The general proposition that freedom of expression upon public questions is secured by the First Amendment has long been settled by our decisions. The constitutional safeguard, we have said, "was fashioned to assure the unfettered interchange of ideas for the bringing about of political and social changes desired by the people." Roth v. United States, 354 U.S. 476, 484. "The maintenance of the opportunity for free political discussion to the end that government may be responsive to the will of the people and that changes may be obtained by lawful means, an opportunity essential to the security of the Republic, is a fundamental principle of our constitutional system." Stromberg v. California, 283 U.S. 359, 369. "It is a prized American privilege to speak one's mind, although not always with perfect good taste, on all public institutions," Bridges v. California, 314 U.S. 252, 270, and this opportunity is to be afforded for "vigorous advocacy" no less than "abstract discussion." N.A.A.C.P. v. Button, 371 U.S. 415, 429. The First Amendment, said Judge Learned Hand, "presupposes that right conclusions are more likely to be gathered out of a multitude of tongues, than through any kind of authoritative selection. To many this is, and always will be, folly; but we have staked upon it our all." United States v. Associated Press, 52 F. Supp. 362, 372

(D.C.S.D. 1943). Mr. Justice Brandeis, in his concurring opinion in Whitney v. California, 274 U.S. 357, 375-376, gave the principle its classic formulation:

"Those who won our independence believed . . . that public discussion is a political duty; and that this should be a fundamental principle of the American Government. They recognized the risks to which all human institutions are subject. But they knew that order cannot be secured merely through fear of punishment for its infraction; that it is hazardous to discourage thought, hope and imagination; that fear breeds repression; that repression breeds hate; that hate menaces stable government; that the path of safety lies in the opportunity to discuss freely supposed grievances and proposed remedies; and that the fitting remedy for evil counsels is good ones. Believing in the power of reason as applied through public discussion, they eschewed silence coerced by law—the argument of force in its worst form. Recognizing the occasional tyrannies of governing majorities, they amended the Constitution so that free speech and assembly should be guaranteed."

Thus we consider this case against the background of a profound national commitment to the principle that debate on public issues should be uninhibited, robust, and wide-open, and that it may well include vehement, caustic, and sometimes unpleasantly sharp attacks on government and public officials. See Terminiello v. Chicago, 337 U. S. 1, 4; De Jonge v. Oregon 299 U. S. 353, 365. The present advertisement, as an expression of grievance and protest on one of the major public issues of our time, would seem clearly to qualify for the constitutional protection. The question is whether it forfeits that protection by the falsity of some of its factual statements and by its alleged defamation of respondent.

Authoritative interpretations of the First Amendment guarantees have consistently refused to recognize an exception for any test of truth, whether administered by judges, juries, or administrative officials—and especially not one that puts the burden of providing truth on the speaker. Cf. Speiser v. Randall, 357 U. S. 513, 525-526.

The constitutional protection does not turn upon "the truth, popularity, or social utility of the ideas and beliefs which are offered." N.A.A.C.P. v. Button, 371 U. S. 415, 445. As Madison said, "Some degree of abuse is inseparable from the proper use of every thing; and in no instance is this more true than in that of the press." 4 Elliot's Debates on the Federal Constitution (1876), P. 571. In Cantwell v. Connecticut, 310 U.S. 296, 310, the court declared:

"In the realm of religious faith, and in that of political belief, sharp differences arise. In both fields the tenets of one man may seem the rankest error to his neighbor. To persuade others to his own point of view, the pleader, as we know, at times, resorts to exaggeration, to villification of men who have been, or are, prominent in church or state, and even to false statement. But the people of this nation have ordained in the light of history, that, in spite of the probability of excesses and abuses, these liberties are, in the long view, essential to enlightened opinion and right conduct on the part of the citizens of a democracy."

That erroneous statement is inevitable in free debate, and that it must be protected if the freedoms of expression are to have the "breathing space" that they "need . . . to survive," N.A.A.C.P. v. Button, 371 U. S. 415, 433, was also recognized by the Court of Appeals for the District of Columbia Circuit in Sweneey v. Patterson, 128 F. 2d 457, 458 (1942). Judge Edgerton spoke for a unanimous court which affirmed the dismissal of a Congressman's libel suit based upon a newspaper article charging him with anti-Semitism in opposing a judicial appointment. He said:

"Cases which impose liability for erroneous reports of the political conduct of officials reflect the obsolete doctrine that the governed must not criticize their governors . . . The interest of the public here outweighs the interest of appellant or any other individual. The protection of the public requires not merely discussion, but information. Political conduct and views which some respectable people approve, and others condemn, are constantly imputed to Congressmen. Errors of fact, particularly in regard to a man's mental states and processes, are inevitable . . . Whatever is added to the field of libel is taken from the field of free debate."

Just as a factual error affords no warrant for repressing speech that would otherwise be free, the same is true of injury to official reputation. Where judicial officers are involved, this court has held that concern for the dignity and reputation of the courts does not justify the punishment as criminal contempt or criticism of the judge or his decision. Bridges v. California, 314 U.S. 252. This is true even though the utterance contains "half-truths" and "misinformation." Pennekamp v. Florida, 328 U. S. 331, 342, 343, No. 5, 345; such repression can be justified, if at all, only by a clear and present danger of the obstruction of justice. See also Craig v. Harney, 331 U. S. 367; Wood v. Georgia, 370 U. S. 376. If judges are to be treated as "men of fortitude, able to thrive in a hardy climate," Craig v. Harney, supra, 331 U. S., at 376, surely the same must be true of other government officials, such as elected city commissioners.

Criticism of their official conduct does not lose its constitutional protection merely because it is effective criticism and hence diminishes their official reputations.

If neither factual error nor defamatory content suffices to remove the constitutional shield from criticism of official conduct, the combination of the two elements is no less inadequate. This is the lesson to be drawn from the great controversy over the Sedition Act of 1798, 1 Stat. 596, which first crystallize a national awareness of the central meaning of the First Amendment. See Levy, Legacy of Suppression (1960), at 258 et seq., Smith, Freedom's Fetters (1956), at 426, 431, and passim. That statute made it a crime, punishable by a $5,000 fine and five years in prison, "if any person shall write, print, utter or publish . . . any false, scandalous and malicious writing or writings against the Government of the United States, or either House of the Congress. . . , or the President . . . , with the intent to defame . . . or to bring them or either of them, into contempt or disrepute; or to excite against them, or either or any of them, the hatred of the good people of the United States."

The act allowed the defendant the defense of truth, and provided that the jury were to be judges both of the law and the facts. Despite these qualifications, the act was vigorously condemned as unconstitutional in an attack joined in by Jefferson and Madison. In the famous Virginia Resolutions of 1798, the General Assembly of Virginia resolved that it "doth particularly protest against the palpable and alarming infractions of the Constitution, in the two late cases of the 'Alien and Sedition Acts' passed at the last session of Congress. . . . Congress [the Sedition Act] exercises . . . a power not delegated by the Constitution, but, on the contrary, expressly and positively forbidden by one of the Amendments thereto—a power which more than any other ought to produce universal alarm, because it is leveled against the right of freely examining public characters and measures, and of free communication among the people thereon, which has ever been justly deemed the only effectual guardian of every other right." 4 Elliot's Debates, supra, pp. 553-554.

Madison prepared the report in support of the protest. His premise was that the Constitution created a form of government under which "the people, not the Government, possess the absolute sovereignty." The structure of the Government dispersed power in reflection of the people's distrust of concentrated power, and of power itself at all levels. This form of government was "altogether different" from the British form, under which the Crown was sovereign and the people were subjects. "It is not natural and necessary, under such different circumstances," he asked, "that a different degree of freedom in the use of the press should be contemplated?" Id., p. 569-570. Earlier, in a debate in the House of Representatives, Madison had said: "If we advert to the nature of republican government, we shall find that the censorial power is in the people over the government, and not in the government over the people." 4. Annals of Congress, p. 934 (1794). Of the exercise of that power by the press, his report said:

"In every state, probably, in the Union, the press has exerted a freedom of canvassing the merits and measures of public men, of every description, which has not been confined to the strict limits of the common law. On this footing the freedom of the press has stood; on this foundation it yet stands. . . ." 4 Elliot's Debates, supra, p. 570. The right of free public discussion of the stewardship of public officials was thus, in Madison's view, a fundamental principle of the American form of government.

Although the Sedition Act was never tested in this Court, the attack upon its validity has carried the day in the court of history. Fines levied in its prosecution were repaid by Act of Congress on the ground that it was unconstitutional. See e.g., Act of July 4, 1840, C. 45, 6 Stat. 802, accompanied by H. R. Rep. No. 86, 26th Cong., 1st Sess. (1840). Calhoun, reporting to the Senate on Feb. 4, 1836, assumed that its invalidity was a matter "which no one now doubts." Report with Senate bill No. 122, 24th Cong., 1st Sess., p. 3. Jefferson, as President, pardoned those who had been convicted and sentenced under the act and remitted their fines, stating:

"I discharged every person under punishment or prosecution under the Sedition Law because I considered, and now consider, that law to be a nullity as absolute and palpable as if Congress had ordered us to fall down and worship a golden image." Letter to Mrs. Adams, July 22, 1804, 4. Jefferson's Works (Washington Ed.) pp. 555-556. The invalidity of the act has also been assumed by justices of this Court. Holmes, J., dissenting and joined by Brandeis, J., in Abrams v. United States, 250 U.S. 616, 630; Jackson, J., dissenting in Beauharnais v. Illinois, 343 U.S., 250, 288-289; Douglas, The Right of the People (1958), p. 47. See also Cooley, Chafee, Constitutional Limitations (8th Ed., Carrington, 1927), pp. 899-900; Free Speech in the United States (1924), pp. 27-28. These views reflect a broad consensus that the act, because of the restraint it imposed upon criticism of government and public officials, was inconsistent with the First Amendment.

There is no force in respondent's argument that the constitutional limitations implicit in the history of the Sedition Act apply only to Congress and not to the states. It is true that the First Amendment was originally addressed only to action by the Federal Government, and that Jefferson, for one, while denying the power of Congress "to control the freedom of the press," recognized such a power in the states. See the 1804 letter to Abigail Adams quoted in Dennis v. United States, 341 U.S. 494, 522, n. 4 (concurring opinion). But this distinction was eliminated with the adoption of the 14th Amendment and the application to the states of the First Amendment's restrictions, see, e.g., Gitlow v. New York, 268 U.S. 652, 666; Schneider v. State, 308 U.S. 147, 160; Bridges v. California, 314 U.S. 252, 268; Edwards v. South Carolina, 372 U.S. 229, 235.

What a state may not constitutionally bring about by means of a criminal statute is likewise beyond the reach of its civil law of libel. The fear of damage awards under a rule such as that invoked by the Alabama courts here may be markedly more inhibiting than the fear of prosecution under a criminal statute. See City of Chicago v. Tribune Co., 307 Ill. 596, 607, 139 N.E. 86, 90 (1923). Alabama, for example, has a criminal libel law which subjects to prosecution "any person who speaks, writes, or prints of and concerning another any accusation falsely and maliciously importing the commission by such person of a felony, or any other indictable offense involving moral turpitude," and which allows as punishment upon conviction a fine not exceeding $500 and a prison sentence of six months. Alabama Code, Title 14, Section 350.

Presumably a person charged with violation of this statute enjoys ordinary criminal-law safeguards such as the requirements of an indictment and of proof beyond a reasonable doubt. These safeguards are not available to the defendant in a civil action. The judgment awarded in this case—without the need for any proof of actual pecuniary loss—was one thousand times greater than the maximum fine provided by the Alabama criminal statute, and one hundred times greater than that provided by the Sedition Act. And since there is no doublejeapardy limitation applicable to civil lawsuits, this is not the only judgment that may be awarded against petitioners for the same publication. Whether or not a newspaper can survive a succession of such judgments, the pall of fear and timidity imposed upon those who would give voice to public criticism is an atmosphere in which the First Amendment freedoms cannot survive.

Plainly the Alabama law of civil libel is "a form of regulation that creates hazards to protected freedoms markedly greater than those that attend reliance upon the criminal law." Bantam Books, Inc. v. Sullivan, 372 U.S. 58, up.

The state rule of law is not saved by its allowance of the defense of truth. A defense for erroneous statements honestly made is no less essential here than was the requirement of proof of guilty knowledge which, in Smith v. California, 361 U.S. 147, we held indispensable to a valid conviction of a bookseller for possessing obscene writings for sale. We said:

"For if the bookseller is criminally liable without knowledge of the contents, . . . he will tend to restrict the books he sells to those he has inspected; and thus the state will have imposed a restriction upon the distribution of constitutionally protected as well as obscene literature . . . and the bookseller's burden would become the public's burden, for by restricting him the public's access to reading matter would be restricted . . . (his) timidity in the face of his absolute criminal liability, thus would tend to restrict the public's access to forms of the printed word which the state could not constitutionally suppress directly. The bookseller's self-censorship, compelled by the state, would be a censorship affecting the whole public, hardly less virulent for being privately administered. Through it, the distribution of all books, both obscene and not obscene, would be impeded." (361 U. S. 147, 153-154.)

A rule compelling the critic of official conduct to guarantee the truth of all his factual assertions—and to do so on pain of libel judgments virtually unlimited in amount—leads to a comparable "self-censorship."

Allowance of the defense of truth, with the burden of proving it on the defendant, does not mean that only false speech will be deterred. Even courts accepting this defense as an adequate safeguard have recognized the difficulties of adducing legal proofs that the alleged libel was true in all its factual particulars. See, e.g., Post Publishing Co. v. Hallam, 59 f. 530, 540 (6th Cir. 1893); see also Noel 49 Col. L. Rev. 875, 892 (1949). Under such a rule, would-be critics of official conduct may be deterred from voicing their criticism, even though it is believed to be true and even though it is in fact true, because of doubt whether it can be proved in court or fear of the expense of having to do so. They tend to make only statements which "steer far wider of the unlawful zone." Speiser v. Randall, supra, 357 U. S., at 526. The rule thus dampens the vigor and limits the variety of public debate. It is inconsistent with the First and 14th Amendments.

The constitutional guarantees require, we think, a Federal rule that prohibits a public official from recovering damages for a defamatory falsehood relating to his official conduct unless he proves that the statement was made with "actual malice"—that is, with knowledge that it was false or with reckless disregard of whether it was false or not. An oft-cited statement of a like rule, which has been adopted by a number of state courts, is found in the Kansas case of Coleman v. MacLennan, 78 Kan. 711, 98 p. 281 (1908). The State Attorney General, a candidate for re-election and a member of the commission charged with the management and control of the state school fund, sued a newspaper publisher for alleged libel in an article purporting to state facts relating to his official conduct in connection with a school-fund transaction. The defendant pleaded privilege and the trial judge, over the plaintiff's objection, instructed the jury that "where an article is published and circulated among voters for the sole purpose of giving what the defendant believes to be truthful information concerning a candidate for public office and for the purpose of enabling such voters to cast their ballot more intelligently, and the whole thing is done in good faith and without malice, the article is privileged, although the principal matters contained in the article may be untrue in fact and derogatory to the character of the plaintiff; and in such a case the burden is on the plaintiff to show actual malice in the publication of the article."

In answer to a special question, the jury found that the plaintiff had not proved actual malice, and a general verdict was returned for the defendant. On appeal the Supreme Court of Kansas, in an opinion by Justice Burch, reasoned as follows (78 Kan., at 724, 98 P., at 286):

"It is of the utmost consequence that the people should discuss the character and qualifications of candidates for their suffrages. The importance to the state and to society of such discussions is so vast, and the advantages derived are so great, that they more than counterbalance the inconvenience of private persons whose conduct may be involved, and occasional injury to the reputations of individuals must yield to the public welfare, although at times such injury may be great. The public benefit from publicity is so great, and the chance of injury to private character so small, that such discussion must be privileged."

The court thus sustained the trial court's instruction as a correct statement of the law, saying:

"In such a case the occasion gives rise to a privilege, qualified to this extent: Anyone claiming to be defamed by the communication must show actual malice or go remediless. This privilege extends to a great variety of subjects, and includes matters of public concern, public men, and candidates for office." 78 Kan., at 723.

Such a privilege for criticism of official conduct is appropriately analogous to the protection accorded a public official when he is sued for libel by a private citizen. In Barr v. Matteo, 360 U.S. 564, 575, this court held the utterance of a Federal official to be absolutely privileged if made "within the outer perimeter" of his duties. The states accord the same immunity to statements of their highest officers, although some differentiate their lesser officials and qualify the privilege they enjoy.

But all hold that all officials are protected unless actual malice can be proved. The reason for the official privilege is said to be that the threat of damage suits would otherwise "inhibit the fearless, vigorous and effective administration of policies of government" and "dampen the ardor of all but the most resolute, or the most irresponsible, in the unflinching discharge of their duties." Barr v. Matteo, supra, 360 U.S., at 571. Analogous considerations support the privilege for the citizen-critic of government. It is as much his duty to criticize as it is the official's duty to administer. See Whitney v. California, 274 U.S. 357, 375 (concurring opinion of Mr. Justice Brandeis), quoted ante, p. 15. As Madison said, see ante, p. 20, "the censorial power is in the people over the government, and not in the government over the people." It would give public servants an unjustified preference over the public they serve, if critics of official conduct did not have a fair equivalent of the immunity granted to the officials themselves.

We conclude that such a privilege is required by the First and 14th Amendments.

III

We hold today that the Constitution delimits a state's power to award damages for libel in actions brought by public officials against critics of their official conduct.

Since this is such an action, the rule requiring proof of actual malice is applicable. While Alabama law apparently requires proof of actual malice for an award of punitive damages where general damages are concerned malice is "presumed." Such a presumption is inconsistent with the Federal rule. The power to create presumptions is not a means of escape from constitutional restrictions," Bailey v. Alabama, 219 U. S. 219, 239; "The showing of malice required for the forfeiture of the privilege is not presumed but is a matter for proof by the plaintiff . . ." Lawrence v. Fox, 357 Mich. 134, 146, 97 N. W. 2d 719, 725 (1959). Since the trial judge did not instruct the jury to differentiate between general and punitive damages, it may be that the verdict was wholly an award of one or the other. But it is impossible to know, in view of the general verdict returned. Because of this uncertainty, the judgment must be reversed and the case remanded. Stromberg v. California, 283 U. S. 359, 367-368; Williams v. North Carolina, 317, U. S. 287, 291-292; see Yates v. United States, 354, U. S. 298, 311-312; Cramer v. United States, 325 U. S. 1, 36, N. 45.

Since respondent may seek a new trial, we deem that considerations of effective judicial administration require us to review the evidence in the present record to determine whether it could constitutionally support a judgment for respondent. This court's duty is not limited to the elaboration of constitutional principles; we must also in proper cases review the evidence to make certain that those principles have been constitutionally applied. This is such a case, particularly since the question is one of alleged trespass across "the line between speech unconditionally guaranteed and speech which may legitimately be regulated." Speiser v. Randal, 357 U.S. 513, 525. In cases where the line must be drawn, the rule is that we "examine for ourselves the statements in issue and the circumstances under which they were made to see . . . whether they are of a character which the principles of the First Amendment, as adopted by the due process clause of the 14th Amendment, protect." Pennekamp v. Florida, 328 U.S. 331, 335; see also One, Inc., v. Olesen, 355 U.S. 371; Sunshine Book Co. v. Summerfield, 355 U.S. 372. We must "make an independent examination of the whole record," Edwards v. South Carolina, 372 U.S. 229, 235, so as to assure ourselves that the judgment does not constitute a forbidden intrusion on the field of free expression.

Applying these standards, we consider that the proof presented to show actual malice lacks the convincing clarity which the constitutional standard demands, and hence that it would not constitutionally sustain the judgment for respondent under the proper rule of law.

The case of the individual petitioners requires little discussion. Even assuming that they could constitutionally be found to have authorized the use of their names on the advertisement, there was no evidence whatever that they were aware of any erroneous statements or were in any way reckless in that regard. The judgment against them is thus without constitutional support.

As to The Times, we similarly conclude that the facts do not support a finding of actual malice. The statement by The Times secretary that, apart from the padlocking allegation, he thought the advertisement was "substantially correct," affords no constitutional warrant for the Alabama Supreme Court's conclusion that it was a "cavalier ignoring of the falsity of the advertisement [from which] the jury could not have but been impressed with the bad faith of The Times, and its maliciousness inferable therefrom." The statement does not indicate malice at the time of the publication; even if the advertisement was not "substantially correct"—although respondent's own proofs tend to show that it was—that opinion was at least a reasonable one, and there was no evidence to impeach the witness's good faith in holding it.

The Times's failure to retract upon respondent's demand, although it later retracted upon the demand of Governor Patterson, is likewise not adequate evidence of malice for constitutional purposes. Whether or not a failure to retract may ever constitute such evidence, there are two reasons why it does not here. First, the letter written by The Times reflected a reasonable doubt on its part as to whether the advertisement could reasonably be taken to refer to respondent at all. Second, it was not a final refusal, since it asked for an explanation on this point—a request that respondent chose to ignore. Nor does the retraction upon the demand of the Governor supply the necessary proof. It may be doubted that a failure to retract which is not itself evidence of malice can retroactively become such by virtue of a retraction subsequently made to another party. But in any event that did not happen here, since the explanation given by The Times' secretary for the distinction drawn between respondent and the Governor was a reasonable one, the good faith of which was not impeached.

Finally, there is evidence that The Times published the ad vertisement without checking its accuracy against the news stories in The Times's own files. The mere presence of the stories in the files does not, of course, establish that The Times "knew" the advertisement was false, since the state of mind required for actual malice would have to be brought home to the persons in The Times organization having responsibility for the publication of the advertisement. With respect to the failure of those persons to make the check, the record shows that they relied upon their knowledge of the good reputation of many of those whose names were listed as sponsors of the advertisement, and upon the letter from A. Philip Randolph, known to them as a responsible individual, certifying that the use of the names was authorized.

There was testimony that the persons handling the advertisement saw nothing in it that would render it unacceptable under The Times's policy of rejecting advertisements containing "attacks of a personal character"; their failure to reject it on this ground was not unreasonable. We think the evidence against The Times supports at most a finding of negligence in failing to discover the misstatements, and is constitutionally insufficient to show the recklessness that is required for a finding of actual malice. Cf. Charles Parker Co. v. Silver City Crystal Co., 142 Conn. 605, 618, 116 A. 2D 440, 446 (1955); Phoenix Newspapers, Inc. v. Choisser, 82 Ariz. 271, 277-278, 312 P. 2D 150, 154-155 (1957).

We also think the evidence was constitutionally defective in another respect: it was incapable of supporting the jury's finding that the allegedly libelous statements were made "of and concerning" respondent. Respondent relies on the words of the advertisement and the testimony of six witnesses to establish a connection between it and himself. Thus, in his brief to this court, he states:

"The reference to respondent as Police Commissioner is clear from the ad. In addition, the jury heard the testimony of a newspaper editor . . . ; a real estate and insurance man . . . ; the sales manager of a men's clothing store . . . ; a food equipment man . . . ; a service station operator . . . ; and the operator of a truck line for whom respondent had formerly worked . . . each of these witnesses stated that he associated the statements with respondent . . ."

There was no reference to respondent in the advertisement, either by name or official position. A number of the allegedly libelous statements—the charges that the dining hall was padlocked and that Dr. King's home was bombed, his person assaulted, and a perjury prosecution instituted against him—did not even concern the police; despite the ingenuity of the arguments which would attach this significance to the word "they," it is plain that these statements could not reasonably be read as accusing respondent of personal involvement in the acts in question. The statements upon which respondent principally relies as referring to him are the two allegations that did concern the police or police functions: that "truckloads of police . . . ringed the Alabama State College campus" after the demonstration on the State Capitol steps, and that Dr. King had been "arrested . . . seven times."

These statements were false only in that the police had been "deployed near" the campus but had not actually "ringed" it and had not gone there in connection with the State Capitol demonstration, and in that Dr. King had been arrested only four times. The ruling that these discrepancies between what was true and what was asserted were sufficient to injure respondent's reputation may itself raise constitutional problems, but we need not consider them here. Although the statements may be taken as referring to the police, they did not, on their face, make even an oblique reference to respondent as an individual. Support for the asserted reference must, therefore, be sought in the testimony of respondent's witnesses. But none of them suggested any basis for the belief that respondent himself was attacked in the advertisement beyond the bare fact that he was in over-all charge of the Police Department and thus bore official responsibility for police conduct; to the extent that some of the witnesses thought respondent to have been charged with ordering or approving the conduct, or otherwise being personally involved in it, they based this notion not on any statements in the advertisement and not on any evidence that he had, in fact, been so involved, but solely on the unsupported assumption that because of his official position, he must have been.

This reliance on the bare fact of respondent's official position was made explicit by the Supreme Court of Alabama. That court in holding that the trial court "did not err in overruling the demurrer (of The Times) in the aspect that the libelous matter was not of and concerning the plaintiffs," based its ruling on the proposition that:

"We think it common knowledge that the average person knows that municipal agents, such as police and firemen and others, are under the control and direction of the city governing body, and more particularly, under the direction and control of a single commissioner. In measuring the performance or deficiencies of such groups, praise or criticism is usually attached to the official in complete control of the body." (273 Ala., At 674-675.)

This proposition has disquieting implications for criticism of governmental conduct. For good reason "no court of last resort in this country has ever held, or even suggested, that prosecutions for libel on government have any place in the American system of jurisprudence." (City of Chicago v. Tribune Co., 307 Ill. 595, 601, 139 N.E. 86, 88, 1923.) The present proposition would sidestep this obstacle by transmitting criticism of government, however impersonal it may seem on its face, into personal criticism, and hence potential libel, of the officials of whom the government is composed. There is no legal alchemy by which a state may thus create the cause of action that would otherwise be denied for a publication which, as respondent himself said of the advertisement, "reflects not only on me, but on the other commissioners and the community." Raising, as it does, the possibility that a good-faith critic of government will be penalized for his criticism, the proposition relied on by the Alabama courts strikes at the very center of the constitutionally protected area of free expression. We hold that such a proposition may not constitutionally be utilized to establish that an otherwise impersonal attack on governmental operations was a libel of an official responsible for those operations. Since it was relied on exclusively here, and there was no other evidence to connect the statements with respondent, the evidence was constitutionally insufficient to support a finding that the statements referred to respondent.

The judgment of the Supreme Court of Alabama is reversed, and the case is remanded to that court for further proceedings not inconsistent with this opinion.

Reversed and remanded.

CONCURRING OPINIONS

Mr. Justice Goldberg with whom *Mr. Justice Douglas* joins, concurring in the result.

The Court today announces a constitutional standard which prohibits "a public official from recovering damages for a defamatory falsehood relating to his official conduct unless he proves that the statement was made with 'actual malice'—that is, with knowledge that it was false or with reckless disregard of whether it was false or not." Ante, at 25. The Court thus rules that the Constitution gives citizens and newspapers a "conditional privilege" immunizing nonmalicious misstatements of fact regarding the official conduct of a government officer. The impressive array of history and precedent marshaled by the Court, however, confirms my belief that the Constitution affords greater protection than that provided by the Court's standard to citizen and press in exercising the right of public criticism.

In my view, the First and 14th Amendments to the Constitution afford to the citizen and to the press an absolute, unconditional privilege to criticize official conduct despite the harm which may flow from excesses and abuses. The prized American right "to speak one's mind," cf. Bridges v. California, 314 U. S. 252, 270, about public officials and affairs needs "breathing space to survive," N.A.A.C.P. v. Button, 371 U. S. 415, 433. The right should not depend upon a probing by the jury of the motivation of the citizen or press. The theory of our Constitution is that every citizen may speak his mind and every newspaper express its view on matters of public concern and may not be barred from speaking or publishing because those in control of government think that what is said or written is unwise, unfair, false, or malicious. In a democratic society, one who assumes to act for the citizens in an executive, legislative, or judicial capacity must expect that his official acts will be commented upon and criticized. Such criticism cannot, in my opinion, be muzzled or deterred by the courts at the instance of public officials under the label of libel.

It has been recognized that "prosecutions for libel on government have (no) place in the American system of jurisprudence," City of Chicago v. Tribune Co., 307 Ill. 595, 601, 139 N.E. 86, 88. I fully agree. Government, however, is not an abstraction; it is made up of individuals—of governors responsible to the governed. In a democratic society where men are free by ballots to remove those in power, any statement critical of governmental action is necessarily "of and concerning" the governors and any statement critical of the governors' official conduct is necessarily "of and concerning" the government. If the rule that libel on government has no place in our Constitution is to have real meaning, then libel on the official conduct of the governors likewise can have no place in our Constitution.

We must recognize that we are writing upon a clean slate. As the court notes, although there have been "statements of this court to the effect that the Constitution does not protect libelous publications . . . (n)one of the cases sustained the use of libel laws to impose sanctions upon expression critical of the official conduct of public officials." Ante, at 13-14. We should be particularly careful, therefore, adequately to protect the liberties which are embodied in the First and 14th Amendments. It may be urged that deliberately and maliciously false statements have no conceivable value as free speech. That argument, however, is not responsive to the real issue presented by this case, which is whether that freedom of speech which all agree is constitutionally protected can be effectively safeguarded by a rule allowing the imposition of liability upon a jury's evaluation of the speaker's state of mind.

If individual citizens may be held liable in damages for strong words, which a jury finds false and maliciously motivated, there can be little doubt that public debate and advocacy will be constrained. And if newspapers, publishing advertisements dealing with public issues, thereby risk liability, there can also be little doubt that the ability of minority groups to secure publication of their views on public affairs and to seek support for their causes will be greatly diminished. Cf. Farmers Educational & Coop. Union v. WDAY, Inc., 360 U.S. 525, 530. The opinion of the Court conclusively demonstrates the chilling effect of the Alabama libel laws on First Amendment freedoms in the area of race relations. The American Colonists were not willing, nor should we be, to take that risk that "(m)en who injure and oppress the people under their administration (and) provoke them to cry out and complain" will also be empowered to "make that very complaint the foundation for new oppressions and prosecutions." The Trial of John Peter Zenger, 17 Howell's St. Tr. 675, 721-722 (1735) (Argument of counsel to the jury.)

To impose liability for critical, albeit erroneous or even malicious, comments on official conduct would effectively resurrect "the obsolete doctrine that the governed must not criticize their governors." Cf. Sweeney v. Patterson, 128 F. 2d 457, 458.

Our national experience teaches that repressions breed hate and "that hate menaces stable government." Whitney v. California, 274 U.S. 357, 375 (Brandeis, J., concurring). We should be ever mindful of the wise counsel of Chief Justice Hughes:

"Imperative is the need to preserve inviolate the constitutional rights of free speech, free press and free assembly in order to maintain the opportunity for free political discussion, to the end that government may be responsive to the will of the people and that changes, if desired, may be obtained by peaceful means. Therein lies the security of the Republic, the very foundation of constitutional government," De Jonge v. Oregon, 299 U.S. 353, 365.

This is not to say that the Constitution protects defamatory statements directed against the private conduct of a public official or private citizen. Freedom of press and of speech insure that government will respond to the will of the people and that changes may be obtained by peaceful means. Purely private defamation has little to do with the political ends of a self-governing society. The imposition of liability for private defamation does not abridge the freedom of public speech. This, of course, cannot be said "where public officials are concerned or where public matters are involved . . . (O)ne main function of the First Amendment is to ensure ample opportunity for the people to determine and resolve public issues. "Where public matters are involved, the doubts should be resolved in favor of freedom of expression rather than against it." Douglas, The Right of the People (1958), P. 41.

In many jurisdictions, legislators, judges and executive officers are clothed with absolute immunity against liability for defamatory words uttered in the discharge of their public duties. See, e.g., Barr v. Matteo, 360 U.S. 564; City of Chicago v. Tribune Co., 307 Ill., at 610; 139 N.E., at 91. Judge Learned Hand ably summarized the policies underlying the rule:

"It does indeed go without saying that an official, who is in fact guilty of using his powers to vent his spleen upon others, or for any other personal motive not connected with the public good, should not escape liability for the injuries he may so cause; and if it were possible in practice to confine such complaints to the guilty, it would be monstrous to deny recovery. The justification for doing so is that it is impossible to know whether the claim is well founded until the case has been tried, and that to submit all officials, the innocent as well as the guilty, to the burden of a trial and to the inevitable danger of its outcome, would dampen the ardor of all but the most resolute, or the most irresponsible, in the unflinching discharge of their duties. Again and again the public interest calls for action which may turn out to be founded on a mistake, in the face of which an official may later find himself hard put to it to satisfy a jury of his good faith. There must indeed be means of punishing public officers who have been truant to their duties; but that is quite another matter from exposing anyone who has suffered from their errors. As is so often the case, the answer must be found in a balance between the evils inevitable in either alternative. In this instance it has been thought in the end better to leave unredressed the wrongs done by dishonest officers than to subject those who try to do their duty to the constant dread of retaliation. . . .

"The decisions have, indeed, always imposed as a limitation upon the immunity that the official's act must have been within the scope of his powers; and it can be argued that official powers, since they exist only for the public good, never cover occasions where the public good is not their aim, and hence that to exercise a power dishonestly is necessarily to overstep its bounds. A moment's reflection shows, however, that that cannot be the meaning of the limitation without defeating the whole doctrine. What is meant by saying that the officer must be acting within his power cannot be more than that the occasion must be such as would have justified the act, if he had been using his power for any of the purposes on whose account it was vested in him . . ." Gregoire v. Biddle, 177 F. 2d 579, 581.

If the government official should be immune from libel actions so that his ardor to serve the public will not be dampened and "fearless, vigorous, and effective administration of policies of government" not be inhibited, Barr v. Matteo supra, at 571, then the citizen and the press should likewise be immune from libel actions for their criticism of official conduct. Their ardor as citizens will thus not be dampened and they will be free "to applaud or to criticize the way public employes do their jobs, from the least to the most important." If liability can attach to political criticism because it damages the reputation of a public official as a public official, then no critical citizen can safely utter anything but faint praise about the government or its officials. The vigorous criticism by press and citizen of the conduct of the government of the day by the officials of the day will soon yield to silence if officials in control of government agencies, instead of answering criticisms, can resort to friendly juries to forestall criticism of their official conduct.

The conclusion that the Constitution affords the citizen and the press an absolute privilege for criticism of official conduct does not leave the public official without defenses against unsubstantiated opinions or deliberate misstatements. "Under our system of government, counterargument and education are the weapons available to expose those matters, not abridgement . . . of free speech . . ." Wood v. Georgia, 370 U.S. 375, 389. The public official certainly has equal if not greater access than most private citizens to media of communication. In any event, despite the possibility that some excesses and abuses may go unremedied, we must recognize that "the people of this nation have ordained in the light of history, that, in spite of the probability of excesses and abuses, (certain) liberties are, in the long view, essential to enlightened opinion and right conduct on the part of the citizens of a democracy." Cantwell v. Connecticut, 310 U.S. 296, 310. As Mr. Justice Brandeis correctly observed, "Sunlight is the most powerful of all disinfectants."

For these reasons, I strongly believe that the Constitution accords citizens and press an unconditional freedom to criticize official conduct. It necessarily follows that in a case such as this, where all agree that the allegedly defamatory statements related to official conduct, the judgments for libel cannot constitutionally be sustained.

Justice Black

Mr. Justice Black, with whom *Mr. Justice Douglas* joins, concurring.

I concur in reversing this half-million-dollar judgment against The New York Times and the four individual defendants. In reversing the Court holds that "the First and 14th Amendments delimit a state's power to award damages for libel in an action brought by a public official against critics of his official conduct." Ante, P. 28. I base my vote to reverse on the belief that the First and 14th Amendments not merely "delimit" a state's power to award damages to "a public official against critics of his official conduct" but completely prohibit a state from exercising such a power. The Court goes on to hold that a state can subject such critics to damages if "actual malice" can be proved against them. "Malice," even as defined by the Court, is an elusive, abstract concept, hard to prove and hard to disprove. The requirement that malice be proved provides at best an evanescent protection for the right critically to discuss public affairs and certainly does not measure up to the sturdy safeguard embodied in the First Amendment. Unlike the Court, therefore, I vote to reverse exclusively on the ground that The Times and the individual defendants had an absolute, unconditional constitutional right to publish in The Times advertisement their criticisms of the Montgomery agencies and officials. I do not base my vote to reverse on any failure to prove that these individual defendants signed the advertisement or that their criticism of the Police Department was aimed at the respondent Sullivan, who was then the Montgomery City Commissioner having supervision of the city's police; for present purposes I assume these things were proved. Nor is my reason for reversal the size of the half-million-dollar judgment, large as it is. If Alabama has constitutional power to use its civil libel law to impose damages on the press for criticizing the way public officials perform or fail to perform their duties, I know of no provision in the Federal Constitution which either expressly or impliedly bars the state from fixing the amount of damages.

The half-million-dollar verdict does give dramatic proof, however, that state libel laws threaten the very existence of an American press virile enough to publish unpopular views on public affairs and bold enough to criticize the conduct of public officials. The factual background of this case emphasizes the imminence and enormity of that threat. One of the acute and highly emotional issues in this country arises out of efforts of many people, even including some public officials, to continue state-commanded segregation of races in the public schools and other public places, despite our several holdings that such a state practice is forbidden by the 14th Amendment. Montgomery is one of the localities in which widespread hostility to desegregation has been manifested. This hostility has sometimes extended itself to persons who favor desegregation, particularly to so-called "outside agitators," a term which can be made to fit papers like The Times, which is published in New York.

The scarcity of testimony to show that Commissioner Sullivan suffered any actual damages at all suggests that these feelings of hostility had at least as much to do with rendition of this half-million-dollar verdict as did an appraisal of damages. Viewed realistically, this record lends support to an inference that instead of being damaged Commissioner Sullivan's political, social, and financial prestige has likely been enhanced by The Times's publication. Moreover, a second half-million-dollar libel verdict against The Times based on the same advertisement has already been awarded to another commissioner. There a jury again gave the full amount claimed. There is no reason to believe that there are not more such huge verdicts lurking just around the corner for The Times or any other newspaper or broadcaster which might dare to criticize public officials.

In fact, briefs before us show that in Alabama there are now pending 11 libel suits by local and state officials against The Times seeking $5,600,000, and five such suits against the Columbia Broadcasting System seeking $1,700,000. Moreover, this technique for harassing and punishing a free press—now that it has been shown to be possible—is by no means limited to cases with racial overtones; it can be used in other fields where public feelings may make local as well as out-of-state newspapers easy prey for libel verdict seekers.

In my opinion the Federal Constitution has dealt with this deadly danger to the press in the only way possible without leaving the free press open to destruction—by granting the press an absolute immunity for criticism of the way public officials do their public duty. Compare Barr v. Matteo, 360 U.S. 564.

Stop-gap measures like those the court adopts are in my judgment not enough. This record certainly does not indicate that any different verdict would have been rendered here whatever the court had charged the jury about "malice," "truth," "good motives," "justifiable ends," or any other legal formulas which in theory would protect the press. Nor does the record indicate that any of these legalistic words would have caused the courts below to set aside or to reduce the half-million-dollar verdict in any amount.

I agree with the Court that the 14th Amendment made the First applicable to the states. This means to me that since the adoption of the 14th Amendment a state has no more power than the Federal Government to use a civil libel law or any other law to impose damages for merely discussing public affairs and criticizing public officials.

The power of the United States to do that is, in my judgment, precisely nil. Such was the general view held when the First Amendment was adopted and ever since. Congress never had sought to challenge the viewpoint by passing any civil libel law. It did pass the Sedition Act in 1798, which made it a crime—"seditious libel"—to criticize Federal officials or the Federal Government. As the Court's opinion correctly points out, however, ante, pp. 19-21, that act came to an ignominious end and by common consent has generally been treated as having been a wholly unjustifiable and much to be regretted violation of the First Amendment. Since the First Amendment is now made applicable to the states by the 14th, it no more permits the states to impose damages for libel than it does the Federal Government.

We would, I think, more faithfully interpret the first Amendment by holding that at the very least it leaves the people and the press free to criticize officials and discuss public affairs with impunity. This nation of ours elects many of its important officials; so do the states, the municipalities, the counties, and even many precincts. These officials are responsible to the people for the way they perform their duties. While our Court has held that some kinds of speech and writings, such as "obscenity." Roth v. United States, 354 U. S. 476, and "fighting words," Chaplinsky v. New Hampshire, 315 U. S. 568, are not expression within the protection of the First Amendment, freedom to discuss public affairs and public officials is unquestionably, as the Court today holds, the kind of speech the First Amendment was primarily designed to keep within the area of free discussion. To punish the exercise of this right to discuss public affairs or to penalize it through libel judgments is to abridge or shut off discussion of the very kind most needed. This nation, I suspect, can live in peace without libel suits based on public discussions of public affairs and public officials. But I doubt that a country can live in freedom where its people can be made to suffer physically or financially for criticizing their government, its actions, or its officials. "For a representative democracy ceases to exist the moment that the public functionaries are by any means absolved from their responsibility to their constituents; and this happens whenever the constituent can be restrained in any manner from speaking, writing, or publishing his opinions upon any public measure, or upon the conduct of those who may advise or execute." An unconditional right to say what one pleases about public affairs is what I consider to be the minimum guarantee of the First Amendment.

I regret that the Court has stopped short of this holding indispensable to preserve our free press from destruction.

Index